Critical Acclai

*Also by Patricia Scanlan
and published by Bantam Books*

FOREIGN AFFAIRS

FINISHING TOUCHES

PROMISES, PROMISES

Patricia Scanlan

BANTAM BOOKS

TORONTO · NEW YORK · LONDON · SYDNEY · AUCKLAND

PROMISES, PROMISES
A BANTAM BOOK: 0 553 409425

Originally published by Poolbeg Press Ltd, Dublin, Ireland

PRINTING HISTORY
Poolbeg edition published 1996
Bantam edition published 1997

Set in 10/11 pt Linotron Sabon by Deltatype Ltd, Birkenhead

Bantam Books are published by Transworld Publishers Ltd,
61–63 Uxbridge Road, London W5 5SA,
in Australia by Transworld Publishers (Australia) Pty Ltd,
15–25 Helles Avenue, Moorebank, NSW 2170,
and in New Zealand by Transworld Publishers (NZ) Ltd,
3 William Pickering Drive, Albany, Auckland.

Reproduced, printed and bound in Great Britain by
Cox & Wyman Ltd, Reading, Berks

Acknowledgements

Sometimes I feel I should call this book *Miracle Miracle* because looking back on the year I spent writing it, it is a miracle that it got written. It was a tough year certainly but when the chips were down for me I had dear and true friends who took care of me and got me through the bad times. And so it is with the deepest gratitude and love I thank:

God: *I give you thanks, O Lord, with my whole heart, before the angels I sing your praise.* Psalm 138: 1

My wonderful family, especially my mother and father who looked after me with such love and kindness when I came out of hospital.

My sister Mary – my best friend. (It was the best New Year's Eve, ever!)

My brothers, Donald, Hugh, Paul and Dermot, who take the greatest care of me.

My sister-in-law Yvonne – my candle in the dark.

Lucy, Rose and Catherine, thanks for reading the manuscript and giving me great encouragement.

Henry, who makes great fried bread.

* * *

Not only are Poolbeg my publishers, they are also caring, kind friends who give me so much support in every way.

To Kate Cruise O'Brien, who is a friend first and then an editor. Dear Kate, thank you for *everything* . . .

To Philip MacDermott who in spite of his own desperately sad bereavement was always there for me.

To Kieran Devlin, who holds us all together. Thanks for all the hospital visits, the cream cakes, and all the little kindnesses that made the last year much easier for me. You're a real pal. And thanks to Barbara for reading the manuscript.

To Nicole Hodson, another real pal. Thanks for the printing out, the photocopying, the advice and the fun. I promise I'll do my ellipses properly!

To Paula Campbell. Let's hit the road and have a ball. (Or a McDonald's anyway!) Thanks for a bulging itinerary.

To Ivan Kerr. Wong's here we come! Thanks, Ivan, for all the hard work, and especially for the phone call with the best news ever!

To Brenda Dermody for my wonderful covers.

To Karen, Nicole, Lucy, Terry, Paula, Conor and Audrey. For all the help and support – thanks.

* * *

To my dearest agents, Sarah Lutyens and Felicity Rubenstein, who make it all great fun and treat me like royalty when I visit them in London as do Francesca Liversidge, my dear kind UK editor, and all in Transworld. Can't wait to see you at Christmas.

* * *

Some friends never let you down no matter what, and I know I can always count on them.

To my godmother, Maureen Halligan, Cinderella eat your heart out! She's mine!

To Margaret Daly, my wise, caring, loving friend whose phone calls made the hard times much easier for me.

To Deirdre Purcell, my dear, for all the belly laughs and for being a cheerleader of the highest order, I thank you from the bottom of my heart.

To Breda Purdue. She read my manuscript. She gave me lifts when I couldn't drive. She makes me laugh. She's the best in the world.

To Annette Tallon – *no man is my enemy, no man is my friend, every man is my teacher* – For all that you have taught me, Annette, there are not enough words of thanks. May the Divine pattern of your life be filled with serenity and joy.

To Anne Schulman who makes the best toasted sandwiches ever! And to Ruth Bernstein whose memories I raided.

To Audrey, Brenda, Olive and Emma in Mac's Gym. Don't give up hope!

To Nikki and Susan for the hair and beauty bits.

To Michael McLoughlin who listens to my sob stories, then I listen to his and we end up guffawing! Thanks *mon ami*.

To Kieran Connolly my favourite computer buff . . . even if I'm still waiting to be shown how to use mail merge . . .

To Tony Kavanagh who's a brilliant writer and who makes me eat my greens! Thanks for reading the manuscript and for the Christmas card that still makes me laugh.

To Noel Cleary. Sorry I drenched you at Mary's barbie. Told you I'd put you in a book. Ha ha!

To John Condon in RTÉ. Thanks for the beautiful flowers on the day of my op, and for all the support during the last year. 'Raiders' was great fun. Hollywood here we come!

To Mr John Byrne, Maria, Betty, Tina, and all who looked after me in the Bons.

To Dr Frankie Fine who looks after me all the time with such kindness.

Thank you all. How lucky I am.

*This book is dedicated in loving memory to
Bernadette MacDermott, a dear and cherished friend*

If at first you don't succeed . . .
Don't make the same stupid mistake again . . .
(anon.)

PART ONE

Chapter One

1961
Glenree, North County Dublin

I wonder what she'll be like, Miriam Munroe thought as she strolled along the leafy back road that led to her mother-in-law Sheila's house. She was going to meet Emma Connolly, her sister-in-law-to-be, for the first time. She'd heard a lot about Emma from Sheila Munroe.

'She's a judge's daughter, you know,' was Sheila's constant refrain. 'She mixes with the best of high society.' All Glenree knew that Vincent Munroe was dating a judge's daughter. Vincent was an estate agent. He was young, ambitious and hard-working. Vincent was going places. He'd sold a property to Judge Connolly and met Emma when she'd accompanied the judge to the viewing. It was love at first sight, Sheila declared proudly. When they announced their engagement, she was ecstatic. She had made a triumphant entrance into the Women's Guild meeting that night and accepted the congratulations of the ladies of the town with regal composure.

Poor Sheila was a terrible snob. Miriam knew she was a bit of a disappointment to her mother-in-law. She was just a farmer's daughter. And he'd been a relatively small farmer at that. The old, familiar hurt welled up as she thought of her late father. Even after four years of happy marriage to Ben, the memory of her father's rejection of her still had the power to wound. 'Don't think about it,' she muttered fiercely.

13

She stopped walking and leaned her elbows on top of the old wooden gate that led into Blackbird's Field. Miriam liked this shady little hollow. The rich emerald sward rippled in the breeze. Beyond that, Ned Doyle's combine plundered a field of golden corn. A blackbird sang in a blackberry bush that was laden with ripe juicy berries. The scent of autumn perfumed the air. Miriam felt a measure of ease. The past was the past. She should let it go.

It was just the unfairness of it all. When her father's will had been read out it was as if he'd risen up from his grave and slapped her in the face. Even now Miriam could vividly recall the moment when she knew what she'd always suspected . . . that she meant little or nothing to her father. Tears pricked her eyes. She'd slogged her heart out at home until she was twenty-five, but her loyalty and effort had gone unacknowledged. For three years, she'd kept house for her elderly parents. She'd given up a good secretarial job in Limerick to go home to the farm on the banks of Lough Derg where she'd nursed her mother until she died of cancer.

It hadn't been easy. As well as nursing her mother, and running the house, Miriam had helped her father on the farm. Each morning she rose at six, prepared breakfast and then went to help him feed the stock, hail, rain or shine. She could still remember the cold dark wild winter mornings when howling gales lashed torrents of icy sleet against her face and the land, edged by the meandering Shannon river, was sodden underfoot.

Her father, Martin, was a taciturn self-contained man who worked hard for his family out of a sense of duty rather than love. He had never shown her or her brothers any affection. He simply didn't know how. He'd never been given affection as a child and he had none to show his own children.

Once, he'd been in hospital for a minor operation and she'd gone to visit him. He was standing by a window gazing out. Miriam knew he hated being trapped inside a strange building. She suspected he was worrying about the farm. He looked smaller, less authoritative, in his new pyjamas and dressing gown bought specially for his hospital stay. It was as if he was diminished by his unfamiliar surroundings. Miriam felt a surge of unexpected concern for him and, when she reached him, she'd put her arms out and hugged him. Her father stood in the circle of her embrace as stiff as a board. He gave a grunt and muttered, 'Howya . . . there's no need for all that.'

Rebuffed, Miriam drew back as embarrassed as he was. She'd never hugged her father again.

When the doctor told him that Maeve's illness was terminal he said gravely, ''Tis God's will. Do your best for her.' He never referred to the matter again. As his wife's condition grew progressively worse, Martin spent more of his time working the land. It was as though he was preparing for the time when she'd no longer be there.

Maeve McGrath passively accepted her fate with the quiet resignation that she'd shown in life. She bore her pain stoically and tried to be as little a burden as possible. She never complained, or showed any anger about the cancer that was ravaging her thin angular body.

Only once had she made an oblique reference to death. 'Look after your father and, when the time comes, you'll find the sick call set for the priest in the middle drawer of the dressing table. Ask Lizzie Conway to help you out. She'll know what to do.' Lizzie was the village midwife and she always helped to lay out the dead.

Miriam didn't know what to say to her mother. Seeing her distress, Maeve squeezed her hand and said comfortingly:

'You're a good daughter, Miriam, and I'm lucky to have you. But when I'm gone, go and make a life for yourself in Dublin or Cork, or you'll be stuck here like I was all my life. I never did anything. There's an old saying. *She spent a life of going to do . . . and died with nothing done!* You don't be like that. Go and do all the things you want to do. Make plenty of friends. Go places. Promise me now,' her mother said earnestly.

15

'I promise.' Miriam leaned down and kissed her mother. Soon after that, Maeve slipped into a coma from which she never recovered.

As she watched her mother's coffin being lowered into the grave, Miriam remembered the promise she'd made to her. No matter what, she was going to leave home and get a job. She'd stay at home for a few more weeks to get her father settled into a routine. She'd organize for a woman to come in from the village to do a bit of cleaning and cooking. But then she was going to go to Dublin to try her luck.

The day the postman arrived with a letter to tell her that she'd been successful in her application for the position of secretary in a clothing firm in Dublin, Martin had a stroke. Miriam's plans were shattered.

She nursed him and employed a man from the village to help her keep the farm going.

Her brothers Sean and Johnny were too busy with their own lives to help out. Sean and his wife, Della, lived in Athlone. Sean was a lock-keeper on the Shannon. Johnny, her youngest brother, was a dining-car attendant on the Dublin to Limerick train. Neither of them had any desire to live at home and take over the responsibilities of the farm and be subject to the dictates of their father.

And so it had been left to Miriam to shoulder the burden again. She'd argued fiercely about the unfairness of it. Sean and Della reluctantly agreed that they would take Martin into their home in the future if Miriam would stay at home and look after him for the next year. Since the doctor had told her that her father wouldn't last the year, this meant nothing. Miriam felt thoroughly taken for granted and manipulated by her family.

Her father lived for eighteen months after his stroke. Della got pregnant and told Miriam she couldn't take care of her sick father-in-law and a baby. Johnny, who had a flat in Limerick, rarely came home and couldn't have cared less about his father.

It was a relief when Martin died. Miriam felt terribly

guilty and could hardly admit it to herself but, as his coffin was lowered into the grave beside her mother, she felt a huge burden lift from her shoulders. She watched Della, weeping into her handkerchief for the neighbours' benefit, and felt utter contempt for her hypocrisy.

'I suppose we better get the will read as soon as possible,' Sean suggested. They'd gone back to the house, as was the custom, to provide refreshments for the neighbours after the funeral. Her brother stuffed a thick skelp of buttered brack into his mouth and ate it with relish.

'For God's sake! The man's not cold in his coffin and you're talking about the will. Sean, will you at least wait until we've taken care of the neighbours.'

'I just can't be hanging around and I don't want to have to come back down from Athlone, if we can get it sorted out now. Couldn't you ring the solicitor and see if he can meet us.'

'Right, right. I'll speak to Mr Finnerty about it. Maybe he could see us all tomorrow.' Miriam was at her wit's end. She hadn't given the will a thought. But it was something that had to be attended to. Now that Sean had brought it up, the sooner the reading was over, the better. She slipped out into the hall and phoned the solicitor's office. He agreed to read the will the following day. Miriam didn't give it another thought as she poured endless cups of tea and washed numerous dishes for neighbours and acquaintances who came from far and wide to pay their condolences.

It was only as the family settled themselves in Mr Finnerty's office the next day that it dawned on Miriam that the reading of the will could radically affect her future. As she sat and listened to the elderly lawyer reading the terms of her father's will, Miriam was shocked beyond belief.

Her father had chosen to ignore her sacrifice. She'd done her duty, he expected nothing less. It was not something to be rewarded. Tradition dictated that the eldest son inherit the estate, so Sean inherited the house and farm that she had slaved over. Johnny inherited fifty acres and she was left three hundred pounds.

Three hundred pounds after years of exhausting slogging. No roof over her head. No land. Just three hundred pounds to see her through the rest of her days. Tears smarted her eyes. Pressure like a vice grip encircled her chest so that she could hardly breathe. She felt bitterness, rage, despair ... but most of all an aching feeling of rejection. Had her father put so little value on what she had done for him and her mother? So it seemed.

'Della and I will have to talk about what we're going to do. When we know ourselves, we'll have a chat with you to see what your plans are.' Sean was gruff, embarrassed.

Miriam, suddenly anxious about her future, noted the emphasis on her 'plans'.

'Fine,' she snapped, hurt that he hadn't hastened to assure her that there was no need for her to leave her home. He and Della needn't think for a moment that she'd be under a compliment to them. She could stand on her own two feet. And she would. She wouldn't hang around waiting to be *evicted*.

It was just as well she'd decided that. Two weeks later Sean and Della arrived at the farm. They informed Miriam that they'd decided to move back and live in the house and farm the land themselves. Della made it abundantly clear that there was no place for Miriam in what would soon be *her* house. 'I know how keen you were to go to Dublin after your mother died, now you'll be able to go and get on with your life and you won't have anyone to worry about but yourself.' Della was as sweet as could be.

Hypocritical wagon! Miriam raged silently. But as usual she couldn't speak of her anger or disgust and kept all her resentment bubbling deep inside. She was twenty-five, without a job or a home and, as they said in the village, 'with no prospects'.

It was a very bitter young woman who travelled on the train to Dublin with everything she possessed packed into two shabby suitcases. She took a room in a small guesthouse near Amiens Street and set off on the task of finding work.

Her first job had been as a typist in a solicitor's office. Mr Bartholomew Cunningham BL was crotchety and dictatorial and Miriam started looking for another job almost immediately. Second time around she was lucky. She got a job in an insurance company, a much nicer place to work. The other girls were friendly and, some months after joining the firm, she moved into a flat with two of them.

Then she met Ben Munroe. At the time, meeting a fella was not of great importance. After her treatment at the hands of her father and brothers, Miriam was off men.

Ben was a clerk in Aer Lingus. Miriam met him at a dance in the Olympic Ballroom and they hit it off immediately. She felt as though she'd known him all her life. He asked her to lunch the following day and to her surprise she found herself saying yes. Although she was nervous as she waited for him at the corner of Henry Street, she looked forward to seeing him again. He walked towards her with his long loping stride and smiled. Miriam smiled back, happy to see him. He was tall and gangly and somewhat bashful which Miriam found unthreatening and attractive. Ben was a great listener. He drew her out of herself. They chatted away and she couldn't even remember what she'd had for lunch when she went back to work.

He'd asked her to the pictures the following Sunday, and as she waited for him to call, she fussed anxiously over her hair. She'd been trying to curl it into a flick but it just kinked up and wouldn't do what she wanted it to do. It was typical. The very time she wanted to look sophisticated and with-it, and her hair just wouldn't behave. The ding-dong of the doorbell sent her into a tizzy but when she opened it and saw him standing there, smiling, she didn't care about her hair.

'Howya,' he said.

'Hi Ben.' She felt shy. Knowing he felt the same helped and, impulsively, she hugged him as he stepped into the hall. The warmth of his hug in return made her feel delightfully cherished. A new and totally unfamiliar feeling for her. She liked it very much. Never having received much attention before then, Ben's hug was a turning point in her life.

Some months later when she'd got to know and really trust him she found herself telling him about the will and how hurt she felt. He was horrified. His face darkened in anger and she was utterly touched that he felt so moved for her. He became extremely protective of her and Miriam realised that her feelings towards him had changed from friendship to love. She wanted to be with him always. She loved the way he made her feel precious and wanted. When he told her that he loved her she knew that she was the luckiest girl in the world.

Ben brought her to Glenree to meet his family. It was a small rural town about ten miles north of Dublin, near the airport. The Munroes lived in a rambling farmhouse just outside the town. Mr Munroe was the town butcher. He didn't farm his land himself, he had it set to a neighbour. Mr Munroe was a nice man, very different to her father. Miriam liked him, but Mrs Munroe was a bit stand-offish. Miriam knew Ben's mother felt that Miriam wasn't good enough for her son.

Even to this day, after four years of marriage, Sheila Munroe never lost an opportunity to let her know that Miriam was very fortunate to have married into the Munroe clan. Sheila Munroe was certainly a cross she had to bear.

Miriam sighed as she came back to reality. Looking back always depressed her and brought back the familiar feelings of hurt and rejection. She ate a plump juicy blackberry, and enjoyed its tangy taste. Yes, she was lucky to have met a man like Ben, certainly. But *he* was lucky to have met her. She was a very good wife. Ben's sister, Ellen, was always saying she spoilt Ben rotten.

Miriam liked Ellen. She was in her late twenties, as mad as a hatter and always in the throes of a great romance that was going wrong. Ellen thrived on trauma.

Miriam grinned. Ellen had already met Emma Connolly and was not impressed. 'She's a right little consequence if you ask me. A right Lady Lala. Vincent must be mad. She'll never settle down out here in the sticks,' Ellen scoffed after the first encounter.

But it seemed as though Emma was indeed going to settle in Glenree because Vincent was already drawing up plans for a magnificent house to be built on the site that was his parents' wedding gift to the couple.

Miriam glanced at her watch, she'd want to get a move on. Sheila had asked her to come early to help with the preparations for 'The Tea'. Ben was minding their two children, he'd bring them over later. She could see the farmhouse nestled between two great oak trees that had just the faintest touch of autumn gold and russets. Smoke curled from the chimney. The fire was lit in the parlour. Sheila meant business. Tea was only held in the parlour on rare occasions such as a visit by the priest or after a funeral. She'd had to make do with tea in the kitchen, Miriam thought with a wry smile as she headed towards the farmhouse.

*   *   *

Sheila Munroe tutted in disgust as the stem of a pink gladioli snapped. 'Typical!' she muttered. Just when you needed things to go right. She'd arranged gladioli hundreds of times. Arranged them for the altar, arranged them for the Women's Guild. Arranged them for her own sideboard on occasions too numerous to count, but today, when she needed everything to be perfect, she was all fingers and thumbs. It was a particularly nice shade of pink too, she thought crossly, as she laid it aside.

She glanced out of the kitchen window. Where was that Miriam one? She'd promised to come and help. Ellen was useless, she had made a batch of scones that Sheila couldn't possibly put on the table, they were so big and untidy.

21

Sheila gave a martyred sniff. She should have made them herself. The only way to get things right was to do them yourself and not be depending on that other pair.

She wanted everything just so. Emma might be a judge's daughter but she'd not eat a better meal anywhere than at Sheila's table. She cooked the choicest meat every day, thanks to Mick and his butcher's shop. Sheila's cooking couldn't be topped. She was the best cook in the guild. She had certificates and awards to prove it. Her sponges, tarts and scones had won many an award. There was no better fed family in the country, Sheila assured herself as she tidied up leaves and stalks and stood back to admire her handiwork. She fiddled a bit more before she was finally satisfied with the flower arrangement. She carried it in to the table in the parlour and placed it on top of the pristine Irish linen tablecloth. She picked up one of the silver knives and rubbed it with her apron until it gleamed.

She had been in a bit of a dither as to whether she should serve wine. It would have been a fine excuse to show off her Waterford Crystal wineglasses. But Emma had been invited to tea. Not lunch, not dinner. Sheila wasn't quite sure, but she didn't think it was quite the done thing to serve wine at tea. Maybe sophisticated people like the Connollys didn't have tea. Maybe she should have invited her to lunch.

'Oh dear,' Sheila muttered, beginning to get into a right tizzy. It was hard to know what to do with young ladies from high society. It was all very well boasting to the ladies of the guild that Vincent was engaged to a judge's daughter, but right this minute she wished he hadn't been quite so highbrow in his choice of wife-to-be.

*   *   *

Emma Connolly drew deep on her filter-tipped cigarette and exhaled a thin plume of smoke through her nostrils. She wished this tea thing was over. She'd visited Vincent's family twice before. Just fleeting visits on Sunday

22

afternoons before she and Vincent headed off to go for a walk on the pier in Howth. Mrs Munroe had fussed over her. Ellen hadn't been over-friendly. Only Mr Munroe seemed anyway normal. Now she was going to have to endure at least three solid hours of being fussed over when she'd much rather be having a drink and some fun with her set. Still, needs must. After all they were Vincent's family and they hadn't even seen her engagement ring. But Vincent needn't think that Sunday tea with the Munroes was going to become a habit. Once she was married and in her own house Emma would do her own Sunday entertaining. And Mr and Mrs Munroe and sourpuss Ellen would definitely not be on the guest list.

Emma stifled a yawn. She and Vincent had been at a party the night before and it was all hours when he brought her home. Friends of theirs, Gillian and Frank, had thrown a house-warming party and, Emma had to admit, she was impressed. They'd had an interior decorator redo the Victorian house from top to bottom. They'd had a pine kitchen fitted. Pine was very 'in' these days. And they had an antique four-poster bed with lots of frilly broderie anglaise pillows. Emma was pea-green with envy when she saw it. They even had a nursery, which Emma thought was tempting fate a bit. They'd just got married. What was the big rush? *She* didn't intend ruining her perfect size ten figure for years.

Still, Gillian and Frank had set a very high standard in the house stakes. Emma had no intention of lagging behind. That was why she had agreed to come to live in this godforsaken back of beyond in North County Dublin. She sighed deeply. Mr and Mrs Munroe were giving Vincent a site as a wedding present. Vincent said they could build their own house from scratch and it would be much less expensive than buying a Victorian pile in Sandycove or the like. When this suggestion was first mooted, she put her foot down and said a very emphatic no!

There was no way she was going to live in the country.

Even if it *was* only ten minutes from the airport and twenty-five into the city. She wanted to live near her friends on the southside. She wanted to be able to pop into Grafton Street to shop, without making a grand safari. Glenree was miles away from all her favourite haunts. And miles away from Mummy and Daddy. In vain did Vincent point out that, if they built their own house, they could design it whatever way they wanted. In vain did he point out that she could zip in and out of town in the little red Mini her parents had given her for her twenty-first birthday. She wanted to live in the civilized suburbs, not the backwoods.

And then when she was having lunch with Gillian one day, in the Russell, she told her friend what Vincent was proposing. She'd said it with her eyes thrown up to heaven in a 'isn't he absolutely crazy' tone. Gillian gave a little squeal and exclaimed, 'Oh how wonderful!' Emma was flabbergasted.

'It's our dream to live in the country. Frank wants to be a Lord of the Manor. How lovely for you. And you'll be able to build your house whatever way you want. You can have ensuite bedrooms, a utility room, a huge dining-room, not like our little cubby-hole,' she said enviously. Privately Emma thought Gillian and Frank's little 'cubby-hole' was most impressive with its oval mahogany dining-suite and the heavy flock wallpaper and red velvet curtains.

'Are you going to have stables? If you're living in the country you'll be able to keep horses,' Gillian asked breathlessly. 'Oh trust you, Connolly, to land a catch like Vincent. A gorgeous hunk with land as well. My dad says land out there is going to sell for zillions because of the building boom.'

'Mmm,' Emma murmured non-committally. This was news to her. She couldn't believe her friend's reaction. It really would be one up on all her friends if she had horses and stables. They all loved riding and had to pay a fortune on stabling fees. Maybe living in the sticks might have its advantages after all. And Vincent was right. She had the Mini, it wouldn't take that long to get into Dublin.

'If I agree to live in Glenree can I have a horse and stables?' Emma asked Vincent that evening, when he came to take her out to dinner. Her fiancé's eyes lit up.

'You certainly can. In fact I'll buy you a horse for a wedding present. How would you like that?'

'Oh Vincent, you are good to me,' she murmured, nestling close against him. 'And can we have ensuite bedrooms and a utility room and a *huge* dining-room?'

'We can have whatever you like.' Vincent kissed the tip of her nose.

The set were deeply impressed when they heard these plans. Overnight Gillian and Frank were relegated to the second division in the keeping-up-with stakes. Vincent and Emma's magnificent new pad was the talk of every dinner party in town.

Emma lit another cigarette as they drove into the town of Glenree. Well the inhabitants called it a town. She'd call it a village, Emma sniffed as she gazed around her. It didn't have one decent boutique. And the small hotel was a hoot. She'd had a glass of white wine there once and it was actually *warm*. It was a very clean town, she had to admit. And the main street was quite wide, not like some of those awful narrow windy streets of some of the towns they drove through on the way to Cork.

They got stuck behind a car with a horsebox moving at a snail's pace so Emma sat back and viewed Glenree with renewed interest. Now that she was going to be living here she might as well see what it had to offer. The first building was a garage, *Noel Doyle Motors*. There were a few ancient Morris Minors and several Minis and a Ford Cortina on the forecourt and a pair of gleaming petrol pumps. Next to the garage there was a betting shop. She wouldn't be frequenting the bookies, she thought dryly. Then came *Egan's Foodstore*, and beside it a bakery. And then her father-in-law-to-be's butcher shop. Emma had to admit *Munroe's Meats and Poultry* looked very impressive from the outside. Mr Munroe had recently had new windows installed. Big plate windows that made the shop

25

look very modern indeed. He had nice tile work on the front of the building and a big red and white striped canopy which was unfurled during working days. It was immaculately clean and he even had two baskets with gorgeous flowering geraniums on each side of the door. It was the most impressive-looking shop on the street, Emma decided. She wouldn't fancy working in it though. Ellen, his daughter, was the cashier. It sounded quite boring. Emma did secretarial work for her father. It wasn't very taxing and she had a lot of free time, unlike Ellen, who had to work from eight-thirty to six.

Next to Mr Munroe's was a small coffee shop which had faded blue and white gingham curtains to match the tablecloths. It looked a bit twee. The church stood in its own neatly kept grounds. Big beds of flowering shrubs lined the grey stone walls that enclosed the grounds and a gravel walkway led to the entrance. It wasn't a very big church, from the outside. Emma had never been in it, but she knew Mrs Munroe was on the committee that kept it clean and did flower arranging and so on.

Emma frowned as they drove slowly past St Joseph's. She didn't bother going to Mass that often now. Her parents always went to the Hibernian for Sunday lunch with friends and they left the house before twelve. They assumed that Emma went to twelve-thirty Mass in the parish church. She'd got into the habit of turning over and having a lie-in, especially if she'd been out on the town the night before, as was usually the case. When she came to Glenree, she'd probably have to put in an appearance on Sunday mornings. It wouldn't go down too well with her in-laws that their son was married to a heathen.

It was such a nuisance. It wasn't as if they were living in the fifties any more. They were in a new decade. It was nineteen sixty-one. Times were changing. She'd had a taste of it only this summer. She'd gone to London to stay with her newly married sister, Jane. She'd had a ball away from the restrictions of home. London was paradise. The clothes, the markets, the shops and restaurants, were unbelievable. Emma loved to go to the theatre or cinema and then go on to one of the coffee bars with Jane and her friends. The coffee bars were so hip with their with-it cane furniture, rubber plants and jukeboxes. The steaming Gaggia machines made the frothiest coffee. There was nothing at home to compare with such cool sophistication.

It was exciting to listen to people discussing the films of Truffaut and Fellini. She'd listened to animated debates about the superiority of Pinter's plays to John Osborne's. And someone called Eugene Ionesco caused fierce argument. He was someone you either loved or hated . . . seemingly. Not that Emma had a clue. Most of the names were unknown to her, but she nodded and murmured 'Mmm' at what she judged were the right moments and nobody seemed to notice that she was completely at sea. They were too busy impressing the hell out of each other with their witty incisive observations and repartee.

She'd gone to a jazz night and heard the great George Melly play and then gone on to a party where people were smoking pot and drinking gallons of wine. It was very 'way out' as Jane would say. But the most exciting moment of her holiday was when she'd joined the hundreds of thousands of cheering people who'd lined President Kennedy and Jackie's route from London airport. Getting a glimpse of the golden couple had been the biggest thrill.

Jackie was Emma's heroine. Her style, her poise, her sophistication was everything she aspired to. When she was in London Emma changed her long flowing hairstyle to the ultra-chic bouffant style that Jackie sported with such élan.

Gillian and the gang were deeply impressed and lost no time in following suit. Vincent said the hairdo was nice, but he missed her long hair and hoped she'd grow it again. But as long as Jackie and her bouffant ruled supreme, Emma would be a faithful disciple.

She'd gone to immense trouble this morning to get her hair just right for the occasion. She wanted to look her best when she met the rest of Vincent's family. Today she was wearing an elegant sleeveless A-line pastel pink dress, slightly above the knee, à la Jackie. She wore a single strand of pearls around her slender neck. A pair of patent pumps and a black patent shoulder bag completed the ensemble. Emma was very pleased with the stylish result. Although it would probably be wasted on the Mary Hicks of Glenree. She sighed. They were passing the Glenree Arms just at the end of town, another few minutes and they'd be at the Munroes'.

'Are you hungry?' Vincent turned and smiled at her. He had a lovely smile. Even though she was fed up at the thought of going to tea with his family, she would give an Oscar-winning performance because it was important to her fiancé.

'I'm ravenous,' she assured him.

'Great. Mam's been cooking all morning. She wants to make a good impression.' Vincent glanced at her.

'There's no need, really.'

'You know what mothers are like,' Vincent laughed.

'Yeah, I know,' Emma agreed. When her mother wanted to impress people she took them out to dinner. Pamela Connolly wouldn't be caught dead slaving over a cooker. Privately Emma thought Mrs Munroe was crazy to be doing all this cooking for her. Had the woman no cop-on at all? How did she think Emma kept her size ten figure? It certainly wasn't by guzzling sponges and tarts and cream cakes and the like. Well, even if it hurt Sheila's feelings, Emma was not going to stuff herself with fattening food. Some things were more important than making an impression. Not for anyone would Emma jeopardize her envied figure.

*   *   *

'For crying out loud, you'd think it was the Queen of bloody Sheba that was coming to tea,' Ellen muttered out of the side of her mouth as she savagely cut the crusts off the ham sandwiches and cut them into neat triangles.

Miriam giggled. Ellen was not in a good humour. She was nursing a broken heart (her ex had ditched her for an eighteen-year-old nubile). She had a raging hangover acquired in the effort to erase all memories of He-Whose-Name-Would-Never-Pass-Her-Lips-Again. Bed was where she wanted to be. The last thing she wanted was to have to entertain Her Highness Connolly. To add insult to injury, she'd been informed by her mother that her scones did not pass muster.

'Maybe once we get to know her she'll be quite nice,' Miriam ventured.

'Are you kidding?' Ellen snorted. 'She looks down her cute little button nose at the likes of us and I for one don't like being patronized. Miriam, the day I like her, snowballs will roast in hell! And if Vincent can't see what a superficial little snob she is, he's an idiot. But then what do you expect? He's so busy social climbing these days.' She viciously sliced a tomato in quarters. Miriam prudently kept quiet.

One thing about Ellen, if she took a dislike to you, she took a dislike to you. Fortunately they got on extremely well. Miriam was dying to meet Emma. She couldn't help feeling a little hurt when she saw all the trouble Sheila was going to for her guest. Tea set out in the parlour. The best china and silverware. Fancy sandwiches and all sorts of cakes and tarts. When Ben had brought her to visit her in-laws for the first time, tea had been served at the big square table in the kitchen. She hadn't merited the linen tablecloth or posh napkins. It had been ordinary everyday red check gingham for her. And the crusts certainly hadn't been cut off the sandwiches.

Miriam felt a surge of resentment. Who was to say Emma Connolly was any better than she was, just because she was a judge's daughter? Mrs Munroe was always quick to come to Miriam for help when she was entertaining the guild ladies or having the priest say The Stations of the Cross in her house. Would she be as quick to ask Emma to lend a hand when she became her daughter-in-law?

It was the same old thing she'd been used to at home. Good old obliging Miriam who could always be relied upon. Well a bit of thanks now and again wouldn't go amiss. She'd never got thanked at home. She was a fool to expect it here, she thought sourly. A cloud of bad humour enveloped her. She wished this damn tea was over so that she could go home to her own house. There at least she was queen. She was loved and cherished by her husband and her little girl, Connie, and Daniel, her baby son. They were the important ones. To hell with the rest of them!

'Cheer up.' Ellen grinned. 'Wait until it's time to entertain the judge and his wife. Then we'll be in *real* trouble.' Miriam had to laugh. Thank God for Ellen. She was a good pal.

'Here, have a sanger,' Ellen offered. The two of them were munching on the tiny triangles when Sheila arrived looking flustered.

'Now what did I do with my handbag?' She caught sight of the girls chomping on the sandwiches.

'For goodness' sake, would you pair leave the food alone or there'll be nothing left for tea. You're worse than children,' she scolded.

'Oh Ma, would you stop getting into a flap. There's plenty of food, for God's sake!' Ellen said irritably.

'Oh heavens! They're here.' Sheila heard the crunch of gravel as Vincent's car drove up. 'Quick, bring those sandwiches in to the table.' She whipped her apron off and hurried out to the hall to greet her guests.

'Mick. They're here! Come out to the door with me,' she ordered her husband. Ellen raised her eyes to heaven.

'Can I move in and live with you, Miriam, if this is going to happen every time she comes to visit? My nerves will be shot to hell!' She grabbed the plate of sandwiches and held them aloft. 'Come on, let's go charm the pants off dear Ems before Mother has hysterics altogether.'

'Aah, Miriam dear,' Sheila said sweetly as Miriam preceded Ellen into the parlour. Her mother-in-law was using her posh voice, Miriam noted with amusement.

'Miriam, let me introduce you to Emma Connolly. Emma, this is Miriam, Ben's wife. Ben will be here shortly with the children.'

'How do you do?' Miriam murmured politely. She shook hands with the petite dark-haired girl standing in front of her. She saw an extremely pretty girl with wide dark almond eyes under sharply defined eyebrows. Her cheekbones were high, classical. Her mouth a Bardot-like pout. Emma was dressed in the height of fashion, and beside her, Miriam felt gauche and dowdy in her white blouse, pale blue cardigan and full skirt.

'Nice to meet you,' Emma murmured. She gave a limp handshake and Miriam noticed the other girl's perfectly manicured nails with their coating of smooth pink nail varnish. Some people were just naturally elegant. Emma was one of them.

'Hi Emma,' Ellen said breezily. 'Let's have a look at the sparkler.' Emma extended her left hand. A diamond solitaire gleamed on her third finger. Ellen whistled. 'Liz Taylor eat your heart out! Very nice, Emma. Congratulations.'

'Oh. Thank you.' Emma's cool tones took on a note of warmth.

'When do you plan to get married?' Miriam asked as Sheila urged them all to sit down.

'Valentine's Day, next spring,' Emma said coyly.

'How romantic!' Ellen declared. 'Vincent, I never knew you had it in you.'

'Well now you know.' Vincent grinned. 'We didn't want to get married too soon after Christmas, but we didn't want to hang around either.'

'That's the way to do it.' Mick beamed. He was dying to get his hands on the sausage rolls with the golden flaky pastry, fresh out of the oven, the way he liked them.

'Have you any idea where you're going to have the wedding breakfast, dear?' Sheila asked delicately. Miriam knew her mother-in-law was extremely anxious to know where the reception was to be held. It would set the tone of

31

the whole wedding. She'd know then if it was going to be posh, ultra-posh, or the wedding of the season, even.

Emma turned her limpid gaze on Sheila. 'Oh Daddy wants to hold it in the Shelbourne,' she said airily and Miriam knew by her mother-in-law's reaction that she was somewhat relieved. It would be posh, but not too intimidatingly so. 'But Mummy and I want to hold it in the International,' Emma chirruped gaily. 'It's modern and sophisticated. Much more me. We're working on Daddy. I think he's wavering.'

'I see,' Sheila said faintly. Miriam could tell she was horrified. The International was very very posh indeed. Sheila would be way out of her depth. As she would be herself, Miriam thought glumly. At least she'd have Ellen to have a bit of a laugh with. If the wedding was in February, she had almost six months to lose a stone. I'll start tomorrow, Miriam decided. There was no point starting now. Not with all those goodies Sheila had baked. She'd love to be able to wear her hair in that bouffant style, but it was curly so that was out. Maybe she might get it cut very short, or even straightened for the day. But she was definitely going to look elegant. It would probably be her first and last time in the International Hotel. She was going to look her best.

Sheila was dispensing sherry. Although she was putting on a good front, she was rattled. She was going to have to have a serious talk to Vincent about this wedding nonsense. The International Hotel was much too grand. Even if the judge and his wife were paying for the wedding. She glanced at her husband. He didn't seem the slightest bit concerned. But that was Mick for you. He took people as he found them and expected the same in return. It wouldn't make the slightest bit of difference to him if the reception was held in the International, the Glenree Arms, or here in the parlour.

'We're going to start the house next week, we have the plans drawn up and the planning permission's come through,' Vincent declared as he took Emma's hand in his.

'Are you going to build a bungalow?' Miriam asked.

'Oh no,' Emma's tone was dismissive. 'Bungalows are so boring!'

Miriam stiffened in her chair. The cheek of her looking down her pert little stuck-up nose at bungalows. Just because she lived in a mansion in Foxrock.

'It's kind of split-level. It's an American design,' Vincent explained hastily.

'It's fabulous,' Emma enthused. 'It's semi-open-plan. We're going to have a lot of wood panelling. Plenty of glass to let in natural light and make the most of the view of the valley. I hate poky little windows.'

Sheila flushed and Ellen flashed Miriam a glance. The windows in the farmhouse, while not exactly poky, were not very large. Emma's remark was in rather poor taste. She didn't notice her faux pas and rattled on artlessly about her ensuite bedrooms and huge dining-room. Vincent looked a little uncomfortable.

'It's just a good opportunity to do something a little different, seeing as we can start from scratch,' he said placatingly.

'I see,' Sheila said stiffly. 'It all sounds very interesting, I'm sure.' Fortunately Ben and the children arrived just then. Miriam smiled at her husband. Many would judge Vincent the more handsome of the two brothers but in Miriam's view Ben's craggy face had much more character. Her husband had dark chestnut hair, hazel eyes ringed by silky black lashes, a straight nose and a wide well-shaped mouth that smiled easily. He was tall and lean, and his temperament was very calm and easygoing. Vincent was much more go-ahead and ambitious.

'Hi.' Ben leaned down and kissed Miriam on the cheek and smiled at her. He gave her the tiniest wink and she smiled back, warmed by his empathy. He had already met Emma. Vincent and she had called in to see him in the reservations office in O'Connell Street and they'd all gone to the Gresham for lunch. So he'd seen Emma in action, he knew what to expect.

Daniel squirmed in his father's arms. At fifteen months he was a handful. Connie stood shyly behind Ben. The parlour was new territory to her. Miriam drew her towards her and put her arm around her. 'Did you help Daddy mind Daniel?'

'Yes. An' Mammy he had a filthy poohy nappy an' it was all over his bottom. An' I wiped it for Daddy with the blue sponge,' she said breathlessly.

Sheila shot them a daggers look. 'Such things to be talking about and we ready to sit down to our tea.'

'I'll mind the kids if you'd like to have tea in peace,' Ellen offered.

'Not at all, Ellen.' Miriam knew precisely what her sister-in-law was up to. She needn't think she was getting off that lightly.

'I need you to make the tea, Ellen,' Sheila ordered. 'And Miriam, would you bring in the strawberries and cream from the larder.'

'Would it be very awkward if I asked for coffee instead of tea?' Emma asked demurely.

'Not at all, dear. Miriam will make it for you.'

'Just black, please, Miriam. Thank you very much.'

'Certainly,' said Miriam, feeling more like Wee Slavey every minute.

'This is the last time I'm getting involved in this carry-on,' Ellen grumbled as she boiled the water for the tea. 'I'm not wasting every Sunday entertaining Vincent and Ems. Who does she think she is? Did you hear her about bungalows and poky windows? Patronizing snob.' Ellen's voice rose indignantly. 'And did you ever see anything like the hair? A swallow's nest has nothing on it. I had my escape route all planned. I was going to take Daniel and Connie out picking blackberries. You could have encouraged it.'

Miriam laughed. 'Yeah, thanks. You didn't mind a bit, me being stuck with her. I don't know what to say to the girl. I've nothing in common with her.'

'Has anyone? She's from another planet,' Ellen said

34

tartly. 'Ma nearly fainted when she heard about the International. Vincent will get a right earbashing tonight. He needn't think he's going to act the lord with his handmaidens waiting on him. He can bloody well do the washing-up,' Ellen decreed as she heated the teapot. 'Do you want some water to make Madame's coffee?'

'What's keeping you?' Sheila appeared. 'Miriam, could you give Daniel a bottle or something, he's very boisterous? He nearly pulled the tablecloth off the table.'

'I'll bring him home if you like?' Miriam said hopefully. Ellen glowered at her.

'I need you here. Put him in his pram and give him a bottle,' Sheila ordered. 'But bring in that coffee to Emma first. Hurry along with that tea, Ellen.' She bustled out of the kitchen.

'Heil Hitler,' snorted Ellen, goose-stepping around the kitchen with the kettle. Miriam could hear Ben giving out to Daniel in the other room. Her heart sank. It was always the same when you wanted them to be on their best behaviour.

'I better get Daniel out of there. Come on, stop messing around and bring the tea in.' She brightened. 'At least I've an excuse to go home early with the children. They come in very handy sometimes.'

'Some friend you are,' Ellen said grumpily.

'You get free flights?' Emma was saying to Ben as Miriam handed her the cup of coffee. 'Lucky you.' She smiled at Miriam. 'Did you go abroad this year? Is that where you got your tan from?'

'We just went to Paris for a weekend. I got my tan here in Glenree.' Miriam laughed.

'Oh. Paris must have been nice. I'm trying to persuade Vincent to bring me there.'

'By the time we get the house of your dreams built, plus the horse, plus the stable, we'll be lucky to afford a weekend in Bray,' Vincent joked as he tucked into the plate of sandwiches.

Emma nibbled on one of hers. 'Don't be silly, Vincent,' she rebuked.

'Any jobs going in Aer Lingus, Ben?' Vincent winked at his brother.

Emma was not amused. You'd think Vincent hadn't a penny. Going on about the cost of the house and horse and everything. Implying that all his money was being spent on her. Wait until she got him on his own. She took another sip of coffee. Miriam hadn't a clue how to make coffee. It was terribly bitter. She seemed a nice enough girl. Much nicer than that dreadful Ellen. The state of her in her slacks and stilettos. She hadn't bothered to dress up at all. Which was rather rude in Emma's opinion. At least Miriam seemed to have made an effort, even if the result was somewhat dowdy.

As for the mother! Emma sighed. Sheila was going to drive her mad. If only she'd stop *fussing*. Handing her the plate of sandwiches before she'd even finished the one she was eating. Pressing buns and slices of rich fruit cake and tarts on her. She'd never seen anyone eat like Mr Munroe. He'd scoffed three sausage rolls, one after the other. This was definitely the last time she was going through this ordeal, Emma vowed. They'd all seen the ring. She'd met the family. That was more than enough.

*   *   *

'She's got a very poor appetite,' Sheila said disapprovingly. She was making another cup of coffee for Emma before she went home.

'Stop worrying, Sheila,' her husband said.

'Maybe she didn't like my cooking? She hardly ate a thing,' Sheila fretted.

'She's a skinny little thing. Two bites of a sandwich would fill her,' Mick comforted.

Sheila was not one bit happy. The tea had not gone well. Ellen had a face on her. The children had misbehaved. Sheila couldn't even face the thought of the wedding breakfast. Maybe it wouldn't come to that. Maybe she could persuade Vincent that Emma was not the girl for him. Things were not working out as planned at all. The Connollys were too posh for the likes of them. And that was something that Sheila Munroe had never thought she'd admit to anyone. Well she wouldn't admit it to anyone, she was just thinking it to herself, she thought crossly as she poured water over the coffee and hoped that she hadn't made it too strong.

*   *   *

'What did you make of Emma then?' Ben asked as he deftly changed his son's nappy.

'She's a bit silly if you ask me. With all those airs and graces. And Mummy this and Daddy that. I thought she'd an awful cheek saying that about the windows and dismissing bungalows as if they were slums,' Miriam retorted. She'd told Ben what Emma had said.

She was glad the tea was over. She had a thumping headache. Daniel had got extremely cantankerous and Connie had knocked her cup of milk all over Sheila's good tablecloth. Miriam had been on edge until they left.

'She'll get sense. She'll suit Vincent though. They'll be a glamorous couple, climbing to the top. Not like us pair of fuddy-duddies.'

'I like being a fuddy-duddy.' Miriam leaned over and gave her husband a kiss. 'I don't want a split-level house and a horse and stables. I'm perfectly happy here with you in our little bungalow with poky windows.'

'Me too,' Ben grinned. 'Did you see the face of Ellen when Vincent offered to wash up and Mam told him it was all right, Ellen would do it. I thought she was going to burst. I went out to give her a hand and by heavens Mam was lucky to get all her crockery washed up in one piece. Ellen was sizzling. I can tell you one thing, I'm glad I'm in my own little peaceful abode tonight.'

Miriam laughed. She knew Ellen wouldn't put up with such treatment in silence. There'd be fireworks when she got Sheila on her own tonight. It served her mother-in-law right, Miriam thought unsympathetically. She knew Sheila was in a right state too about the International. Well, they'd all had the judge's daughter shoved down their necks, ever since Vincent started dating her. Now Mrs Munroe was just going to have to put up with the consequences of getting involved with high society. Emma's arrival into the Munroe family was going to make for some very interesting times ahead, thought Miriam as she took Daniel from Ben and began to feed him his bottle. Now, Sheila Munroe just might realize how lucky she was with her other daughter-in-law. Even if she was only a farmer's daughter. Miriam had enjoyed her mother-in-law's discomfiture today. It helped make up for all the many little barbs that had been cast in her direction over the years. Miriam thought that Emma was just what Sheila deserved.

Chapter Two

'Come on. Let's have a peek at the mansion to see how much more they've done,' Ellen suggested with a glint in her eye.

'But they might drive up and catch us,' Miriam demurred. 'That would be really embarrassing.'

'They won't catch us, they're gone racing at the Curragh. It's the perfect opportunity. Although why they can't just show us around like you and Ben did when you were building your house, I can't figure out. It's ridiculous having to sneak around peering in through windows. Mind you,' she laughed, 'there's plenty of windows to peer through. I'd hate to have to clean them.'

'I'm sure Emma will have someone in to "do",' Miriam remarked.

'I don't know if they'll have the money. They're spending an absolute fortune. They can't have a lot left with the wedding coming up and a honeymoon in Italy.' Ellen steered Daniel's pram around a muddy puddle. It was New Year's Day and they'd gone for a walk in an effort to liven themselves up after the big turkey dinner they'd had.

Miriam was disgusted with herself. Through strict dieting, she'd managed to lose almost a stone between September and Christmas, but she'd put back on half of it during the festive season. It was very disheartening. She wanted to be slim for the wedding.

'Come on, I'll put Connie in the pram as well and we'll walk really fast. Dawdling along is no good for us,' she urged Ellen.

'Just let's have a quick look,' Ellen wheedled. 'It's only down the road.'

'You're as nosy—'

'Give over, Miriam. Be honest, you're dying to see the mansion too,' Ellen retorted.

Miriam laughed. She was curious. It was six weeks since she and Ellen had last ventured to have a look and by all accounts the house was almost completed. Emma didn't want anyone to see it until it was just right so they had to make do with whatever they were told about its progress. Much to Ellen's chagrin. It didn't bother Miriam to the same extent. Sometimes she thought Ellen was a bit jealous of Emma and Vincent. If only her sister-in-law could find a nice chap and settle down herself.

The black-tiled roof and redbrick walls of the new house could be seen through the tangles of bare-branched trees. In summer the foliage would hide it from view of the road. The house was the talk of Glenree. Vincent had hired a building firm recommended by his architect. Much to the disgust of local builders. Only the best of material was being used and the strange design of the house led to much comment.

'Too posh for the likes of us,' Mrs Whelan said snootily to Sheila at the guild one evening. Sheila was furious. But she couldn't think of a suitable riposte, and privately she agreed with the remark. It was nice to be able to show off, but floor to ceiling windows and strange sharp angles were a bit much. Instead of being the object of envy, the house was becoming the object of ridicule. Houses like that were all right in Hollywood, but not in the quiet backwaters of Glenree.

Miriam and Ellen walked through the churned-up dirt track that led towards the house. They were used to conventional bungalows and cottages and two-storey houses; the angular redbrick building ahead of them was unlike anything either of them had ever seen.

A huge plate glass window dominated the front of the house. This seemed to be the sitting-room and Miriam had to admit that in summer the views would be superb. Redbrick walls jutted out to form an alcove where the big balustraded porch stood with its double white wood doors. Further along, a long narrow floor-to-ceiling window gave a church-like impression. The driveway dipped to a lower level and two large garages. Above them, the bedrooms. The master bedroom had an ornately decorated wrought-iron balcony.

The nearer they got to the house, the muckier it got. Connie was having great fun, dancing in and out of puddles in her little red wellies.

'I think we should turn back,' Miriam said doubtfully.

'Never say die,' declared the intrepid Ellen as she sidestepped a particularly muddy patch. 'Come on, I want to see how they've decorated it.' She put the brake on Daniel's pram and clambered over bricks and planks. Moments later she had her nose pressed to the window of the sitting-room.

'Jeepers! Miriam, look at this!'

Miriam hastened to her side and peered in through the window.

'Wow!' she breathed. 'It's all painted white. And look, they've got a television set—'

'And a radiogram,' Ellen said enviously. 'Look at the size of the room. I don't like the white though. It's a bit cold if you ask me.'

'Yeah, but they have a big fireplace and Vincent told Ben that they're going to get that new sort of heating. Oil heating.'

'Let's have a goo at the kitchen.' Ellen edged her way around to the back of the house.

'Look at the presses. They're all fitted. It's so modern. They've got a fridge too. It's huge. Ben and I are saving for one.' Miriam's tone was wistful.

'Da wanted to buy Ma one but she wouldn't have it. Her larder's her pride and joy,' Ellen said ruefully. 'To be honest, I think a kitchen like that is wasted on Ems. I wouldn't say she could cook an egg.'

'Don't be so nasty, Ellen. Give her a chance. I think she's nice enough,' Miriam argued.

'Saint Miriam,' jeered Ellen. 'You're such a softie, you know.'

'I know. But we're going to have to get used to having her in the family. We should make an effort to get on with her.'

'Listen, she gets up my nose and that's it. Don't expect me to be watching my Ps and Qs for the next fifty years.'

Miriam laughed. 'You couldn't watch your Ps and Qs for five minutes, let alone fifty years. Come on, let's get out of here and walk as far as Glenree.'

'Do we have to?' Ellen made a face.

'Yes we do,' Miriam said firmly. 'We're going shopping for our wedding outfits in a couple of weeks. I want to have a few pounds off.'

'Yeah you're right. We don't want to look like elephants beside Miss Skinnymalinks Emma.' Ellen set off at a brisk pace around to the front of the house.

'Wait for me, Mammy!' Connie said anxiously.

'I'm waiting, pet.' Miriam stretched out a helping hand to her daughter.

'What's a . . . a . . . skinnyinks, Mammy?'

Miriam stared down into Connie's wide blue trusting eyes. 'What?' she asked, puzzled.

'Don't say what. Say pardon, Mammy,' Connie reproved, primly echoing her mother's oft-repeated instruction.

'Sorry. Pardon.' Miriam hid a smile.

'What's a . . . a you know, what Auntie Ellen called the new lady?'

Holy God, I'll kill her, Miriam thought in horror. Ellen frequently forgot little ears were listening to her and was apt to be most indiscreet.

'She wasn't talking about the new lady,' Miriam said lightly, and then came her salvation. 'Oh look! There's a little robin. Isn't he gorgeous.' Connie's attention was immediately diverted. She stood very still and watched the bird hopping across the muck. Miriam heaved a sigh of relief when her daughter announced that the robin was looking for his tea and wondered if he would like to come home and have some of their turkey.

'Maybe he'll follow us home.'

'Maybe he will, now let's go and catch up with Auntie Ellen and Daniel. If you're very good I'll buy you a treat in Glenree.' Connie squealed with delight and skipped along-side her mother, all questions about skinnymalinks forgotten.

*   *   *

Sheila stood in front of the old polished wardrobe in her bedroom and eyed her clothes with a jaundiced eye. Nothing that she could see was at all suitable to wear for her forthcoming meeting with the judge and Mrs Connolly. The judge and his wife had invited Mick and herself to lunch in the Russell. It would be their first encounter. Mrs Connolly had been extremely pleasant on the phone. She'd said how pleased they were that Emma was marrying such a nice young man as Vincent. And how wonderful and generous it was of the Munroes to give them a site as a wedding present. Such a practical and expensive gift, she'd said. 'Well we've sites set out for all our children,' Sheila couldn't resist boasting. The Connollys might have a magnificent house in Foxrock, and lashings of money, but the Munroes were landowners. That counted for a lot.

'We thought the Russell might be nice. The food is wonderful,' Mrs Connolly suggested.

'Delightful,' Sheila said in her posh phone voice. As if to imply that she dined in the Russell morning, noon and night. They'd agreed on the Sunday after New Year.

Ever since then she'd been trying on outfits and discard-ing them. Ellen had bought her a lovely new dusky pink twinset for Christmas which looked very smart with her grey skirt. She could wear her pearls and her cameo brooch and her fur stole. Mick kept telling her to go and buy herself a new outfit, but she'd already spent a fortune on her wedding outfit. She'd bought it in Switzers and it was most elegant. It was a pity she couldn't wear it to the lunch but of course that was out of the question.

'If a twinset and pearls is good enough for the Queen to wear, it will be good enough for you to wear,' Sheila addressed her reflection in the mirror. She'd had her hair permed for Christmas. She'd go to the hairdressers for a set on Friday. By this time next week, the ordeal would be over, she comforted herself. She was going to buy Mick a new shirt and tie though. She'd get that in Kelly's drapery in town. It would save her having to traipse into the city. She'd do that first thing in the morning. Now that she'd finally decided on her outfit she felt more relaxed. Then a thought struck her. Should she wear a hat? Sheila's heart sank. No doubt Mrs Connolly would be wearing a hat. Smart ladies always did. Sheila hated hats. She always wore a lace mantilla to Mass and she had one navy one for occasions. She'd bought a flower petal creation for the wedding. Would the navy hat do or should she buy a new one? This was even worse than the wedding, Sheila thought crossly as she took out the hat and held it up against the twinset. No! Definitely not. Now she was going to have to rethink her whole outfit. It was very vexing indeed.

*　　*　　*

The Connollys were thoroughly enjoying the races. It was a crisp sunny day with just a hint of chill in the breeze. 'I've been thinking, darling.' Pamela Connolly arched an eyebrow at her daughter and handed her a glass of champagne. 'Perhaps we should make it dinner rather than lunch, with the Munroes. I don't want them to think we're being mean. After all they are going to be your in-laws and that site they gave you is worth quite a bit of money. They might think we're cheapskates.'

'Oh Mummy, don't be silly. Lunch will be fine. They don't go out that much. They're not that sort of people. Lunch in the Russell will be a treat for them.' Emma's tone was dismissive. She took a sip of her champagne and waved at Gillian and Frank, who were heading in their direction.

'I'll speak to your father about it, Emma, and see what he has to say. We don't want Vincent to think that meeting his parents isn't important,' Pamela said firmly.

'Oh do what you want. I wish this blasted ordeal was over. If you ask me, dinner in the Russell will be wasted on them. They're more used to roast chicken and tinned peas in that dreadful Glenree Arms,' Emma retorted rudely. Fortunately Vincent was studying form with her father so he didn't hear her condescending remarks.

'Emma!' Pamela frowned. 'That's no way to talk about Vincent's parents and don't ever let him hear you talk like that about them. Otherwise I can promise you, my dear, you'll end up rowing. It's all right for Vincent to criticize his parents or for you to criticize your father and me, but one of the golden rules of marriage is not to criticize each other's parents.'

'But you're always giving out about Grandad Connolly,' Emma said huffily.

'Yes, maybe, but not in front of your father. I warned you at the beginning that you might have been better marrying someone from your own set—'

'Vincent fits in perfectly with us,' Emma responded quickly. 'It's just his parents aren't very sophisticated.'

'Well if you're marrying Vincent you've got to put up with his parents. So be gracious about it, Emma. Your father and I wanted you to wait. Sometimes I think you're too immature to be getting married at all.'

'I'm going to join Gillian and Frank, see you later.' Emma turned on her heel, furious with her mother and her lectures. We'll see how gracious she is when she meets the rest of the clodhopper relations at the wedding, she fumed as she flounced her way across the muddy track. If only

45

Vincent's family were upper-class southsiders everything would be perfect. She could have married Oliver Singleton or Conan Rafter if she'd wanted to. Both of them were crazy about her. But once she'd met Vincent, Emma knew he was the one for her. Vincent was a *real* man. He was ambitious, he could fit in at dinner parties. And he was strong and fit and didn't mind doing physical work. She loved watching him help the builders at the weekend, stripped to his white short-sleeved T-shirt, like the one Marlon Brando wore in *Streetcar Named Desire*, his muscles rippling as he lifted the heavy blocks. Oliver and Conan hadn't any muscles to speak of and they certainly wouldn't have the strength to lift a block in each hand the way Vincent could.

She was dying for their wedding night. Vincent wouldn't go the whole way, even though she wouldn't really object if he did. He didn't want to risk her getting pregnant. The wait would be worth it, he told her when she lay in his arms tingling with frustration during one of their passionate petting sessions. She had no intention of getting pregnant, married or not. Her sister had told her about a great new discovery called the contraceptive pill. All the girls in London were on it. Jane was on it. She said you just took a little tablet for twenty-one days and then took a break for seven days and it prevented you from getting pregnant. It wasn't available in Ireland but Emma had got a six-month supply the last time she was in London. She'd been on it for two months. The only difference she noticed was that her breasts were a little bit fuller and she didn't mind that at all. It really turned Vincent on.

Emma glanced over at her beloved. He looked very dashing in his sheepskin coat. She'd bought it for him for Christmas. He'd bought her an exquisite gold charm bracelet with a gold heart charm. He was going to buy her a charm every Christmas for the rest of their lives, he'd told her as he fastened it around her wrist on Christmas morning. Emma thought it was the most romantic gesture. She shouldn't have snapped at her mother, she thought ruefully. It was just pre-wedding nerves. The sooner she was married and all this fuss and faddle was over the better.

'How's the bride-to-be?' Gillian trilled. Emma put on her couldn't-be-happier smile.

'Wonderful. Just wonderful.'

'Well just wait,' Gillian warned. 'The next few weeks are going to be hell. Take it from one who's been there. By the time you've argued about the number of tiers on the cake, and about who's sitting where in the church and at what table in the hotel and so on, you'll be ready for divorce. Frank and I had a row the night before the wedding. The *night* before! Didn't we, darling?' Gillian beamed up at her husband.

'That was because you insisted I wear that ridiculous top hat,' Frank growled.

'You looked very distinguished in it,' his wife purred. 'Is Vincent going to wear one?'

'We haven't decided yet.' This was an outright fib. Vincent's language when she had told him she wanted him to wear top hat and tails was unrepeatable. Emma was doing her best to get around him but it looked as if the most he'd do would be to wear a morning suit. As she listened to Gillian rattling on, Emma couldn't help thinking that an elopement was beginning to seem like a most attractive proposition.

*   *   *

Sheila sat beside Mick in the cosy warmth of the car and stared out at the Christmas lights strung across Grafton Street. Coming through town had been like driving through wonderland. All the shop windows festooned with lights and decorations. The trees in O'Connell Street sparkled like diamonds as frosty moonbeams caught their light. Normally Sheila loved the magical atmosphere of Dublin at night during the festive season, but tonight she was too tense and wound up to give more than a cursory glance out of the car window.

47

When Mrs Connolly phoned to suggest changing the Sunday lunch invitation to Saturday dinner, Sheila was horrified. Lunch was bad enough, but dinner could go on for hours and hours. She certainly wouldn't be able to wear her twinset to dinner. She had to beg Ellen to go into town with her the following day to buy an outfit. Dinner in the Russell meant serious dressing up. After much traipsing through shops, and trying on and discarding, and interference from condescending sales ladies, Sheila had finally selected an evening dress in shades of muted pinks and lilacs. She'd bought it in Madame Nora's and she'd treated herself to a beautiful pair of long black gloves to go with it. Ellen assured her she looked like royalty.

She certainly didn't feel like royalty, composed and regal and poised, as Mick drove slowly past the Shelbourne and turned right along Stephen's Green. Her stomach was tied up in knots. She wouldn't be able to eat a thing, Sheila fretted. Her palms felt sweaty as they drove towards the Harcourt Street corner of the Green and the long gleaming elegant windows of the Russell came into view. Sheila could see the silhouettes of diners already seated and the warm subdued glow of the lamp lights.

'Cheer up. At least we'll get a good meal. This is one of the best hotels in Europe, we might as well enjoy it,' Mick said cheerfully as he manoeuvred the car into a parking place. Mick wasn't the slightest bit perturbed. He was looking forward to the evening. Mick felt he was anyone's equal, he didn't suffer the anxieties she was feeling about this meeting.

'You look lovely, Sheila. I've never seen you look as well, so best foot forward now,' he encouraged as he held open the car door for her and took her arm to lead her across the street. Her breath curled white in the frosty sharp air as they walked briskly towards the hotel, her high heels tapping on the ground. Couples strolled hand in hand, laughing and chatting, looking forward to their night out. Sheila would have given a million pounds to be sitting beside her blazing fire at home listening to the Saturday night concert on the wireless.

Before she knew it, she was marched up the steps and into the foyer of the luxurious hotel. A wave of warmth enveloped them. Swiftly, discreetly, their coats were taken.

'We're joining Judge and Mrs Connolly for dinner,' Mick informed the formally attired man at the desk. They were led into a lounge which had a huge fire flaming merrily in the grate. Cosy sofas dotted the room. A hum of chat and convivial laughter gave the room a friendly atmosphere. Sheila saw Vincent and Emma seated by a tall distinguished grey-haired man and a petite radiant woman, striking in rich emerald silk. Sheila was stunned. That couldn't be Emma's mother. She was far too young-looking. She was the most elegant sophisticated woman Sheila had ever seen.

'Mam, Dad.' Vincent stood up to greet them and make the introductions.

'How do you do, Mrs Munroe?' Her hand was taken in a strong clasp and Judge Connolly smiled down at her. He had nice eyes, Sheila thought, flustered.

'A pleasure, at last,' Pamela Connolly said graciously, offering a dainty, perfectly manicured hand. Sheila felt ashamed of her own work-worn paw.

'What will you have to drink now, Mick? A whiskey?' Judge Connolly said expansively.

'That would hit the spot nicely,' Mick approved, rubbing his hands.

'A dry sherry for me, please,' Sheila murmured.

'And I'll have another dry Martini, darling.' Pamela smiled.

'And a Babycham for me,' Emma said. She was looking exquisite in black shantung. The drinks were served from a trolley and, after Sheila had taken a few sips of her sherry, she began to relax a little. Mick and the judge were chatting away about the building boom and land prices. Vincent was keeping a conversation going with Pamela and Emma. He was quite at home and relaxed.

Sheila felt very proud that her son was at ease in such company.

'Are you looking forward to the wedding?' Pamela asked, smiling. She really was an exceptionally beautiful woman whose fine porcelain skin and big brown eyes were enhanced by her shimmering emerald gown.

'I am of course, but then I don't have the worry of it like you do,' Sheila responded.

'Oh we have everything under control.' Pamela laughed. Sheila had no doubt she had.

'I'm making the most of it. Emma is the last to go, so I'll never get the chance again. Poor Edmund', she smiled in her husband's direction, 'doesn't know whether he's coming or going. But of course you've been through it before.'

'Well yes, when Ben and Miriam got married. But I suppose it's not the same unless it's a daughter who's getting married. There's no sign of my Ellen taking the plunge yet.'

'She's right,' Pamela said, surprisingly. 'It was different in our days. But nowadays young girls can do so much more with their lives. I'd love to have had a career.'

'Really?' Sheila was amazed. In her view Pamela had everything.

'Maybe I'm just feeling middle-aged. It's hard to believe Emma's fleeing the nest,' the other woman said a little sadly. Sheila warmed to her. She wasn't at all stand-offish.

'You don't look the slightest bit middle-aged, my dear. You look more like Emma's older sister than her mother. And just think when the grandchildren come along you'll be able to spoil them. I know I do with my two,' she fibbed. Sheila didn't believe in spoiling children, but it seemed like the right thing to say.

'I'm looking forward to that.' Pamela smiled. 'I would have liked more children. I had two miscarriages after Jane and before I had Emma. After she was born, I couldn't have any more.'

'How sad,' Sheila murmured, patting the other woman's

hand. Pamela didn't seem the slightest bit snobby. In fact, to her surprise, Sheila rather liked her.

The waiter arrived with the menus. 'We can order here, and then go in to the dining-room when our meal is ready,' Pamela explained. 'There's a fish tank just off the lounge and you can select your choice of fish. The lobster and trout are divine. And for the first course I really do recommend the *crêpe-de-mer*. It's out of this world.'

Pamela did not exaggerate. The *crêpe-de-mer* was filled with mixed seafood in a mouth-watering cheesy sauce. It was the most delicious thing Sheila had ever eaten. They sat in the long dining-room, at a table by one of the large windows overlooking Stephen's Green. Mick tucked into an immense prawn cocktail. Vincent and Emma chose smoked salmon and the judge and his wife had the *crêpe-de-mer*.

Sheila gazed around her with interest. The dining-room was full and everyone seemed to know everyone else. It was like a private little club with regulars saluting each other, stopping to chat at each other's tables. Everyone was dressed to the nines and jewels glittered on necks and wrists. A beautiful hand-painted pastoral mural decorated the length of the room. The tables were round or oblong, dressed in the finest white linen, with sparkling silverware and crystal. The waiters were formally dressed and most discreet. The atmosphere was one of gracious, timeless elegance.

Mick and the judge were getting on like a house on fire. They had discovered a mutual interest in fishing and the talk was all of this fly and that, casting rods and sinkers, which made Pamela and Sheila throw their eyes up to heaven in mock bad humour. Sheila decided to be adventurous and had the wild duck in orange sauce, while Mick had a thick juicy steak that nearly covered his plate.

They lingered over coffee, relaxed after the superb meal and fine wines. The ordeal which she had so dreaded turned into a most pleasurable occasion. One that Sheila intended to boast about for all she was worth to the ladies of the guild the following week.

*　　*　　*

'Nice people,' Edmund Connolly said as he belched behind his hand and eased himself into bed. 'Mick's going to take me to a river out his way to fish. It's full of trout.'

'Sheila was a bit out of her depth at first. She'd put on a grand voice and then forget. But she's a good soul, even if they aren't quite our sort,' Pamela mused as she cold-creamed her face.

'Emma will be all right with them. They've good values,' Edmund declared. 'Did you hear that that young rip Shaun Redmond is having an affair with Martin Desmond's wife?'

'Good God!' exclaimed Pamela. 'But he's only married a year.'

'I know. I'll tell you frankly, Pamela, that set Emma mixes with is too fast. Vincent Munroe is a very nice young man. I'm glad Emma's going to live out in Glenree. The Munroes might not be upper-crust but they're decent people. I'll worry much less about Emma knowing she's married to someone like Vincent. To think that that young cur, Redmond, was sniffing around her before she met Vincent and she encouraged him. God knows where it would have ended. In tears I'd say.'

'Well to be honest, I'd have liked Emma to marry someone like us, but I suppose you might be right.'

'I know I'm right. Now hurry on and get in here beside me. My feet are freezing and you're the only one that can warm them.'

'Charmer,' Pamela laughed but she snuggled in beside her husband and wrapped her arms around him. 'If Vincent is as good to Emma as you've been to me she'll be a very lucky girl.'

'I think we need have no fears on that score,' Edmund Connolly murmured and in seconds was fast asleep.

'Wasn't it wonderful? Some evening you and I will go there ourselves and really enjoy it. Did you see the cutlery and the silverware? And the style of the ladies! Did you see the woman sitting opposite us with the ruby necklace? It was exquisite.' Sheila couldn't stop talking. She was full of beans even though it was long after midnight and Mick was valiantly trying to stay awake over his cup of cocoa. The embers of the fire glowed orange as they sat in the sitting-room reliving their night out.

'The poor soul had two miscarriages before she had Emma but honestly, it's hard to credit that she's the mother of two girls in their twenties. Did you see how youthful her skin was? And the tiny waist of her. And wasn't the judge a good-looking man?' A rumbling snore was all the response she got as Mick's head drooped on his chest. Sheila looked at him regretfully. She wanted to go over every second of the evening that had turned out to be such a delightful occasion. How silly she'd been to get herself in such a tizzy. Wait until she told the women of the guild how she'd been hobnobbing with high society.

'Come on, Mick.' She poked her husband in the shoulder. There was no point in waiting up for Vincent. He'd be in at all hours. She'd just have to go to bed and remember every delicious detail. She was far too wound up to sleep.

*   *   *

'It went well, didn't it?' Vincent nuzzled Emma's ear.

'Dad got on very well with your father. They're going fishing next week.'

'Mam really enjoyed it once she relaxed. The sherry and wine went to her head a bit,' Vincent grinned.

'At least that's over.' She snuggled into his arms. They were sitting in the back seat of the car, high on a hill overlooking Killiney. 'It won't be long now to the wedding.'

'Hmmmm.' Vincent slid his hand inside the neckband of her dress and cupped one full breast.

'Oh Vincent,' Emma breathed. 'I love when you do that.' They kissed passionately and she slid her hand up along his inner thigh, feeling the hot hardness swelling against the thin material of his trousers.

'And I love when you do that,' he groaned, wishing it was their wedding night and he could throw caution to the winds and make love to her with all the passion he'd been suppressing for months and months.

Chapter Three

'I now pronounce you man and wife.' The priest smiled benevolently on Vincent and Emma as they stood before him at the altar rails. Emma beamed at her new husband and he smiled back, squeezing her hand. She felt utterly happy. After all the hectic running around of the last few weeks, everything had clicked nicely into place. It was a beautiful spring day. The skies were as blue as the Mediterranean. There was a hint of warmth in the sun and, now that the ceremony was almost over, she was going to enjoy every minute of her special day.

It had been extremely gratifying to hear the chorus of oohs and aahs as she walked up the aisle beside her father. She looked stunning. Her dress, a vision of silk and lace, looked like something from a fairytale. She'd had it made in a similar style to Princess Margaret's dazzling wedding gown of almost two years ago. Emma thought it was exquisite when she'd seen photos of it. There and then she decided she was going to have something like it. Her dressmaker had done a superb job. It had cost a fortune but it was well worth it. And the diamanté tiara that Jane bought for her in London set off the yards of white veil to perfection. She felt like a princess today, Emma thought in exhilaration as she admired the slim gold band on her finger.

*   *   *

So far so good, Pamela thought with satisfaction as she watched her daughter become Vincent Munroe's wife. They were a gloriously stylish couple. Emma looked very beautiful and ethereal and Vincent looked extremely handsome in his grey morning suit. She would have liked him to wear top hat and tails, but he'd been adamant. Despite her disappointment, she'd been impressed by his polite but firm refusal. Vincent was his own man. Emma needed someone who wouldn't stand for any nonsense. She was rather spoilt, Pamela acknowledged ruefully. The apple of her father's eye.

She cast an approving eye around the church. The florist had decorated it beautifully. Her theme was spring and the posies of crocuses and primroses and snowdrops and pansies entwined in curling ivy vines were exquisite. Emma had wanted roses on the altar but Karen Selby, Dublin's new up-and-coming floral designer, as she liked to describe herself, told her that everyone had roses and she should dare to be different. Emma was persuaded so the altar bloomed like a spring garden with boughs of cherry and apple blossom and vases brimful of tulips and daffodils. Pamela noted Noeleen Farrell taking it all in. Noeleen's daughter was getting married in May. The Connolly wedding would be a hard act to follow, Pamela thought a little smugly. Wait until they saw the room in the International! And as for the menu . . . she could feel her mouth watering already at the thought of fresh salmon *en croûte* with new baby potatoes and buttered asparagus spears.

She glanced across at Vincent's family and sighed. The one little fly in the ointment, she thought regretfully. Sheila's hat was unlike anything she'd ever seen before. A multicoloured petalled creation that made Pamela wonder if its creator had been high on LSD. And that fur stole with the fox's head was extremely passé. Poor Mick looked as if his morning suit was too small for him. And the daughter, Ellen, was wearing a low-cut empire-line dress which was quite revealing. Vulgar actually, Pamela thought crossly.

There was an array of aunts and uncles and friends who obviously weren't used to sophisticated occasions and were rather overawed by it all. If only Vincent's family were more, well, *suitable*, it would have been the perfect wedding.

*   *   *

Lucky cow! Ellen thought enviously as she watched Vincent slide the ring onto Emma's finger. Emma was only twenty-two and she'd managed to snare a husband. Ellen was heading for twenty-nine and, unless a miracle happened, it looked as if she was going to be left on the shelf. It was extremely depressing.

For years she'd gone out dancing every weekend with her pals. She'd had a wild time dancing and drinking and getting off with fellas. It was a great life. She hadn't wanted to settle down, she was having too much fun. Then she'd started to go out with Joseph McManus two years ago and she'd sort of felt he was the one she'd marry. Nothing had ever been said, it was like an unspoken agreement between them.

It wasn't that she'd been madly in love with him or anything, Ellen sniffed, remembering her ex-boyfriend. He was nice, good company, worked in the civil service and didn't take life too seriously. They were well matched. Or so she'd thought until he'd upped and left her for an eighteen-year-old child. A child who didn't smoke or drink and knew how to behave in public. Traits that attracted him to her, he'd said coldly when she'd blown a fuse and ranted and raved at him for his duplicity. He'd been seeing this Lolita for six months before he'd broken it off with her. Ellen's lips tightened and her hands clenched into fists as she thought of Joseph. His hypocrisy sickened her. *She'd* been all right to get drunk with and smoke with and have fun with, not to mention . . . have sex with. The bastard! Ellen fumed.

About a year into their relationship, they'd slept with

each other. Ellen hadn't wanted to be the last of the red-hot virgins and besides she'd assumed that sleeping together meant a total commitment. Marriage in other words. Her friends thought she was very daring. Most of them had been virgins when they married. They thought she was modern and with-it. Ellen enjoyed their admiration. They looked up to her and thought of her as a woman of the world. What they didn't realize, and what Ellen kept to herself, was what a disappointment sex was. She'd been so looking forward to it after all the months of panting frustration in the back seat of the Anglia when Joseph had done his best to persuade her to lose her virginity. All she'd read in romantic novels, all she'd seen in the movies, had led her to believe that, when she finally did it, it would be wonderful.

The first time had been quick and painful. Ellen couldn't believe it was all over when Joseph, flushed and breathless, had asked her had it been good for her.

'It was great,' she assured him, lying through her teeth, and all the time she was thinking, is this it? Is this what all the fuss is about? She'd bled, it being her first time, and Joseph's expression of repulsion when he removed the condom did nothing to reassure her. She was sore for a day after, but nevertheless she looked forward to their next lovemaking, thinking that it would be much better than the first time. It wasn't. Joseph came quickly, kissed her, looked at his watch and told her they'd make last orders down at the pub if they hurried. That was to be the pattern. Ellen thought it must be normal and blamed herself because sex disappointed her. Modern 'with-it' women were supposed to enjoy sex as much as men. At sex she was obviously a failure. It was a failure she would admit to no one.

Then Joseph dumped her for a moon-faced nymphet who didn't smoke or drink or make a show of herself in public and who most certainly would wait until marriage to be deflowered.

The last six months since the break-up had been the

most miserable of Ellen's life. Most of her friends were now married and producing offspring at a great rate. She spent her time going to christenings, for heaven's sake! She didn't seem to have much in common with them any more. All they could talk about was baby's first tooth, or worse, detailed descriptions of labour and childbirth. It gave Ellen the willies even to think about it, it all sounded so gory and painful. It was hard to watch friends who'd been a great gas and ready for anything on a night out, change into boring matrons, more interested in changing nappies and getting dinners than going out on the hunt for whatever man they fancied. It was difficult to accept that her friends were no longer free agents. It was hard to find someone to go out for a jar with on a Friday and Saturday. Much and all as she liked Miriam and Ben, they didn't exactly set the world on fire when they were out for the night. Ellen felt more and more out of step with the world since her split with Joseph. If you weren't married and either expecting a baby or rearing children, you were the odd one out.

Surreptitiously she scanned the guests lining the altar rails for Communion. One fine thing caught her eye. He looked in his early thirties. He was of medium build, but taller than she, which was most important. He had dark brown hair and, when he turned to walk back to his seat and she had a closer look, she saw that he was quite good-looking. She wondered if he was eligible. He wasn't one of Vincent's friends, that she knew. Maybe he was a colleague from work or maybe he was one of Emma's relations. That would be just her luck. To meet Mr Right and discover he was related to Ems.

Don't think about that right now, she instructed herself. Meet him first and worry about his family tree later. Maybe he was married or engaged, or going with someone. Ellen felt impatient for the Mass to end so that she could satisfy her curiosity about the man who had quite unexpectedly caught her fancy.

* * *

Ben looked so handsome standing at Vincent's side, Miriam thought proudly as she watched her husband murmur something to his brother. This was a far cry from their quiet wedding in Glenree. Sean and Della had come, Johnny had emigrated to Australia. She had two aunts and an uncle and three of the girls from work and that was it. Ben's relations and friends had been invited, of course, but there'd only been thirty people at the wedding.

The wedding had been held in Glenree's little church. She certainly hadn't had a floral designer. The altar had been decorated with sprays of gladioli from Sheila's garden. The wedding breakfast had been held in the Glenree Arms and it had been nothing like today's occasion promised to be. Sheila certainly hadn't made the fuss about Ben and Miriam's wedding that she'd made about Vincent and Emma's.

It hurt Miriam to think that her mother-in-law thought so little of her. It was all Emma and Vincent this and Emma and Vincent that now. Miriam knew she shouldn't let it get her down. Maybe if her own mother were alive, she'd feel differently. If her father had treated her better in his will, her self-confidence might not be so poor and she wouldn't suffer these silly feelings of rejection.

She couldn't help noticing how proud Judge Connolly was of Emma. Every look, every gesture as he'd walked up the aisle and placed her hand in Vincent's, showed immense pride. Her own father had never once by deed or word made Miriam feel he was proud of her. As far as he was concerned, Miriam was there to look after her parents. Daughters were drudges. Sons were what counted. Judge Connolly certainly didn't feel like that. Emma was his little princess. She seemed to take it for granted. She just didn't know how lucky she was. Emma took it all as her due.

She had immense self-confidence for one so young. No doubt a result of the love and pride lavished on her by her parents. It was ridiculous, but Miriam felt in awe of Emma. She was nine years older than the other girl and yet

Miriam invariably felt inadequate beside her. She sighed. This was silly. She was supposed to be enjoying herself. It was a day out. She looked good. She'd lost a stone in weight through rigid dieting. And it was worth it to get into a size twelve dress again. Why was she sitting here feeling all glum and gloomy? Miriam clasped her hands over her stomach. No one knew it yet, not even Ben, but she guessed that she was about two months pregnant and she was nauseous with it. This was definitely going to be her last. Three children was enough for anyone.

*   *   *

Sheila Munroe nearly burst with pride as she sat at the top table in the Tara suite of the International Hotel. Sophisticated hotels held no fear for her now. After all she had dined at the Russell.

It was an impressively beautiful room. She'd overheard one of Pamela Connolly's friends say approvingly, 'Very much like the Ritz.' Mirrored gilt-edged doors led into a large pillared room. White columns reached to the gold-filigreed ceiling. Luscious ferns in huge terracotta tubs stood at the base of each column. Crystal chandeliers glittered and sparkled like diamonds. A plush deep-pile royal blue and gold carpet covered the floor. The walls were painted in palest primrose which matched the colour of the table linen exactly. A pianist, in a secluded corner near the mirrored doors, played soothing classical music throughout. It was all so elegant. So classy. Pamela Connolly really had good taste, Sheila thought approvingly as she sipped her coffee and helped herself to a *petit four*.

The meal had been delicious. She was definitely going to try cooking salmon in flaky pastry some day at home. It was exceedingly tasty and it couldn't be that difficult to do. The sauce – hollandaise, she thought it was called – that had dressed the asparagus was out of this world. The asparagus itself was a bit of a disappointment. It was her first time to taste it and she'd expected something with a bit more zing to it. Still it had been a superb meal and the sumptuous pavlova that followed had caused a ripple of delight from the approving guests when it was served.

Sheila glanced down at the round table at the far end of the room. She could see Mona Cullen and Bonnie Daly deep in conversation. Sheila sat back and delicately patted the side of her mouth with her pale primrose napkin. No doubt her friends were deeply impressed. Bonnie was a know-all. An expert on every matter. She could bake, sew, crochet, embroider, arrange flowers. Anything. There was an unspoken rivalry between them and always had been even though they were friends.

Bonnie had really tried to rub Sheila's nose in it when her daughter, Maura, got engaged and then married to a Doctor Flynn's son. The wedding breakfast had been held in the Hibernian. A judge's daughter outranked a doctor's son any time. And nothing could top this, Sheila thought with satisfaction. That was why, when Pamela had told her to invite as many guests as she wanted, Sheila invited Bonnie Daly. Bonnie would blab everything to the rest of the guild. This wedding would be the talk of Glenree for months to come. It was one of the best days of Sheila's life.

*   *   *

'I'm Emma's cousin. Chris Wallace. Let's split and go down to the bar and have a drink,' suggested the man who'd caught Ellen's fancy in the church, with a charming grin.

'You're on,' Ellen agreed enthusiastically. She was bored stiff. There wasn't one person here she could have a bit of gas with. All Emma's posh friends could talk about were horses, and holidays on the Costa del Sol. Miriam was feeling sick and she wasn't much fun, so when Ellen had seen Mr Dishy heading in her direction, her heart lifted. He'd given her cleavage a good inspection as he'd introduced himself.

What a pity he was related to Emma. Still, she wouldn't let it stand in the way of progress, she decided, as he guided her out through the mirrored door and they headed in the direction of the lounge downstairs.

'You looked as bored as I felt.' Chris smiled and Ellen thought he had the most beautiful eyes. Blue and darkly lashed, they were his best feature.

'This isn't my scene.' Ellen giggled.

'Or mine. What can I get you to drink?'

'A dry Martini, please.' Ellen sat back in the secluded corner of the lounge and prepared to enjoy herself. It was exciting fancying someone and she certainly fancied Chris. The way he looked at her so admiringly was a turn-on. She wouldn't mind having a good snog with him at all, she decided happily.

She had a wonderful time. Chris was very entertaining. He was an insurance salesman, a junior partner in a developing firm. Insurance was booming, he confided. When the time came he had every intention of going out on his own. Ellen was fascinated. He was full of confidence. She couldn't understand why a good-looking successful young man like him had come to a wedding unaccompanied.

Later, after several drinks, he told her that he'd just broken up with his girlfriend of two years.

Ellen's heart went out to him. He looked so sad when he said it. Impulsively, she reached across and touched his hand. 'It's very hard, I know. It's not long since I broke up with my ex. That was why a wedding was the last place I wanted to be.'

'Exactly!' Chris nodded in agreement. 'Let's get out of here. We could go out to Howth or up to Killiney and then go for a drink and a bite to eat if we're hungry. Nobody will miss us, there's so many guests at the wedding.'

'I'll just get my bag and coat.' Ellen was thrilled.

'Miriam, I'm in love,' she whispered as she collected her belongings.

'Where are you going? You can't leave the wedding!' Miriam was scandalized.

63

'Of course I can. No one's going to miss me. If Ma's looking for me, tell her I'm out in the grounds with Chris.'

'Is that his name?'

'Chris Wallace. Doesn't it have a nice ring to it? Ellen Wallace. Sounds good to me.' Ellen giggled. She was slightly tipsy. 'Guess what, Miriam? He's just broken up with his girlfriend. Maybe it was fate that we met at this wedding. Maybe he's the one. He's got gorgeous eyes and a lovely smile, even if he is dear Em's second cousin.'

'For God's sake you've only just met him. Would you calm down.' Miriam was alarmed. Ellen Wallace indeed. Her sister-in-law was so impulsive. Here she was practically marrying the guy and she didn't know him from Adam.

'See you later,' Ellen murmured, as she cast a wary glance around to see where her mother was. Sheila was deep in conversation with Bonnie Daly, so she made her escape unnoticed.

*   *   *

'I can't believe it's all over.' Emma snuggled into Vincent as the plane swayed from side to side on its descent into London airport. They'd had to fly to London to catch a flight to Rome as it wasn't possible to fly direct from Dublin. They were heading off to Italy for their honeymoon the following morning.

'It was a great day,' Vincent said as the plane landed with a bump. 'And now we're going to have a great night.'

Emma laughed and ran her fingers along his thigh.

'You bet,' she murmured huskily.

They snogged the whole way into London in the back of the big black cab. It was so erotic knowing that they were going to make love properly very soon. Emma quivered with anticipation as Vincent filled in the form at the reception desk. Minutes later they were in their room tearing the clothes off one another. Touching, tasting, caressing. Frantic for each other. All the months of frustration were forgotten as they made love twice in quick succession.

*   *   *

'Any phone calls for me?' Ellen asked anxiously. It was almost noon the following day and she had a fierce hangover. Chris had promised he'd call to make arrangements about taking her out that night.

'No,' Sheila said curtly. She was extremely annoyed with Ellen for gadding off with a stranger when she should have been at her brother's wedding. It had been all hours before she'd got home that morning.

'Would you go down to the shops and get me a pound of butter? I've run short.'

Oh Ma not now, Ellen wanted to yell. It would be just her luck for Chris to ring when she was out. She didn't want to take any chances. But her mother was so irate with her about yesterday, Ellen had to try and get on her right side.

'Right, I'll go,' she said. Maybe Chris wasn't up yet. She'd scoot down on the bike as quick as she could. She threw her coat on and went out into the hall. The black phone stood on a little table by the door. Ellen lifted the receiver slightly so that it was off the hook. She'd replace it when she got back.

By seven that evening she was a nervous wreck. Maybe he'd lost her number. But he could have phoned Mrs Connolly and got it from her if that was the case, Ellen argued with herself. They'd got on so well and they'd had a steamy courting session in the car when he'd brought her home. It had been so sexy. Chris was very experienced compared to Joseph. In fact the more Chris kissed her and caressed her, the more she realized just how little Joseph had known about being sensual and loving.

He hadn't got a clue! Ellen thought in delight as Chris expertly eased her breasts free from the constraints of her new long-line bra, bought for the wedding, and gently and then more firmly kissed and suckled her nipples until she moaned with pleasure. Thank heavens I've got my new bra, she thought for one fleeting moment as he moved the straps down lower. Her old one had been washed so many times it was practically grey.

'What's good for you, honey?' he asked huskily. 'Tell me.'

'This is, this is,' she whispered breathlessly, arching against him. She'd never felt like this before. It was exquisite. Then he eased her dress and slip up around her waist and traced his hands lightly along the top of her inner thighs. Oh God, if only I wasn't so fat, Ellen thought in embarrassment as she looked down and saw his tanned fingers, so dark against the dimpled whiteness of her legs. She hadn't minded her shape with Joseph, she was used to him and he was used to her. But this gorgeous man with his sensual ways and come-to-bed eyes made her want to be thin and sexy and uninhibited. How could you be un-inhibited when you knew you had orange peel skin on your thighs and flab all over. Ellen stiffened and Chris stopped.

'Relax sweetie. It's all right,' he murmured against her ear. 'Let me touch you. I want to make love to you. You're not a virgin, are you?'

Ellen shook her head.

'Well then . . .'

I want you to make love to me too, she wanted to blurt out, but she didn't want him to think she was cheap. Going all the way on a first date was out.

'Let me just touch you,' he urged. 'You really turn me on. I won't take advantage, I promise.' He kissed her passionately and Ellen returned his kisses hungrily, not protesting at all when he slid his hands along her thighs once more and resumed his mind-blowing stroking, moving further up until he slid his thumbs inside the elastic of her panties. His feather-light touch was a revelation to her compared to Joseph's inexperienced rubbing.

'Oooh . . .' she murmured in delight. 'Oh Chris. Oh Chris don't stop . . .' she begged. Butterfly ripples of

66

pleasure came faster and faster and he teased and tormented her, sliding his thumbs back down her thighs until she ached to feel his fingers touching her again in that unbelievably sensuous way.

'Touch me. Touch me,' she pleaded, reaching for his hand.

'Soon,' he murmured against the pulsing hollow of her throat.

'Please.' She arched against him and felt wild un-inhibited joy as his fingers caressed where she guided them until, overwhelmed by the new delicious sensations, she shuddered and called his name as she experienced her first orgasm.

Chris looked at her and smiled with satisfaction as he saw the almost shocked wide-eyed sultry delight in her eyes. He'd seen that first-time look of rapture before. 'My turn now,' he said huskily and Ellen willingly did the whispered things he told her turned him on.

'Let's do this again ... soon. Tomorrow night.' He smiled at her, his eyes dark and inviting. 'I'll call you in the morning and fix a time to collect you when I've sorted out my appointments.'

'Promise?' Ellen felt almost shy.

'I promise, sweetie.' Chris gave her a last lingering kiss before opening the car door to let her out. She waved after him until the tail lights of his car disappeared into the inky darkness.

Ellen floated upstairs to her bedroom. She was ecstatically happy. Her body still quivered at the memory of his touch. Chris was the most gorgeous, handsome, sexy hunk, so tender and sensual. And he wanted to see her again!

'Eat your heart out, Joseph baby.' It was worth going through all the heartache to meet Chris. She smiled at her reflection in the mirror. Her eyes were shining. Her face flushed and tingling from beard rash. She didn't mind. It had been nice feeling the stubbly abrasiveness of his jaw against her cheeks and breasts. She felt alive, invigorated, and giddily tipsy. Sleep was a long time coming as she replayed every memory of him.

And then the waiting. That long long day that frayed her nerves to ribbons. The stomach-churning worry when the phone didn't ring.

He must want to see her again. He must. He'd promised to phone. Ellen was distraught.

The phone remained stubbornly silent. She picked up the receiver as she'd done a hundred times that day already and checked to see if there was a dial tone. There was. Maybe he'd had a crash on the way home and was stuck in hospital somewhere. After all he'd had a good few drinks on him.

'Do you want to come down to the Glenree Arms for a drink with Miriam and me?' Ben stuck his head around the kitchen door.

'Maybe later,' she said glumly. She'd wait until nine and, if there was no call, that was it! At half nine Ellen went to bed and cried her eyes out.

*   *   *

'What can I get you to drink?' Chris Wallace asked the beautiful blonde he'd been chatting up for the last ten minutes.

'Champagne, please,' she said coolly. Chris was impressed. He was going to have to work hard to get anywhere with her. Not like Ellen Munroe yesterday. She'd fallen at his feet after two minutes. Chris liked a challenge. Ellen had got him through yesterday, but she wasn't really his type. He liked sophisticated women and there was something a little desperate about Ellen. Still, she'd been very responsive to his lovemaking. She was soft and voluptuous and he knew, if he persevered, he'd get to first base with her. It was a pity she didn't live in town. That Glenree place was in the back of beyond. He didn't feel like traipsing all the way over to North County Dublin. He knew he'd said he'd phone her. But that's what you always said at the end of an evening. It meant nothing.

This blonde was very much to his liking, even if she was a bit on the bony side. He was going to make sure she ended up liking him. He'd keep Ellen in reserve, Chris decided as he lit a cigarette and ordered champagne for the cosmopolitan woman at his side.

*   *   *

'Oh my God! I've forgotten to take my pills for the past few days.' Emma was horrified as she unpacked her toilet bag in the magnificent hotel room overlooking the Bay of Naples.

'Take them now,' Vincent suggested, coming up behind her and putting his arms around her. 'I'm sure missing a couple won't make any difference.'

'I hope not,' Emma said worriedly. She swallowed two of the little white pills.

'It won't. Don't worry,' Vincent reassured her as he nibbled her earlobe.

'Anyway I don't think you can get pregnant the first time you do it,' Emma comforted herself.

'Well now you've taken two, so that means we can do it all night.' Vincent laughed as he cupped her breasts and sent the most delightful tingles shooting through her.

Emma giggled. 'I wonder am I turning into a nymphomaniac?'

'I hope so.' Vincent turned her to him and kissed her passionately as the sun began to set. Dusk filled the sky and their room was bathed in a soft golden glow.

Chapter Four

Emma took a last look at the mouth-watering buffet laid out on her gleaming chrome and glass dining-table. There was enough food to feed an army. Her mother had kindly offered Emma Mrs Gilligan's services. Mrs Gilligan was a superb cook. She'd worked for the Connollys since Emma was a child. Mrs Munroe had provided tarts and sponges and flans. Emma struggled against a wave of nausea. The look of the food was making her sick. She didn't know what was wrong with her lately. Since she'd come back from her honeymoon, she hadn't been feeling at all well. It was nothing she could put her finger on. Just a vague nausea and a lethargy that was unlike her. She must have picked up some bug in Italy. It was annoying because she wanted to enjoy her house-warming party. She'd been looking forward to it since they'd started building the house. The thought of the look of envy on Gillian's and Frank's faces as she graciously accepted their effusive compliments had given her many a pleasant daydream. Right now, she couldn't care less about compliments or envious faces. All she wanted to do was to go and lie down and bawl her eyes out, she felt so ghastly.

'Will I open the red wine to let it breathe?' Vincent stuck his head around the door.

'You might as well,' Emma said dispiritedly.

'What's wrong, pet?' Vincent walked over to her and put his arms around her. Emma nestled in close to him, enjoying his embrace.

'I just feel a bit off. I don't think I could eat a bite of food.'

'I think you should go and see the doctor tomorrow. You're not yourself this last few days. I'm worried about you.' Vincent was concerned.

'Ah, it's some sort of a bug or something. It's just a nuisance. I was really looking forward to tonight. It'll pass.' Emma tried to brighten her tone.

'Tell you what! I'll get you a brandy. That'll settle your stomach quicker than anything.' Vincent smiled down at her and Emma felt utterly protected. She loved Vincent very much. He was so good to her. She raised her head and drew his down to her and kissed him. His arms tightened around her. They kissed passionately, hungrily. No matter how many times they made love, Emma would never have enough of him, she thought happily as Vincent slowly traced his fingers down along her spine before encircling her slim waist with his hands. A discreet cough ended their kiss. Mrs Gilligan, cheeks pink, stood in the doorway bearing an enormous dish of trifle.

'I'll just put this on the sideboard,' she murmured.

Vincent winked at Emma. 'I'll go and look after the wine. Put on some music. Put on some Elvis.'

'OK,' Emma agreed. She felt a little better. The doorbell chimed. The first guest had arrived. She peered excitedly out the window and saw her parents-in-law. Her excitement petered away. It wasn't any of the gang. It wasn't that she didn't like Vincent's family. She just found them boring. The entire family irritated her. Miriam was an awful old granny and Ellen was too loud by far. Ben was nice enough. She would have preferred not to have had to invite them, but they were Vincent's family and they only lived down the road. It would be very pointed not to. But they needn't think they'd be invited every time there was a party, Emma thought crossly. If they wanted parties they could throw some of their own.

She heard Vincent open the door and then the murmur

of voices and laughter. Emma took a deep breath, banished the scowl from her face, and glided out to greet her guests.

*   *   *

'Hello! Surprise, surprise!' Miriam stood in shock as her sister-in-law, Della, stood beaming on the front step. Sean was coming up the path behind her.

'Hello, Della, Sean,' she said weakly, stepping back to let her unexpected, and if the truth be admitted unwelcome, guests into the house.

'We had to come to Dublin for the day and we decided we couldn't go home without calling to say hello,' Della dripped with honeyed insincerity as her eyes darted inquisitively around. The hall was full of toys and Miriam was disgusted with herself for being caught with an untidy house.

'Actually we were wondering if there was any chance of a bed for the night?' Sean came straight to the point. 'It's a bit late to be trekking back home. We were delayed in town unfortunately. Della wanted to shop.' He glowered at his wife. 'And the kids are knackered.'

'Don't mind him, Miriam. You couldn't come to Dublin and not do a bit of shopping. We just wanted to pop in and say hello. We'll find a B&B somewhere. We can't land in on top of you.'

'Of course you must stay the night,' Miriam said hastily. 'But Ben and I are going out. We've been invited to Emma and Vincent's house-warming and we have to put in an appearance.'

'We'll babysit!' Della announced, giving the impression that her arrival was an answer to prayer.

'I had got a girl from the village to do it but I suppose I could give her a ring and cancel.' Miriam led the way into the kitchen.

'Of course you will. You and Ben go off to your party and leave everything to Sean and me. Sean, go and get the children out of the car. We'll have a bite of tea and I'll get them ready for bed. Just show me where to go.' Della began issuing orders. Taking over as usual.

Miriam felt silent rage bubblir up. The cheek of Della McGrath making free in her house as if she owned it. And the cheek of her and Sean to arrive on her doorstep without a bit of notice expecting to be put up for the night. She wasn't fooled at all by their protestations that they'd get a B&B. It was typical of them to take her so much for granted. If she did the same to them, she'd be given short shrift.

'Well feck the pair of you,' she muttered as she put the kettle on and started making preparations for her unwelcome guests' tea. Miriam was not one to use bad language, but this was an occasion that definitely called for cursing.

By the time she cooked a fry-up, changed the sheets on the bed, and got the children settled, she was in a thoroughly bad humour.

'We'll just go to Vincent's for an hour or so,' Ben said comfortingly as he changed into a clean shirt. 'We'll flop tomorrow when Sean and Della and their darlings are gone.'

'I wouldn't put it past them to stay for the weekend. Have I got "doormat" written in red ink on my forehead or something? I hate being used, Ben,' Miriam fumed. 'Did you see the way she was nosing around my kitchen presses? I ask you. Would you go into someone else's kitchen and start poking around? She's an ignorant cow and she always was. I hate the thought of going out and leaving her in my house.'

'We'll stay at home then?' Ben paused in the act of knotting his tie.

'Emma'd have a face on her if we didn't go. And so would your mother. You know how she likes all the family to get together for things like this.'

'Look, Miriam, if you don't want to go we won't go. Forget Ma and Emma's hurt feelings. Do what *you* want to do, love.'

73

Miriam sighed. Ben was always saying that to her. He was constantly telling her to stand up for herself. It was something she found extremely difficult to do.

'Well?' He eyed her quizzically.

'Let's go,' she said decisively. 'I don't want to spend the night listening to Della pontificating.'

'Me neither.' Ben gave her a hug. 'Let's go and listen to Emma pontificating instead. Then we'll stagger home singing and I'll ravish you on the sitting-room floor and Della'll think you're a wild racy woman.' Miriam laughed.

'You're a nutter, but I love you like crazy.' She flung her arms around him and he gave her a bear-hug back. Ben always made her feel good about herself, and she'd been looking forward to this night out for ages. Besides she was dying finally to get to see the inside of the house. By all accounts it was something to behold.

* * *

'What do you think of the four-poster bed?' Ellen murmured to Miriam as she tried to spear a sliver of smoked ham onto a piece of brown bread. It was difficult to hold her plate and her wineglass and try and eat. The dining-room was jammed with people. There wasn't a seat to be had in the sitting-room. All the white leather sofas were full.

'It's gorgeous! All those fluffy pillows. Come on, let's go and sit on the stairs,' Miriam suggested. She was worn out after her tiring evening.

'I bet she thinks she's Grace Kelly with a bed like that and a house like this. Stuck-up little cat.' Ellen scowled as they pushed and shoved their way out to the hall. She was most annoyed with Emma. She'd been trying to find out, in a roundabout way, if Chris Wallace was coming to the party. She'd casually asked while they'd been sipping aperitifs before the rest of the guests arrived.

Emma gave a dry laugh. 'Try and keep Chris away. I've warned him he'd not to go pestering people to take out life

74

insurance but I can promise you he'll have a client or two before the night's out. He's such a smooth operator.' Then she'd stared at Ellen with her catlike almond eyes. 'Why do you ask?'

'Oh, I was just wondering. I met him at the wedding,' Ellen replied airily. But her heart was beating fast, and she was in danger of blushing.

'A word of advice, Ellen,' Emma said coolly. 'Although he's my cousin and I'm very fond of him, Chris is a shit. His last girlfriend caught him in bed with her sister. He's dating a blonde secretary at the moment. Steer well clear of him.'

Ellen was furious. Emma had just succeeded in making her feel gauche and silly. How dare she, a slip of a twenty-two-year-old, presume to offer her advice. And in such a cool bored tone. Ellen felt like slapping her face.

'Emma's right,' Vincent agreed. 'Ellen, if you know what's good for you, don't touch him with a bargepole.'

'For God's sake, I just asked if he was going to be at the party!' Ellen exploded. 'He's the only one I remember from the wedding. That's all. It's no big deal.'

Emma gave her a knowing look, but refrained from saying anything else. To break the awkwardness, Miriam babbled brightly. 'It must be wonderful having a TV. Ben and I are saving for one.'

'Any time you want to look at it, come over,' Vincent invited. He was very fond of his sister-in-law. He failed to notice Emma's expression of dismay. Fortunately the doorbell rang just then and a crowd of Emma's horsy friends arrived. After that, every time the doorbell chimed, Ellen's heart lurched in case it was Chris.

She knew she was mad. She knew that Emma and Vincent were right about Chris. Deep down she wasn't surprised to find out that his girlfriend had caught him cheating, although it was shocking to know it was with her sister. *That* was low. But, fool that she was, she still wanted to see him again. That was how much he'd got to her. When he'd come over to her and invited her to have a

75

drink at the wedding, Ellen had felt that fate had intervened in her life. There was something about him,
something about the way he looked at her, something
about the way they'd laughed and joked all that day,
something *right* about it all, especially after the way he'd
made love to her.

When he hadn't phoned she'd been devastated. She
hadn't gone out once after work all that week in case he
might phone. She'd cursed him and called him all the
names under the sun and wished she'd never gone off with
him that day. But she knew very well that she'd go out with
him again if she got the chance.

Her heart had soared when she'd heard about the
house-warming party. Maybe he would be at it. She'd been
sick with nerves all week, dreaming of the moment she
might see him again. Tonight she was dressed to kill in
skintight trousers and a red sweater that clung in all the
right places. She'd even lost a few pounds because she
couldn't eat. She'd taken immense care with her make-up.
Trying to get the kohl right had taken ages but it was worth
the effort. It made her eyes look as luminous as Liz
Taylor's. Miriam had told her she looked fabulous.

The doorbell pealed again. Ellen tensed. Emma went to
open the door. Chris stood framed in the doorway. As
handsome as she remembered. He had his arm around a
stunning blonde. Ellen felt sick. Her heart landed with a
dull thud in the pit of her stomach. The smoked ham in her
mouth turned to sawdust. This wasn't the way it was
meant to be. The bastard! she thought frantically. How
could he do that? Hadn't he given a thought to the fact that
she might be here? Had that precious day together meant
so little to him? Ellen felt demeaned and worthless.

Miriam gave her hand a sympathetic squeeze. Tears
blurred Ellen's eyes as she hung her head and hoped that
Chris hadn't noticed her sitting halfway up the stairs.

He didn't even look in her direction. He followed Emma
into the sitting-room and disappeared among the throng.

'Are you OK?' Miriam whispered.

Ellen shook her head and swallowed hard as she angrily wiped the tears from her eyes. 'I know you think I'm mad but I really fancy him and I thought he fancied me.'

'Maybe it's just as well he doesn't, after what Emma told you about him,' Miriam suggested gently.

'Why is it that bastards are always so bloody attractive?' Ellen growled. 'I'm going up to the loo to fix my make-up and then Chris Wallace and the blonde bombshell better watch out because I'm going to party. And how!' She marched up the stairs leaving Miriam staring after her anxiously.

Ellen closed the bathroom door and locked it firmly behind her. No way was she going to skulk off home. A girl had her pride. Let Chris be embarrassed if he wanted to. She was going to ignore him, have a couple of drinks to get her in the mood, and then she was going to boogie for the night.

She stared at her reflection in the mirror. She wasn't beautiful like Emma and the blonde dame but she wasn't unattractive either, she thought grimly. She had nice hazel eyes with flecks of gold, ringed by long dark lashes. Her mouth was a bit too wide, her nose had a smattering of freckles but she had good cheekbones that gave definition to her face. Her hair was a rich dark chestnut and she wore it to her shoulders. Tonight it was tied back with a chiffon scarf which was all the fashion. It didn't look as elegant as Emma's soignée chignon, or as glamorous as the blonde's bob, maybe she should wear it loose so that it would swing around her shoulders when she danced. Ellen whipped off the scarf and shook her hair. She wiped under her eyes where her tears had made her mascara run, then redid her make-up. She took a deep breath, and studied her reflection once more in the wide mirror of the bathroom unit. It was the best she could do. Head high she unlocked the bathroom door and descended the stairs. Of Miriam, there was no sign, so Ellen lit a cigarette, poured herself a generous gin and tonic, and prepared to mingle.

*   *   *

'Everybody . . .' Vincent tinkled a fork against his glass as he tried to get a bit of hush.

'Sshh,' Emma ordered.

'Just a few words to say welcome to all of you, and we hope you're enjoying the party—' Loud whistles and hollers assured him that the assembled guests were indeed enjoying themselves.

'I just want to say', continued Vincent, 'that this is the first party of many and Emma and I want to thank you all for your good wishes. And, before we really get down to serious partying, would you all come out to the front porch with me?' A murmur of anticipation rippled among the intrigued visitors.

Emma looked at her husband in surprise. What was this all about?

Vincent came over to her and put his arm around her. 'Close your eyes.'

'What's happening?'

'Just close your eyes, darling.' Vincent took her hand and led her through the dining-room, into the hall.

'Keep them closed.' He flung open the front door and a gasp from the onlookers made Emma open her eyes wide. She saw a beautiful chestnut mare standing patiently on the marble steps, as a youth from the village murmured soothingly in her ear. A big yellow bow hung from her halter. Her coat gleamed russet and gold in the setting sun and her long silky tail swished from side to side as she gazed on the proceedings with huge alert brown eyes. A brand new horsebox stood on the driveway.

'Oh Vincent!' Emma squealed as she ran out and put her arms around the mare's neck. 'Oh she's gorgeous.'

Vincent smiled proudly at his wife. He'd been planning this surprise for ages. 'Do you like her?'

'Like her . . . I *love* her. I can't wait to ride her.' Emma was ecstatic. She gazed around at her friends and said delightedly, 'Haven't I got the best husband in the world?' There was a murmur of assent.

'Pass me the sick bucket,' Gillian muttered to her

78

husband through thinned lips as people moved forward to get a closer look. 'What a bloody show-off that Vincent Munroe is. Waiting until we were all here to give Emma her horse so that we could see how well off they are. Pretentious asshole.'

Ellen gazed at the horse and wondered how it was that some women were steeped in luck. Emma had a little Mini to zip around in. Now she had a horse to go cantering around the countryside. Ellen had a High Nellie of a bike and, unless she found herself a rich husband, it was all she was ever going to have.

Miriam grinned at Ben and said teasingly, 'My birthday's next week . . . beat that.'

Sheila was as proud as Punch as she watched her son kiss his wife. What a pity Bonnie Daly wasn't at the party to see this grand gesture. Sheila'd make sure to let her know all about it.

'Sheila, let's head for home and leave the young people to it. That racket is giving me a headache.' Mick frowned. The sound of the Hollies blared from the radiogram. Modern music was not to his taste. The sight of all the young people jiving and twisting and worse, wrapped around each other, kissing and pawing, shocked him to the core. It was different when he'd been at parties in his youth. He wouldn't have dreamed of treating Sheila with such disrespect. He noticed Ellen had started dancing to the beat of the music, swinging her hair and her hips. Making a show of herself.

'Look at that one,' he murmured to Sheila. 'Those trousers are far too tight.'

'It's the fashion, dear,' Sheila placated. She was somewhat shocked herself. She'd never been to a party like this. She'd gone upstairs to the toilet and spied a couple sneaking into Vincent and Emma's bedroom. She was horrified. She told Vincent but he just told her not to worry about it. Sheila was glad Pamela Connolly wasn't here to see the carry-on. She and the judge were in Cheltenham for the races. Surely they wouldn't approve of such permissiveness. She certainly wouldn't want them to get the impression that this was how Vincent was reared.

'I think you're right. I think we'll go home,' Sheila murmured as a young man, wearing the most pointy winkle-pickers she'd ever seen, spilt a glass of red wine on the new hall carpet. She'd be crying if it were her house. All those stiletto heels were gouging into the lovely rugs and carpets as well. It was a disgrace. She collected her coat from the hallstand and went to find Vincent.

'We're going, dear. It was a lovely party,' she fibbed. Then indignation got the better of her. 'It's a shame though the way some of those . . .' her nostrils flared as she pointed in the direction of the jiving masses '. . . those uncouth brats have no respect for other people's property. Your lovely new hall carpet is ruined with drink.'

'It will come out, Ma, don't worry about it,' Vincent soothed. 'Emma,' he called. 'Mam and Dad are going.'

Emma disengaged herself from the horse and made her way over to them.

'Thanks a million for coming and thanks for all the sweet things.' Her tone was effusive. She kissed each of them on both cheeks, French style.

'Not at all, dear. Give our regards to your parents when they arrive back.'

'Oh I will. Cheers,' Emma said airily and then headed back to the horse. 'Isn't she a dream?' she exclaimed to another friend who was admiring the mare. 'I think I'll call her Cleopatra.'

Sheila was not pleased to be brushed off so casually. The least Madame could have done was to see them off the premises. Cheers indeed!

'We'll see you, Vincent.' Sheila pursed her lips in a little moue of disapproval but Vincent didn't notice her annoyance as he greeted some latecomers.

'Young people now get things too easy,' Sheila grumbled as she got into the car. 'It wasn't like our day when we had to work hard for everything we got. And we had to wait until we could afford it. Now it's all hire purchase and the never-never. No wonder they don't put value on what they've got. And I'll tell you another thing, Mick,' she continued as they drove slowly down the drive, 'it would match that young madam better if she learned how to do a bit of baking rather than be off gadding about the countryside on that horse. Vincent would want to make a firm stand there.'

'Now don't go interfering, Sheila. It's their business what they do,' Mick warned. He knew his wife of old. She liked to poke her nose in. She was forever bossing Miriam around and telling her how to rear her children. Emma wasn't one to be bossed, he thought in some amusement.

'I have no intention of interfering,' Sheila retorted haughtily. 'I was merely saying the girl should learn how to bake.'

'Mmm.' Mick's tone was sceptical. Sheila pursed her lips and maintained an aloof silence for the rest of the short journey home.

*　　*　　*

'This soup is nice, isn't it? Imagine serving soup cold,' Miriam murmured to Ben as they sampled the buffet.

'I think it's called vichyssoise. There's potatoes and leaks in it and cream. I had it once in a restaurant,' Ben explained as he sampled a portion of egg mayonnaise.

'There's some spread here. Vincent and Emma certainly have expensive tastes. I don't know how they can afford it all. New house. All mod cons. Horse and horsebox. Just look at the furniture, Ben. White leather!'

'Vincent's doing really well in the business,' Ben observed as he helped himself to coleslaw. 'Property prices have gone sky-high. There's a huge building boom and he's on big commission. Do you think you married the wrong brother?'

'Never!' Miriam reached out and gave him a hug. 'Do you think you married the wrong girl? Here I am pregnant and getting fat again.'

81

'You're beautiful, Miriam. I know the baby was a bit of a shock but I'm happy about it.' Ben caressed her cheek.

'So am I but this is definitely the last one,' Miriam declared.

'Definitely,' Ben agreed with a twinkle in his eye and they both burst out laughing.

Emma swanned past giggling at something Chris Wallace was saying to her. Miriam looked at her sylph-like figure enviously. She was wearing a stunning black dress that clung to every curve. No matter how hard Miriam dieted, she'd never have a figure like Emma's. Besides it was too late for all that now, Miriam thought stoically as she helped herself to a portion of cold turkey. The dress she'd worn to the wedding no longer fitted her. Her waist had thickened noticeably and she couldn't get into a size twelve any longer. Now that the first three months of her pregnancy were over and the dreadful nausea was gone, she might as well enjoy her food. Especially as it was food she hadn't had to cook herself. She hadn't bothered to have anything with Della and Sean, she'd been so put out. Now she was hungry.

'Have some of this, it tastes nice. I don't know what it is. It's spicy,' Ben suggested, pointing to an interesting dish. 'It looks like chilli.'

'Mmm,' murmured Miriam. 'This food is scrumptious. It makes our meat and two veg dinners seem so boring. I must start experimenting. The party's fun, isn't it? Better than being stuck with Sean and Della. I wonder how Ellen's getting on?' She peered around but couldn't see any sign of her sister-in-law. She'd go looking for her as soon as she'd finished her meal, Miriam decided, as she and Ben edged their way to a corner where there were two empty chairs.

*   *   *

'Why did you bother to ask me to this party if you're going to spend the evening trying to sell insurance policies?' Suzy

Kenny snapped furiously as she cornered Chris Wallace in the hall. She took another slug of her Martini. It was her sixth this evening, but what was a girl to do when she was dropped like a hot potato by her escort, just because he wanted to flog insurance. He'd spent the past half-hour in conversation with some business associate of Vincent's. Suzy had been left to her own devices and she didn't like it one bit. She didn't know a single soul at this party. It was very lively and the food was great, but she wasn't in the humour for flying solo. She wanted Chris's attention. She was used to men dancing attendance on her and Chris had been very attentive when she'd started dating him a few weeks ago. In fact, the more she kept him at his distance, the more eager he'd been to please her. But lately it was as if he was growing bored with her. He didn't phone when he said he would and sometimes he even cancelled dates. It was very distressing, especially as she'd started to feel very strongly about him. She couldn't help it. There was just something so appealing about Chris. When he turned on that little boy charm he was irresistible. Nevertheless, charm or not, she'd had enough of being on her own. If Chris didn't start paying her some attention she was going to split. Although that would be difficult, seeing as they were stuck out in the back of beyond somewhere.

'Dance with me,' she demanded aggressively.

'OK, doll.' Chris drew her into his arms. Suzy was fairly tight, he reflected as alcohol fumes wafted past his nostrils. She'd been drinking steadily since she came to the party. He sighed. Women! They were all the same. Attention! Attention! They all craved attention and, while he was happy enough to supply it, he had to make a living. Occasions like this were ideal for making business contacts. As they danced, his eyes scanned the room to see if there were any more suitable candidates for the terrific opportunities he could put their way. Life insurance was an absolute necessity. If only people could be persuaded. He noticed a woman with a shapely figure, dressed in skintight trousers that clung to her voluptuous curves. She was dancing uninhibitedly, jiving to the sound of Buddy Holly. Very nice, thought Chris. Suzy, though sophisticated and with-it, was a bit on the skinny side. He liked curves. The woman turned and shimmied low, laughing at her partner who was trying to copy her moves. Chris looked again.

Well fancy that, he thought as he recognized her. It was Vincent's sister. The bird he'd shifted at the wedding. Helen . . . No, Ellen. She was looking good. She knew how to enjoy herself, not like Suzy who lurched limply against him.

'I think you'd better lie down for a while,' Chris suggested.

'With you?' Suzy slurred.

'Who else?' he murmured as he led her out of the room and upstairs. He eased her down onto the bed in one of the guest rooms and Suzy drew him down beside her. They kissed. Then Suzy's eyes rolled in her head and she passed out.

'Sweet dreams, babe.' Chris drew the coverlet over her and left her to it. He had other fish to fry.

Downstairs, he saw Ellen chatting to the bloke she'd been dancing with. Not one to let a consideration like that stand in his way, he strode over and said with pretend surprise, 'Ellen! Hi. It's good to see you again. I was hoping I might bump into you. I lost your phone number and I kept meaning to ask Emma for it.'

Ellen's heart soared as she turned and found herself staring into his vivid blue eyes. It was as if everyone in the room had faded into oblivion. She saw his lips move but couldn't concentrate, her heart was beating so fast. She heard him say something about asking Emma for her phone number. Liar! she thought to herself as she heard his pathetic excuse. Still, he'd made a point of coming to say hello and there was no sign of the blonde bombshell. Play it cool, she warned herself. She didn't want Chris Wallace to think that she was ready to fall into his arms after the shabby way he'd treated her.

'Hi, Chris.' Her voice was admirably cool. 'Are you enjoying the party? Let me introduce Larry Ryan.' She introduced the two men and tried to compose herself.

'Larry, do you mind if I have a dance with Ellen? I haven't seen her for ages,' Chris asked smoothly.

The nerve of him! Ellen thought crossly. Swanning over to her and expecting her to drop everything to dance with him.

'Actually, Chris, we were just going to the buffet to get something to eat,' Ellen fibbed. 'Maybe later.'

'Oh! Right.' It was clear he was taken aback.

Good enough for you, Ellen thought bitterly as she took Larry's arm and steered him towards the dining-room.

'I hope you don't mind,' she said apologetically to her partner. 'I didn't particularly want to dance with him.'

'I should think not, you're with me. Do you want to get something to eat?'

'Yeah, sure.' Ellen tried to keep her voice light. Food was the last thing she wanted now that she'd actually spoken to Chris. She was already beginning to regret her rejection of him. It was most annoying. Larry just wasn't interesting in comparison. He was a bit of a geek, actually, she thought glumly as she watched him fill his plate with goodies. He seemed to think that she was with him for the evening, wherever he'd got that idea! This was the big chance she'd been waiting for and she'd got on her high horse and ruined it.

But a girl has to have some pride, she argued silently. Chris had to have some respect for her. He'd used her the day of Emma's wedding. She couldn't let him see how much of a doormat she was prepared to be for him. Ellen took a mouthful of salad and felt her throat close. She could barely swallow the food. Her heart filled with pain. Oh Chris, I wish I'd never met you, she thought unhappily. Why had she said no when she so badly wanted to say yes? If only she had the nerve to throw her pride to the winds and go and dance with him.

Chris watched Ellen walk away. He'd misjudged her, he

thought in some surprise. He wasn't used to being refused by women. He was sure she'd have been delighted to see him. They'd got on extremely well at the wedding. He could see no reason why Ellen should refuse to dance with him. Maybe she was just being polite because of the other guy. He'd try and catch her on her own later. In the meantime, he'd just spotted Eric Flood, who owned a building outfit. A potential candidate for life insurance, Chris thought with satisfaction.

An hour later, he spotted Ellen on her own. He made his move.

'Where's lover-boy?' he murmured into her ear as he came up behind her. Ellen whirled around.

'Oh, oh it's you.'

'Yeah, it's me. Hiya, tetchy.' Chris grinned and Ellen couldn't resist grinning back. When he smiled at her like that she couldn't help herself. This was another chance, to hell with it, she was going to make the most of it. She knew she'd regret it for the rest of her life if she didn't.

'Where's the other guy?'

'He's gone to the loo. Where's your girlfriend?'

'Oh, she's not my girlfriend. She's someone I know and she wanted to come to the party. She's flaked out upstairs.' Chris was dismissive. 'Are you going to dance with me now?'

'Sure. Why not?' Ellen said as if it was no big deal but the minute she slipped into his arms she knew she was lost. They danced to the slow number, bodies entwined. Larry arrived back, but she ignored his reproachful gaze and gave herself up to the bliss of being in Chris's arms.

'Let's split,' he murmured huskily against her ear.

'What about the girl you came with?'

'I told you, she just came to the party. She's in no condition to go anywhere. Come on, let's go back to my place.'

Ellen wavered. Chris was a swine, to leave that girl on her own. But she was very flattered that he wanted to be with her instead of the blonde Barbie. And she wanted to be with him. Swine or not, she'd fallen for him, hook, line and sinker. If she didn't go with him now, that might be the last she'd see of him. Who knew when Emma and Vincent would throw another party.

'Come on, let's get away by ourselves,' he urged. 'There's too many people here.' He ran his fingers down the length of her spine and let his hand rest lightly on the top of her hip. She could feel him getting aroused as he pressed close against her. He kissed her. The pressure of his mouth firm against her own. His tongue seeking the softness of hers as he teased her with feather-light touches.

Ellen drew away, dazed. It was lovely experiencing all those sensations she remembered from their first time together. She wanted more.

'OK,' she whispered. 'I'll just get my coat.'

'I'll meet you outside at the car,' Chris said as they walked towards the hall. Ellen rooted impatiently for her coat amidst the piles on the telephone seat.

'You're not leaving with him, are you, Ellen?' Miriam appeared at her shoulder.

'Oh Miriam, don't give out to me,' Ellen snapped.

'Ellen, you can't. You heard what Emma and Vincent had to say about him. He's trouble. And what about that girl he came with?'

'Look, Miriam, that's her problem. I'm a big girl now, I don't need people telling me what to do. OK?'

'Well I think you're mad.'

'Fine. I'm mad. See you when I see you.' Ellen took her coat and marched out the door. She was practically thirty, for God's sake, she didn't need Miriam's advice. It was all right for her, she had someone. Ellen was lonely and panicky. Her twenties were nearly over. Thirty loomed like a dark threatening cloud on the horizon. Once she was thirty she could forget men and marriage. She'd be over the hill, facing a life of barren desolation, just like Miss Coony the postmistress, who was known to drink cooking sherry. All because she'd been let down by a man who'd broken their engagement and upped and married someone else, many years ago. Miss Coony was a crabby spinster who hadn't a good word for anyone. Who'd want to end up like that? Ellen had to take her chance. And what was more she *wanted* to take her chance with Chris. The minute she'd laid eyes on him, she'd known he was the man for her. Much more so than Joseph Boring McManus, she thought viciously, remembering her ex and the trauma he'd put her through.

Chris revved the engine of his Cortina and she hurried to get into the car beside him. He leaned over and kissed her and sped off down the drive, gravel spitting in his wake.

* * *

'I shouldn't have eaten all that food,' Miriam moaned. She was feeling slightly queasy. She pulled her nightdress over her head, brushed her teeth and followed Ben down the hallway. She shivered. There was still a nip in the air and the hall was cold. Not like Vincent and Emma's house, so snug with its central heating system. She passed her bedroom door and thought enviously of Della and Sean ensconced in her big double bed. Ben and herself were sleeping on the bed settee in the sitting-room.

'It was a good night, wasn't it?' Ben held the covers back for her.

'I wouldn't like to be doing the washing-up after it.' Miriam yawned. It was much later than she usually went to bed and she was whacked. She snuggled in close to Ben. 'Night, love,' she murmured sleepily as Ben's arms tightened around her. Sleeping on the settee wasn't that bad and there was still a glow from the dying embers in the fireplace that gave the room a cosy hue. Her eyes were just closing when she heard Daniel howl.

'Oh no.' The groan came from the depths of her soul. Ben was already snoring. Miriam gave him a dig in the ribs. It was Friday night, he didn't have to get up for work in the morning. She'd been up every night this week.

'Wha—'

'Daniel's crying.'

'Aw hell.' Ben sat up groggily.

'Thanks, Ben.' Miriam stretched out her limbs to the four corners of the settee. She heard Ben go down the hall into the baby's room. The crying stopped soon after. Thank God for that, she thought drowsily. All she craved was a decent night's sleep. A fleeting thought of Ellen came to mind. Where was she, Miriam wondered. She was heading for trouble by getting involved with the likes of Chris Wallace. But Ellen was terribly stubborn and single-minded once she got an idea into her head. Nothing Miriam or anyone else said would make the slightest bit of difference. Miriam said a little prayer for her sister-in-law and fell asleep.

* * *

'Promise you'll pull out in time,' Ellen urged Chris as he eased down her panties and caressed her soft curvy flesh.

'Mmmm, don't worry. You've got a great ass.' Chris groaned with pleasure as she unzipped his trousers and slid them down over his hips. He kissed her fiercely, bruising the softness of her lips. Ellen returned his kisses and caresses ardently. This was what she'd been hungry for. The feel of him in her arms again, the joy of being held close, the power of being wanted. When he entered her she felt immense happiness. She was special to Chris, she knew it. There was a bond between them that had been there from the beginning. This was the man who was going to marry her and grow old with her. She gave herself up to the pleasure he was giving her, and touched and caressed him until his harsh breathing and frantic thrusts told her that he was near orgasm.

'Now, Chris. Pull out now,' she gasped.

'Yeah, babe.' He groaned, moving against her.

'Now, Chris!' she said in alarm, feeling his orgasm start.

'All right,' he gasped as he drew away from her. Ellen felt his wetness against her and hoped against hope that he hadn't left it too late.

89

Chris gazed down at Ellen as she slept in his arms. Her chestnut hair fanned out across his chest, her face was flushed after lovemaking and a little smile curled around her lips. Chris inhaled his cigarette. Tonight had been good. Really good. Ellen was made for lovemaking. She was so responsive, much less inhibited than Suzy. He was blown out with Suzy now for sure. He supposed that he shouldn't have left her sleeping it off in Emma's. But she was out for the count. Pissed out of her skull. Short of slinging her over his shoulder in a fireman's lift, there was nothing else to do. Right now he didn't particularly care. Suzy could be abrasive at times. It jarred. Though they'd only been together twice, Ellen was much more gentle and affectionate with him. He liked that. It was vaguely comforting. He stubbed out his cigarette and leaned over and softly nuzzled her earlobe. Ellen murmured something and stirred.

'Come on, Ellen, put your arms around me. Kiss me, baby,' he whispered and was immensely gratified when her arms tightened around him and her lips sought his.

*   *   *

'Can you imagine the nerve of Chris leaving that girl asleep in our guest room?' Emma grumbled as she cold-creamed her face. She looked extremely fetching in her frilly ice-blue baby-doll pyjamas and matching mules. Vincent's favourite night-time outfit.

'I didn't see him leave.' Vincent lay back against the pillows, waiting for his wife to join him. 'I wonder did he shift someone?'

'I wouldn't doubt it!'

'He's got a way with women all right.' Vincent grinned.

A thought struck Emma. 'I didn't see Ellen leave . . . you don't think—'

'She's crazy if she went with him, after what we told her about him. I really don't think Ellen's that stupid.' Vincent frowned.

Emma wasn't so sure. But she said nothing. It was awkward. She didn't want that loony sister of Vincent's getting involved with a relation of hers. She'd probably get blamed if it ended in tears.

'It was a great party all the same,' Vincent said with satisfaction.

'Yeah, it was. And did you see Gillian and Frank's faces when you gave me the horse? They were pea-green with envy.' Emma giggled. That moment had made her night.

'They're always trying to impress, but it was them who were impressed this evening. Frank will be busting a gut now to try and outdo us. He's very competitive. But he's such an idiot he'll spend beyond his means. I won't. We'll draw in our horns now for a little while and get on an even keel again. Maybe we could have another party at Easter.'

'Lovely,' Emma approved as she slid into bed beside him.

'How are you feeling now?' Vincent was solicitous as he put his arms around her.

'I don't feel as bad as I did. I'd love to have been able to eat some of the buffet, it looked gorgeous.'

'It was. Mrs Gilligan really surpassed herself. Everybody was talking about it.'

'Miriam certainly enjoyed it,' Emma remarked tartly. Every time she'd seen the other girl she was stuffing her face. It made Emma feel ill to think about it. No wonder her sister-in-law was putting on so much weight. She was bursting out of that dreadful navy crimplene trouser suit she'd been wearing.

'Well she *is* eating for two.' Vincent yawned.

'She's what!'

'Oh! Of course you didn't know. Ben told me tonight. Miriam's expecting. Seemingly she was very sick for the first three months. She couldn't eat and she was exhausted.

But that's all passed and she's fine now and well able to enjoy her food. They're going to tell Mam and Dad at dinner on Sunday,' Vincent explained.

A chill enveloped Emma. Not able to eat. Tired for no reason. Crikey, she thought in horror, remembering those missed pills. She couldn't be. Surely a few missed pills couldn't make a difference. Don't think about it. Just go to sleep and you'll be fine in the morning. It's a bug, Emma tried to reassure herself. Being pregnant was unthinkable. It couldn't possibly happen to her.

* * *

'You bastard, Chris Wallace. How could you do that to me?' Suzy screamed down the phone the following afternoon.

'Calm down, angel. You were pissed. What else could I do?'

'Don't you angel me, you fucker. You left me in a stranger's house. I didn't know what to say to them this morning. I was mortified.'

'Well you shouldn't drink so much if you don't want to black out in strangers' houses,' Chris drawled. A shrill virago was the last thing he needed. He had a very important client coming in at two, he wanted to have all his facts at his fingertips.

'Listen you pig, I've had enough of you. Go find someone else to treat like shit, because *nobody* treats me like that.'

Chris winced as the receiver at the other end was slammed down with a vengeance. 'Suit yourself,' he growled as he resumed studying his figures.

He had found someone else. Ellen. He'd been telling her all about today's meeting and she'd been *fascinated*. Suzy got bored when he started talking about work. Ellen was genuinely interested and wanted to know more. He liked a woman with *brains*. Suzy was only interested in clothes and make-up. He scowled. He wasn't used to being

92

dumped by a woman. Still, give Suzy a few days to cool off, send her a bunch of red roses and she'd be fine.

On the other hand, maybe he wouldn't bother. He'd get some roses for Ellen, she'd really appreciate them. The second time last night had been sensational. She'd been sleepy and relaxed and very giving. He was looking forward to seeing her again. As soon as his client was gone, he'd phone her and make a date. Chris leaned back in his chair and thought of the night before and was almost sorry when his secretary interrupted his reverie to announce the arrival of his client.

*   *   *

'Oh Miriam! I'm so happy,' Ellen bubbled. She was dying to talk about Chris. She'd wanted to talk about him all day. If she didn't talk about it soon she'd burst.

'Ellen, Ellen, Ellen, what am I going to do with you?' Miriam shook her head, half amused, half dismayed at her sister-in-law's impetuosity.

'Are your visitors gone?' Ellen plonked down on a kitchen chair and lit a cigarette.

'Thank God. They went early this morning. I really thought I was going to be stuck with them. Sean is discovering how tied down you are when you have a farm,' Miriam said dryly. 'Forget about them. What about you and Chris? Where did you go last night?'

'Quick, put the kettle on and we'll have a cuppa. I've got to go home and bathe and change. I'm going out on a date. Can you believe it. He *phoned*! He wants to see me again tonight. I just want to dance.' She stood up and did an exuberant twirl around the kitchen as Miriam filled the kettle.

'Would you calm down! What about the other one he was with?' Miriam scolded.

'Ah Miriam, don't be like that! I know you think he's a bit of a playboy. But he's not really. Honest. He's lovely. He's very kind and tender. And she's not really his

93

girlfriend. Just someone he brought to the party,' Ellen assured her earnestly.

Miriam eyed her sceptically. She was tempted to ask Ellen what was his excuse for not phoning after the wedding. But then she looked at her sister-in-law's shining eyes and joyful expression and she couldn't bring herself to do it. 'So where did you go last night?' she enquired as she busied herself with cups and saucers.

Ellen hesitated. Miriam was much more strait-laced than she was. She hadn't approved of her sleeping with Joseph. She'd probably think she was a right slut for sleeping with Chris on the second date. But she wanted to tell her, badly. She wanted someone to confide in and Miriam was a great confidante.

She took a deep breath. 'Um . . . well . . . actually we went back to his place . . .'

'Did you take precautions?' Miriam asked quietly.

'He was very careful, Miriam,' Ellen assured her, trying to suppress the memory of the second time. The second time had been like no other lovemaking she'd ever experienced. It had been exquisite but Chris hadn't withdrawn. She hadn't wanted him to, it was so good. He'd promised to use Frenchies from now on.

'Be careful, Ellen.'

'I will, I will. I promise. Oh Miriam it was fantastic. I had one of those orgasms.' She giggled.

Miriam blushed to the roots of her hair. 'Ellen!' she expostulated.

'Well I did! I never had one with Over-In-Two-Seconds-Flat-McManus. That's for sure,' she scoffed. 'He was pathetic when I think of it.'

'You're something else, you know. Could you imagine the faces of your Ma and Bonnie Daly if they could hear you.'

'Huh! Bonnie Daly wouldn't know what an orgasm was in a million years. I bet she had sex three times in her life to conceive her three treasures. Wouldn't you know by the look of poor old Tommy that he's deprived. I've never seen such a miserable sod in my life.'

Miriam tittered. 'Ellen Munroe, I fear for you!'

'Well don't. I'm as happy as can be. And I never thought I *would* be happy. This is going to work out. I know it. We get on like a house on fire and I don't care who disapproves. I can't live my life to accommodate other people's feelings. I only have one life to live and if people don't like the way I live it, tough. And if Emma and Vincent say anything to me, by God I'll let them have it.' Her tone was defiant.

'People worry about you because they care about you, Ellen.' Miriam handed her a cup of tea.

'Just be happy for me, Miriam,' Ellen pleaded.

'I am, I am,' Miriam said gently. There was no point in going on about it. Ellen would only dig her heels in. She was as stubborn as a mule.

'What are you going to wear?'

Ellen's eyes lit up. 'I was thinking I might wear my new red hipsters and my black sleeveless ribbed polo.'

'Hmm,' Miriam approved. 'I wish I could wear hipsters, I'd look like Bunty the elephant.'

'Let's go on a strict diet. Starting tomorrow,' Ellen said eagerly as she munched on a Marietta biscuit liberally spread with butter.

'Well I can't really because of the baby!' Miriam demurred. 'But I could cut out rubbish. I'll give up bread and chocolate. And we'll start walking as well.'

'Yeah, and we'll eat loads of fruit and drink gallons of water. That's what models do to keep their figures.' Ellen was resolute. 'I want to be as thin as a rake for the summer. I want to be able to wear a bikini.'

'I wouldn't have the nerve to wear one.' Miriam rubbed a hand over her rounded tummy. 'Not with my stretch marks.'

'Who cares about them if you've got the figure to wear one. And I'm determined to have the figure. It's mortifying being chubby when Chris and I are . . . well you know . . . in bed. I keep thinking how slim that Suzy one is and I wonder how can he fancy me.'

'You're not chubby, you idiot,' Miriam snorted. 'You just need to lose a few pounds.'

'A stone at least. But this is it.' She beamed. 'I better go home and beautify myself. Chris is picking me up in town at eight. Is it OK to say I'm staying the night with you, if I don't come home?'

'Ellen, for God's sake be careful. Say your mother phones looking for you?'

'She *won't*, Miriam.' Ellen's tone was a little testy. 'Just this once.'

'OK.' Miriam wasn't happy about the idea.

'Living at home is so restrictive,' Ellen grumbled. 'I think I'll start looking for a job in Dublin and get a flat there. It would make life much simpler and I'd be as free as a bird.'

'Just wait until you see how things go with Chris,' Miriam cautioned. In Ellen's reckless state, she was liable to do something daft.

'This is going to work, I know it. Chris is special. I've never felt like this about anyone.'

But how does he feel about you? Miriam wanted to ask, but she restrained herself. 'It's early days yet. Stay cool.'

'I sure will. *Ciao baby*, as Emma would say.' Ellen grinned, kissed Miriam and huried off home to prepare for her date.

As she watched her sister-in-law race down the garden path Miriam shook her head. Ellen was so naïve. So trusting and open. She'd been devastated when Joseph McManus dumped her. If this Chris geezer let her down it would be disastrous. And Miriam didn't think much of what she'd seen of him so far. 'Please, God, don't let her get hurt,' she murmured as she poured hot water over the dirty crockery in the sink.

Ellen had no such fears as she dropped a scented bath cube into her bath. She rubbed soap between her hands and made a lather which she smeared on her legs. She began to shave her right leg. She wanted her skin to be smooth and silky for Chris. She'd paint her toenails as well, she decided, humming to the sound of Dean Martin singing *Return to Me* on her transistor which was perched precariously on the side of the bath. Ellen smiled to herself. Right now it seemed as if every love song that had ever been written was written for her. She was halfway through her left leg when Elvis came on crooning *Can't Help Falling In Love.* His deep, husky musical voice breathed life into the beautiful words. Ellen paused, closed her eyes and listened intently. The song described *exactly* her feelings for Chris. Only Elvis could sing it like that. Elvis was unique. Ellen shivered, soon she'd be in Chris's arms. It was all she wanted.

When Chris presented her with a beautiful bouquet of roses when he met her outside the GPO, Ellen's heart soared. She was exquisitely happy. They went to the Gresham for a drink and he told her all about the new client he'd persuaded to take out a large insurance policy the previous day. He was in great form as he explained the policy in detail. His bonus would be pretty substantial, he assured her. Soon he'd be able to think about going out on his own.

'You can be my secretary,' he said light-heartedly and she jumped at the idea.

'I could get a place in Dublin, I really want to leave home and do my own thing. It would be great! I know about running a business. I do all the paperwork for my dad. And you could explain all about insurance to me. I'm sure I'd grasp it.' Ellen was bubbling with enthusiasm.

'I'm sure you would.' Chris smiled deep into her eyes and squeezed her hand. 'We'd make a terrific team.'

A terrific team she repeated over and over to herself, hugging his words to her. He took her home and they made love for hours. She didn't need any persuading to stay the night. She was where she wanted to be . . . always.

Chapter Five

'There must be some mistake, Doctor. I couldn't possibly be pregnant.' Emma's voice was sharp and high-pitched. 'I don't plan on having children for a long time yet.'

'I'm afraid, my dear, it's a case of the best-laid plans and all that.' Doctor Waldron patted her shoulder and sat down behind his desk. 'If you'd come to me before you started taking those pills, I wouldn't have let you go near them. It was very irresponsible of your sister to give them to you. And no one knows what the side effects are going to be like in years to come.'

'I just didn't want to get pregnant,' Emma said sulkily, not relishing the lecture. 'It's not fair!'

'Ach, you'll be fine, my dear. It's a bit of a shock now, I know. But you'll get used to the idea. Won't it be wonderful to have a little baby to keep you occupied when your husband's at work?' Doctor Waldron said jovially.

Emma burst into tears. What did that fat old idiot know? She'd only gone to him because he was her own family doctor and she didn't know anyone else. She hadn't needed to see a doctor in years. Now she'd be seeing a lot more of him. The thought made her cry harder.

'There, there,' Doctor Waldron said gruffly, giving a surreptitious glance at his watch. He had half a dozen calls to make and his wife liked him to be home at one-fifteen sharp, for his lunch. It was tears of happiness young Emma Munroe should be crying. Wasn't a baby what every young wife wanted? It would be different if it was her sixth. Then she'd have something to bawl about. All this nonsense about contraceptives and planned pregnancies. These newfangled notions were beyond him. Retirement seemed an ever more enticing prospect, he reflected glumly as he listened to his patient's heart-rending sobs.

'Come along now, Emma. That won't do you or the baby any good. Wipe your eyes and go out and give your husband the happy news with a smile on your face. You don't want to upset him, now do you?'

Emma shook her head and took some deep breaths. Poor Vincent. What was he going to say? Babies hadn't figured in his plans either. He was out in the waiting-room. He'd taken the morning off work to accompany her. He'd have a blue fit when he heard. She hadn't confided her pregnancy fears to him, just in case she'd been mistaken. Her lip started to wobble again.

'Now, now.' Doctor Waldron had had enough. He ushered Emma out the door to where Vincent was patiently waiting. He jumped up when he saw them.

'Everything OK?'

'Everything's fine,' Doctor Waldron said reassuringly. 'Your wife is perfectly healthy. I'll leave her to tell you all about it. Good day to you both and congratulations.' He patted Emma paternally on the shoulder and left the room.

'What did he mean? Congratulations?' Vincent looked mystified.

'Oooohhh Vincent.' Emma buried her head in his chest and started crying again.

'What is it? What's wrong? Tell me, Emma.'

'I'm pregnant,' Emma howled.

'What?' Vincent's jaw dropped.

'I'm sorry, Vincent. I really am.'

He stared down at her. 'A baby!'

Emma couldn't talk, she was so upset.

'It's all right, love. Stop crying.' Vincent cuddled her close. 'Let's get out of here.' He led his weeping wife out to the car.

'Come on now, Emma, I know it's an awful shock and not what we'd planned, but we'll get used to the idea,' he said, weakly. 'We would have had children at some stage. We'd agreed that.' He was trying to be positive about it. But it *was* a shock. He'd thought that pill thing guaranteed freedom from pregnancy from the way Jane and Emma raved about it. So much for *that* idea, he thought as he sat in the car with his arms around Emma. He should have used johnnies.

'It won't be so bad, Emma. Look at Ben and Miriam, their kids are nice little things.' The thought of Miriam bursting out of her navy crimplene trouser suit made Emma cry even harder. She'd be like that soon. Not in a navy crimplene trouser suit. *Never* that. But soon her clothes wouldn't fit her and she'd have to get bigger sizes and she'd be FAT. It was a horrible thought. Another thought struck her. Childbirth was supposed to be excruciatingly painful. How would she cope with that? It was bad enough if she got a headache. Tentacles of fear squeezed her insides. This was a nightmare. One that wasn't going to go away.

'Just take me home, Vincent,' Emma wept. 'My life is over.'

* * *

'Nonsense. Of course your life isn't over, you silly girl. This is great news. Your father will be thrilled. He's dying to be a grandfather,' Pamela Connolly said soothingly as she tried to comfort her distraught daughter. It was two weeks since Emma had found out about her pregnancy and she'd broken the news to Pamela, who'd returned from a spring break in England.

'I don't want to have a baby, Mum.' Emma glared at her mother frustratedly. Why would no-one listen to her and believe her when she kept saying she didn't want this child? Mrs Munroe and Miriam had dismissed her fears and assured her she'd be fine once she got used to the idea. They'd been thrilled. Full of delight for her. And her mother was just the same. Fierce resentment surged. She didn't want this child. Nothing was going to change that. Not Mrs Munroe or Miriam or her mother or father or even Vincent who was at his wit's end over her misery.

'You're better to have your children when you're young, darling. You have the energy for them when they're toddlers and then, before you know it, they're all grown up and you've a whole new life for yourself.' Pamela was brisk. She observed her daughter, noting Emma's pale pinched expression and the dark circles around her eyes. She did feel sorry for Emma. It was tough being brought to earth with a bang. A honeymoon baby was always a bit of a shock. She knew her daughter had been looking forward to having fun, and entertaining and riding her lovely new mare. Emma was not one for responsibilities. Pamela was well aware of that.

Well unfortunately responsibilities were part of life and life was tough. It was time for her darling daughter to grow up.

'I hope, dear, that you're not making life miserable for Vincent?' Pamela arched a perfectly plucked eyebrow. Emma hung her head and said nothing. What did her mother want? For her to go around singing *Que Sera, Sera* like Doris Day and pretend that she was over the moon with happiness. If she couldn't be dejected in front of Vincent, who could she be dejected in front of? He was her husband. She didn't have to put on an act in front of him.

'Now that's not fair, Emma,' Pamela rebuked sternly. 'You can't think of yourself all the time.'

'Oh for God's sake, Mother, leave me alone!' Emma exploded. She hadn't driven all the way from Glenree to Foxrock for a lecture. She wanted sympathy and she certainly wasn't getting any. Why did everyone think she should be thrilled to be pregnant? Was she some sort of a freak because she hated the idea? Did no-one understand how she felt?

*   *   *

She was always as regular as clockwork. She had a twenty-eight-day cycle come hell or high water. Now it was thirty-three days – five days over – and Ellen was very scared. Maybe worry had stopped her period from coming. If she could forget about it and relax, it would arrive.

'You've given me too much change, Ellen,' Bonnie Daly said sweetly, as she handed Ellen back a ten-shilling note.

'Oh . . . oh . . . sorry.' Ellen was flustered. She hoped her father hadn't noticed.

'And how is Emma settling in to our little backwater?' Bonnie inquired.

Nosy cow, Ellen thought grumpily. She wished Bonnie Daly would shag off and leave her alone. 'She's settling in fine.'

'And your mother tells me, she'll be hearing the patter of tiny feet before the end of the year. Isn't that wonderful news?' Bonnie gushed.

Ellen's heart started to pound.

'Great news,' she managed to say. If she was pregnant, she'd have to leave Glenree. Bonnie Daly would have a field day. Sheila would never be able to hold her head up in the town again. It was a huge disgrace to be expecting a baby before marriage. Chris would have to marry her. But would he? Ellen didn't dare think about it.

'No sign of you taking the plunge?' Bonnie smiled coyly, knowing full well that Ellen had no prospects.

'The sea's too cold and I can't swim.' Ellen scowled. 'Now you must excuse me, Mrs Daly. I've some figures to do.'

Rude hussy, Bonnie Daly thought crossly as she marched out of the shop. The cheek of Ellen Munroe, snubbing her like that. No wonder she hadn't got a ring on her finger. What man would have a moody madam like her?

Please let Chris ring, she prayed. He hadn't been in touch for the past few days. The weekend was coming up. Surely he'd phone to make plans. They were having such fun. He was wonderful to be with, so attentive and charming. He had class. He took her to expensive restaurants. He took her dancing. He made her laugh with his dry humour and caustic comments. He always wanted to be out and about. He was popular and well known around town and, although Ellen was having a hectic, exciting time, there were times when she'd much prefer to be on her own with him. To talk to him, and listen to him tell about his great plans for his own company. The company she was going to work in as his secretary. She wanted to be close to him, in every way. She'd never felt like this about a man before.

Joseph, her ex, had never taken her over, mind, body and soul, the way Chris had. She hadn't spent all her waking hours thinking about *him*. On reflection, Ellen had to admit that, when Joseph had walked out on her, it was her pride rather than her heart that was injured. Ellen knew she'd never have any pride with Chris. He had her heart. He'd had it from the moment he'd looked into her eyes and smiled that devil-may-care smile. She'd always sneered at the idea of love at first sight – before she'd met him. But it had happened to her. Absolutely!

Miriam said that it was infatuation. But she didn't understand. Ellen knew it wasn't infatuation. The feelings she had for Chris overwhelmed her completely. He was all she wanted. Her days and nights were filled with thoughts of him. It was crazy and she knew she wasn't being rational. Just as she knew that Chris, with his reputation as a womanizer, was not the man she should fall in love with. She knew she was heading for trouble. She knew she'd never have a minute's peace with him. For every hour of ecstasy she'd had with him, she'd had *days* of misery. Days when she waited patiently and in vain for him to phone. Days when she knew she was just an afterthought in his life.

If only she knew how he really felt about her. When they made love he told her he loved her and she wanted desperately to believe him. But when she was alone and waiting for his call, all her fears and anxieties surfaced. Did he not want to be with her? How could he let two or three days go by without phoning her? Did that mean that for three whole days he didn't once think of her? And, if that was the case, how could he be in love with her? Because she was so obsessed she couldn't stop thinking about him, morning, noon or night. She couldn't wait to hear his voice on the phone. Or be with him and feel his arms around her. *That* surely was love and why could he not feel the same?

When, in despair, she'd pour her heart out to Miriam, and ask her questions she couldn't answer, her sister-in-law would sigh and say, 'Ellen, I don't know, love. Why don't you just end it now and stop tormenting yourself? Love isn't something that torments. What you have with him isn't love.'

'It is, it is. He's busy, up to his eyes. He's going out on his own soon. When this is all over things will be different.' She'd make excuses for him, trying to find reassurance in them herself.

Sometimes, alone in bed, she'd acknowledge the truth of Miriam's words and vow to end it. To get on with her life and find someone who would value her. But then he'd phone and make her laugh and they'd meet and she'd know that he was the one she wanted to be with. Chris only had to look at her with his intense blue-eyed gaze and her stomach would tighten in knots of delicious anticipation. Making love with him satisfied every fibre of her being. Ellen could think of no greater pleasure. Each time they dated they'd ended up at his house, in bed. After that first night he'd used French letters. She'd insisted. But deep down, Ellen knew it was too late for all that. She was knocked up and she was in deep trouble. No matter how hard she pretended she wasn't. The shrill ring of the phone made her jump. She picked up the heavy black receiver willing Chris to be at the other end. Her heart was pounding.

'Hello?' she said hopefully.

'Hello, Ellen, would you bring me home a pound of

streaky rashers when you come back at lunchtime? And would you bring me an oxtail? I'm going to make some soup for poor little Emma. Vincent tells me she isn't eating a thing, God love her. I know what it's like, especially with your first child. It's a worrying time. All the fears and uncertainties. We must be kind to her. I've told Miriam to make a fuss of her and try and reassure her. She might listen to Miriam. They're closer in age.' Sheila was in full spate. Her words twisted like a knife in Ellen's heart.

She knew she'd be able to cope with the physical side of pregnancy, the labour and the birth. But what she dreaded more than anything else was telling her mother and father. They'd never forgive her.

Please Chris, ring me. Please, please, please, she beseeched as her mother launched into a litany of the kind of advice she intended giving Emma.

'I have to go, Ma. I've a queue,' Ellen fibbed five minutes later as the flow continued unabated. She hung up and felt she was going to be sick. The phone rang. She snatched up the receiver.

'Hello?'

'Is that the butcher's?' Ellen felt a lump in her throat. Her eyes smarted with tears.

'Yes,' she murmured.

'This is Mrs Nugent. I want four gigot chops and a pound of round steak when he's delivering this morning.'

'Certainly,' Ellen responded heavily. There was a knot of pain right in the middle of her breastbone. How could emotional feelings be so physically painful, she wondered dully as she took a note of the order. If only he'd ring and put her out of her misery. Ellen could stand it no longer. She picked up the phone and dialled Chris's office number. Only to be told by his secretary that he was out of the office meeting clients and would be gone for the rest of the day.

What am I going to do? she thought in panic.

'Any more orders?' Mick stuck his head into the little cubicle, where she sat on a high chair surveying the shop through a plastic partition.

'Ellen, Ellen, are you listening to me?'

'Sorry, Da.' Ellen felt so tempted to blurt out her fears. Her father was a kind man. He wouldn't turn on her, surely. If only she could tell someone.

'Any more orders? Eamonn's off on the delivery round.'

'Just Mrs Nugent. Four gigots and a pound of round.'

'Right.'

Ellen watched her father take his big knife from his belt as he walked over to the big wooden table where he chopped the meat. Imagine if she told him. There'd be ructions. Maybe she was mistaken, she thought forlornly. It was best to say nothing to anyone, until she found out one way or the other.

* * *

'You're a shit, Chris Wallace.' Suzy Kenny took a sip of her white wine and stared coldly at the man sitting in front of her.

'I've been called worse.' Chris grinned. His vivid blue eyes smiled into hers. 'Maybe you could reform me.'

'I don't know if I'd want to.'

'Oh come on! You know you can't resist a challenge,' he teased. Suzy laughed and he knew he was halfway there. He'd bumped into her quite by accident and, although she'd been snooty enough at first, he'd persuaded her to have lunch. She was looking very elegant in her powder-blue suit, her sunglasses perched atop her blonde bouffant. Suzy was always so groomed, unlike Ellen who, although she looked very curvaceous and sexy, never seemed to get her look together. You could take Suzy anywhere, any time. He's forgotten how provocative Suzy's cool 'keep your distance' air could be.

'How about dinner tonight?' he invited.

'Can't. I'm seeing someone tonight.' Suzy drew on her filter-tipped cigarette and exhaled a long thin stream of smoke.

'Tomorrow then?'

'I'm going to the pictures with Alexandra, a friend of mine.'

'I remember her.' Chris frowned. He had never got on with Alexandra Johnston. 'Cancel it.'

'Certainly not,' Suzy said coolly.

'Saturday then,' Chris persisted.

'I'm booked up for the weekend.'

'You're a busy woman,' Chris said dryly.

'That's me.' Suzy stood up. 'Thanks for lunch.'

'I'll call you.' Chris stood up politely.

'Whatever.'

Her air of indifference infuriated him. Challenged him. Excited him. He'd seduced her once. He'd do it again if he put his mind to it. Suzy was no pushover. Not like Ellen, the thought came unbidden.

Chris watched his former girlfriend glide out the door of the restaurant, watched by every man there.

She could play hard to get all she liked, Chris reflected. She'd be his again if he wanted her. He had no doubt whatsoever on that score. She was cool though, very cool, he thought admiringly as he paid the bill. And he liked it. He was feeling a bit smothered by Ellen lately. She was falling for him and, while it was very nice and very flattering, he didn't want her to get too serious. He had no intention of settling down yet. The thought made him feel claustrophobic. Maybe he'd cool things with Ellen for a while. She'd be expecting him to phone to make plans for the weekend. Maybe he'd give it a miss this weekend and catch up on some paperwork.

He'd phone her on Monday and arrange to see her midweek. He knew she'd be upset. His heart softened. Ellen was a loving, giving woman, if only she could distance herself a bit and be cool about it. Not be clinging and emotionally demanding. He found that hard to handle. Chris sighed. Women, he loved them, but they certainly were complicated creatures.

*　　*　　*

'You had lunch with him!' Alexandra shrieked down the line. 'I'm coming straight over. I want to hear *everything*.' Alexandra Johnston was Suzy's best friend and she knew all about Chris.

Suzy smiled as she hung up. She wrapped a towel turban-wise around her blonde hair. She'd fibbed when she'd told Chris she was seeing someone this evening. But if he thought she was going to fall headlong into his arms, he had another think coming. Not that she didn't want to fall headlong into his arms. She most certainly did. When he'd dumped her, she'd been in bits. She'd lost half a stone in a week. She couldn't sleep. She couldn't concentrate on her work. Her boss had called her into his office and told her she'd have to sharpen up. All her letters had mistakes in them. Suzy had wanted to tell him to piss off, her heart was broken and all he cared about was his piddling letters.

Chris thought he'd bumped into her by chance today, little did he know that she'd staked him out and followed him into town and pretended to bump into him. A girl in love had to take desperate measures, and she was in love. She was crazy about the bastard. Suzy bit her lip. Maybe she'd overdone the not interested bit. Maybe he wouldn't call.

'No! He'll call. You played a blinder. You handled him perfectly,' Alexandra assured her half an hour later as they sat by the fire drinking dry Martinis.

'I don't know.' Now she was racked by self-doubt.

'I'm telling you, Suzy, you keep putting him off and he'll be panting for you. You play your cards right and you'll be Mrs Chris Wallace yet. Trust me. Have I ever led you astray?' Alexandra popped a black olive into her mouth.

'Do you think so? Really?' Suzy felt much more hopeful.

'I certainly do. Men like him need to have women falling at their feet. You play cool with him. Keep your distance. Don't let him sleep with you this time and I promise you he'll have a ring on your finger before you know it,' Alexandra said confidently. 'How did he look?'

Suzy's eyes took on a dreamy faraway look. 'Gorgeous.

You know when he smiles at you and looks into your eyes and you feel you're the only woman on the planet?'

'Hmm.' Alexandra was dubious. 'Don't let him get to you. The strategy is to keep him dangling.'

'I know.' Suzy sighed. 'I just wanted him to take me back to his place and go to bed. It's very hard to keep your distance when he turns on the charm. I really miss sleeping with him.'

'Don't let your hormones rule your head, ducky. There'll be plenty of time for that when he's hooked.'

'I know. You're right. I'll play it cool like I did today. Once bitten, twice shy.'

'That's my girl. Now pour me another drink and have one yourself and let's devise a strategy that will ensure that Mr Chris Wallace pops the question.'

Giggling, Suzy complied.

*   *   *

Miriam was fuming as she dusted the dried flour off the soda scone she'd just baked and placed it on the window sill to cool. The cheek of her mother-in-law to suggest that Miriam wasn't being helpful enough to Emma now that she was pregnant.

The utter cheek of her! Miriam wiped her floury fingers on her apron, her cheeks flushed with anger. Mrs Munroe had had the nerve to suggest that Miriam bake Emma a soda scone or a tart or a sponge to tempt her appetite. Then she'd hinted that Miriam could give her a hand with her housework. It might be too taxing for Emma in her condition.

'In her condition!' Miriam muttered indignantly as she picked up the laundry basket full of boiled nappies and headed for the line.

'What about my condition? I'm pregnant too and I've got two small children. Who's going to bake for me and give me a hand with my housework? Interfering old busybody,' she grumbled aloud as she began to peg nappies on the line with grim determination. But *had* she told her mother-in-law that she was up to her eyes herself without having to bake and do housework for Emma? Of course not, Miriam thought in self-disgust. She always had these fantasies of telling Sheila where to get off. She'd practise saying things like, 'I'm sorry, Mrs Munroe, I can't come over to help cook for your guild evening. It's inconvenient.' Or, 'I can't come to your card night tonight, I have another engagement.' How she longed to summon up the nerve to tell her mother-in-law, politely but firmly, to get lost. The only reason Sheila invited her to her card game was so that she could help serve the supper and wash up after it. Ellen flatly refused to have anything to do with it and usually made sure she was out for the evening.

Sheila had invited Emma to a card game soon after she'd come back from her honeymoon and Emma refused outright, saying that she couldn't stand playing cards. Sheila was terribly huffed. Miriam couldn't help admiring the younger girl's nerve.

She sighed deeply and rubbed her back. She was suffering dreadful backache this pregnancy. She pulled up the line and stood enjoying the freshness of the lovely spring day. An invigorating breeze lifted her hair away from her face and caused the line full of snowy-white nappies to flutter to and fro. They'd be dry in no time, she thought with satisfaction. There was a hint of warmth in the sun, the first time she'd felt it this spring.

Her daffodils were out. Great clumps of them under the trees. Their yellow heads a vibrant contrast to the delicate clusters of snowdrops that grew alongside them. Primroses, crocuses, and vivid purple grape hyacinths edged the green sward that sloped gently down to the street that ran along the end of their garden. Miriam loved her garden. It was her haven. When she was annoyed with her mother-in-law an hour spent weeding or planting or dead-heading and pruning always restored her equilibrium. It was such a fine day Miriam decided she'd work on her flower beds for a while. The soil had dried out. It would be easy enough to break it up with a fork.

Daniel was having a nap in his pram by the back door and Connie was playing with a neighbour's child. It was much too nice to be indoors baking, she thought defiantly, glaring in the direction of Sheila's house which was two fields away to the west. To the south, between the budding branches of the trees, Miriam could see the black-tiled roof of Vincent and Emma's house. Smoke curled from the chimney, its thin plumes wafting away into the deep blue of the sky. Even though they had central heating, Vincent always lit a fire for Emma, so that she could loll in front of it and read magazines or romantic novels if she wasn't off in Dublin visiting her mother or shopping or meeting her friends for lunch. Miriam felt a pang of envy. It must be wonderful to have a car of your own and be able to come and go as you pleased. Ben needed their car to get into work and she'd never bothered to learn to drive. Well maybe she just might, she decided as she saw, with a sinking heart, her mother-in-law appear around the back of the house wheeling her bike.

'I see you've baked the bread for poor Emma.' Sheila indicated the loaf cooling on the window sill. 'I'll bring it with me, I'm on my way down to call in.'

Tell her it's not for Emma, Miriam silently ordered herself. She took a deep breath. 'Actually, Mrs Munroe – '

'You know, you shouldn't let him sleep in the daytime, he doesn't need it now. No wonder he won't sleep for you at night,' Sheila interrupted. She leaned into the pram and gave Daniel a prod. 'Wake up, you lazy lump, and say hello to Nannie,' she chided. Miriam was horrified. The last thing she wanted was for Daniel to wake up. He was as cranky as hell with his teeth and he needed whatever sleep he could get, the poor little fellow.

'Don't wake him,' she said hastily, but it was too late. Daniel started to bawl lustily.

'Oh Lord!' Miriam was disgusted.

'He's probably hungry.' Sheila sniffed. She wasn't used to Miriam showing displeasure.

'He was only fed before he was put down. I didn't want him woken,' Miriam said sharply as she rocked the pram gently.

'I was only trying to help,' Sheila retorted, miffed. 'When you come complaining to me that he isn't sleeping at night, I try and give you the benefit of my experience. I used never let mine sleep in the daytime at his age. You young mothers do things differently it seems.' Her nostrils flared and her lips pursed the way they always did when she was annoyed. 'I'll take that bread and be off. I'll tell Emma you'll be down to see if she wants a hand.' She removed the bread from the kitchen window, put it in her bicycle basket, and cycled off in high dudgeon.

Miriam stood staring after her. She was filled with anger, resentment, frustration, and self-disgust. For the first time in her marriage, she'd stood up to Sheila and let her know that she was annoyed by her unwanted interference. But instead of keeping it up, she'd chickened out and let her mother-in-law take the loaf of bread she'd baked for her own family. And to add insult to injury, by remaining silent, she'd allowed Sheila to tell Emma she'd go and do housework for her. She was furious with Sheila, but she was far more angry and disgusted with herself.

Chapter Six

'You're putting on weight,' Chris remarked as Ellen plonked herself into the car beside him. So would you be if you were five months pregnant, she was tempted to blurt out. But she said nothing. He'd kept her waiting under Clerys clock for nearly three quarters of an hour and not a word of apology. The best he could do was, 'You're putting on weight.' He eased into the traffic and cast a glance in her direction.

'Sorry about cancelling at the last moment the other night. I got one of those awful stomach bugs. Spent the day in the loo.' Chris did his poor me voice.

She wanted to shout 'Liar!' at the top of her voice and rake her nails down his face. Do you think I'm a fool, she wanted to scream. But she couldn't. She daren't. She was only hanging on by her fingernails. She knew that Chris held the strings and she came running when he pulled them. She rarely saw him on a Friday night or Saturday night any more. At the beginning, she'd seen him twice a week at the weekends. But then he'd started making excuses, saying that he was working. Tonight was a rare exception. He'd phoned her unexpectedly this morning and asked her if she wanted to see him later. Usually it was Wednesday or Thursday when they met and she hardly ever slept over because she had to get the last bus to Glenree. Otherwise she wouldn't be able to get to work on time the following morning. She couldn't use the excuse of staying in Miriam's midweek.

Usually Chris took her for a quick meal and then he took

her home and they had sex. Then he drove her back into town to get the last bus. Ellen hated the arrangement. She hated having to get up out of bed and get dressed after making love, and then go rushing into town to catch the last bus. It seemed sordid, somehow. But if she started moaning about it that would be the end of it. Once when she'd lost her temper, when he'd cancelled their date at the last minute, he'd told her coldly that he didn't like nagging women. The implied threat chilled her. If Chris stopped seeing her, she was in real trouble.

She'd humoured him in the hope that, when she finally told him about her pregnancy, he'd think that marriage wouldn't be such a bad thing. Though she suspected he was still seeing the blonde, she'd said nothing. She was pathetic, she knew. But the fact that he still made dates with her and seemed to enjoy them gave her comfort. Maybe he would come to understand that she was the one who would love him and cherish him as no other woman would or could. If he only realized what was there for him, he'd never look at another woman again.

'You're very quiet. I suppose you're annoyed because I'm late.' He was sulky.

'I was just worried about you. I thought something might have happened.'

'Daft woman.' Chris grinned. 'Something did happen. I made a great deal. I sold a massive insurance policy to a punter who's loaded. I'm going to get a hefty commission. You know something, Ellen, I think the time is come for me to branch out on my own.' He was brimming with enthusiasm and excitement, his blue eyes bright and happy as he smiled at her. All her anger and resentment melted away. She was delighted for him.

'Oh Chris, that's brilliant. I think you should go for it. You should definitely be working for yourself. You've been talking about it long enough. What's the point in you slaving for someone else and making great deals when you don't get the benefit of it? I think you'll make a big success of your own company.'

'That's what I like about you, Ellen. You're interested. I know I can make it on my own. It gives me great encouragement when someone else thinks so too.' Chris was exuberant. Ellen suddenly felt very happy. She was special to him, she knew it. His blonde bombshell would never give him the support and encouragement she could.

'I'll be your secretary, like you said, and we'll make a great go of it,' she offered eagerly.

'Hmm.' Chris didn't sound as enthusiastic as she did about it. She could have kicked herself for being so pushy.

'You've a good job with your dad. I might not be able to afford as good wages as you're getting.'

'That doesn't matter, Chris. Honest.'

'We'll see.' He looked away.

Ellen's heart sank. Oh God, he doesn't want me, she thought in desperation and turned her head away so that he wouldn't see that she was close to tears.

*　　*　　*

He should never have suggested that Ellen would be his secretary, Chris thought angrily as he drove towards Ringsend. It had been a flippant remark. Trust her to take it to heart. He didn't want to hurt her feelings. That was the last thing he wanted to do. Ellen was a great girl. Why did she have to be so intense about everything? It put pressure on him and the last thing he needed was pressure. She was totally the opposite to Suzy.

Suzy had phoned him up at lunchtime to announce that she wouldn't be seeing him as planned that evening. She'd got an unexpected invitation to a house party in Wicklow and was planning to stay in the country for the weekend. He was flabbergasted. 'But I'd booked tickets for the theatre, and I'd planned on bringing you out to dinner.'

'Sorry, darling, another time. This is just too good to miss,' had been her airy response. Suzy was so goddamn offhand. Her indifference about whether she saw him or not infuriated him. He'd assumed they'd take up where they'd left off after their short split following Emma's party. After all it hadn't been that much of a row. No big deal.

He'd assumed wrongly. She was keeping him at arm's length. They'd been seeing each other for months and she was still acting like a bloody virgin. If it wasn't for Ellen he'd have exploded from frustration. Thinking of Suzy made him feel horny.

He turned to Ellen and said placatingly, 'Come on, let's get a bottle of bubbly and bring it home and celebrate doing what we do best.' He let his hand slip down along her thigh and caressed it lightly. He heard her sigh and felt her hand reach out to cover his.

'That's my sweet girl,' he murmured huskily. Ellen never let him down.

* * *

'I don't know if I should have let you persuade me to come. Chris was furious,' Suzy moaned as she gazed out through the window at a sullen grey sky that smothered the tops of the Wicklow hills in its gloom. 'Oh Christ, there's a magpie!' She scanned the skies anxiously looking for its mate. '*One for sorrow* – not a good omen!'

'Calm down, will you,' Alexandra drawled from the divan where she was sprawled. 'Let him be furious. Be *glad* he's furious. It shows you're getting to him. And you are, you know. Just trust me and hang in there.'

'I bet he'll ask someone else out tonight.' Suzy was not to be soothed. She'd been keeping Chris at bay for months and it was getting very difficult. She wanted to sleep with him.

'So what if he takes someone else out. Suzy, you're the one he's going to marry. You're driving him bananas and it's working. I've seen him looking at you. If you tumble into bed with him now, he's got you where he wants you and he'll be in no hurry to pop the question. He's taken the line, reel him in slowly.' Alexandra lit a cigarette and inhaled with satisfaction. 'In fact I think you should say you met a rather dishy someone down here. Tell Chris you had a wonderful weekend and that this guy wants to see you again. Say he's a lawyer. It sounds ever so suave . . . much better than an insurance salesman.'

'Chris might tell me to get lost.'

'Suzy! I'm losing patience with you. That will make him even more eager. Don't you know anything about men?'

'Well if you know so much about them how come you haven't a ring on your finger yet?'

Alexandra laughed. 'Believe me. When I see the one I want . . . I'll have him. Who knows, he might be at the party tonight. Now take that miserable look off your face. We're going to have fun this weekend. You'll have a lot to tell Lover-boy Wallace by the time I'm finished with you.'

A second magpie joined its mate down on the lawn, much to Suzy's relief. *Two for joy.* Alexandra's no-nonsense lecture had restored her courage. It gave her a great sense of power to have Chris dangling on *her* rope for a change. To lose her nerve now would be disastrous.

*   *   *

Ellen watched Chris disappear through the doors of the off-licence. If only she knew where she stood with him. It was he who'd suggested that she should be his secretary. And they'd talked about it since then. As far as she was concerned it was a foregone conclusion. Men! They were all the same. Promises. Promises.

'Oh stop it,' she muttered. Maybe she was being oversensitive. It was the strain of being pregnant and keeping it to herself. The uncertainty, the fear of not knowing how he'd react was making her paranoid. She shouldn't ruin her precious evening with him. Tonight was going to be wonderful.

She loved going to Chris's house. She especially loved his bedroom. Decorated in terracotta and blue, it had an almost foreign atmosphere. The polished wooden floor had leopardskin rugs which gave the room an exotic air.

Chris had lamps everywhere. The light, subtle and soft and romantic, made her feel as if she was in another world. There was a huge double bed and smart fitted wardrobes which were much more modern than her antique double-doored monstrosity. Chris had good taste. Much better than Emma, whose decor was way over the top. A night in that luxurious romantic room with Chris was all she desired.

It was Friday night too. She could stay over. She'd warned Miriam that she'd told her mother she'd be staying overnight in her house. Poor Miriam was always in a state the nights Ellen stayed with Chris for fear that Sheila would come looking for her. It had never happened yet. Miriam didn't approve of her sleeping with Chris. Her sister-in-law was very old-fashioned. This was the sixties and lots of couples were doing it. Ellen would try and explain, but Miriam was not impressed. 'If he respected you, he'd wait until you were married,' she warned. Ellen hated when she said that. It was too near the bone. Sometimes she was afraid that she wouldn't see Chris at all if she wasn't sleeping with him. Don't think about it now, she pushed the thought to the back of her mind as Chris drove up his drive and leaned over and kissed her hungrily.

It was the nicest night she had ever spent with him. All her fears and worries receded into the background as they made love, drank champagne and talked for hours about his plans. She didn't mention anything about being his secretary again. Later as she watched him sleeping Ellen studied every detail of his face. His long silky black lashes, his firm well-shapen mouth, the little dent in his chin, now darkened by five o'clock shadow. In sleep he looked boyish and she felt a fierce surge of almost maternal affection. She wanted so much to take care of him and be part of his life. She had such love to lavish on him, if only he would let her. She lay cradling him in her arms daring to plan and dream of a future with him.

She'd have to tell him about her pregnancy. So far it hadn't been too difficult to conceal. She'd worn loose tops and trousers and, because she'd always been on the voluptuous side, her weight gain hadn't been too noticeable. Nothing like Miriam who was now eight months pregnant and as heavy as a walrus. Emma was as petite as anything, apart from her small rounded bump, which was causing her immense distress.

But in the last few weeks, Ellen had felt herself get bigger. She'd asked Miriam very casually about it. Miriam said that one minute it seemed as though you could pass for being overweight and all of a sudden your body just spread out all over, boobs and belly everywhere. 'It always happens to me around the fifth month,' Miriam said, unaware of the consternation she was causing Ellen.

She knew the time was coming when not even the best roll-on was going to contain her. Besides she was beginning to get dreadful heartburn from squashing herself into the one she wore to conceal her pregnancy.

Chris had told her last night she'd have to go on a diet but then he'd laughed as he caressed her breasts and said not to. He loved big girls. She'd almost told him there and then, but something stopped her. She wanted one more perfect night with him before she told him about their child. Sleep was a long time coming. Her mind raced hither and yon as she tried to anticipate what her lover's reaction would be to her news. Dawn was breaking before Ellen finally fell into a deep sleep.

She woke to feel Chris nuzzling her neck and shoulders. His hands touched her breasts and then moved down over the curve of her belly. Then the baby kicked. Hard.

'What the hell was that?' Chris murmured drowsily.

Ellen's mouth went dry. It was now or never. 'That was your son . . . or daughter,' she said softly.

Chris wrenched his hand away as if he'd been scalded. He shot up in the bed and stared down at her.

'What did you say?' He was pale, his blue eyes dark with alarm.

'I'm five months pregnant,' Ellen said quietly. Her heart began to pound with fear and dread.

'Jesus Christ! I don't believe it.' He was horrified. 'Five months! Why the hell didn't you tell me?'

'I couldn't bring myself to, Chris.'

'You stupid cow! You should have told me at the beginning. You could have got rid of it. It's too bloody late now,' he raged.

Ellen paled. 'Chris, for God's sake, it's your child we're talking about. How could you suggest such a thing?'

'Oh for crying out loud, Ellen, don't give me that crap.' Chris was so furious he was trembling. 'A child means nothing to me. I don't want children now. I can't have a wife and child hanging out of me just when I'm starting off my business.' He glared at her. 'How do you know it's mine?'

'You bastard!' Ellen felt as if she'd been kicked in the stomach. She jumped out of bed and lunged at him.

'Bastard! Pig! You fucking shit!' she yelled at him hysterically, clawing at him, wanting to hurt and maim him.

'How could you say that? Have you no idea how much I love you? How do you think I could look at another man? Does what we did last night mean so little to you?' She flailed at him, but he was much stronger than she and he held her away from him with some difficulty.

'For Christ's sake, Ellen, cut it out!' he yelled. He held her wrists in a vice-like grip as she twisted and turned. All the fight went out of her. She slumped to her knees, sobbing as though her heart would break.

'I love you,' she wept. 'How could you say that to me?'

He let her go and walked out of the room. She watched him leave and knew that he would never marry her. She was on her own.

Even though it was a bright sunny day, she suddenly felt icy cold. Her teeth started to chatter. She was shaking. She got back into bed and curled up in a tight foetal position. She felt sick. All the months of keeping her secret to herself, pretending that everything was normal, all the fears and anxieties she'd endured were nothing to the pain his words caused her. Her heart felt as if it was cut to ribbons. She wanted to die. How could she have deluded herself so badly?

It could have been minutes but it felt like hours that she lay there before he came back into the room again. He had a dressing-gown on. His face was white.

'Let's get some things straight, Ellen,' he said coldly as if he was speaking to a stranger. 'I won't marry you. I can't marry you. I can't be tied down with a wife and child. Not now when I'm going out on my own. I'll give you money, but that's as far as it goes.'

'Please, Chris,' she pleaded, fear, desperation, love, dispelling all pride. 'You have to marry me. I'll be ruined. I can't go through this on my own. I love you. I'll be a good wife. You'll never be sorry you married me. I swear I'll love you more than you've ever been loved. I promise you won't be sorry. Please, Chris. Please,' she begged.

'Look, I'm sorry already. I'm sorry I ever met you. I don't need this hassle, Ellen. I'm not going to marry you. I'm not going to ruin my life so forget the idea of marriage,' he said harshly. He went over to a bureau and took something out of the drawer. 'Here, it's a hundred pounds. I'll give you more when it's born. We can't see each other any more. I'm going out. Get a taxi home.' He dropped another fiver on the bed beside the bundle of notes already there. Ellen couldn't speak. Her throat constricted. Through blurred eyes she watched him gather his clothes and shoes. Then he was gone. She could hear him moving around in the adjoining bedroom. Five minutes later she heard the front door slam. A funereal silence descended on the house. The only sound the racing rhythm of her heart, thumping against her ribs. She sat motionless, unable to think.

Eventually, she dragged herself out of bed and dressed. She took a last look around the bright airy bedroom with its leopardskin rugs and the huge double bed where she'd experienced the most intense happiness of her life and, an hour ago, the most devastating hell. Her hand hovered over the money. With all her heart, she longed to leave it there and walk away with that much of her pride intact at least. But she was in no position to indulge her pride. If she was thrown out of home when her parents found out, she was going to need that money badly. She snatched it up, stuffed it in her bag and walked out of the bedroom with tears streaming down her face.

She stood by the phone in the hall, struggling to compose herself. She dialled for a taxi and then sat huddled on the bottom step of the stairs waiting for it. Ten minutes later she heard it pull up outside. Ellen stood up, took a deep breath, and walked out of her lover's house without a backward glance.

She gave the driver directions and settled back into the depths of the rather shabby seat. The driver made several attempts to engage her in conversation, but she answered him in monosyllables and he took the hint and gave up. Numb, she stared out the window, oblivious to everything. Her worst nightmare had come true. Chris had dumped her. It was only the beginning. Her parents had to be told. Her shame and disgrace would be known to everyone in Glenree unless she left home and came to Dublin to fend for herself. Suddenly she was scared. She didn't want to come and live in Dublin. She knew very few people in the city. She'd be alone. Alone with a baby to care for. She'd never been so frightened in her entire life. She couldn't tell them at home yet. She hadn't the nerve. Maybe Chris would have a rethink once the shock wore off. A glimmer of hope pierced her misery. Maybe when he had time to think he'd realize what he was losing and decide he'd made a mistake. She'd give him a week. If she hadn't heard anything by then, she'd have to face the fact that she was on her own. And she'd have to tell her parents.

God please let him come back to me. Please let him change his mind, she prayed fervently as the taxi left the suburbs and took the route through country roads past the airport towards home.

*　*　*

122

Chris lit a fag and drew deep on it, inhaling the tobacco down into his lungs. He took a slug of whiskey from the double in front of him. He needed it badly. He actually had the shakes. He couldn't believe it. When Ellen told him she was pregnant it was as if someone had punched him in the gut. Hard. The memory of that determined little kick made him shudder.

Why hadn't she told him at the beginning? He would have made arrangements for her to go to London for an abortion. It would have been so simple. The end of the problem. Jim Devlin had knocked up his girlfriend and they'd had the problem sorted out in a couple of days. It was no big deal.

Chris sighed and settled back into the dark anonymous corner of Hallin's pub. The sun was splitting the trees outside, but the Gothic gloom of the bar suited him at the moment. Maybe Ellen hadn't told him because she didn't want the problem solved. He scowled. Obviously she'd expected him to marry her. Most fellas did in that situation. Two of his mates had had shotgun weddings. They were miserable. Well Chris Wallace wasn't going to be trapped into marriage that easily.

It wasn't that he didn't like Ellen, he did. She was good fun. And she was a good listener. She was always encouraging him to go out on his own. If he sold a big policy, she was interested in the details. Suzy wasn't a bit interested in that side of him. As long as he had money to spend on her she didn't care where he got it from. Suzy found insurance boring. She was much more sophisticated than Ellen and she ran with a fast crowd who were more to his taste than any of Ellen's friends or relations. But Chris had to admit he always enjoyed his midweek dates with Ellen. He loved her soft curvy body. He'd miss Ellen's warmth and enthusiasm. He liked her. She didn't expect much from him and was content with what he gave her. That took a lot of pressure off a bloke. He didn't always have to be entertaining and witty and in good form. If he had a bad day, he could slump and be himself. She didn't mind.

But marriage was out of the question. He was too young. He had too much to do. He'd help financially. He wasn't that much of a cad. But Ellen could forget about anything else. A clean break was the best thing for both of them. If she had any sense she'd put the baby up for adoption and get on with her life. Just as he intended getting on with his. He glanced at his watch, midday, she should be gone by now, he thought hopefully. He hated scenes. He'd have another whiskey, just in case.

It was after two when Chris got home. He'd met a friend of his, and bought him a pint. They'd chatted. He felt a niggle of apprehension as he put his key in the front door. What would he do if Ellen was still there? The house was quiet. Only the drone of a bluebottle caught in the net curtains broke the silence. He swatted it viciously. He hated bluebottles. For some reason they reminded him of death and decay.

She'd taken the money, he noted with satisfaction, as he stood beside the bed. That meant she must have accepted it was the end. He didn't want to be at the receiving end of bleeding-heart phone calls. The least she could have done was made the bed, he thought crossly as he tweaked the blankets into place. He supposed he should change the sheets in case by some miracle he got Suzy into bed after her weekend away. He scowled. Now that Ellen wouldn't be there for him he hoped Suzy would loosen up. Enforced celibacy was not his idea of fun.

He eyed the sheets unenthusiastically. They were stained. Tough! He'd keep the lights off. Suzy wouldn't know the difference in the light of day. Women, they were all the same! Hysterical – if they thought another woman was on the scene.

Ellen, to give her her due, hadn't been possessive. Chris suspected she'd known he was still seeing Suzy, but she'd never reproached him. He liked that about her. She'd always let him do his own thing. If only she hadn't gone and got herself pregnant they could have carried on their perfect affair. He opened his bureau to check on his supply of Frenchies. If Ellen really had got pregnant at the beginning then he needn't have worn the blasted things for the last five months. He hated wearing condoms. He supposed Emma'd have something to say about his getting her sister-in-law pregnant. The best thing to do was to keep a low profile for a while. It was Ellen's fault for not telling him when there was time to do something about it, Chris thought angrily as he undressed and went to have a shower.

*　　*　　*

'Mam's birthday is coming up next week and Ellen and Miriam will be doing a little party for her. We'll have to put in an appearance,' Vincent said, a little gingerly.

Emma threw her eyes up to heaven. 'Oh Vincent, you go. I'm not in the form for socializing. You know I feel sick all the time.'

'I know, pet. We'll just pop over and give her her present and then we can come home.'

'OK,' Emma said sulkily. She picked up a copy of *Vogue* and flicked through the pages. Vincent sighed deeply. Emma ignored him.

'I'll be off to work then.'

'Bye,' Emma said coolly. Vincent decided against proffering a kiss. In the humour Emma was in, he'd only be rebuffed. She always seemed worse in the morning for some reason. If she felt queasy all the time, he'd be moody too, he reasoned as he started the ignition and sped off down the drive. Miriam's morning sickness had only lasted three months with all of her pregnancies. Poor Emma was now in her seventh month but she was still as sick as ever.

It happened to some women, Doctor Waldron said matter-of-factly when Vincent hopefully inquired if Emma'd ever have some respite. Vincent had watched Miriam take pregnancy in her stride and he'd hoped Emma would get to that stage too. But it never happened. Emma did not bloom. She wilted. Even drinking the milk that was so necessary for the baby's good health made her gag. Once, they'd been driving home from Dublin and the farmers had been spreading silage and the smell of that had made her retch. She cried her eyes out and said she hated being pregnant, she hated living in the countryside and she hated looking fat and frumpy. In vain Vincent insisted that she looked lovely and that her small round bump was not in the slightest bit off-putting. Emma stopped wearing her sexy baby-dolls and enveloped herself in a voluminous cotton tent and told him there was no more sex until she was a size ten again.

Fortunately that phase hadn't lasted too long. But she insisted on making love in the dark and he missed the way she used to flaunt herself sexily at him, enjoying it as much as he did. Vincent sighed as he drove along the back roads towards the airport. At least there were only a couple of months left before this endurance test was over.

He saw a woman cantering her mare around a field. Her long black hair streamed behind her in the summer breeze. She had a look of exhilaration on her face. Poor old Emma couldn't even ride Cleopatra. The motion made her too queasy. He was very glad he wasn't a woman, he thought fervently as the airport came into sight and he turned left in the direction of Swords. He was selling a house and site there and he was late for the meeting with the prospective buyer.

*　　*　　*

Emma flung down her magazine and stared out the kitchen window. It was another hot, humid day. Grey thunderous clouds hung oppressively low. The sunny weather had broken and for the past few days they'd endured sultry airless still days that left her feeling hot and sticky and uncomfortable. A bluebottle buzzed incessantly, driving her nuts. The sight of the watery egg yolk on Vincent's plate made her want to puke. How he could eat soft egg like that was beyond her. Even the look of it made her nauseous.

She got up from the breakfast counter, took an apple and walked out the back door. The new lawn looked parched and dried out, despite Vincent's constant watering. The earth in the flower beds was cracked and dry. It was the way she felt, Emma thought despondently as she licked a bead of perspiration off her top lip. Even though it was still early in the morning, it was very warm. A low rumble of thunder far in the east warned of storms to come. She didn't care. She'd welcome a thunderstorm to clear away the hot fetid air. She could hear Cleopatra whinnying in the stable down by the river. Poor Cleo hated thunder. Emma hastened her steps. She loved her mare. It killed her that she couldn't ride her. Nothing had worked out the way it was supposed to, and all because of this baby, she thought resentfully as her child reminded her of its presence with a fandango of little kicks.

By rights she should have been taking Cleo out for her morning ride. Then she should have been flitting into town to do some shopping in Grafton Street and then having lunch with Gillian or some of the gang.

Then a visit to her mother and, following that, dinner with Vincent after work and maybe a trip to the theatre or to the pictures.

They'd planned to have barbecues at weekends all this summer and they'd only had two because she felt so miserable. Poor Cleo was getting as fat as she was because she had no exercise. And now, Emma thought irritatedly, as she handed Cleo her apple and received a rapturous welcome, Vincent wanted her to go to Mrs Munroe's do. What a pain in the ass having to endure the nosy questions and sycophantic sympathy. If only her mother-in-law would stop *fussing* and leave her alone. Emma knew she meant to be kind. Not a day passed that she didn't have some advice to give her. She still came back for more no matter how short Emma was with her.

'Just say yes and nod your head from time to time and

think of something else,' Miriam advised her on one occasion. Miriam was quite nice really, Emma mused. She'd called up to the house when Emma was in her early pregnancy and offered to help with the housework. Emma told her that a lady from the town came in two days a week so she was fine and then inexplicably she'd burst into tears. Miriam was most comforting as Emma sobbed out all her frustration and fears about the pregnancy. She explained a few things that Emma couldn't bring herself to ask Doctor Waldron. Like why she kept wanting to pee all the time. And why her boobs were expanding alarmingly.

Miriam was very reassuring and told her why. She was a veteran after all. This was her third time. Whenever Emma felt anything new happening, like the first time she felt the tiny little flutters deep in the pit of her stomach, she asked Miriam about it. 'That's called "quickening",' Miriam told her. 'I always get really excited when that happens. It's a very precious feeling when the baby moves.' Emma hadn't felt very excited, just vaguely curious. She knew she was unnatural but, as her pregnancy progressed, her resentment against the child grew. This being had taken over her whole body. Distorted it, so that she looked like a little fat penguin. It had made her sick, made her wee at the most awkward moments, kept her awake at night with heartburn. It had taken control of her and there was nothing Emma could do about it. How she envied Miriam her joyful anticipation. Her serenity, even. Emma knew she was spoiling it for Vincent and she tried hard to pretend some excitement for his sake. But her life had changed completely and was about to change even more dramatically when the baby arrived. She felt frustrated, angry and very very trapped.

*   *   *

Ellen was baked alive. She was helping Miriam with the preparations for Sheila's party. She had just opened the oven door to take out the tray of cocktail sausages and the oven blast of heat rushed to her face and made her feel very hot and dizzy. She managed to put the tray on top of the cooker and then sank onto a chair.

'What's wrong, Ellen?' She could hear Miriam's concerned voice from a distance and then her face swam into view as Ellen tried to focus on her.

'Put your head down between your legs.' Miriam pressed between her shoulder blades forcing her head down. The dizziness eased a little and Ellen sat up gingerly.

'You're as white as a sheet. What are you wearing a big heavy jumper like that for on a day like today? It's so muggy out. I'm boiled alive in this and it's only gingham.' She shook her maternity dress away from her to try and create an airflow. 'Go up and change into something cooler. I'll finish off here.'

Ellen's heart started to pound. She couldn't change into anything else. Nothing else would fit her. In the two weeks since Chris had walked out on her, she'd really ballooned. Her bump had exploded outwards and the constraints of the roll-on couldn't hide and flatten it any more. She was so warm wearing the roll-on. She was permanently soaked in perspiration. She couldn't fasten her jeans so she had to wear a big loose jumper to camouflage the gap. It was one of the warmest summers she could ever remember.

Since Chris had disowned her and her child she hadn't heard one word from him. He hadn't phoned and his secretary told her that he was unavailable when she'd tried to reach him at work. When she'd phoned him at home, he'd silently hung up. His rejection of her devastated Ellen. She lay awake at night replaying their entire relationship in her head, from start to finish. Especially the finish. All she could think about was Chris. He was in her thoughts first thing in the morning and last thing at night and every other minute besides. He drove a red Cortina. She'd stare out the window of the shop looking for red cars and her heart would leap when she'd see one coming down the main street, only to plummet when it went by and it was the wrong make and model. Every time the phone rang hope would rise, only to be dashed. Her nerves were in shreds. She was having dreadful palpitations and panic attacks, especially late at night when she tossed and turned in bed, desperate for sleep. She knew the time was coming when she'd have to tell her parents she was pregnant. It was either that or disappear off into the night and never be seen again. She knew she wasn't brave enough to go it alone.

'Ellen, are you all right? Will I call your mother?'

'Jesus, no! Don't do that!' Ellen exclaimed in alarm. 'I'm all right.'

'You don't look all right. You look ghastly.'

Ellen burst into tears. The strain of keeping it to herself was unbearable. 'Miriam, I'm pregnant. What am I going to do?'

'Oh my God!' Miriam paled and sat down quickly herself. 'How far gone are you?'

'Nearly five and a half months, I think.' Ellen tried to compose herself as the tears streamed down her cheeks and great sobs racked her body.

'Ssshhh, Ellen. Someone might come in,' Miriam said frantically. 'Come into the pantry and close the door. We'll talk in there, it's nice and cool.'

They walked over to the door leading off the kitchen. Miriam was right, the pantry was cool. The familiar childhood smell of freshly cooked bread and scones was faintly comforting. Jars of pickled onions and jams and chutneys and preserves stood in serried rows along oilcloth-lined shelves. Pots of butter and jugs of cream and buttermilk filled a small recess under the tiny muslin-covered window through which a prism of sunlight lightened the cool dimness. A dozen freshly laid eggs gleamed speckled gold and brown in a blue ceramic dish that had been passed down from her great-grandmother. Emma might have a big modern fridge, but nothing could compare with Sheila's spotless well-stocked pantry.

A calmness came over Ellen. Now that she'd actually told Miriam she felt somewhat unburdened.

'Have you been to a doctor yet?' Miriam asked worriedly.

Ellen shook her head.

'God, Ellen. You'll have to go and see one soon. You've got to get yourself checked out. You should be taking iron tablets.'

'I know.' Ellen wiped her eyes with her sleeve. 'I've just been putting it off.'

'What about Chris?' Miriam asked delicately.

'He's dumped me.'

'The *bastard*!'

'It's my own fault. I was warned. I should have listened to you and Vincent. But I love him and I always will.' She broke down in tears again.

Miriam put her arms around her. 'Don't cry, Ellen. Don't! He's not worth it. You'll find someone who's worthy of you.'

'Me and an illegitimate baby. No one's going to take us on, Miriam. My life is ruined. Can you imagine Bonnie Daly and the gossips around here? They'll have a field day. Mam and Dad will probably throw me out. I don't know what I'm going to do.'

'They won't throw you out,' Miriam comforted. 'Anyway, if the worst comes to the worst, you can always move in with me and Ben.'

'Thanks, Miriam, you're the best friend a girl could have.' Ellen was utterly grateful that Miriam hadn't uttered one word of reproach. It was a huge relief to know she had at least one ally.

She turned to hug Miriam and their bumps collided. They started to giggle. The more they laughed, the worse they got.

'I'm going to wet myself, please stop,' Ellen gasped hysterically.

'It's not funny, I don't know why I'm laughing,' wheezed Miriam as tears rolled down her face. 'I just know how Humpty Dumpty felt. Look at the size of me. Emma looks like she's got a pea in her pod compared to me.'

'Oh Lord!' Ellen stopped laughing. 'I'll have to tell them too. Vincent's going to eat the face off me.'

'It's not his business to eat the face off you.' Miriam scowled.

'He warned me about Chris.' Ellen grimaced.

'It's too late to think about that now,' Miriam said firmly. 'I think the best thing you can do is tell your parents and get that over with and see how it goes from there.'

'Yeah, you're right.' Ellen sighed. The ordeal had to be faced.

'What on earth are you doing in here? Bonnie and Mona Cullen have arrived. Could we have a cup of tea or do I have to come out and make it myself on my birthday?' Sheila peered into the pantry.

'Coming right up.' Miriam pretended cheeriness.

'I'll bring in these cocktail sausages seeing as they're cooked. Oh and here's Vincent and Emma. You can make tea for them too,' Sheila ordered as she went to greet the new arrivals.

'If Madame thinks I'm waiting hand and foot on her she's got another think coming,' Ellen muttered as they walked back into the kitchen. 'How come she's not over here mucking in the way you do?'

'Ah, she's really sick, Ellen,' Miriam said placatingly.

'Huh.' Ellen wasn't impressed. Time hadn't improved her relationship with Emma.

'I feel very sorry for her, getting caught on her honeymoon. She doesn't want this baby at all,' Miriam remarked as she heated the teapot.

'It's a pity about her, at least she's got a husband,' Ellen said tartly as she dolloped fresh cream on the trifle and sprinkled it with hundreds and thousands.

Miriam said nothing. There was nothing she could say. Ellen was in the very worst predicament a girl could be in and when Sheila heard the news all hell was going to break loose. When a young single girl in the town had got pregnant last year, Sheila had been vociferous in her condemnation. As indeed had most of the women's guild.

There hadn't been one ounce of Christianity towards the poor unfortunate who'd been made to give her child up for adoption. She'd been treated as a pariah in the town ever since. Ellen was going to get the very same treatment. Sheila's social standing would be damaged beyond repair. She and Ellen would be the subject of gossip and conjecture. Miriam's heart sank at the thought of the undoubted traumas ahead.

'Right, let's get this show on the road.' Ellen jabbed some candles into the icing on the cake and marched into the front parlour where the guests were assembled. Miriam brought up the rear with the pot of tea.

Ellen thought the evening would never end. Sheila sat, queen-like, in her winged high-back chair, accepting congratulations and good wishes from family and friends. She was in her element. Bonnie Daly and Mona Cullen made a great fuss over Miriam and Emma and were all questions about the pregnancies and imminent arrival of the new offspring. Ellen could see that Emma hated every minute of it. She empathized with that at least.

Emma looked palely delicate in a beautiful embroidered cheesecloth maternity top and loose-fitting trousers. Her bump was very neat. She hardly looked pregnant at all. She'd have had no problem concealing her state had that been necessary, Ellen thought crossly. She felt big and ungainly in comparison. She was terribly warm and uncomfortable. As soon as she told her mother about the baby she was going to take off that damned roll-on for the rest of her pregnancy and to hell with concealment.

A sing-song started. Oh God! They'd be at this for hours. Ellen groaned in dismay as Tim Nolan, a neighbour, went to get his accordion. The older people were in great form, singing lustily with enjoyment. As a rousing rendition of *The Boys of Wexford* ended, Bonnie launched into a solo, quavering in a thrilling high-pitched soprano voice, '*This is my happy day . . . This is the day I will remember, the day I'm dying . . .*'

Ellen caught Miriam's eye and snorted into her tea,

spluttering it all over herself. 'Excuse me,' she murmured weakly. Trying to contain hysterical laughter she made for the kitchen. She collapsed onto a chair and muffled her laughter in a tea towel.

Miriam followed, giggling. Tears streamed down Ellen's face as she gasped for air. 'I surely will remember this the day I'm dying, all right. How apt. Maria Callas has nothing on her.'

Emma appeared at the door. She stopped short when she saw her two sisters-in-law bent double.

'Don't mind us,' Miriam chortled. 'But have you ever heard anything like Bonnie Daly in your life?'

A smile lightened Emma's pale face. 'She's awful, isn't she? Did you hear her saying she always wanted a dildo rail like the one I have in the hall. I thought Vincent was going to burst.'

The other two couldn't contain their heavy guffaws. Emma laughed in spite of herself.

'Oh dear.' Miriam wiped her eyes. 'I don't know how I'm going to keep my face straight when I go back in there.'

'Do you think Mrs Munroe would feel insulted if I went home? I don't feel very well,' Emma asked.

'She wouldn't be a bit insulted,' Miriam said reassuringly. It was a pity about her if she was, she thought privately.

'Go while the going is good,' Ellen said dryly. 'They're only warming up in there. Bonnie Daly's had two glasses of sherry. She'll sing for the night.'

'Oh God!' Miriam paled and gave a gasp.

'What's wrong?' the other pair queried in unison.

Miriam drew a sharp breath. 'I think I've started.'

'But you're not nine months yet.' Emma was horrified.

'I know. Maybe it's a false alarm. Get Ben. I better go home.'

Emma flew out the door as if the devil was on her heels.

Miriam groaned. 'Oh Jesus, Mary and Joseph. This isn't a false alarm, Ellen. You better ring Doctor Elliot.'

Ben and Sheila rushed in. 'What's wrong?' Ben put

his arm around Miriam's shoulders as she doubled up in pain.

'The baby's coming. I better get home. I'm very sorry, Mrs Munroe, for spoiling your party.'

'Now you don't worry about a thing, dear. I'll come with you. Bonnie and Mick will look after the children here. Vincent's phoning for the doctor. Ellen, you come with us,' Sheila ordered briskly. She was not one to panic in a crisis. 'Vincent is going to give us a lift, seeing as you walked over.'

Miriam groaned again as another contraction overwhelmed her. 'They're very close together. It's not at all like Connie and Daniel,' she gasped.

'Thank God for small mercies,' Sheila said. 'A nice quick birth is always a blessing. When I had Ellen I was only in labour for an hour before she popped out.'

Vincent came into the kitchen. He looked anxious. 'Will we go?' He was petrified Miriam was going to have the baby in the back of his car. Emma was in floods of tears upstairs. The sight of Miriam in pain had frightened the daylights out of her.

Ellen felt scared herself. Miriam was going through what she was going to have to endure in another few months. She didn't want to see the baby being born. She didn't want to have to think about it. But she couldn't leave Miriam in the lurch, especially as it was an emergency.

'Come on out to the car. We'll go around the back so all the neighbours don't see you,' she suggested, taking Miriam's hand. Miriam gripped it hard.

'Don't come if you don't want to,' she whispered.

'I want to,' Ellen lied.

The journey took less than five minutes. 'Boil the kettle,' Sheila instructed Ben as she and Ellen assisted Miriam to her bedroom.

'Do you want me to stay?' Vincent asked, hoping against hope that the answer would be no.

'You go back to Emma, she got a bit of a fright, I think,'

his mother advised. Vincent's relief was almost palpable as he hurried out the door.

They helped Miriam undress. The contractions were very severe and perspiration dripped down her face.

'I hope the baby is all right,' she whimpered, as Ellen sponged her with a damp facecloth. 'I hope Doctor Elliot gets here in time.'

So do I, Ellen thought fervently. It was awful to see Miriam in such pain. It seemed like hours but it was only twenty minutes before Doctor Elliot arrived. Ellen was never so glad to see anyone in her life.

'Now Miriam, I'm just going to examine you,' he said reassuringly as he pulled back the bedclothes and eased up her nightdress.

'This one's in a hurry to get out,' he remarked as he gently made his investigations. 'It won't be long now.'

It all happened so quickly, Ellen didn't have time to be scared. She held Miriam's hand while Sheila supported her daughter-in-law's legs as the doctor gave instructions about when to push and when not to. The baby slid out as Miriam yelped in pain, her eyes bulging out of their sockets.

'Good girl,' Doctor Elliot said with satisfaction as he held the baby aloft and gave her a smart slap on her little bottom. A little cry made them all sigh with relief. 'I'll cut the cord now, pet, and then you can hold her,' he said as Sheila stood, beaming, with a towel ready to wipe the baby off.

'Go and tell Ben, he's got a fine little baby girl,' Doctor Elliot smiled at Ellen. 'And put the kettle on for a cup of tea.'

Ellen was shaking as she left the bedroom. In four months, maybe sooner, she'd give birth to a tiny little human being. She was going to have to tell her parents and she was going to have to decide about her future.

She'd deliberately not thought beyond the birth. It was time to take her head out of the sand and stop behaving like the proverbial ostrich.

'It's a girl, Ben. She's fine and so is Miriam,' she said shakily to her brother who was pacing around the kitchen, smoking.

'Thank God for that,' Ben exclaimed. 'I shouldn't have let Miriam do all that work for Ma's birthday party. It wasn't fair to expect it of her. I should have put my foot down. Ma expects too much of her. No fear of Emma mucking in.'

Ellen said nothing. She knew it annoyed Ben the way Sheila treated Miriam like an unpaid servant. But it was up to him and Miriam to have it out with Sheila. She had enough problems of her own without getting involved in a family squabble.

'Just make a pot of tea,' she said wearily. 'I'll look after Connie and Daniel tonight. They can stay over. I'll go and get some clothes for them.'

'Thanks, Ellen. I'm very grateful.'

Suddenly she wanted to tell her brother that she was pregnant. She wanted to get it over with. But she knew it would be selfish to tell him now. He was harassed enough.

'No problem.' She patted him on the shoulder affectionately. She and Ben had always been close.

When she went back into Miriam's bedroom, she felt a lump rise to her throat when she saw her weary sister-in-law beaming down at the dark downy little head nestled close against her.

'Isn't she lovely? We're going to call her Rebecca,' Miriam said proudly.

'That's a pretty name. She's beautiful,' Ellen murmured.

'Any sign of the tea?' Doctor Elliot inquired cheerfully as he packed away his instruments. Sheila was folding the soiled bedlinen.

'It's on its way. I'm going back over to the house. Connie and Daniel can stay there for the night. I'll look after them.'

'Thanks a million, Ellen. Thanks for everything.' Miriam leaned up and kissed Ellen on the cheek.

'See you tomorrow.' Ellen was almost too choked up to

talk. She slipped out of the room and hurried along the hall to the front door. As she walked down the garden path the tears she'd been keeping in check overflowed.

Why couldn't it have been like this for her and Chris? Why couldn't they have shared precious moments with their new baby as Miriam and Ben would? Instead of love and pride and happiness, she'd suffer fear and shame and guilt.

She leaned against the old wooden gate overlooking Blackbird's Field and sobbed her heart out. She'd never felt as scared in her life. The sight of Miriam's newborn baby brought it home to her that she had more than herself to consider. Would it be better to hand up her own baby for adoption, so that it would have a normal life with a mother *and* father? Something it wouldn't have if Ellen decided to bring it up herself. Chris was finished with her. That was obvious. She'd meant nothing to him. The pain of that was worse than any pain she'd feel in labour. She'd never be able to think about him without anguish. That was Chris's legacy to her. That and the child who kicked and moved inside her. Ellen laid her palms on the round curve of her belly. She wondered if her baby was a boy or a girl. She hoped it was a girl. A boy would make her think of Chris. She'd be worried that he'd grow up as mean and as selfish as his father. It was illogical, she knew, but logic had long flown out the window. One minute she wanted to keep the baby, the next she wanted to put it up for adoption. One minute she hated Chris, the next she was crying her eyes out over him. She was in such turmoil she couldn't think straight.

Eventually, she composed herself. It was long past the children's bedtime. After she'd got them to bed, she'd wait for Sheila to come home and then she'd tell her. There was no point in putting it off any longer.

Chapter Seven

'What a wonderful way to remember my birthday. I think Rebecca is a lovely name for the baby.' Sheila was as proud as Punch as she sat down opposite Mick. She sipped from a glass of sherry, a treat to celebrate her birthday and the birth of her new granddaughter. She beamed at Ellen, and waited for a response. Ellen was sitting in the old rocking-chair beside the wireless. She was listening to a concert. She looked pale and strained. Come to think of it, she hadn't been in good form for ages and she'd stopped talking about this Chris fella she'd been seeing. Sheila suspected that he'd dropped Ellen. She was always waiting for the phone to ring. Always the first to answer it when it did. That was a sure sign. Not that she was sorry. Ellen could do much better for herself. That Chris had notions about himself. On the few occasions he'd called for Ellen she'd felt as if he was looking down his nose at her and Mick. Not that he'd collected Ellen that often, Sheila sniffed. Most of the time Ellen had to make her own way into Dublin. He wasn't half as attentive as he should be. Not compared to the way Vincent and Ben had treated their girlfriends. No doubt Ellen would be upset, if it was all off. But she'd find someone else. Although she was getting a bit long in the tooth, as Bonnie Daly had so ungraciously put it. What was it about Ellen that she couldn't keep a man? It was most annoying. Sheila hadn't planned for her daughter to end up a spinster. That's what she would end up as, if she didn't straighten herself out and find a nice lad to marry her.

Sheila frowned over at her daughter. She really did look washed out. The birth must have been a shock. The first birth you saw always was.

'Why don't you have a sherry, dear? To celebrate,' she suggested magnanimously. She didn't approve of young women drinking in pubs. She and Ellen had had bitter rows about it in the past. But a glass of sherry now and again in the privacy of one's own home was perfectly acceptable.

'No thanks, Mam,' Ellen murmured.

'I wonder how poor Emma—'

'Mam, Dad, I'm . . . I'm pregnant.' Ellen's voice shook. Sheila stared at her uncomprehendingly.

'What did you say, Ellen?' She felt a frisson of alarm. She'd been wondering how Emma had got over her fright and Ellen . . . no she couldn't have . . . she must have misheard.

Sheila lowered her sherry glass. 'I'm going to have a baby,' she heard her only daughter say. The words sounded like a roaring in her brain. Her heart started to thump. She couldn't speak. She looked at Mick. He looked at her. Stunned. Sheila felt her insides dissolve as her world came crashing down around her ears. As long as she had lived in Glenree, she had been respected, admired, even envied by her peers. She was proud of her husband and her family. And justifiably so. Mick had his own business and was a pillar of the community. Vincent and Ben were doing very well for themselves in their respective careers. Especially Vincent who was going from strength to strength. His marriage to Emma, and even their magnificent house, were a source of great pride to her. Now, it was all for nothing. Ellen had just put the entire family beyond the pale.

Tears came to her eyes. Her hands trembled. Anger ripped through her.

'How far gone are you?' Her eyes were like ice chips.

'Five months,' Ellen muttered.

'Jesus, Mary and Joseph!' Sheila was horrified. Mick

covered his face with his hands. He didn't know what to say.

'Well, my lady, you can marry the fella that's done this to you and you'll marry him quietly in the next fortnight. We'll have to go and talk to Father Kelly. You have that Chris come and meet your father and myself tomorrow night so we can make the arrangements.' Sheila's voice shook with emotion. She felt like slapping her daughter's face.

'Chris won't marry me,' Ellen said quietly. 'He's finished with me.'

'By God, he's not finished with you. And he *will* marry you. No daughter of mine is going to have an illegitimate child.'

'I'm telling you, Mam. He's left me. He won't see me. I haven't seen or spoken to him in two weeks.'

'We'll see about that. Won't we, Mick?' Sheila glared at her husband, demanding that he back her up.

'We'll go and talk to him on Monday,' Mick fumed. 'He'll accept his responsibilities if I have anything to do with it.'

'I'm telling you, Mam—'

'Enough! Get out of my sight. I don't want to hear another word out of you. Your father and I will handle this. What will Pamela and Judge Connolly think when they find out about this sorry mess? You've disgraced us, Ellen.' Sheila sat ramrod-straight, pale and utterly unforgiving.

'I'm sorry,' was all Ellen could say.

'It's too late for that. Go to bed. Your father and I have to talk.'

'But I have to talk too.'

'You'll just do as you're told. You . . . you . . . *tramp*.'

'That's enough, Sheila!' Mick warned. 'Ellen, go to bed. Now, Sheila, what's done is done. Ellen's our daughter and there'll be no name-calling,' Mick ordered quietly as Ellen walked out of the room.

'How could she? How could she, Mick?' Sheila was

distraught. 'She was always the same. Running after fellas. Down there in that pub acting like a slattern. Drinking beer! Oh Bonnie Daly was always rubbing it in. Wait until she hears about this. She'll be in her element. They all will. I'll never be able to show my face in the guild again.' Sheila burst into tears. Tears of anger, rage, frustration and shame. She'd never forgive Ellen, never.

'Let's go to bed. It's been a long day. We'll talk about it in the morning. Ellen's not the first girl to get into trouble and she won't be the last.' Mick rubbed his eyes wearily.

'She's the first on my side and your side of the family,' Sheila retorted sharply. 'Imagine how I'll feel telling the relations about this. If that Wallace brat thinks he's running away from our daughter after getting her into this mess, he's got another think coming. First thing Monday morning, Mick. Do you hear me? The three of us are going to tell that young man just where his responsibilities lie. You go to bed if you want to. I couldn't possibly sleep.' Sheila marched out into the kitchen and started to clean the top of the cooker even though it was after eleven. She had to do something to keep herself occupied. Either that, or go and strangle her daughter with her bare hands.

*   *   *

Ellen removed the hated roll-on, with a strange sense of liberation. Her bump protruded, round and smooth. She needn't try to hide it any more. She'd go and see Doctor Elliot sometime during the week. Miriam was right, she should be taking iron tablets. She didn't want to harm her baby. It was bad enough denying its existence for the past five months.

She'd been right about her mother, she thought wearily as she pulled off the heavy sweater that had imprisoned her all day. She stank of stale perspiration. She'd love to have a bath, but it was a bit late and besides it would take ages for the water to heat up if she switched on the hot water tank.

She sat on the bed and listened to the murmur of her

parents' voices downstairs. It was hard to believe that she'd finally told them about being pregnant. Never, as long as she lived, would she forget the unbearable tension of waiting for Sheila to come home from Miriam's. Every minute had seemed like an hour. She'd been so tempted to blurt it out to Mick as he sat doing his crossword puzzle. But she'd resisted the urge. What was the point in having to make the same confession twice? Do it once when her parents were together and lessen the ordeal.

Ellen winced as she remembered the expression in her mother's eyes when she'd told her. Fury and utter disgust. The boys had always been her mother's favourites anyway, Ellen thought bitterly. She'd been a grave disappointment as a daughter. She didn't like cooking or sewing or gardening or housework. She'd resented the way the boys got off scot-free from doing household chores when they'd lived at home and had often argued long and loudly about the unfairness of it. Much to her parents' annoyance.

Sheila was furious when Bonnie Daly asked her did she not mind about Ellen drinking beer in the Glenree Arms. Bonnie had more or less implied that Ellen was behaving in a most unladylike fashion. There'd been an almighty row when Sheila confronted Ellen about the fact that she was drinking behind her parents' backs.

Ellen was enraged by her mother's double standard. Her brothers were allowed to drink, why wasn't she? She told Sheila not to be so bloody old-fashioned and to take no notice of that nosy old crab, Daly, whose own daughter wasn't slow to lower the odd sneaky short.

'Why can't you settle down and get married like other girls and stop behaving like someone with no rearing?' Sheila fumed.

It hurt Ellen that her mother was so disappointed in her. But she had to live her own life. If she lived the way her mother wanted her to live, she'd end up a loony. When Joseph ditched her for his whey-faced Miss Goody-Two-Shoes, Sheila was bitterly disappointed. She'd been planning the wedding for ages in her mind. Needless to say, she'd blamed Ellen for losing him. Another failure, another mark against her. Now, finally, Ellen had given her mother the biggest blow any mother could suffer.

There would be no forgiveness. Ellen didn't expect any. Sheila had meant it when she'd called her a tramp. There was no going back.

Mick was disappointed in her. But he was easygoing. He'd get over it. He, unlike Sheila, couldn't care less about what neighbours thought.

Ellen sighed. She heard Mick's heavy footstep on the stairs. As soon as he went to bed she'd go into the bathroom and wash herself. A breeze whispered through the window, the white lace curtains fluttered in the moonlight. Ellen went and stood by the window. It was a beautiful night. A full moon shone brightly between the gently swaying treetops. The stars glittered against an inky sky. The Plough so clear she felt she could trace it with her finger. The breeze made a shushing sound through the trees, like the sound of the sea. Where was Chris, she wondered. Who was he with? Was he walking along Killiney beach with Suzy? Pain so sharp it made her catch her breath pierced her heart. Didn't he care about her at all? Maybe when he was faced with her parents he'd come to his senses. It was a forlorn hope but it was all she had. Ellen stood in the moonlight, crying silent tears.

* * *

'You're going to Wicklow to another house party?' Chris fumed. He and Suzy were having lunch in the Capitol restaurant and his girlfriend had just dropped her bombshell.

'They're nice people. I like them. I like getting out of Dublin for the weekend now and again. It's not as if I'm away *every* weekend. It's ages since the last one.' Suzy was so offhand he could have strangled her.

'It's not that long ago. Why can't I come with you?'

'Because you weren't invited, darling,' she said patiently.

'But I don't want you to go away for the weekend,' Chris argued petulantly. He'd worked his butt off morning, noon and night for the last two weeks, setting up on on his own. It had been exhausting. And now that he'd finally gone solo he was feeling apprehensive. Working alone was exhilarating and nerve-racking at the same time. He wanted to talk to Suzy about it, but he knew it bored her. Now, just when he'd been looking forward to a weekend of relaxation, she announced she was off to Wicklow without a thought for him. He wanted to relax and he wanted to get Suzy into bed. He hadn't had sex since his last night with Ellen.

At the thought of Ellen Chris suddenly felt very lonely. It was strange, but he missed her. If she'd still been a part of his life he'd be able to tell her all about his new business. *Wallace Insurance Brokers Ltd.* She would have been thrilled and proud to see the impressive lettering on the shiny brass plate beside the door of his new office. Suzy had just murmured 'very nice' when he'd shown it to her. She didn't approve of him going out on his own. She thought it was too big a risk to take.

Ellen had been all for it. She'd have listened to all his plans and given good advice. More importantly, she would have given him a hand setting up the office. She would have made a good secretary. Ellen had brains, unlike the dozy young woman he'd hastily hired. He'd actually caught her painting her toenails in the office and she was forever on the phone wittering on about this bloke and that to one of her equally dozy girlfriends. She wasn't going to last the pace . . . for sure. As soon as he was established, she was out on her ear. He needed a secretary with a bit of get up and go.

Chris sighed as he watched Suzy take a delicate bite out of her sandwich. She was a very ladylike eater. Nibbling this and that. Suddenly he felt enormously irritated. Ellen had never *nibbled* at food. She enjoyed her food, just like he did. Ellen would never have announced that she was taking off just like that for a weekend. She'd never have left him in the lurch. She'd have cherished him and soothed him and made a fuss of him, especially at this most stressful time in his life. If only she hadn't got bloody well pregnant they'd still be together. He pushed away his bowl of oxtail soup. He didn't fancy it now. To tell the truth he felt extremely guilty about Ellen. He knew she'd been phoning him at work. He'd even gone so far as to hang up when she phoned him at home. He'd felt a right heel after that. He'd gone and got pissed. She'd sounded so forlorn on the phone. He just couldn't handle it.

He couldn't possibly take on a wife and child right now, he argued silently with himself as the waitress in her smart black dress and white apron and little frilly cap removed his half-eaten soup. If only Ellen had told him earlier, he could have taken care of it. Sent her to London to have a little job done. They'd still be together. She'd probably be working for him. Maybe they would have married eventually. Ellen loved him. She knew how to take care of him.

Chris glowered at Suzy sitting opposite him sipping her coffee. That was more than he could say about her right at this moment . . . the stupid cow . . . he thought irritably.

*   *   *

'I mean it, Alexandra. I think I'm pushing it. He was in a foul humour. He barely gave me a peck on the cheek when I was leaving.' Suzy unpacked her cocktail dress and smoothed it out before hanging it up.

'Well that's just what he needs.' Alexandra was un-impressed by Lover-boy Wallace's foul humours.

'He's up to his eyes with his new business. I think he was crazy going out on his own. If it fails he'll have no money. I can't marry a pauper,' Suzy moaned.

'Chris Wallace won't fail,' Alexandra assured her. 'Anyway his family's loaded, he'll always be jammy.'

'True.' Suzy brightened. 'He was as mad as hell, though, about me going. He said it was the first free weekend he'd got since going out on his own and he wanted to relax, eat out, go for a walk in Killiney, go to a film. It would have been nice.'

'Yeah, maybe we have to change our tack a little,' Alexandra conceded as she stepped out of her white silk lingerie and headed for the bathroom where a foamy scented bath awaited her. 'It might be a good time to overwhelm him with some TLC. Perhaps it's time to spend a night with him.'

'Do you think so?' Suzy asked eagerly as she perched on the edge of the bath. She lit two cigarettes and handed one to Alexandra who was now reclining up to her neck in frothy white bubbles.

'Hmm. He'll be feeling *sooo* sorry for himself he'll fall all over you. Now the plan is: You go home early Sunday afternoon and surprise him. Seduce the daylights out of him this once, just to remind him of what he's missing. Only once mind . . .' Alexandra warned. 'And we'll proceed from there.'

'I can't wait.' Suzy gave a long languorous stretch. She wished it was Sunday afternoon. The prospect of spending the night with Chris made her tingle with anticipation. He certainly knew how to turn her on. For two pins she'd have dumped her clothes back into her suitcase and gone haring back to Dublin this minute. But that wasn't cool behaviour. After a weekend without her, he'd really appreciate her all the more, Suzy assured herself.

* * *

He'd been thinking about Ellen all weekend. Twice on Friday afternoon he'd picked up the phone to call her. But lost his nerve. Then by chance he'd bumped into Emma at her mother's where he'd gone to deliver a few of his business cards and prospectuses in case Pamela or his uncle might know of a few potential clients. 'How's all in the back of beyond?' he asked lightly. 'How are all the culchies?' It annoyed Emma when he said things like that about her in-laws.

'Glenree is not the back of beyond,' Emma snapped. 'And don't you dare refer to Vincent as a culchie. He's got more money and a better business than you have, buster.'

'I was just teasing.' Chris grinned. His cousin was looking very prettily pregnant. How ironic that Ellen was in the same boat. Chris wondered whether she'd told her family yet. It was only when he'd really looked at Ellen that he'd seen the signs. To most people it would probably look as though she'd put on weight.

'Well it is the back of beyond sometimes,' Emma agreed, grimacing. 'I've to go to a party at my mother-in-law's. How ghastly!'

'How's Ellen?' he asked offhandedly.

'She's a moody madam. I don't see that much of her,' Emma drawled. 'You're not still interested in *her*, are you?'

'I was just wondering. She was a bit of a gas,' Chris said lightly. By unspoken agreement, neither he nor Ellen had told Emma and Vincent that they were seeing each other again. It was obvious Emma didn't know that Ellen was pregnant. He felt vaguely relieved. Somehow the thought of Emma looking down her superior little nose at Ellen, as she surely would when she found out about the pregnancy, bothered him.

Maybe if he phoned Ellen and arranged to meet, they could talk about him providing some money towards the baby's keep. Maybe Ellen could come and work for him as a secretary. It was the best he could offer, but marriage was definitely out of the question at the moment.

He felt much better having come to that decision. Less of a heel. He went home, showered and shaved, and went out on the town for the night with a few pals. He'd a hell of a hangover the next morning and stayed in bed until well after one. And by the time he got his head together and made up his mind to phone Ellen, it was after four. He was

148

apprehensive as he dialled the number. What would she say to him? Would she be glad he'd called or would she never want to speak to him again? He wasn't sure which he'd prefer. But at least she couldn't say he *hadn't* called.

Vincent answered the phone. In the background, Chris could hear laughter and chat. Of course, the mother's party.

'Hello!' Vincent said again.

Damn! Why hadn't Ellen answered? Chris hung up. Vincent would have recognized him if he'd spoken and he'd surely wonder why he was looking for Ellen. He'd leave it until Sunday afternoon. Maybe he'd catch her then.

*   *   *

Suzy's heart was beating fast as she rang the doorbell. She'd been petrified that Chris wouldn't be at home. The relief when she saw his car in the drive was immense. The look of surprise on his face when he opened the door was gratifying.

'You're back early!' he remarked as he stepped aside to let her in.

'I missed you, darling.' Suzy flung her arms around him. She gazed into his deep blue eyes. 'I really missed you.'

'Show me how much,' Chris said huskily. His arms tightened around her. She kissed him. A long slow deep wet French kiss that left him in no doubt as to how much he'd been missed. His eyes darkened with desire.

'Let's go upstairs,' Suzy murmured. She took him by the hand and led him up to the bedroom.

*   *   *

Ellen's stomach lurched as she saw the familiar red car in the driveway. It was eight-fifteen on Monday morning as Mick pulled up outside Chris's house. She'd persuaded her parents to confront Chris in his house rather than at work.

He'd never forgive her if they made a show of him at the office. She had no idea that he'd moved offices and gone out on his own.

Sheila stepped out of the car with grim resolve. She hadn't spoken once on the trip into town. Ellen followed her. She felt as if she were in a dream and that her life was no longer hers to control. She was fearful, hopeful, desperate to see him once more. Sheila gave a smart rap on the dull brass knocker. Mick shuffled from one foot to the other, and cleared his throat. Ellen's palms began to sweat as panic overcame her. She could see Chris's outline against the glass panel.

He opened the door and the look of shocked dismay on his face made her feel sick.

'What the hell?' he swore.

He looked very handsome in his smart business suit. Despite all that had happened between them, Ellen longed to fling herself into his arms and have him hug her.

'We want a word with you, young man.' Sheila glared at him. 'If you don't mind, we'll step inside. I'm sure you don't want the neighbours to know your business.'

'Who is it, Chris?' Ellen wanted to die as she saw Suzy glide down the stairs looking cool and soignée and reed-thin in a Prince of Wales check suit with a short boxy jacket, edged in black velvet.

'I . . . I . . . have some business to do with the Munroes. I'll call you later.' Chris flushed as he ushered the surprised girl past the trio at the door.

'Oh . . . OK.' It was obvious she was extremely disconcerted.

Sheila's lips thinned. Her nostrils flared. She stepped inside as if she was walking into a slurry-pit. Mick followed sheepishly. Ellen couldn't look Chris in the eye. He closed the door and glared at Ellen. Sheila gave Mick a dig in the ribs.

He cleared his throat. 'You know Ellen's pregnant with your child. We want to know how soon you can marry her. We want to make the arrangements,' Mick said bluntly.

'Look, I've told Ellen I'll support her financially if she doesn't want to hand the baby up for adoption. But marriage is out of the question,' Chris blustered.

'Now, son, it's like this. Where I come from, if a man gets a girl into trouble, he marries her and he faces up to his responsibilities. My daughter's reputation is ruined. But it can be salvaged. And you, young man, will do the proper thing.'

'Indeed you will.' Sheila couldn't contain herself. 'And very soon, too, if you don't want your child to be born out of wedlock.'

'Ellen, tell them. Tell them I can't marry you. I've just set up in business,' Chris said angrily. 'I can't afford to get married.'

'I'll see to it that you have a roof over your heads.' Mick was unimpressed. 'I'll build a house on the site we've kept for Ellen. So apart from taking care of your wife and child, you'll be very little the worse off.'

'No!' Chris sounded desperate. How dare she bring her parents to his house to browbeat him!

Ellen looked at him. His eyes were hard and angry. His mouth drawn in a thin line. Nothing would make him change his mind. She'd been a fool to think otherwise.

'Young man, have you no shame? What do your parents think of this?'

'They don't know about it. But if they did, they wouldn't expect me to get married when I've said I'd take care of Ellen financially. And don't talk to me about shame. Ellen didn't have to sleep with me. And she wasn't a virgin either when she did. It might not be mine at all.' Chris was incandescent with rage as he lashed out mercilessly, unmoved by Ellen's stricken face.

Mick's hands clenched into fists. Sheila looked as if she was about to faint.

'I should knock your head off for that. But I won't lower myself to your level in the sewers. Come on, Sheila, Ellen.' He flung open the front door and directed the two women out before him. Red-faced with anger and contempt he turned to Chris. 'I'll take care of the child. I wouldn't see my daughter humble herself by taking one penny of your money.'

'But Mick,' protested Sheila as her one vain hope of redemption disappeared, 'he's got to marry her.'

'I wouldn't allow Ellen to marry him under any circumstances. Let's get home,' her husband said curtly.

Ellen had never seen her father so angry. She felt dirty and humiliated and shamed. The shock she felt couldn't be more if he'd physically hit her. How could Chris have told them she wasn't a virgin before he'd slept with her? How low could he get? She'd never rise above this. She'd never be able to look her parents in the eye again. She was at their mercy. She got into the car and struggled to keep her composure. If she started crying, she'd never stop.

'You can go and stay with Aunt Lily in Navan until the baby is born. I'll phone her immediately. And then you can have the child adopted. No one need ever know.' Sheila was distracted.

'She won't go to Lily's and she won't put the child up for adoption either unless she wants to. She'll stay with us, Sheila. I won't avoid my responsibilities, and neither will you. That's the end of it. Ellen's our daughter and we'll stand by her.'

Sheila swallowed hard. Mick rarely laid down the law but, when he did, he was implacable. There was no arguing with him. He had set his face against the wind and there was no turning back. Sheila knew that sending Ellen to her sister Lily and having the baby put up for adoption was the last chance the family had of retaining their respectability now that Chris had refused to do the honourable thing. But Mick had stepped in and put a stop to that, with his talk of accepting responsibility. All because of his stubborn pride. She was the one who was going to have to suffer the snide gossip and pointing fingers. Sheila felt thoroughly defeated.

Ellen sat in the back of her father's car, her mind in turmoil. Perhaps her mother was right. Maybe she should go to her aunt's for the rest of her pregnancy. Maybe she should hand the baby up for adoption. Would it be the best thing to do for her child's future? Her father's reaction wasn't a total surprise to her. He was a good man. He looked after his own. Her baby might never know its father, but Mick would not disown it. And neither will I, Ellen thought fiercely. Somehow or another, with his help, she'd get through it. Sheila would never forgive her. Ellen would have to live with that.

*   *   *

'Christ Almighty!' Chris slammed the door after his unwelcome guests. He was so stunned and angry, he was shaking. That was it. Definitely! He was finished with Ellen. He never wanted to see her or her dreadful parents again. The nerve of them, landing on his doorstep making demands and threats. How dare that . . . that provincial butcher and his hick dragon of a wife look down their noses at him as if he was some sort of worm. He'd had every intention of phoning Ellen until Suzy's unexpected arrival. But then, they'd gone to bed and all thoughts of his former girlfriend had disappeared as he and Suzy spent hours making passionate love.

He'd have phoned Ellen at work today and tried to come to some satisfactory arrangement. But she'd ruined her chances by pulling this morning's crazy stunt. Ellen's father could look after the child. Chris was having nothing to do with them. Ever.

He thought of the stricken look of deep pain and hurt that had darkened Ellen's eyes when he said the child might not be his and felt horribly guilty. He shouldn't have said that. It was rage and the feeling of being trapped that had made him blurt it out. It was her own fault, he thought angrily. Guilt was not a feeling he was familiar with. And he didn't like it. He drove to work and banished all memories of the morning's debacle from his mind and immersed himself in his paperwork. When Suzy phoned him an hour later demanding to know what was going on, he bluntly told her to mind her own business. It was nothing to do with her and she wasn't ever to ask him about it again.

The vehemence of his tone told her he was deadly serious. Although she was dying with curiosity, Suzy knew he meant every word he said. Instinctively she knew this was a topic to be left alone. Suzy wasn't too worried. For some strange reason she felt much more confident of her chances of becoming Mrs Chris Wallace.

*   *   *

'Why, Miriam? Why has he done this to me? How could he say a thing like that? And in front of my parents? Why can't he love me the way I love him? He said he loved me. How could he lie about that? How could he say it if he didn't mean it?' Ellen was almost incoherent as grief, hurt and pain overwhelmed her. She was sobbing like a child in her sister-in-law's kitchen. Mick had told her to take the day off work.

'I would have done anything for him. Anything. And he knows that. Why has he treated me like I was his worst enemy?'

'Because he's a bastard of the highest order. He's a selfish, lying, cheating shit who doesn't know the meaning of the word love. There's only one person in this world that Chris Wallace loves, Ellen, and that's himself. I'm telling you now. You're better off without him. Forget him.' Miriam, nearly in tears herself, was flushed with anger. If she could have got her hands on Chris she would have murdered him without a qualm for inflicting such suffering on Ellen.

Ellen was speechless at her sister-in-law's tirade. Miriam only used bad language under extreme provocation. It was painful to hear her say such things about Chris. Especially as, in her heart of hearts, Ellen knew there was a lot of truth in what Miriam said.

'Ellen, you're shattered. Why don't you go and have a lie-down for a while and I'll bring you up a bite of lunch later on,' Miriam urged.

Ellen hiccuped and nodded. She felt immensely weary. Ten minutes later she was lying in Miriam's big brass bed. The curtains were drawn and she curled up tightly in the dark and tried to ignore the panicky racing of her heart.

'Please, God, take this pain away. Please, please, please, let me forget Chris. Please get him out of my head and my heart. And help me to be strong for my baby. Saint Michael, archangel of God, give me courage. Saint Anthony help me to find peace of mind,' she prayed frantically, desperate to find solace in this, the worst trauma of her life.

Chapter Eight

Rebecca Catherine Munroe whimpered as Father Kelly poured holy water over her forehead and christened her. The whimper turned into a howl. Emma watched Ellen try to soothe her new goddaughter. She wasn't having much success. Babies were very noisy. There was so much fuss attached to them. All the feeding and bathing and changing. It was never-ending. She hadn't really realized how much attention babies needed until Rebecca's arrival.

Emma knew she was unnatural, but the thought of having to give her life over completely to a demanding baby made her feel most resentful. This hadn't been the plan at all. And besides, what did she know about babies? Nothing! And now she was expected suddenly to know all about feeds and nappy rash and colic and something called cradle-cap. It was horrendous. And the thought of breast-feeding gave her the shivers. How did you know if it was getting enough milk? She definitely wasn't going to breastfeed. Besides she certainly didn't want a bosom like Liz Taylor's. She liked her pert firm breasts. Would they ever return to normal, she wondered despondently. She'd gone up a bra size already. She was enormous.

Rebecca quietened down, thankfully. What did you do if your baby wouldn't stop crying? How did you know what was wrong with it? It couldn't tell you. The idea of it all petrified Emma. Why should she have to be a mother when she didn't want to be one?

Emma looked at Ellen rocking the baby gently in her arms. She looked drawn and pale and desperately unhappy. Dark shadows ringed her eyes. She was a stupid girl not to have listened to her and Vincent's advice about Chris. Sheila had told Vincent the news about her pregnancy this morning. Vincent was as mad as hell. Especially when he'd heard that Chris had no intention of marrying Ellen. He'd wanted to go and flatten him. It was most embarrassing to have her cousin behave so badly. She wouldn't have cared if it was some girl she didn't know. But Vincent's sister. Sheila had been rather frosty with Emma that morning as if it were her fault. It was most unfair. Especially when Ellen had been warned. Stupid idiot, Emma thought angrily. Vincent was so furious, he'd demanded that Emma go and talk to Chris to get him to see sense.

'I'm not getting involved, Vincent. It's nothing to do with me. I warned her not to have anything to do with him, so forget it,' she snapped. 'He'll never marry her.'

He was right too, she thought defiantly. Why on earth would Chris want to marry Ellen Munroe when he could have his pick of the crème de la crème. She wasn't glitzy or glamorous enough for high-flying Chris Wallace and she was a fool ever to think she was, Emma thought contemptuously.

Vincent was so annoyed by her response that he was now in a huff. He hadn't spoken a word to her on the drive to the church and, when they were waiting for the christening to start, he just sat with his arms folded, his face like thunder, ignoring her. Now he was up at the foot of the altar, performing his godfatherly duties, looking as if he'd like to murder Ellen. When he'd heard that Ellen was actually going to go through with being godmother and had gone to Mass that morning as if nothing had happened, he'd nearly had a blue fit.

'She can't go to church in her condition. She can't stand up at the altar as brazen as you like for the christening. She'll make a show of us,' he raged to Sheila.

'Miriam and Ben want her as godmother and there's nothing I can do about it,' Sheila hissed. 'For God's sake don't start a row at the church and make a disgrace of us. Things are bad enough as they are. That's what comes of mixing with riff-raff.' She cast a cold look in Emma's direction before she marched out to the car where Mick was waiting.

Emma was incensed. If Sheila Munroe thought she was going to look down her aquiline nose at Emma and blame her for Chris's misdemeanours she had another think coming. Marrying into this culchie clodhopping family was the biggest mistake she'd ever made in her life, she decided as she glowered at her husband who gave her an equally icy stare in return. For two pins, she wouldn't bother going back to Miriam's for tea and sandwiches and christening cake. Let Vincent go on his own. It was his bloody family. She'd had enough of them.

'You can bring me home. I'm not going back to Miriam's. I don't feel well,' Emma muttered as Vincent came back to the seat.

'You can come back for ten minutes. Miriam's been very good to you. *Then* we'll leave.' Vincent was uncharacteristically stern. Emma wanted to argue. She hated being bossed about. But it was true that Miriam had been very good to her. It would have been insulting not to go back to her house to congratulate her on her daughter's christening. She'd be pleasant to Miriam and Ben but Vincent, Sheila and Ellen could go and get lost, Emma decided crossly as she preceded her husband out the door of St Joseph's.

Ellen was getting into Ben's car with Rebecca. Now that she knew what to look for, Emma could see the unmistakable signs of pregnancy. Before she'd thought that her sister-in-law was putting on weight which she covered up with bulky clothes. Now that she knew the reason, Emma couldn't help having a good look. Today Ellen was wearing a loose blouse over a kilt-type skirt. Very untidy, Emma thought. She'd definitely have to start wearing maternity clothes soon and then the tongues would start wagging. It would certainly take Sheila down a peg or two, she thought vindictively, still smarting from her mother-in-law's insulting remark earlier.

They drove to Miriam's house in silence. She had no intention of breaking the ice. *He* would have to apologize to her first. The nerve of Vincent, treating her like that just because she refused to confront Chris. She wondered what her parents would say when they heard the news. Pamela would be mortified that a member of her side of the family had got Ellen into trouble. Why hadn't Ellen listened to them? She was so bloody sure of herself, she thought she knew it all. Now look at her, and all the trouble she was causing. Well Ellen needn't think she'd get any sympathy from her. Emma was so annoyed she felt like giving her sister-in-law a piece of her mind.

* * *

Ellen could see Emma scowling at her. Obviously she knew. Vincent certainly knew. He'd glared at her through the ceremony and Ellen knew he was going to let her have it. She settled into the car with the baby in her arms. Emma turned her head away dismissively as Ben drove past. Well fuck her with her airs and graces. It was none of her business anyway, Ellen raged. It wasn't anyone's business and they needn't think they were going to make her feel bad. Thank God for Miriam and Ben, if it wasn't for them, she'd never get through it.

Miriam had told Ben about the baby. When Ellen went over to the house the next day, he told her that he and Miriam would help as much as they could and that she was to do what she felt was right, about keeping the baby. Sheila was keeping the pressure on about her going to her aunt's in Navan and having the baby adopted.

There'd been a mighty row when Ben told Sheila that they had asked Ellen to be godmother. Ellen was doing the washing-up and Sheila was icing a cake at the kitchen table when Ben told his mother of their plans. Sheila glared at Ellen and turned on her son.

'What kind of a person is she to be godmother to any child? She's in a state of mortal sin. She can't parade up to the altar in St Joseph's. What will people say? A godparent is supposed to undertake to look out for the moral welfare of the child. That one has the morals of an alley cat.'

Ellen walked out of the kitchen, white-faced.

Ben held his ground. 'It's what Miriam wants, Mam. Ellen's been very good to her.'

'Can't she ask Emma? It would be altogether more fitting. Especially as Vincent is the godfather,' Sheila argued.

'No, Mam, and don't cause a fuss. I won't have Miriam upset. She's tired and a bit weepy still.'

Sheila gave an eloquent snort. 'And what about me? Does anyone care about *me* being upset? My daughter's disgraced the family name. Your father won't let me handle the matter the way it should be handled. *You* won't listen to my advice and have Emma as godmother. I'm just your mother and my feelings don't count for anything. Is that it?'

'No, Mam, of course not. And I know it's a very unfortunate situation. But Miriam wants Ellen to be godmother to show her some solidarity and I think she's right.'

'Oh, so Ellen's to get sympathy and a pat on the back for behaving like a slut.' Sheila was fit to be tied.

'Mam, don't talk about Ellen like that. She's going to be godmother and that's it.' Ben turned on his heel and left.

Sheila hurried upstairs and marched furiously into Ellen's bedroom.

'If you had any sense of decency, you'd tell Miriam no. That child deserves better.'

'Emma doesn't even want to be a mother. She'd hate to be asked to be godmother. Miriam asked me and I'm going to do it. And if you don't like it, you can lump it,' Ellen spat. Her mother's words had cut her to the quick.

'Don't you talk to me like that, my girl. Don't think you're too old to feel my hand on that cheeky puss of yours.' Two bright spots of red stained Sheila's cheeks. Her hands itched to slap Ellen's face. She wanted to physically hurt her for the anguish and shame she was causing. The two women stared at each other. Then Sheila turned and walked out of the room, quivering with anger.

Ellen sighed, remembering the altercation. Things were going to get worse. Only the immediate family knew of her pregnancy at the moment. Once the relations and neighbours knew, Sheila's anger and resentment would increase. And Ellen would bear the brunt of it.

Rebecca gave a little cough. Ellen gazed down at her admiringly. She was lovely. So dainty and perfect with her big blue eyes and shock of dark hair. If she had a little girl, they'd be pals, just like her and Miriam. The thought gave Ellen some comfort as Ben swung the car into the drive and Miriam prepared to receive her guests.

*　　*　　*

'Have a sandwich.' Ellen held out the plate of sandwiches to Emma and Vincent. She'd decided to act as though everything was normal. Tough luck if they couldn't handle her pregnancy. She wasn't going to go around with her head bowed no matter how much they expected her to.

'No thank you,' Emma said snootily.

'Vincent?'

'Have you no shame?' Vincent growled. 'It's bad enough getting pregnant before you're married when you were warned not to get involved with Chris Wallace. But to flaunt yourself before Father Kelly, and promise to look after Rebecca's moral welfare, that takes the biscuit.'

'It's none of your business,' Ellen gritted.

'You're damn right it's my business. When you devastate our parents, *that's* my business. Imagine how Mam's going to feel when she has to meet Mr and Mrs Connolly. When you make a show of the family, *that's* my business. And I'm going to make it my business to make sure that Chris Wallace marries you, no matter what he or Dad says.'

'You stay out of it, Vincent. I don't interfere in your life. Don't you go interfering in mine,' Ellen argued heatedly.

'Why couldn't you listen to Vincent and me, when we told you to stay away from Chris?' Emma couldn't contain herself.

'Listen, you. I don't have to take any crap from you, and I won't.'

'Vincent, don't let her talk to me like that. I'm your wife.' Emma bristled.

'Shut up, Ellen.' Vincent's voice rose. 'Don't talk to Emma like that. She's every right to say that to you. She warned you about that creep.'

'You fuck off, Vincent Munroe, and stay out of my business. I didn't interfere when you married that stuck-up little bitch, even though I knew you were making a big mistake. Did I? I let you make your own mistakes without lecturing you. So you let me make mine.' Ellen was so mad she said the most hurtful thing she could think of and she didn't care who heard.

'How dare you!' Emma stuttered.

'Oh grow up,' Ellen snorted. 'You're pathetic.'

Vincent was purple with fury.

'You're a vicious little—'

'Vincent, Ellen!' Miriam exclaimed, coming to stand between them. Emma was weeping at this stage. 'This is my daughter's christening. If you want to have a row, do it somewhere else. Please.' Her voice shook. It took a lot of effort to assert herself but she was determined. Enough was enough.

'Take me home, Vincent. Miriam, I'm sorry about this. You can blame *her*,' Emma blubbered.

'I'm sorry, Miriam.' Ellen was suddenly contrite. It wasn't fair brawling at Rebecca's christening party.

'So you should be,' Vincent exploded.

Ellen bit her lip. She badly wanted to retort that he'd started it but Miriam was upset so she said nothing.

'Are you satisfied now?' Sheila demanded as Vincent led his sobbing wife from the room.

'Be quiet, Sheila,' Mick said quietly. 'Ellen, go and get me another cup of tea, please.'

Ellen went out to the kitchen. She was trembling. Vincent's venom had taken her by surprise. She knew he'd be mad. But the strength of his feelings surprised her. If it had been anyone else other than Chris he wouldn't have been so annoyed. It was an awkward situation and his in-laws wouldn't be impressed. But so what? Blood was thicker than water for God's sake and what the hell was so special about Pamela and Judge Connolly? They didn't live in Glenree. They'd never have anything to do with her. There was no need for Vincent to get his Y-fronts in such a twist. He was always the same anyway, doing the older brother act. If he wanted to come the heavy with Emma, fine, but Ellen wasn't going to put up with it.

She poured her father a cup of tea. Mick hadn't referred to the incident with Chris or made any comment about her pregnancy. His attitude towards her wasn't angry or reproachful like Sheila's. He was supporting her in his own quiet way. It gave her comfort. She'd never really appreciated her father until now. In this, the biggest crisis of her life, he was her strongest ally. She'd never realized how much he loved her until he'd done his best to restore her dignity in front of Chris. She was lucky to have him. She was going to need his strength in the next few months.

*   *   *

Miriam opened her top and put Rebecca to her breast. The baby fed contentedly. Miriam felt desperately tired. It had been a long day. She was glad it was almost over. She'd been dreading the family coming back to the house after the christening. Sheila was like an Antichrist these days and Vincent was very annoyed about Ellen's pregnancy. He'd phoned Ben and asked him to reconsider having her as godmother.

The row that afternoon was distressing. Miriam felt sorry for Ellen but she'd been annoyed that her daughter's christening party was marred by the Munroe's family squabble. That was why she'd intervened.

Miriam sighed. She was sick to death of being stuck in the middle of them. Sheila whinged in her ear about how Ellen had disgraced the family. Ellen was forever making snide remarks about Emma. Emma was always giving out about Sheila. It was very wearing. From now on, Miriam decided, she was just going to concentrate on her own little family. She wasn't going to take everyone else's burden on her shoulders. She had enough of her own.

*　　*　　*

'Vincent, Vincent! I've got a terrible pain. Quick! We've got to get to the hospital.' Vincent woke from a deep sleep to see Emma peering down frantically at him.

'Emma, it's just cramp. Relax,' he muttered groggily.

'No, I think I've started. This time I know it's for real.' Emma was nearly in tears. Ever since Miriam had gone into labour prematurely she was petrified the same thing was going to happen to her. Her greatest fear was that she wouldn't get to the hospital on time. She didn't want a home birth. She wanted to be in hospital where there were drugs and anaesthetics to knock her out so that she wouldn't feel any pain. The nearer she came to giving birth the more frightened she became. She'd lie awake at night having dreadful panic attacks. Poor Vincent wasn't getting any sleep at all because of her.

'Please take me to the hospital,' she begged.

'Well just wait another little while and if the pain gets worse we'll go,' Vincent promised.

'But Vincent, I might be the same as Miriam. It might come really quickly.' Emma jumped out of bed and began to dress.

'Emma! Will you get back into bed? It's four a.m. You're not going anywhere. You're not going to be like Miriam. It was Miriam's *third* child. Labours are much longer on the first.' He tried to keep the impatience out of his tone. He was dead tired. This was Emma's third false alarm since Miriam had given birth. Each time he'd managed to calm her down and had avoided a trip to the hospital.

'Please, Vincent. I'm telling you it's different this time.' Emma was insistent. 'If you don't drive me to hospital I'm going to phone for a taxi.'

'Emma, for God's sake—'

'Don't for God's sake me,' she yelled. 'I'm scared and you won't help me. I hate you. And I hate your stupid bloody family. And I hate this baby and I wish I wasn't having it. I'm going to the hospital whether you like it or not.' She pulled her dress down over her head and rushed out of the bedroom to the phone downstairs.

Vincent shot out of bed, cursing. He got to the phone just as Emma was about to order the taxi. He grabbed the phone off her and hung up. 'It's all right, Emma, I'll bring you to the hospital if that's what you want,' he growled.

'I want to go now!'

'Right, I'll get dressed.'

Emma sat rigid with fear as they drove through the back lanes of North County Dublin past the twinkling lights of the airport, towards the city. The pain was still there. Not coming in spasms like Miriam's had. Just constant. Maybe there was something wrong with the baby. Terror engulfed her. It would be all her fault if there was. Hadn't she said she hated it? She didn't want it? Maybe she'd wished this on the child. Just say it was a handicapped baby. What would she do then? She broke down, sobbing.

'Stop crying, Emma. We'll be there soon.' Vincent was at his wits' end. Never again, he vowed silently as he scorched down The Meatpackers' Hill, past Hedigan's field where the gymkhanas were held. This child would be their first and last. He hoped it was a boy. He'd have a son and heir to carry on his name. But even if it wasn't a boy, there'd be no more. Once was enough to go through this trauma. It was causing too much stress in their marriage.

Emma wasn't able to cope with it, and right now, neither was he.

It was a long night. Emma was whisked away for examination as soon as they got into the hospital. Vincent expected they'd both be leaving for home in less than an hour but some time later a doctor came and told him that, although Emma was certainly not in labour, her blood pressure was alarmingly high and there were some signs of slight toxaemia. They would keep her in for observation. If the blood pressure went higher and the toxaemia worsened, they'd have to do a Caesarean. Vincent, remembering how he'd tried to pass it off as another false alarm, felt like a heel. He was allowed to see Emma for a few minutes. She lay in her hospital bed, pale as a ghost against the pristine whiteness of the starched sheets and pillows. Her eyes, huge in the thinness of her face, were bright with apprehension and exhaustion.

'You'll be all right,' he whispered, conscious of the other sleeping women in the darkened ward.

'I'm scared,' she whispered back, gripping his hand.

'Don't be. The nurses and doctors know what they're about. They'll look after you. The doctor said it's nothing to worry about and they're just keeping you in as a precaution,' Vincent fibbed.

'I'm sorry I said I hated you and the baby and your family. I didn't mean it. I love you, Vincent.' Emma's bottom lip quivered.

Vincent felt like crying himself. She looked so small and scared and vulnerable.

'I love you, Emma. More than anything. This will all be over in another few weeks and I promise you, when the baby's born, we'll get someone in to help and when you're better you can ride Cleo and go to lunch with the girls and do all the things you wanted to do.'

'That sounds lovely.' Emma reached up and caressed Vincent's cheek.

'I'm afraid you have to leave now, Mr Munroe.' A nurse

slipped quietly between the drawn curtains. She reached for the blood pressure kit on the locker.

'I'll see you tomorrow, darling.' Vincent kissed her gently and left the nurse to her work.

The days that followed were fraught with anxiety. Emma's blood pressure soared and dipped. The toxaemia worsened. A week after she was hospitalized, the doctors decided to perform a Caesarean. Emma was frantic with worry. The baby was going to be born weeks premature. It was all her fault for not wanting it. She was riddled with guilt. Guilt she couldn't share with anyone, because they would think she was a horrible person if they knew why.

Secretly though, she was most relieved to be giving birth by Caesarean. She'd be asleep, she wouldn't know anything about it. She wouldn't have the indignity of lying with her legs apart in stirrups, panting and groaning in front of some man she hardly knew. She wouldn't have the awful pain that Miriam had endured. It would be sore afterwards. But she wouldn't care about that. At least the ordeal would be over. The only thing that worried her was the scar after the operation. She didn't want to be disfigured. It was bad enough having stretch marks. Silver streaks across her belly that nothing would erase no matter how much baby oil she rubbed into them. The doctor had promised her that he would do a neat cut and she'd be able to wear a bikini with no unsightly scars. People might think it was vain of her to worry about such trivialities when her baby's life was in danger, Emma knew. But these little things mattered to her. It was bad enough having a baby she didn't want and going through all this trauma without looking like Frankenstein's monster afterwards.

When the nurse came to shave her, she was absolutely mortified. When they gave her an enema she wanted to die with embarrassment. Miriam hadn't told her about any of this. No one had! Not even her mother.

Pamela visited every day, full of concern. She'd assured Vincent that he and Emma were welcome to stay with her and the judge as long as they wanted to after the birth, until Emma got on her feet again. Vincent accepted the invitation gratefully. Pamela thought he looked ghastly. Grey and strained and exhausted. He was spending as much time as he was allowed with Emma as well as working all hours. He was desperately worried about Emma. As was Pamela. She hadn't given her daughter much sympathy during her pregnancy. She'd been brisk and matter-of-fact, hoping that Emma would stop panicking and start looking forward to her new baby. It hadn't happened. Emma did not want the child. She was afraid but, worse than that, she was resentful. Pamela hoped against hope that when her daughter held her newborn baby in her arms for the first time, some maternal spark would ignite in her. Emma had been a very much wanted child. Pamela found it difficult to accept that her expected grandchild was not.

She was allowed in to visit Emma shortly before the operation. Vincent was already there. Emma had been given her premedication and was already drowsily drugged.

'You'll be fine, and so will the baby,' Pamela said reassuringly. 'And you'll be thrilled when you hold it in your arms. All this will be worth it, won't it, Vincent?'

'Absolutely, pet. Just think when you wake up, it will be all over and we'll have a new baby.'

'Time to leave, please.' The nurse whisked back the curtains and an orderly with a trolley arrived. The nurse and orderly assisted Emma onto the trolley. It was hard and cold after the warmth of her hospital bed. Emma flopped back against the pillow. She gave Vincent and her mother a feeble wave. She felt floaty and light-headed as if it were all a dream. It wasn't an unpleasant sensation. It was rather nice, she thought drowsily as she was pushed down a long corridor. Now that it was actually happening, she didn't care. She wanted to go on being pushed along corridors for ever. She didn't want to wake up and suddenly be a mother. She wanted to stay in this cotton-woolly twilight world with people taking care of her, where she had no worries and no responsibilities. The lights overhead flashed by as the nurse and orderly pushed the trolley along. They stopped at a lift and manoeuvred her in. It rattled and groaned and came to a halt with a jerking shudder that made her stomach lurch slightly.

She was vaguely aware of passing through green plastic doors. A very strong sweet sickly smell made her feel queasy. Ether. Overhead, a huge white light gleamed in the morning sun. She was lifted onto another hard surface and a nurse covered her with a green blanket. A man with a green mask peered down at her. He had kind brown eyes. 'You'll just feel a little prick, Mrs Munroe,' he murmured as he rubbed the skin on the top of her hand. 'Count to ten.'

Emma felt the needle and then, before she'd counted to three, it was as if the lights had suddenly been switched off. Darkness enveloped her and she remembered no more.

*   *   *

Vincent stood peering in at his tiny daughter as she lay asleep in the incubator behind the glass partition. Her little matchstick limbs looked as fragile as a sparrow's legs. Vincent feared for her. She only weighed two and a half pounds, the size of two and a half bags of sugar. She was so small, how could she possibly survive? She'd been baptized immediately. He'd called her Julie Ann. That was the name he and Emma had chosen for her the night before she'd been born. Tears smarted in his eyes. She had to survive. She might be all that was left to him. Emma was seriously ill. She had a raging temperature and her blood pressure was dangerously high. She was still unconscious. Vincent wanted to bury his head in his hands and bawl his eyes out. But he was a man, he wasn't supposed to cry. Only cissies cried. His wife was at death's door, his daughter might not survive either, he had every right to cry, he told himself fiercely as he furtively wiped the tears from his cheeks. He straightened his shoulders, took one last look at his little girl and headed for the Intensive Care Unit to see if there was any change in Emma's condition.

*   *   *

Her eyes flickered open. The strong late afternoon sun hurt so she closed them again quickly. She felt a raging thirst. Her mouth was parched and dry and her throat felt as if it had been cut. Swallowing was immensely painful. Her whole body felt like a dead weight but, through the wooziness, a sharp stabbing pain twisted itself through her abdomen with a viciousness that took her breath away.

'Oh Jesus,' Emma muttered, shocked, before drifting back into unconsciousness.

*   *   *

Emma was still unconscious when Vincent arrived. A medical team stood beside the bed working on her. All kinds of monitors and drips were being attached to her. Vincent's heart began to pound with fear.

'Is she all right? What's wrong?' He grabbed a nurse by the arm.

'Please, Mr Munroe, wait outside,' the nurse said calmly.

'Tell me what's wrong with her?' Vincent was frantic.

'Her blood pressure is causing concern. Now you must wait outside.'

'Could she die?'

'Your wife is seriously ill, Mr Munroe. Please, I have work to do. You're not helping her.'

Dazed, Vincent walked through the push doors of the ICU. Emma was dying, and there was nothing he could do to help. And he'd been such a bastard to her, telling her there was nothing wrong. 'Oh Jesus, Jesus, please let her be all right. Please God, don't take her from me.' He buried his head in his hands and felt salty tears pour down his face. Moments later the doors were flung open and orderlies pushed a gurney through at speed. Vincent had a brief glimpse of Emma's waxen face, her inky hair splayed against the pristine white of the pillow.

'What's wrong? Where are you taking her?'

'She's haemorrhaging. We're taking her to theatre.' The nurse hurried past him with Emma's chart and file. Another nurse came over to him as he stood shocked and bewildered watching them disappear behind the grey doors of a lift.

'Why don't you go and have a cup of tea while you're waiting? There's nothing you can do here.'

I don't want tea, he wanted to rage. I want Emma to be all right. He stared down into the nurse's kind eyes. They were dark, like Emma's. 'Is she going to be all right?'

'I don't know, Mr Munroe. We have to wait and see,' she answered honestly.

Vincent felt beads of sweat break out on his forehead. There was nothing he could do to help Emma. He felt helpless, frustrated and utterly out of control. It was the worst moment of his life.

He walked blindly down the corridor. He had to get out of this place or he'd freak. He took the lift to the foyer and walked out through the front door of the hospital. Traffic streamed past. The noise grated on his shattered nerves. People hurried home, tired after a long day at work. A couple overtook him and laughed at some private joke. He wanted to smash his fist in their faces. His wife lay dying, and they were laughing, unaware of her suffering. It seemed obscene. How could people act as though everything was normal? Nothing was normal any more.

It was drizzling steadily. The rain flattened his hair and dripped down the back of his neck. Vincent pulled up his collar, shoved his hands in his pockets and headed for the Pro-Cathedral.

He sat in the dim light of the church for a long time. He was too tired to pray. Too tired and too defeated. He knew he should go back. But he was afraid. Finally he made himself retrace his steps through the wet windswept city streets until he reached the grey imposing pillared entrance to the hospital. He felt sick.

Emma was back in ICU. Her haemorrhaging had been controlled but she was dangerously ill. She was still unconscious. She seemed so fragile and waif-like lying limply against her pillows, attached to all the drips and blood transfusions and monitors that surrounded her. He had never seen anyone so white and drained as Emma was. He feared for her.

The nurses made him go home. There was no place for him there. He was getting in their way. It was the longest night of his life as he, Pamela, and the judge sat in terror waiting for a phone call that would blight their lives for ever.

*   *   *

It was night-time when Emma regained consciousness. A nurse smiled down at her.

'How are you feeling, Mrs Munroe?'

'Thirsty,' she murmured.

'I'll just give you a tiny sip of water, we don't want you to get sick after the anaesthetic,' the nurse said as she held a glass to Emma's lips. Pain shot through her as she raised her head off the pillow. She felt as though she'd been run over by a truck. The water was like nectar to her dry mouth and she sipped greedily.

'That's enough now, good girl.' The nurse withdrew the glass.

Suddenly, Emma felt a wave of nausea. The nurse, experienced in such matters, quickly held a basin to her mouth as Emma was violently ill.

All she wanted to do was die, she thought as she retched uncontrollably, the movements causing excruciating pain in her lower abdomen. When it was over she lay back against her pillows, exhausted. She hadn't the energy to lift her hand to wipe her mouth. The nurse was very kind, and wiped her face and neck with a cool damp cloth as she murmured soothing words about what a good patient she was.

Emma lay dazed. Her eyes flickered open again. She saw a drip and a bag with dark red stuff. Was that blood? God Almighty! What was wrong with her? She felt very frightened. Why was she in pain? What had happened? There was something . . . Something she had to ask about. Her brain was so woozy. It was important though. Think . . . think . . . A fleeting memory drifted through the fog. Emma clung to it. She remembered. The baby! What about the baby?

'Nurse,' she muttered. Her tongue felt so thick she had enormous difficulty in forming the words.

'The baby. . . ?'

'You had a little girl, Mrs Munroe. She's in an incubator downstairs. She's doing as well as can be expected,' the nurse said delicately.

A little girl. Vincent would be disappointed, Emma thought in dismay. Doing as well as could be expected. What did that mean? It didn't sound too good. Tears slid down her cheeks.

'Don't cry. Sister's going to give you an injection now for the pain, and it will make you sleep. Things will look much better in the morning,' the nurse comforted.

Emma wanted to believe her. She was very tired, and scared. She wanted an injection to knock her out so that she'd never wake up. In the distance she heard a baby's cry. Was it hers? The thought made her sob uncontrollably. She was still crying as the needle's jab was followed by welcome black oblivion.

The next time she woke, Vincent and her mother were sitting by her bed. It was reassuring to feel Vincent's strong hand holding her own.

'You're fine,' he soothed. 'And so is the baby. Just rest now and don't worry about a thing.' Emma felt comforted to have Vincent there and she lay quietly with her mother on one side and Vincent on the other and drifted in and out of drugged sleep.

It was a week later before Emma was judged well enough to make the journey by wheelchair to the special care unit to see her daughter for the first time.

She felt terribly weak as Vincent pushed her along the hospital corridor. As they drew near the nursery, her palms began to sweat and a knot of apprehension tightened in her stomach. Vincent wheeled her to the glass partition and pointed in. 'It's the one nearest the window. There she is, isn't she lovely? She's put on six ounces, they're very pleased,' he said proudly, his face wreathed in smiles.

Emma took a deep breath. Her heart was pounding. She gazed in the direction of his pointing finger. All she could see was a tiny scrunched-up red face, and a bony little arm covered in blue veins, flailing the air. She wanted to say she was beautiful but she wasn't. She wasn't like any baby Emma had ever seen. She should be round-cheeked and chubby and adorable. Fear gripped her. She had hoped that a wave of love would move her when she finally saw her child but the feeling that overwhelmed her was one of huge, huge dismay and even worse . . . a vague sense of revulsion.

'Take me back to the ward, Vincent. I don't feel too good,' she whispered in desperation.

'When you're stronger you can go in and hold her. That will make all the difference. I know it's not the same out here.' Vincent mistook her lack of enthusiasm.

'I know.' She tried to smile at him. He'd hate her if he knew that the last thing on earth she wanted to do was to hold that scrawny, mewling being that she had brought forth so reluctantly into the world.

Chapter Nine

'You do it.' Emma handed the bottle back to the nurse. It was feeding time and they wanted her to give Julie Ann her bottle.

'No, Mrs Munroe. You must learn to do it yourself.' The nurse was kind but firm.

'But I'm afraid she'll choke or something,' Emma said agitatedly.

'She'll be fine. Now take her in your arms – no, not like that, like this.' The nurse arranged Julie in the crook of Emma's arm and handed her the bottle. Gingerly, Emma slid the bottle into the baby's mouth. She sucked greedily. Emma sat rigid in her wheelchair. Every fibre tense.

'Relax,' the nurse instructed. 'This is meant to be an enjoyable experience for mother and child.'

You must be joking, thought Emma in disbelief. Julie Ann hiccuped and spluttered.

'God! She's choking!' Emma exclaimed in panic as the baby grew red in the face. 'Here take her, you feed her. I feel ill. I have to go back to the ward.' She thrust the baby into the nurse's arms and fled from the nursery as fast as she could manoeuvre herself in her wheelchair, ignoring the nurse's protestations that she wasn't to go anywhere in her wheelchair unaccompanied. She was no good at being a mother. She couldn't even feed her baby without choking her. She got back into her bed and burrowed down under the bedclothes. Her heart was racing, her stomach was sick with nerves. Emma felt utterly beleaguered.

She refused point-blank to go down to the nursery for the next feed despite the nurse's exhortations.

'But darling you must feed your baby yourself. You've got to get used to it. Every new mother feels apprehensive like you do. I was terrified but after a while it was no bother,' Pamela urged. It was evening visiting time, and the nurse wanted Emma to come back down to the nursery to give the baby her two-hourly feed.

'I just feel too exhausted.' Emma lay back against the pillows, tense and unhappy. 'I'll do it tomorrow.'

'Darling, that little baby needs all the love and attention you can give her,' Pamela said quietly as the nurse left. 'I know you're sore and tired and you've had a very rough time and it will be a while before you're feeling anyway normal, but you're a mother now and Julie Ann needs you. You have to think of her.'

Emma was silent. It was all very well for Pamela to lecture. *She* hadn't had a premature baby who was so delicate she looked as if her little limbs could snap like twigs. *She* hadn't been at death's door. *She* hadn't had to get over a Caesarean that made one feel that one's insides had been put through a mangle. All Emma got was lectures, from the nurses, the paediatrician, Sheila, and now Pamela. Why couldn't they just all leave her alone?

* * *

'Where the hell do you think you're going?' Ellen felt her elbow being grabbed. She turned to find Vincent scowling down at her. She had decided to visit Emma in hospital. When she heard about the hard time she'd had with the birth, and that there was concern for the premature baby, Ellen felt a little guilty about her outburst at Rebecca's christening. She decided to visit Emma before she left hospital and apologize.

She got the six p.m. bus into Dublin, bought a bunch of flowers and a box of chocolates, and was walking along the hospital corridor when she was stopped by Vincent.

'I was going in to see Emma,' Ellen said quietly although her first instinct was to tell him to let go of her arm.

'Oh no you're not. I'm not having my wife upset by you. Not after your disgraceful carry-on at the christening.' Vincent's eyes were cold and unfriendly.

'You started it, Vincent. But I'll apologize to Emma, I don't hold a grudge and I'm not petty,' Ellen said pointedly.

'You can apologize some other time, you're not to go in there now. Pamela's in there. She doesn't know anything about you and Chris, and I don't want her to know. She's upset enough as it is.'

Vincent was in no humour for apologies. He was up to ninety. Emma showed no interest in the baby. She didn't seem to be getting any better herself. She just lay there, limp and indifferent. He couldn't let her see any hint of his worry and frustration. He needed someone to take his feelings out on. Ellen was just the one. He was in no mood to make up. He was still very annoyed with her. And, besides, the last thing he wanted to have to do was to explain to Pamela that his sister was expecting her nephew's child.

Ellen stared at her brother and hated him. Hadn't he any idea how hard it was for her to come in and apologize to Emma? Did he think she *liked* grovelling? Were Pamela Connolly's feelings more important to him than his own sister's? Obviously.

She felt like giving him a puck in the jaw. 'Stick these up your ass,' she flared, thrusting the flowers at him. Head high, she marched back down the hospital corridor the way she had come.

Ellen was furious as she stood at the bus stop outside the hospital and waited for a bus back into the city centre.

The nerve of him, she raged, but hurt was what she felt most. He'd made her feel as if she was worth nothing. It was always the same since he'd started going out with that Emma. Once, before they got married, they'd chanced upon her walking home from the Glenree Arms and given her a lift. When they got home, Vincent had fussed around Emma, and made her coffee and ham sandwiches. Ellen hadn't been invited to join them. She'd had to make her own supper. She'd felt excluded.

That was exactly the way she felt today. Excluded, hurt, bitter and angry. Well he could go to hell. She'd never hold out an olive branch again.

*   *   *

Vincent fed his baby daughter and took pleasure from the fact that she finished her bottle to the last drop. She was a little fighter, he thought proudly. She'd put on another couple of ounces and the staff were very pleased with her. It was a pity he couldn't be as pleased about Emma. She was so lethargic and down in the dumps. The nurses said new mothers sometimes got a little overwhelmed but surely she should have been over that by now. Her lack of interest in the baby was extremely worrying. Emma was due to leave hospital in a few days time but Julie Ann would be in her incubator for the next two months at least. Emma would have to make daily visits to the hospital to feed her. They were going to stay with Pamela and the judge. It would give Emma a chance to get back on her feet, and Foxrock was much nearer to the hospital than Glenree. He'd far prefer to be in his own home but Pamela had insisted. Emma wanted to stay with her parents, and he wasn't going to argue.

It was by the grace of God he'd seen Ellen marching along the corridor, en route to Emma's ward. In the humour Emma was in there could very well have been another row. Ellen had an awful nerve anyway. Did she think a bunch of flowers and an apology would make everything all right? Waltzing around as brazen as you like, not a bit ashamed to be pregnant. The trouble with Ellen was that she didn't give a damn about anything.

*   *   *

Several days after her abortive attempt to visit Emma, Ellen sat in Doctor Elliot's waiting-room. She'd finally decided the time had come to see him. The door opened and she tensed. Bonnie Daly walked in and made a beeline for her.

'Thank the Lord, it's not packed,' she said breathlessly, as she plonked down on the chair beside Ellen.

'I've only to renew my blood pressure prescription and do you know, Ellen, every time I've come there's been dozens here. I've never seen so many people down with flu at this time of the year. How's poor Emma and the little dote? Have you seen her yet?'

'She's in an incubator so only Emma and Vincent are allowed to see her. Emma's getting out of hospital tomorrow. She's going to stay with her mother for a while.'

'Hmmm . . .' Bonnie nodded knowledgeably. 'A girl likes to be with her mother after her first. Especially when she's had a hard time like poor Emma. I saw Miriam and her little lass the other day. It was nice that Emma had a baby girl too, they'll be great company for each other.'

'Yeah,' Ellen said unenthusiastically, wishing heartily that Bonnie was a million miles away. Of all the people to be alone in the waiting-room with, it would have to be *her*.

'Isn't it great for Sheila to have two new grand-daughters? Four grandchildren now. She'll be kept busy,' Bonnie prattled on. Ellen was sorely tempted to make a run for it.

'And what's up with yourself that you have to go to the doctor?' Bonnie arched an eyebrow.

'I've a touch of flu,' Ellen lied.

'He'll probably tell you to go on a diet. You've put on a bit of weight. You wouldn't want to get too stout at your age,' Bonnie remarked with her usual tactlessness. 'It puts men off. Is there any sign of a romance at all?'

Ellen had never liked Bonnie Daly at the best of times. She found her nosy, rude, opinionated and sanctimonious, despite her saccharine sweet air and coy genteel manner.

She objected strongly to the way Bonnie felt free to ask rude and objectionable questions and to make personal comments which were extremely intrusive. She longed to turn around and say, 'Mind your own goddamn business, you ignorant old bat.'

A mad impulse overcame Ellen. 'As it happens,' she said coolly, 'I've been seeing someone for quite a while. Since Vincent's wedding actually. I decided not to marry him. I think I prefer my independence. And I'm not putting on weight as such, or getting stout. I'm pregnant. In a couple of months time Mam's going to have another little grandchild.'

It was worth it, Ellen thought with a sense of wild exhilaration, to see the look of utter stupefaction on Bonnie's pinched little face. Her beady sly eyes almost popped out of their sockets. A deep purple flush ran from the base of her wrinkled neck to the top of her blue-rinsed hair. She opened and closed her mouth like a codfish.

'Next please.' Doctor Elliot came to the door.

Ellen stood up, smiled politely at the stricken Bonnie and followed the doctor into his surgery.

She took a deep breath. 'You might have to resuscitate Bonnie Daly,' she said dryly. 'I've just told her I'm pregnant.'

Doctor Elliot raised a pair of bushy eyebrows.

'Fifth or sixth month, I'd say,' he said calmly.

'Nearly six, Doctor,' Ellen responded.

'You should have come to see me sooner,' he admonished. 'Sit down, Ellen, and we'll have a chat and then I'll examine you.' His matter-of-factness was balm to her soul. Another ordeal, but it hadn't turned out as badly as she'd anticipated. And now Bonnie knew. In a couple of hours the rest of the town would know. Once she spoke to her cronies in the guild, it would be all out in the open and they could do their worst.

'Are you and the father going to get married? Is he sticking by you?'

Ellen shook her head.

'Have you told your parents?'

She nodded.

'How are they taking it?'

'Mam is very upset. She's hardly talking to me. Dad's not saying much one way or the other. But he's being kind.' Ellen fiddled with the fringe of her scarf. 'Mam wants me to go to my aunt's place in Navan and have the baby there. She wants me to put it up for adoption. So does the father.'

'What do you want to do?'

'I want to keep it, Doctor Elliot. It was conceived out of love. I love Chris. I don't want to give our baby away. It's all I have left of him. I want to keep it and bring it up myself.' She started to cry. Great gulping sobs. 'I'm sorry,' she apologized, struggling to compose herself. 'Chris never wants to see me again. Mam's not speaking to me. Vincent's not speaking to me. He says I've disgraced the family. My life is a shambles. Is it selfish of me not to give the baby up for adoption?'

Doctor Elliot handed her a tissue. 'Ellen, that's something you have to work out for yourself. You have to weigh up the pros and cons and decide what's best for your baby and also what's best for you. Whatever decision you make, you're going to have to live with its consequences for the rest of your life. It wouldn't be right for me to advise you one way or the other.' He stood up and patted her shoulder. 'You've a good head on your shoulders, Ellen. And it's good to know that your father is standing by you. You'll make the right decision. Now go behind the screen and get undressed and lie down on the couch and I'll examine you.'

Ellen did as she was told. Why had he made that remark about her father standing by her? Was he encouraging her to keep her baby? Somehow she felt he was. He was a kind man, she reflected as he gently examined her. He had passed no judgement on her. If only others could have been like him, she thought bitterly, thinking of Vincent and her mother.

'Everything seems to be fine,' he said reassuringly when she was dressed and sitting in front of his desk again. 'I want you to start taking iron immediately and increase your milk intake.' He handed her a prescription. 'Come back and see me in a month's time. Or any time, if you feel the need. You know where I am.'

'Thanks, Doctor.' Ellen was deeply grateful to have another ally. She didn't feel quite so beleaguered and it was such a relief to have the first visit over and done with.

'I better go and scrape Mrs Daly up off the floor.' His dark eyes twinkled momentarily. 'You do realize that the whole town will know before nightfall.'

'I think that's why I did it. I wanted to get it out in the open,' Ellen said. 'I better go home and tell Mam, so she'll know what's in store.' She made a face.

'Tell your mother to come in to me for a chat. She's going to have a difficult time of it with the likes of herself out there. She might find it a help to come and talk about it.'

'I don't know,' Ellen murmured. 'I think she'll be too mortified. She's got a lot of pride and I've let her down.'

'Time will cure all that, never you worry,' Doctor Elliot said crisply. 'Remember I'm here if you need me.'

Ellen walked down Main Street feeling as though some of the burden had been lifted. Doctor Elliot knew, Bonnie knew and soon the whole town would know. She didn't have to put on a facade any longer. Sheila would have to handle it as best she could.

*　　*　　*

'You told Bonnie you were pregnant, at Doctor Elliot's?' Sheila's heart sank to her boots and a hollow feeling of dread overwhelmed her. If Ellen had told Bonnie, as she'd just said she had, the whole guild would know by tomorrow night's meeting. The escape route to Lily's in Navan, and the adoption after the secret birth, had been her only hope. A hope that was now well and truly dashed. Ellen might as well have announced it from the pulpit as tell it to Bonnie Daly.

'What did she say?' Sheila asked shakily.

'Nothing.' Ellen suddenly felt immensely sorry for her mother. Sheila looked shaken and defenceless as she stood at the kitchen table cleaning her brasses. Her spark was gone, her spirit quenched. Defeated was the word that came to mind as Ellen looked at her mother and felt thoroughly remorseful.

'Doctor Elliot said you could go and have a chat with him if you wanted to,' Ellen said, awkwardly.

'What do I need to go to him for a chat for? I'm not pregnant,' Sheila snapped. She felt very much alone. She knew she had two choices. She could go to that guild meeting tomorrow night with her head held high and brave it out, and ignore the whispers and gossip. Or she could withdraw from the social life of the town and keep to herself. Right now, that seemed like the better idea. Her nerve had gone.

'Would you like a cup of tea?' she heard Ellen ask. Resentment surged. It was all Ellen's fault, tea wasn't going to make things better.

'If I want a cup of tea I'll make it myself, thanks,' Sheila said shortly. She saw the look of hurt on her daughter's face and didn't feel one bit sorry for her. Ellen had got them all into this mess. She could face the consequences. And one of the consequences was that Sheila would never forgive her. She resumed cleaning her brasses with vigour and didn't speak another word to her daughter for the rest of the night.

The following evening, after listening to *The Archers*, Sheila picked up her knitting and began to knit. She was making a little cardigan for Julie Ann. She wasn't mad about the name, Julie Ann. It wasn't a normal sort of name. It was a bit film-starish. She'd secretly hoped that one of her granddaughters might be called Sheila. She'd love to have a grandchild called after her.

She threw a log on the fire and watched as the sparks flew upwards. The nights were drawing in and the evenings were chilly. In a way she was glad winter was coming. Winter gave you an excuse to stay in and hide.

'You'll be late for your guild if you don't go and get ready,' Mick remarked from his armchair at the other side of the hearth. He was smoking his pipe and doing his crossword.

'I don't think I'll bother going tonight,' she said diffidently. 'I want to finish this cardigan for Julie Ann.'

'Would this reluctance to go to your guild have anything to do with the fact that Bonnie Daly told half the parish about Ellen?' Mick peered across at her over his reading glasses.

'How did you know that?' Sheila asked, miserably. She should have known. She could never hide anything from Mick.

'I had the busiest day I've had in a long time,' Mick said dryly. 'Women who never buy meat from me came into the shop today to have a good gawk at Ellen. Bonnie included. She ignored Ellen completely and told me I was a good man to keep her working for me in her condition, and that I deserved better. She asked after you and said you'd hardly be at the guild meeting tonight.'

'And what did you say?' Sheila hardly dared ask.

'I told that sanctimonious old heifer that Ellen would work in my shop as long as she wanted to and that I didn't deserve such a good and supportive daughter. And I told her that of course you'd be at the guild meeting tonight. And why wouldn't you be?'

'Oh you didn't,' Sheila said heavily.

'I did, and you're going, Sheila Munroe. You have nothing to be ashamed of. You get out there and hold your head high and don't let that crowd of old crawthumpers get to you.' Mick was very firm.

'Mick, I don't want to go in there tonight.'

'Sheila, if you don't go tonight, you'll never go again. Now come on and get your hat and coat on. I'll drive you in. You can leave the bike at home tonight.'

With the greatest reluctance, Sheila went upstairs and slipped out of her skirt and jumper. She was flustered. She knew Mick was right, but she didn't feel brave tonight.

What would she wear? She took out her oatmeal tweed skirt. She could wear that with her pink twinset and pearls. Her gaze alighted on her new tartan skirt. It had glorious shades of purples and greens, like the heathers on the hills. She'd never worn it to a guild meeting. She had a lovely emerald blouse to go with it. She could wear her cameo brooch at the neck. It was much easier to make an entrance when you knew you were looking your best, she thought defiantly. Mick was right, she decided as she applied Max Factor powder to her face and dabbed some Avon scented cream on her wrists. The nerve of Bonnie Daly to assume that she wouldn't go to the guild that night. She'd show her, Sheila thought crossly. Let anyone snub her tonight and they'd never get the chance again. She traced a coral lipstick across her lips. Nothing like warpaint for giving you courage, she thought as she looked at her reflection in the mirror. Very smart.

Now that she had decided to go, her adrenalin was flowing.

'I'm ready, Mick.' Sheila marched downstairs and stood in front of her husband.

'That's my girl.' Mick bent down and kissed her on the cheek. 'After tonight it won't be as bad,' he encouraged. Mick was a stalwart man, Sheila reflected as he held her coat for her. She was very lucky to have him.

'I'd be lost without you, Mick,' she said quietly. They didn't usually say things like that to each other.

'And I'd be lost without you, pet. Don't you worry. This will turn out all right in the end. Ellen's a good girl, try not to be too hard on her.'

'Where did I go wrong in the rearing of her?' Sheila shook her head.

'You didn't go wrong anywhere. These things happen, Sheila. It's just very unfair that the girl has to bear the brunt of it. You never hear anyone pointing the finger and saying, he's an unmarried father. Look at Danny O'Leary. He's fathered at least three children with three different girls and there's not a word about it. He's looked upon as a great fella by the young lads.' Mick's eyes flashed with anger.

'That's true.' She hadn't thought of it like that. Mick surprised her sometimes, the way he looked at things.

They set off down the road. Sheila felt tense with anxiety. 'Let's stop at Miriam's for a minute. Maybe she might like to come.'

'Now, Sheila, Miriam's got a lot on her hands with three young children. Don't be annoyed with her if she's too tired to go,' Mick warned.

'I won't,' Sheila snapped. What was wrong with the women of today, she thought crossly as she got out of the car. Whingeing and moaning about how tired they were. That Emma one took the biscuit, the way she lolled back at her mother's and let poor Vincent do all the running around. She wasn't the only one to have had a hard birth. It wasn't like in her day. She hadn't had washing-machines and spin rinses. Sheila's washing had all been done by hand. Women today didn't know what hard work was, she thought scornfully as she rapped on her daughter-in-law's door. If Miriam and Emma had to blacklead a range every day, as she'd had to, they'd have something to moan about.

Miriam opened the door. She was obviously surprised to see Sheila.

'You look very nice, Mrs Munroe.' She smiled.

She did look tired, Sheila observed. Her heart sank. If Miriam didn't go with her she didn't know if she'd have the nerve to go through with it. Imagine if *everyone* snubbed her and she had no-one to talk to.

'I was wondering if you'd like to come to the guild meeting tonight. We're having a talk about flower arranging,' Sheila said hopefully.

'I don't think so, Mrs Munroe. Rebecca's a bit fractious and Daniel's got a cold on him. I wouldn't like to leave them.'

'Sure Ben can look after them. He's a dab hand at it. You could do with a night out.' Sheila was brisk. She knew Miriam wasn't good at saying 'no'.

'I'm not ready or anything,' Miriam said, flustered.

'It won't take you two seconds to put your coat on.' Sheila sensed victory.

'No, honestly. Thanks very much for asking me, Mrs Munroe. Maybe next week,' Miriam murmured.

Sheila was annoyed. Next week was no use. Why couldn't the girl just do as she was asked without all this palaver? It wasn't as if Sheila was always at her to go to guild meetings.

'I'd really prefer if you came tonight.' She tried to keep the irritation out of her tone.

'Why, Mrs Munroe?' Miriam asked wearily.

Sheila looked down at the toes of her shining black patent shoes.

'Well it's like this, Miriam. Ellen told Bonnie Daly about being pregnant and aah . . . Bonnie told Mick that she didn't think I'd be at tonight's guild meeting. I don't want to go but Mick thinks I should and I was hoping you might come with me.' Sheila was cringing with embarrassment. She couldn't look her daughter-in-law in the eye. How awful to be under a compliment to a girl you didn't think was good enough for your son. It wasn't that she didn't like Miriam. She did. Miriam was an obliging girl. But Sheila had always felt superior to her. It wouldn't be easy to feel superior after this. Ellen had a lot to answer for.

'I'll just get my coat,' Miriam said quietly.

'Thank you, dear,' Sheila murmured, still unable to meet the younger woman's eye. 'I'll wait for you in the car.'

As she walked back out to Mick, Sheila had the grace to feel ashamed. She knew that she was using Miriam. She used her quite a lot and never really gave her any credit for her quiet helpful ways. She didn't deserve her support but it had been given unreservedly. In her own quiet way, Miriam was as stalwart as Mick.

*   *   *

Miriam stifled a yawn as she sat in the back seat of the car. She was dead tired and the last place she wanted to go was to a talk on flower arranging in the women's guild. But Sheila was desperate. There was no doubt about that. Otherwise she would never have admitted to Miriam that she didn't want to go to the guild meeting on her own.

For the first time in their relationship, Sheila had treated her as an equal. Miriam had had it in her power to refuse to go, to let Sheila face the music alone. It would have been good enough for her mother-in-law if she *had* refused to go. It would have made up for all the hurtful little snubs that Miriam had had to put up with over the years. She sighed. She'd gone running, as usual. But if she'd said no this time she would really have left Sheila in the lurch. The truth was she'd felt sorry for her mother-in-law. It was a hard thing to do, to face Bonnie Daly and Mona Cullen knowing that they were all talking behind her back. Maybe she was a fool, maybe she was too soft-hearted for her own good, but Miriam couldn't let Sheila go to that meeting alone.

*   *   *

It would have to be the one night that was an open evening when anyone from the town could attend the talk, Sheila thought unhappily as they neared the school hall. Normally guild meetings were for members only.

'Right, I'll pick the pair of you up at eleven.' Mick drew to a halt outside the school grounds. It was dusk, the sky was streaked with amber. Dark clouds encroached from the west. A sharp breeze tossed and swirled crisp red-gold leaves from the big gnarled oak trees around the yard. The yellow glow of light from the hall windows was warm and inviting and the sound of laughter and talk wafted out the door. Normally Sheila would have looked forward immensely to an evening like this.

'Come on, Mrs Munroe,' Miriam said kindly. 'You don't want to be late for your committee meeting.'

Sheila took a deep breath and stepped inside the hall. Most of the committee members were sitting at the big oblong baize-covered table on the stage. A sudden hush descended on the group. All eyes turned to Sheila. She almost faltered but Miriam's steady hand at her back kept her on course. She saw Bonnie Daly in the secretary's chair. *Her* chair. She'd been so sure that Sheila wouldn't show, she was all ready to take over the secretary's duties. The nerve of her, thought Sheila indignantly. It was just the spur she needed.

'Good evening, ladies,' she said brightly. 'I hope I didn't keep you waiting.'

'Not at all, Sheila,' Marcy Nolan, the president of the guild, assured her warmly.

'I thought you mightn't feel like coming,' Bonnie said sweetly as she vacated her chair. 'I was going to do the minutes if you weren't here.'

'And why wouldn't I be here, Bonnie?' Sheila inquired as she laid her notepad and pen on the table.

'Ah . . . you know,' Bonnie said conspiratorially, her little sharp eyes full of knowing.

'Bonnie, I don't know what you're talking about,' Sheila said crisply. 'I never miss committee meetings.'

Bonnie's eyes narrowed. Sheila Munroe was not playing the game. By rights she should be subdued and abashed, not swanning in looking like Lady Lala and taking over, as usual.

'I thought you might be a bit upset over Ellen,' Bonnie murmured coldly.

Sheila lifted her chin. She was aware that the rest of the committee were watching and listening with avid interest. 'And why should I be upset over Ellen?' she challenged, although her stomach was tied up in knots and her knees trembled.

'Well . . . with her being pregnant.' Bonnie's eyes were hard and triumphant. Bertha Reilly gave an audible gasp, aghast at Bonnie's bad manners.

'But Bonnie,' Sheila said coolly, 'Ellen's six months

pregnant, why should I start missing meetings now because of her?'

'Oh!' Bonnie was flabbergasted. This wasn't the way it was supposed to go. Sheila should be embarrassed and humbled, not aggressive and in control.

Sheila gave her an icy glare. She'd snatched victory from the jaws of defeat and turned the tables on her erstwhile friend. But she'd never forgive or forget Judas Daly's betrayal.

'I think we should call this meeting to order. After all we're having a talk on flower arranging and people will be arriving shortly,' Sheila suggested, all business. She sat beside the president and, when the meeting was officially opened, read the minutes of the last meeting in a clear firm voice. Her insides were like jelly, her knees shook, but not by the flicker of an eyelash would Sheila let Bonnie and her cohorts see that she was churned up inside. She'd got through the worst of it, she'd carry it off, she told herself fiercely as discussion raged about whether to hold a whist drive or a beetle drive to make money for the church repairs.

Well done, Sheila, Miriam silently applauded her mother-in-law. Bonnie Daly was livid. Miriam watched her fidget at the table, two mottled pink spots of suppressed rage staining her cheeks. Good enough for her, Miriam thought grimly. Bloody troublemaker. Sheila had really held her own tonight and Miriam had to admire her.

As she was not a committee member, she was not entitled to sit at the table, so she sat near the edge of the stage in the body of the hall. People were beginning to trickle in, determined to get the front seats for a better view.

'Oh look, there's Sheila Munroe. Did you hear about Ellen? I bet that's a right kick in the teeth for Airs-and-Graces Munroe. I wonder who's the father?' Miriam heard a middle-aged woman say to her companion. They obviously didn't recognize her.

'I think she was going with a fella from Dublin. A Flash

190

Harry if ever I saw one. He drives a big car. I believe he's related to the judge's daughter.'

'How did you know that?' The plump middle-aged woman settled in her chair and lit a cigarette.

'Agnes Shaw does a bit of cleaning for Emma Munroe and she heard her and the husband giving out yards about this bloke Ellen was going with. He's supposed to be a real womanizer.'

'Are you serious? Well I heard from Bonnie Daly that he's no intention of marrying Ellen, so she's up the creek rightly.'

'When you get to her age and there's no sign of a ring on your finger you get a bit desperate. It might teach Sheila a bit of humility. You know the way she goes on? *Who but me?*'

They were enjoying their gossip immensely. Miriam made a mental note to advise Emma not to discuss personal business in front of her cleaner. It was inevitable, of course, that people would gossip. That was the way of small towns but it was distressing that the subject was Ellen. She might put on a couldn't-care-less front, but Miriam knew she was finding the going very tough indeed. If only Chris had stuck by her. The poor girl was mad about him, even after all he'd done. How could she keep deluding herself that he cared about her. The only person Chris Wallace cared about was himself. Couldn't she see him for the low-down, selfish skunk he was? It baffled Miriam. The saying 'Love is blind' was certainly true of Ellen.

The committee meeting ended and Sheila made her way down the steps of the stage to join Miriam, who'd kept a seat for her.

'You were great,' she whispered.

'Do you think so?' Sheila whispered back. 'When Bonnie said about Ellen being pregnant, I didn't know whether I was coming or going and that's God's honest truth.'

'No, you were great. No-one would know that you were

at all upset. Bonnie was very taken aback,' Miriam said reassuringly.

'Imagine doing that to a friend! I couldn't believe my ears,' Sheila fumed. Now that the committee meeting was over, and she had time to think, she was beginning to realize the extent of Bonnie's treachery. It hurt.

'Well people know now. And the president was nice to you.'

'Marcy Nolan's a *lady*. Unlike some I could mention,' Sheila declared with a frosty glare in Bonnie's direction. Bonnie bristled. She'd heard that last remark, as she was meant to. Fortunately the lady who was giving the talk began her speech and silence descended upon the fifty or so ladies who all wanted to learn how to arrange flowers.

By the time Sheila got home she had a vicious headache. Nevertheless she triumphantly gave Mick a blow-by-blow account of the evening's events.

'Oh Bonnie thought she'd try and embarrass me all right, Mick. But I settled her hash for her I can tell you.' Sheila fixed her hairnet around her head and got into bed beside her husband. 'And to think I thought of her as a friend.'

'Never you mind about her. We'll find out who our real friends are in adversity. And when we find them, we'll cherish them and to hell with the rest.' Mick yawned, put his arms around Sheila and within minutes was snoring.

Sheila lay in the circle of her husband's arms. A tear slid down her cheek. Tonight had been the most humiliating night of her life. Bonnie had tried to make a show of her. And she was supposed to be a friend. Some friend! Sheila had seen other women eye her curiously, lapping up her discomfort. If only she could be like Mick and not let it affect her. But she wasn't like him. People's opinions mattered to her. She felt heart-scalded and humiliated as she remembered Bonnie's hard triumphant eye when she'd dropped her bombshell. Mick might say to hell with her, but Sheila knew she'd never forgive Bonnie Daly's betrayal. And furthermore, if she could get even, she would. Hours later, after much tossing and turning, Sheila fell asleep planning the most satisfying malevolent, revengeful things she'd do and say if she ever got the opportunity.

Chapter Ten

When Sheila slapped her dinner down in front of her the following evening, Ellen knew she'd been right. Her mother's anger and resentment had increased a hundred-fold now that everyone knew. She might hold her head up high in public and pretend that Ellen's pregnancy was not the trauma that Bonnie and some of the others would have liked it to be, but Sheila seethed with rage and resentment and Ellen was not going to be allowed to forget it. She resigned herself to a long hard winter.

She'd like to get a flat somewhere. Swords, a couple of miles away, would be ideal. But that would upset her father and she was dependent on him. She'd have to give up work when the baby was born. She couldn't possibly expect Sheila to look after it, she'd probably commit infanticide.

Being dependent was a daunting prospect. She'd always had her own money. She'd always been free to come and go as she pleased. She was going to be very beholden once she gave up work. Her father wouldn't rub it in, but Sheila would, at every opportunity.

The months leading up to the birth were ones of quiet desperation. The sleepless nights were long and lonely. The trauma of being pregnant and unmarried was nothing compared to the turmoil she was in over Chris's brutal rejection of her. If she'd felt anger it would have been so much better for her. It would have given her something to focus on and keep her going. But Ellen was too shocked, too hurt to be angry. She'd loved Chris with every fibre of her being. She would have done anything for him. She'd have spent her life trying to make him happy. He knew that and he'd turned his back on it. It made her feel worthless. Her sense of self was shattered.

She spent most of her time in her room or over at Miriam's. She felt like a guest in her own home. She couldn't be herself. Before, if she was in a bad humour everyone would know about it. But these days she couldn't indulge the luxury of letting rip. Sheila was just looking for an excuse for a good row and Ellen wasn't going to give it to her.

When Sheila saw her in her first maternity dress, she burst into tears. 'You make sure you keep your coat on when you're down the town, you don't want half of Glenree to see your shame,' she snapped.

It was just as well that it was the middle of winter, and that she had to wear her overcoat. Even that didn't completely hide her. It was a tight fit. But Ellen was saving as much money as she could for after the birth. She decided to walk into town to the surgery instead of going on her bike. Cycling was a bit awkward now that she was eight months gone. It was a bitterly cold night. A piercing wind whistled through the bare branches of the trees. It was freezing and thin ice that hadn't thawed all day covered the puddles. A full moon with a ring around it forecast storms.

She passed Vincent and Emma's house, looming dark against the sky. They were still living at her parents. Julie Ann would be coming home from hospital the following week. She was now a healthy five and a half pounds. Ellen had never seen her.

'She's tiny and dainty like her mother,' Miriam told Ellen. If it wasn't for Miriam she'd never know what was going on with them. Sheila certainly didn't discuss Vincent and Emma with her.

The house looked empty and cold. Ellen wondered if they'd spend Christmas there. Sheila was baking Christmas cakes and puddings, but her heart wasn't in it this year. It was a chore rather than a chance to impress the guild. She always donated a Christmas cake and pudding to the guild's annual Christmas draw and her offerings were highly prized.

Ellen dreaded Christmas. Her baby was due the week after Christmas. Doctor Elliot had asked her if she'd like to have it in hospital or would she prefer to have him deliver the baby at home, as he had Rebecca. Ellen dithered. At times she thought she'd prefer the anonymity of the hospital. But she didn't want to face people and the thought of seeing other women with their husbands was not one she relished. If her mother had been in any way sympathetic, she would have had the baby at home. But the last person she wanted to have watching her as she writhed in the throes of childbirth was Sheila.

'Why don't you have the baby in my house?' Miriam invited when Ellen confessed her doubts and indecisions. Ellen was overwhelmed by her sister-in-law's kindness. Miriam had her hands full with three young children and yet she was quite willing to have Ellen give birth in her home.

Doctor Elliot gave the idea his full approval. He was keenly aware of the pressure Ellen was under. He knew Sheila was doing nothing to make his patient's life any easier. Miriam was just the person to be there for the birth and he'd warned Nurse Delaney to be available.

The lights of Glenree twinkled in the distance as Ellen rounded the bend and stood at the top of Healy's Hill. She felt very tired. Her back ached and she was dying to go to the loo. She should have gone before she left the house. Still, she comforted herself as she began her descent into the small valley, she'd had a very healthy pregnancy. She hadn't had morning sickness or heartburn like Miriam had had. And so far, her blood pressure was fine, unlike poor Emma.

It was a relief to reach Kirwan's pub. She slipped in through the side door and went into the ladies. Ellen was glad there was no-one else there. She wasn't in the humour for awkward chit-chat. On her way out Dessie Burke passed her in the hall. He was an elderly, stooped man, a friend of her father's.

'Howya, Ellen? Everything all right?'

'Everything's fine,' she replied.

'Good! Good! Give my regards to your dad.'

'I will, Mr Burke.' Ellen smiled as she stepped out of the pub. He was a nice man, nicer than a lot around here, she thought contemptuously as she saw Mona Cullen and a few other holier-than-thou hypocrites leaving the church. They were worse than the Pharisees. Everybody in town knew when Mona and her cohorts had done a good deed. They were forever prostrating themselves in front of the altar, saying rosaries, doing the stations, licking up to the priest. It was sickening. The forty hours adoration was on tonight. Sheila had been to church earlier to do her stint. Ellen paused. She'd always liked the forty hours though. There was something peaceful about it.

On impulse she walked up the pathway to the door of the church. The main lights were out. Only small sidelights shone along the side walls. The altar was aglow from the flickering light of dozens of long slim white candles. The votive lights around the statues on the side altars were all casting a glow to the recessed shadows. Flowers bedecked the main altar and the steps leading to it. The women of the church committee had spent hours arranging them and decorating the altar for this special annual event. It was a beautiful sight. Incense scented the air with its heavy sweet perfume.

A few parishioners knelt scattered throughout the church. Ellen slipped into a seat and sat in the flickering candlelight and was glad she'd come. A sense of calm enveloped her as she sat silently, immersed in the serenity and peace of the chapel.

She stayed a little while, resting, letting her thoughts run hither and yon. She was reluctant to leave this tranquil oasis, but leave she had to. She hauled herself up and walked slowly out of the church. A few youths loitered at the church gates. One of them made a muttered remark to his mate as she walked past. He guffawed. Ellen ignored them. Little shits. That was the trouble with living in a small country town, everyone knew your business. There were times she hated Glenree, she thought viciously. A one-street dump. She stared around. The street lights gave off an orange glare adding to the gloom of the night. A couple walked into the Glenree Arms. They were arm in arm, laughing. Ellen felt suddenly lonely. All the shops were dark. A trio of giggling girls smoked a shared cigarette in the alleyway beside the coffee shop. Two dogs chased each other across the shadowed green opposite the school grounds. Ellen shivered. Everywhere seemed bleak and threatening. It hadn't always felt like this. When she'd been a teenager, she'd smoked cigarettes in the alley and chatted up the fellas. It had been fun, exciting. She'd always looked forward to going out with her friends. But she'd grown up and Glenree had stayed the same and now there was nothing in it for her. Dispiritedly, she headed towards the surgery. She just wanted to get the visit over and go home.

Doctor Elliot pronounced himself pleased with her progress.

'Another couple of weeks now and you'll be able to see your feet again.' He smiled as he helped her on with her coat. 'All is well.'

Bonnie Daly happened to be walking towards her as Ellen left the surgery. She was going to play cards in the hotel. The older woman immediately crossed the street, head averted, as if the very sight of Ellen would contaminate her. Bonnie no longer shopped for her meat in Mick's shop.

Bitch, thought Ellen grimly as she carried on along Main Street. She saw the Dublin bus, heading for the bus stop. How many times had she got that bus into town to go and meet Chris? A terrible aching twisted her heart. She'd give anything to see him, to be with him, to spend the night in his arms. A crazy impulse overcame her and, almost before she knew what she was doing, Ellen hurried to the bus stop and stepped into the ancient old crock that groaned and creaked with every gear change. As the bus increased speed through the town, Ellen sat back in the hard threadbare seat and felt her heart pound with excitement. Maybe Chris might have changed his mind after all this time. Maybe he'd be so delighted when he saw her again he'd realize what he'd been missing.

Exhilarated and happy and full of anticipation, Ellen planned her happy reunion with the love of her life, as the bus left the lights of Glenree for the ebony darkness of the winding country roads that led to the capital.

Later, as the bus drove through the suburbs of the city, Ellen began to question her crazy impulse. Was she mad? How could she possibly want to see Chris again after the abominable way he'd behaved? Even now, she cringed at the memory of him telling her parents that she wasn't a virgin. It had been the most unforgivable betrayal. Yet, she could not sustain the anger. Which was a pity, she thought wryly. If she hated him it would be much easier to get over him. Sadness engulfed her. If only they could get back to the way they were before she'd told him of her pregnancy.

They'd had good times. Times of laughter and happiness when every thought of him had brought a smile to her face. She missed their lovemaking and the feeling of being sexy and attractive to him. She missed touching him, caressing him in the way that lovers do when they can't take their hands off each other. She missed the knowing, intimate shared glances. Most of all Ellen missed not having the opportunity to cherish him the way she used to. She'd liked cooking special dishes for him, sewing buttons on his shirt, buying him little chocolate treats to satisfy his sweet tooth. Did he not miss being cherished and cared for? Suzy was not the sort to pamper a man, Ellen thought unhappily. She had a hard streak to her. Yet, Suzy was the woman he'd chosen. What had Suzy done right and where had *she* gone wrong?

Ellen's high spirits dipped and wavered. She looked

down at her great bulk, concealed under a big navy coat. There was nothing sexy about her now. But their relationship was based on much more than sex, she argued silently. Chris had confided in her about his business deals. He'd listened to her opinions. Her spirits rose exuberantly. Maybe his new business had settled down and he wouldn't be quite so one-track minded. Maybe he'd *want* to see her, to tell her about how it was going. Maybe he'd want her advice about things. Her horoscope in this week's *Woman's Own* had been very positive. Mercury was transiting her star sign and affairs of the heart were well starred. Love would be hers if she had courage and declared herself. Her life would change completely. It was so accurate, it was uncanny, Ellen reflected as she rooted in her bag to find the little cutting. She often kept her horoscope cuttings when her stars were particularly apt. It's an omen, she decided as she read it again. Her life was going to change completely. But maybe it would change even more, if Chris decided to marry her.

The bus turned left off Dorset Street and raced past Walton's and Findlater's down towards O'Connell Street. The queues for the Savoy snaked as far as the Gresham. It was a long time since she'd been to the pictures, Ellen thought ruefully as she saw a young man wrap a protective arm around his girlfriend in an attempt to shelter her from the biting wind.

Three girls stood huddled together hopping from one leg to the other. They were laughing at the efforts of a busker who was murdering *The Rose of Tralee.* Ellen smiled at their giddiness. She'd been like that once, carefree and full of hope. Now she was desperately hoping that Chris would be the light at the end of her long dark tunnel.

She got off the Glenree bus, joined the queue at the stop outside Clerys, and prepared to wait. She was very lucky that she didn't have long to wait for a Number 3. Less than half a minute later a plethora of buses which had been stopped at the North Earl Street lights headed towards them in convoy. There were two Number 3's. Definitely an omen, Ellen encouraged herself as she boarded the bus and it moved off towards O'Connell Bridge and then turned left into Townsend Street. Her heartbeat quickened as they headed out onto Pearse Street. How many times had she made this journey in the past? Who would have thought she'd gather up the courage to do it again? Ellen peered out the grimy window, impatient with the traffic hold-up. Pearse Street was always the same, morning, noon or night. An old wino staggered across the street and stumbled up the steps into the library. The building looked old, gloomy and somewhat dilapidated. He'd have to be drunk to want to go inside, Ellen reflected crossly. She hated Pearse Street, she wanted to get moving. They still had to go through Ringsend. The bus speeded up, briefly, as it passed Boland's Mills, and then as the road narrowed towards the bridge, slowed down again. Ellen was steaming with impatience. Move, move, move, she urged silently as a throng of people crossed over to St Patrick's church for the Rosary. They chugged past Ringsend library and headed for Sandymount. By the time the bus reached the stop up the road from Chris's, she was a jangle of nerves.

It was a relief to stretch her legs. A chilly sea breeze pierced the thick material of her coat and her breath was white in the frosty air. Ellen shivered and began to walk briskly. The bus had been warm and cosy, now she felt as if she were in the Arctic.

She walked along the familiar route and stopped a few doors from Chris's house and took shelter against a large unkempt evergreen hedge. She took out her compact, powdered her nose, retouched her lipstick and sprayed some *Evening in Paris* on her wrists. She slid the dark blue bottle back in her bag, took a deep breath and set off resolutely.

All the lights were on in the house. Typical of Chris, she thought fondly as she opened the gate. He liked having the lights on, he hated dark rooms. The sound of a man's deep guffaw and a woman's laugh brought her up short. The curtains of the sitting-room weren't drawn and she could see through the lamp-lit windows a group of men and women, drinking and talking and laughing. Through the sliding doors in the back room, the table was set for dinner. Red candles flickered invitingly. Chris appeared. A champagne flute in one hand, a wooden spoon in the other. He had a tea towel around his waist. He was laughing and gesticulating, urging his guests into the dining-room. A woman, dressed in slinky black, slid a proprietorial arm around his waist. It was Suzy.

Ellen slipped back into the shadows. A lump, hard and unyielding, lodged in her throat. Tears pricked her eyes. Hurt and bitterness scalded her heart. They all looked so cosy and jaunty and light-hearted. And she felt utterly excluded. She turned away and walked slowly back the way she'd come. She had lost so much. Not only Chris and the chance to be his wife, but the chance to be *anyone's* wife. What man in his right mind would take her on? An unmarried woman with a child. She'd never be able to have a dinner party for friends in a home of her own. She'd never have a home of her own, to decorate as she wished and to invite who she liked to visit. She would never be independent and her own boss. She would always be subject to her mother's domination as long as she lived at home. And that was her only option if she kept the baby. An immense weariness swept over her. Now she had to face a two-bus journey back to Glenree. There was a three-hour wait until the next scheduled bus was set to leave the city centre for home. She could always go and have a cup of tea in the Roma Grill but the thought did not appeal to her.

It took about fifteen minutes for the next Number 3 to arrive and she was chilled to the bone. She had never felt so lonely or despairing. It was worse than breaking up with Chris. At least then she had some hope that they might get together again. After tonight, she had none. Suzy was still with Chris. They were entertaining together. Even when she and Chris had been a couple, she'd never entertained with him. There was no place for her in Chris's life. It was as if she'd never existed in his world. He was happy, enjoying himself. He'd moved on and forgotten all about her. It was obvious he never gave her a thought. She'd just have to forget him and try and make the best out of life.

She was so dispirited and unhappy when she got to the city centre, she couldn't face sitting alone drinking tea in a cafe. In an act of sheer extravagance Ellen hailed a passing taxi and, sinking back into its dingy back seat, she gave the driver her address as she eased her aching feet out of her shoes. This was finally it, she promised herself. She was never going to think of Chris Wallace again. He was a closed chapter in her life. The old familiar heartache swamped her. A terrible sadness that quenched whatever spirit she had left. Did those feelings never go away, she wondered in despair. Just as well no-one knew she'd gone into town to try and see him. It was the most pathetic thing to have done. And she was the most pathetic doormat with not an ounce of pride to make excuses for that bastard and to hope that he would take her back. She was well rid of him. Miriam was right, he wasn't worthy of her. If she kept telling herself that, maybe she might start to believe it.

When they got to Glenree she asked the taxi driver to let her out at Blackbird's Field. She didn't want Sheila to see her driving home in a taxi. Tonight, she couldn't face an inquisition. Fortunately Sheila had gone to bed early with a headache so Ellen said goodnight to her father and slipped quietly upstairs to bed. She was dead tired and she longed for sleep to blot out her unhappiness. Sleep did not oblige her. She twisted and turned for hours before finally falling into a restless slumber punctuated by weird disturbing dreams.

*   *   *

'It was a good evening, wasn't it?' Suzy snuggled up closer to Chris, revelling in the warmth of his body and the cosiness of the big double bed. The weather had turned dirty. Great gusts of wind shrieked along the eaves of the house and rain lashed against the window pane. She felt delightfully tipsy, and tired.

'It was a smashing evening.' Chris smiled down at her. 'You're a terrific hostess. The Kents were impressed. He's put a lot of custom my way. It's good to keep them sweet.'

'Did you see Judith's boots? The leather was so soft. She bought them on the King's Road. And her lipstick was Mary Quant. I'd love to go on a shopping spree in London,' Suzy said wistfully.

'Hmmm. I wouldn't mind seeing you in a pair of those boots,' Chris murmured. Judith's boots had gone practically right up to her ass. They were stunningly sexy. 'Maybe we might go for a weekend sometime in the New Year.'

'Oh Chris, I'd love that! When will we go? What weekend?'

'Well we'll see how the finances are,' he backtracked hastily. Typical of Suzy to want to know the date, the hour, the minute.

In other words, forget it, Suzy thought crossly. Chris was always doing things like that. Making suggestions and plans and then welching on them. Despite all the hints she'd dropped she was no nearer to getting the ring on her finger. Now that she was back in his bed, Chris was once more taking her for granted. It was most unsettling. Her sense of well-being dissolved. Suzy felt utterly disheartened. She moved away from Chris and turned her back on him.

Chris made no move to draw her back. He felt a surge of irritation. If there was one thing that bugged him about Suzy it was the way she always got huffy if she didn't get exactly what she wanted. Ellen had never got huffy. He switched off the bedside lamp and scowled. What the hell was he doing thinking about Ellen? She was history. He'd put her completely out of his head. That was the only way to do it. He certainly didn't want to start thinking about her again. He lay in the dark, willing sleep to come. He was whacked. Suzy was already asleep. Drink always did that to her.

The memory of Ellen's stricken face when he'd declared to her parents that she wasn't a virgin suddenly came to mind. That had been below the belt and he regretted it. It was just he'd been so angry at being . . . ambushed . . . on his doorstep by her and her parents . . . and in front of Suzy. To give Suzy her due she'd never brought up the subject again after he'd told her not to question him about it.

He wondered if Ellen had had the baby yet. Maybe he was a father by now. Had she had a girl or a boy? Did it look like him?

'Oh for fuck sake!' he swore. He got out of bed and went downstairs and poured himself a large whiskey. He knocked it back and waited for it to take effect. Things were going well. What did he want to be tormenting himself with thoughts of Ellen Munroe for? She was out of his life and that was the end of it.

He missed her though, in spite of everything. He'd always felt very loved, especially when she put her arms around him and held him close after they'd made love. It was never like that with Suzy. A lump came to his throat. His eyes moistened. In the dim light of his sitting-room Chris slumped drunkenly onto his sofa and angrily wiped the tears from his cheeks.

*   *   *

The weeks that followed dragged. Miriam assured Ellen that this was normal. The ninth month of pregnancy seemed as long as all the previous eight put together. Ellen tired much more easily and Mick insisted that she leave work at midday. She always went to Miriam's. She hated spending the long dark winter afternoons with Sheila. The atmosphere between them was tense and unfriendly. Ellen felt as if she was living on a knife-edge. Sheila was sure she was being slighted by some of the neighbours. She and Bonnie hadn't spoken since the night of their confrontation. It was causing a strain at the guild meetings. Ellen knew that, though it was all her fault, there was nothing she could do to make amends and she resented her mother's martyred air. Sheila wasn't the only one who had to put up with slights and whispers. She'd certainly been snubbed by some of the women of the town. Eilis Quinn had actually crossed the street rather than say hello to her. Mrs Foley had called her a slut to her face and told her to get home to her mother's and hide her shame and stop parading down the streets of Glenree. Ellen had been tempted to tell her to get lost and mind her own business, but she'd held her tongue. It was the easiest thing to do in the long run. Bawling in the street would only add to the gossips' enjoyment.

About a week before the baby was due, Miriam suggested that Ellen come and stay with them. It was Christmas week.

'Are you sure, Miriam? Maybe I should stay at home and have the baby there.' Ellen didn't want to take advantage of her sister-in-law's good nature.

'Tell your mam that you're coming over to us for a few days to help me out. If she says you should stay at home then you'll stay. How about that?'

'OK,' Ellen agreed.

Secretly she hoped that Sheila would tell her to stay at home. It would be some little sign that she had accepted the situation. But when she said, diffidently, that she was going to stay a few days at Miriam's, Sheila said coldly, 'Suit yourself.'

Ellen packed her case and wished with all her heart that she'd never have to set foot in her mother's house again.

For Miriam's and the children's sake, she tried to make an effort to get involved in the hustle and bustle of Christmas. But, as her date drew near, she became more and more agitated and spent long hours in her room. She was conscious that she was putting Ben and Miriam out. They'd given her Daniel's room and he was sleeping with Connie and Rebecca. It wasn't an ideal situation. The children's excitement at being together meant that they were awake at all hours, much to their parents' annoyance. As soon as the baby was born, she'd go back home. It wasn't fair on Ben and Miriam.

Ellen had been dreading Christmas Day, but it turned out to be much more pleasant than she'd anticipated. She didn't go to Mass or to visit her parents. She had a cold and it was as good an excuse as any to hibernate. She asked Miriam to deliver her gifts to her parents. After all the pandemonium of Santa's arrival and the excitement that followed, Ellen was more than relieved to get back into bed and pull the cosy patchwork quilt tight around her shoulders while the rest of the family went to Mass.

In the unaccustomed peace and quiet she fell fast asleep and had the best sleep of her pregnancy. The smell of cooking woke her. Bleary-eyed she glanced at the clock by her bedside and couldn't believe that it was after one-thirty. Miriam must think she was a lazy lump, she thought guiltily. She'd really enjoyed that sleep, she felt full of beans, so different to the tiredness she'd felt the last few weeks.

'Miriam, you should have woken me,' she reproached, a few minutes later as she joined her sister-in-law in the kitchen.

'You needed your sleep, and I've everything under control here. Ben's taken the kids down to visit the O'Reillys, so I was making the most of the peace and quiet, and the good news is . . .' She smiled at Ellen. 'Vincent and Emma called to your mother's while we were there so there won't be any danger of them calling here. You're safe.'

'Thank God for that.' Ellen gave a heartfelt sigh. She'd been dreading seeing Vincent and Emma over the Christmas.

'How were they? How did she look? Did they have the baby with them?' She was consumed with curiosity. Even though they were at loggerheads, Ellen always pumped Miriam for news and gossip about her brother and his wife.

'Emma looked stunning, as usual.' Miriam removed the

crunchy streaky rashers from the top of the turkey and basted the crispy golden breast. Ellen took a skelp of stuffing before it was put back in the oven.

'What was she wearing?' Ellen began to dry the dishes on the drainer.

'A beautiful red velvet suit, and she'd a red velvet hairband to match. Her beehive was immaculate. When I backcomb I look as if I've been dragged through a bush backwards. How does she do it? Some people just have the knack of looking elegant all the time,' Miriam said enviously. Her cheeks were flushed from the heat of the oven, perspiration beaded her forehead, a strand of fair hair hung down over one eye, one of her pink varnished nails had broken when she was lifting the turkey out of the oven. She looked anything but elegant.

'Were they asking for me?' Ellen asked tartly. 'I bet they were really sorry they missed me.'

Miriam laughed at her sarcasm. 'They didn't mention you once. Well not in front of me anyway,' she amended.

'I suppose they didn't happen to mention anything about Chris?' Ellen asked hopefully. She was always hoping for some little snippet of news about him.

'No, they didn't mention him either. It was all talk about the babies.' Miriam gave her a sympathetic hug.

'What's Julie Ann like?'

'They didn't bring her. They thought it was too cold, especially as she's not long out of the incubator. Your mother was terribly disappointed. I think they're going to go over to the Connollys for dinner some evening next week.'

'Oh, I was dying to hear how Emma was managing her. She could have given me some hints,' she added wickedly.

'Wagon!' Miriam giggled. 'You should have seen the figure of her. She's like a twig! It's disgusting. You'd think she'd have had the decency to have put on a few pounds. She's even thinner than before.'

Ellen looked down at her voluptuous bosom and the

wide circumference of her bump. 'It's not pounds I've put on, it's stones,' she said mournfully.

'I'll tell you what.' Miriam cut two slices off the mouth-watering pink ham with its festive coating of honey, breadcrumbs and cloves, and handed a slice to Ellen. 'When you've had the baby and Christmas and New Year are over and all the goodies are gone, we'll start on a get-fit-and-slim regime. We'll diet, we'll walk every day, we'll do our exercises and by the summer we'll be like two models, OK?'

'You're on. It will be our New Year resolution. And we're *definitely* doing it this time,' Ellen agreed enthusiastically, picturing herself like Audrey Hepburn. Maybe when she was nice and shapely, Chris might start to fancy her again. She'd make sure to see him. She'd bring the baby to see him, Ellen decided. She felt very optimistic today for some reason. Much more positive. It must be her hormones, she decided as she devoured the ham. It was delicious and for the first time in ages she was ravenous.

'The dinner smells gorgeous,' she enthused, tasting the gravy that Miriam had just added a generous measure of sherry to.

'Here, have a streaky rasher, they're crisp. I love them straight out of the oven.' Miriam popped a tasty piece into her mouth.

'Oh yum.' Ellen helped herself from the pile on the plate. Cheeks bulging they worked together harmoniously, all thoughts of their slimming regime banished as they enjoyed the best part of the Christmas dinner . . . the picking.

For a day she hadn't looked forward to it had been very nice, Ellen thought drowsily as she snuggled down in bed under the patchwork quilt that night. Her cold was much better. She'd had loads of energy. She'd even insisted on doing the whole wash-up herself after the meal. Later, she'd made the tea and washed up after that. She felt so energized, she could have hoovered the house from top to bottom. It was wonderful.

Now she felt nicely tired. Not wearily exhausted, just ready for a good night's sleep. Ellen hoped it would be as nice as the one she'd had that morning. She drifted off listening to the pitter-patter of rain against the window and the sound of the wind whispering in the trees.

A niggling little pain woke her some time around four. Ellen turned on her side and tried to ignore it. She wanted to go back to sleep. She'd been having a wonderful dream about her reunion with Chris. The pain sharpened, deepened. She gave an involuntary little gasp. Her eyes widened in the dark.

'Oh jeepers!' she muttered, easing herself up to a sitting position. Was this it? Four days early! It was hard to believe that her time had come.

Ellen felt strangely calm. It was out of her hands now. Her baby was in control now. She felt a flicker of excitement. Soon, she'd hold it in her arms. They'd been through so much together, she and it. She wanted to kiss it and cuddle it and tell it everything would be all right. Another pain gripped. Ellen didn't care. She welcomed it. At last something was happening. She'd lie here in her snug little room and go through as much as she could of her labour before telling Miriam. Just her and the baby, she thought determinedly as she clenched her fists against the pain.

It was nine before she heard anyone stir. The contractions were strong and steady. Ellen was very proud of the way she was coping. A groan was the most she'd allowed herself, and then she muffled it in the pillow.

Connie knocked on the door and bounced into the room. 'Auntie El, will you get up and play hide an' seek with me?' she asked, skipping over to the bed.

Even in the throes of another contraction, Ellen was amused.

'Pet, will you ask Mammy to come into me for a minute?' She grimaced.

'Are you sick?' Connie looked at her curiously. 'You look sick. Why are you making faces like that?'

'I've a pain in my tummy.' Ellen stifled a groan. 'Get Mammy, love.'

'I wanted to play,' Connie said dejectedly, trailing her teddy out of the room behind her.

Miriam arrived bleary-eyed. She took one look at Ellen. 'When did you start?'

'Around four.'

'Ah Ellen! You should have called me,' she scolded.

'There's no point in us both losing a night's sleep,' Ellen gasped. The contractions were much closer together.

'I knew it was going to happen soon the way you were buzzing around yesterday. I always got a burst of energy before I started labour just like you did yesterday. I'll ring Doctor Elliot.' Miriam squeezed her hand. 'Hang on, just keep telling yourself this time tomorrow it will be all over.'

'Jesus, Mary and Joseph I hope it doesn't go on that long,' Ellen exclaimed. 'I've had enough now, I don't want to play this game any more.' She grinned weakly.

'You'll be fine,' Miriam encouraged.

During the following hours, Ellen thanked God and His grace for giving her a friend like Miriam. Her sister-in-law bathed her face, held her hand for the contractions and soothed her with words of encouragement and reassurance. The pain was intense and she groaned in agony and wished she were dead.

'If Emma can fucking do it so can I,' she muttered to Miriam after a particularly vicious contraction left her utterly exhausted.

'Of course you can. She was knocked out for it,' Miriam reminded her.

'Lucky cow.' Ellen licked the sweat off her lip. It tasted salty. She was bathed in perspiration despite Miriam's best efforts to sponge her down and dry her. Think of Emma, she told herself as another contraction took hold.

Proving that she was her despised sister-in-law's equal kept Ellen going throughout the ordeal. Doctor Elliot and the district nurse gave her confidence and encouragement when she felt she couldn't go on. Ellen asked Miriam not to tell Sheila. She couldn't handle having her mother at the birth. Ben took the children into Dublin to see the Christmas fairy lights. Ellen was glad they weren't in the house to hear her groans of pain.

Towards the end she couldn't help feeling that God was truly punishing her for her sinful affair. She could hear Doctor Elliot's deep voice telling her to push. 'And again,' he instructed as she strained to obey.

'Once more,' he commanded.

'I can't, I can't.' She whimpered.

'One more, Ellen. Come on now, the head's through,' he ordered inexorably.

'Come on. It's nearly over, Ellen. One last push and you'll be finished,' Miriam urged.

Summoning every ounce of strength she had left, Ellen pushed as hard as she could and felt as if her body was being rent in two. The pain was excruciating and she howled. A tiny cry, and then a louder one, penetrated her pain.

'It's a little girl, Ellen,' Miriam exclaimed excitedly. 'And she's a head of black hair.'

'Let me see, let me see.' Ellen struggled to sit up.

'Patience,' the nurse chuckled as she wiped the baby and weighed her.

'She's a little bruiser. Eight pounds.' The nurse lifted her out of the scales and placed her gently in Ellen's arms.

Ellen looked down at her tiny daughter whose eyes were tightly closed and burst into tears.

'She's beautiful,' she sobbed. 'Isn't she? Oh my poor little darling, don't worry, I'll look after you,' she crooned, oblivious to the others. She felt indescribable love for her baby. No matter what, she'd cherish her and love her and give her the best she possibly could. No mother would do as much as she would, Ellen vowed to herself as she cuddled her baby daughter close.

Miriam bent down to have a closer look. There were tears in her eyes.

'Congratulations, Ellen. She's a dote,' she murmured.

'Oh Miriam . . .' Ellen couldn't talk. She reached up her free arm and hugged her precious friend.

'Thanks for everything,' she whispered.

'What are you going to call her?'

'I was going to call her Ciara, but seeing as it's the day that's in it, I think it just has to be Stephanie.' Ellen looked at Miriam for affirmation.

'I think you're absolutely right,' Miriam approved. 'Stephanie Munroe . . . Perfect!'

* * *

'Oh . . . did she? What time?' Sheila felt a myriad of emotions as Miriam told her over the phone that Ellen had just had a baby girl. Relief, resignation, sadness, resentment all struggled for supremacy.

'You should have called me. What will Doctor Elliot think?' She was annoyed that she'd been excluded from the birth. Miriam raised her eyes to heaven. That woman was a scourge and no doubt about it. She hadn't two civil words to say to Ellen since she'd found out about the pregnancy. She hadn't wanted her to have the baby at home, she'd put up no objections to Ellen coming to stay at Miriam's so near her time . . . and *now* she was giving out because she wasn't called for the birth.

'I have to go, Mrs Munroe, I'll talk to you later,' Miriam said sharply.

There was no mistaking her daughter-in-law's annoyance. This irked Sheila. 'I'll be over later to see the baby, if *that's* allowed,' she retorted huffily.

'Right, bye.'

Sheila clattered the phone down on its cradle, very annoyed at being given such short shrift.

'Mick,' she called to her husband who, full of turkey and plum pudding, was snoozing by the fire. 'Mick, Ellen's had the baby.'

Mick opened his eyes. 'A boy or a girl?'

'A girl, eight pounds.'

'Aah, I'm delighted! Ellen wanted a little girl.'

'Did she? I never knew that. But then of course I was the last to know anything.'

'She told me a while back.'

'Did she?' Sheila was somewhat miffed to realize that Ellen had confided in Mick.

'Come on, let's get over there and see them.' Mick got up, stretched and went out to the hall to get his overcoat.

Sheila was sorely tempted to tell him to go on his own. She wasn't sure if she wanted to go. Seeing Ellen's child, the fruit of her sin, was something she did not relish.

'Come on, woman. Let's go and see our new grand-child,' Mick said exuberantly.

'I'm coming,' Sheila snapped.

Five minutes later, Miriam ushered them into Ellen's bedroom.

Sheila looked at her pale, exhausted daughter and felt a pang of sympathy.

'Was it hard?' she asked gruffly.

'A bit.' Ellen was hesitant. She wasn't sure about Sheila's reaction.

Sheila reached down and drew the blanket away from the baby's face. She stared at her for a long time.

'What are you going to call her?' she asked finally.

'Stephanie.'

Sheila nodded and reached down and lifted the baby in her arms. 'Stephanie, that's a nice name.' She was glad Ellen wasn't calling it after her. She wouldn't have liked an illegitimate child to be called after her. It wasn't proper. She was a lovely little baby though. Much healthier-looking than either Rebecca or Julie Ann. Sheila crooned a little song at her.

Mick bent down and kissed Ellen. 'Well done, love. She's a lovely baby. I've done up the crib at home, sanded it down and varnished it and it's as good as new for when she comes home.'

'Thanks, Dad.' Ellen burst into tears.

'Ah don't cry now!' Mick exclaimed in horror. Women's tears always made him feel uncomfortable.

'Sorry.' Ellen gulped. 'But thanks for doing the crib.'

'You just rest yourself now. And don't be too long about coming back home to us.' Mick patted her shoulder.

'I've had the chimney cleaned out in your bedroom, so we can light a fire for you,' Sheila said awkwardly, as she handed the baby back to Ellen.

'Oh, oh thanks very much.' Ellen felt a glimmer of hope at this softening in her mother's attitude.

'Well it's very cold.' Sheila sniffed. 'I have some clothes knitted for the baby. I'll bring them over later. That's if it's all right with you?' She arched an eyebrow at Miriam.

'Certainly,' Miriam said politely. 'I'll make a cup of tea for you now.'

'Not at all, Miriam. You have your hands full with this pair. We'll go now,' Mick said kindly.

Sheila nodded in agreement. Now that the baby was here there was nothing she could do about it. She'd just have to hold her head high and live with the shame. It wasn't the child's fault. And she was pretty. Sheila softened. She took a last look at the sleeping baby. 'Don't wrap the blankets too tight,' she instructed.

Ellen lay back against the pillows and watched her parents leave. She felt utterly relieved. Her mother had behaved far better than she'd expected. The first awkward visit was over and at least she'd held Stephanie and not rejected her outright. She looked down at her sleeping daughter and felt strangely happy. Maybe things weren't going to be too bad after all.

Chapter Eleven

'What do you want in here?' Chris demanded. 'I thought you wanted to buy a birthday present for your father.' He and Suzy were in the children's department in Clerys.

'I do, but a friend of mine – you've never met her because she's moved to Cork – has had a baby girl and I want to get something for her. I won't be a minute. Stop moaning.' Suzy picked up a little dress and bonnet and held it up. 'Ah look, Chris. Isn't it adorable?'

'Huh,' Chris grunted. He was feeling most uncomfortable. It was New Year's Eve. Town was packed. This was the last place he wanted to be. Surrounded by babies' clothes. He couldn't *bear* to think about babies. His thoughts strayed to Ellen.

His parents had thrown a party on St Stephen's night. Emma and Vincent had been there. He hadn't seen his cousin since the birth of her baby and, somewhat awkwardly, he'd congratulated her.

'Congratulations are in order for you too,' Emma said coolly.

His heart did a somersault. And *that* response shocked him. He'd always thought he'd be so cool about it. After all Ellen's pregnancy meant nothing to him. Now Emma was telling him that Ellen had had the baby. He was a father. He felt decidedly shook.

'When did she have it? Was it a boy or a girl?' His palms were sweating.

'She had it today. It was a girl and she's going to call her Stephanie. Mrs Munroe phoned Vincent this evening.

Naturally we haven't told the folks. They know nothing so you're safe there,' Emma said dryly.

Chris flushed. But he was grateful that she'd bothered to tell him. Emma was a mate when the chips were down. Vincent, standing at the far end of the room, looked as if he wanted to take him out and murder him.

'Is Ellen OK?' Chris muttered.

'I think she's fine. Are you going to go and see them?' Emma took a sip of her Dubonnet and white and eyed him inquisitively.

'What do you think I should do?' He was curious to see what she'd say.

'Oooh Chris, that's entirely up to you to decide. You certainly won't be made welcome by the family. I don't know how Ellen feels about you now. We're not exactly bosom buddies.' Emma scrutinized Suzy as she made her way towards them. The other girl looked extremely elegant in a black figure-hugging dress. Her blonde bob razor-sharp against the Chinese-style mandarin collar.

'If you ask me, Chris, and you can tell me to mind my own business if you like, Suzy is the type of girl you should marry. She's got style and class and is ideal for an up-and-coming businessman's wife. As I say, it's up to you. See you later.'

Chris watched as Suzy undulated sexily towards him. Emma, as usual, was spot on. Suzy was perfect. She loved him. She could carry herself anywhere. She was good at entertaining. She was a stunner to look at. Other men envied him Suzy.

He thought of Ellen and remembered the warmth of her lovemaking, and her simple, direct, honest love for him. Ellen had never played games the way Suzy did. She said what she felt, straight out. But Ellen wasn't polished or sophisticated and never would be. Posh soirées and refined dinner parties would never be her scene. There was no point in going to see her. If he went to see her it would only hurt her. It wasn't fair to give her false hope. She might think he wanted to get involved again. She was far better off without him. She deserved better.

Surrounded by a laughing chattering throng Chris faced a moment of truth about himself that he would never allow to surface again. He was a coward and a heel. A weak man with no honour or integrity. He had treated Ellen like dirt and deserted her and her child. His daughter Stephanie would grow up never knowing her father. Maybe she was just as well off. Sadness engulfed him. A powerful sense of aloneness that almost took his breath away.

'Hello baby. Talk to me for a while.' Suzy slid a proprietorial hand into the crook of his elbow. He felt a desperate urge to shake it off. Women! They were always the same. Wanting. Needing. Grinding him into the ground with their demands. Why did they all have to take it so seriously? Seeking emotional sustenance twenty-four bloody hours a day.

'Do you love me?'

'Do you miss me?'

'Did you think about me today?'

'Do I make you happy?'

'Is there someone else?'

Christ Almighty! Every woman he'd been with had asked him the same questions at some point in their relationship. Why couldn't they compartmentalize their lives the way men did?

'What's wrong?' Suzy asked, puzzled by the expression in his eyes.

'Nothing. Let's get out of here,' Chris said bleakly. He intended going home and getting smashed in the privacy of his own house.

'But you can't leave! It's your parents' bash and anyway it's a great party. There's lots of your friends here.'

'I don't bloody care. I just want to be on my own,' Chris snarled viciously.

'Be like that then, you moody bastard!' Suzy stalked away head held high. Fuck him! She was going to enjoy the party. He could go home and sulk if he wanted to. Men! They were all the same. You never knew where you stood with them. One minute they were all over you. Especially when they wanted sex. The next they were miles away, on another planet, and you were the last thing on their minds. He must have had a row with Emma, she'd been talking to him last.

Suzy was pissed off. She'd been hoping against hope that Chris would propose before Christmas so that they could have celebrated the announcement during the festive season.

She had as much chance of getting a proposal from Chris Wallace as she had of getting the weekend away to London that he'd promised her. There's been no further mention of *that* either, Suzy thought despondently as she helped herself to another G&T.

Chris heard his mother's husky chuckle across the room. He glanced across at her and had to admit that she looked superb. Slender, poised, her ash-blonde hair elegantly coiffured, her make-up immaculate, the advancing years had only lightly touched her. At fifty-two, she looked ten years younger. How would she feel if she knew she was a grandmother? Not that she was particularly maternal. She didn't go in for hugging and kissing much, Chris thought sourly. Maybe that was why he'd really liked being with Ellen. Ellen was a great hugger. He always felt *comforted* when he was with her. She'd make a great mother.

Sod this! Chris scowled as he eased his way towards the door. His mother would be extremely annoyed at him for leaving her party early. He'd plead a stomach bug or something. But he had to be by himself. Emma's news had left him shattered. If his mother was miffed, she could join the club, Suzy was giving him daggers looks. He went home and got thoroughly sloshed. It had been the worst night of his life.

Chris gave a wry smile as Suzy stood in an agony of indecision oohing and aahing over this tiny outfit and that one. She hadn't spoken to him for two days after the party. She'd gone all cold and reserved and wouldn't let him near her and then he'd got all horny and wanted her and she'd kept him at arm's length until yesterday. Women knew how to punish you . . . for sure.

'I wonder if she fair-haired or dark?' Suzy mused aloud as she picked up and discarded two tiny little dresses.

'Hurry up, will you?' He tried to keep his tone neutral, but this place was giving him the willies.

I bet Stephanie is dark. Dark and blue-eyed like me and creamy-skinned and soft like Ellen. The thought left him slack-jawed with shock. He wasn't thinking of her as just a baby now. He was calling her Stephanie. This was dangerous!

'I'm getting out of here. I'll meet you downstairs in the men's department.' Chris was so agitated he didn't bother to pick up a pair of little booties he'd knocked down in his haste to get away.

Suzy stared after him. He was like a cat on a griddle lately. She wondered distractedly whether he was seeing another woman. She never knew where she stood with Chris. Deep down, Suzy knew he couldn't be trusted. She made a hasty selection, paid for the little outfit, and hurried after him.

Chris stared unseeingly along the rows of suits as Suzy chose a Van Heusen cream shirt for her father's birthday present. What the hell was wrong with him? Was he actually *broody*? The thought scared the living daylights out of him. Ever since Emma had told him about the baby, he'd been fighting the urge to phone Ellen. He wanted to go to Glenree to see them. It was crazy . . . after all that had happened between them. Even though they'd parted on a bitter note, he was sure Ellen wouldn't turn him away. But if he went once he might want to go again. It was a risk he couldn't take.

It was snowing as they left Clerys. Big soft flakes swirled down from a gunmetal-grey sky, dusting the pavements with a white lacy covering. The Christmas lights gladdened the dusky gloom and people hurried home to prepare for a night of revelry.

As they passed McDowell's Suzy automatically slowed down to glance at the diamond rings and brooches and necklaces that filled the jeweller's window. Chris followed her gaze.

'Will you marry me, Suzy?' he blurted out.

'What?' She was stunned.

'Will you marry me?' Chris repeated, feeling suddenly calm.

'Oh Chris! Oh Chris!' Suzy, radiant, flung her arms around him. Chris hugged her tightly. It was almost a relief to have made the decision. Now there'd be no visits to Glenree. That was the end of it. He was off that particular hook.

'Let's go and pick the ring. We can announce it tonight.' He was committed now, he might as well get it over and done with.

'Oh my God, Chris. I can't believe this. You've had it all planned. You've been thinking about me all along. And I actually thought there was someone else.'

'Silly girl,' he chided, glad it was almost dark and that he had his coat collar up so that she couldn't see his face fully.

'I love you, darling.' Suzy reached up and kissed his cheek.

'I love you, too.' It was an automatic response. Suzy was right for him. She'd make a good wife. *But not as devoted as Ellen. No one would ever love him like Ellen did.* The thought was fleeting. He brushed it aside. That was the past. This was his future. There was no going back.

Chapter Twelve

Miriam groaned as Rebecca's whimper turned into a full-throated bawl. 'Ben . . .' she nudged her husband in the ribs. Ben snored on. She glared at him resentfully as she struggled into a sitting position. How was it that men were able to switch off so completely? She always had a subconscious ear attuned to the children. Deep, un-troubled, restful sleep wouldn't be hers again for a long time.

Miriam was so tired she actually felt dizzy. Her head felt as if it was stuffed with cotton wool. A sickly feeling in the pit of her stomach and a dull heavy ache in her back announced the imminent arrival of her period. Her periods were desperately heavy these days. She was always exhausted after them. Rebecca howled again. Miriam got out of her warm bed, shivered, leaned into the cot and lifted her daughter. Her nappy was sodden and the wet had leaked up her back, despite the protection of the rubber pants. Her nightclothes were damp.

'Shuussh, there's a good girl,' Miriam crooned. It was cold in the bedroom, the temperature outside was below freezing. Quietly, she made her way to the bedroom door and slipped out into the hall. She got a complete change of clothes for Rebecca from the hot press and hurried into the warmth of the sitting-room. Ben had left a fire burning all night because it was so cold and the vivid glow of orange-red coals was a welcome sight. Swiftly, expertly, Miriam washed, dried and changed the baby. Her little cheeks were roaring red and she had her thumb jammed into her mouth and was chewing on it frantically. Miriam hoped Rebecca wasn't starting to teeth early. Teething was so hard on babies, she reflected as she lifted her daughter in her arms and put her to her breast. Rebecca fed contentedly, her eyes drooping with tiredness. Please let her sleep the rest of the night, Miriam offered up the fervent prayer as she watched her daughter's eyes close and her mouth slacken against her breast. As quietly as she could, she eased herself up into a standing position. Rebecca's eyes flickered open. Miriam froze. Rebecca tried . . . hard . . . to keep awake but she couldn't last and it was with weary relief that Miriam placed her back in her cot and covered her up snugly.

She was just dropping off to sleep when a slice of light pierced the dark and she raised her head to see Connie in the doorway, silhouetted against the hall light.

'Mammy I went blah an' it's all over my clothes an' in the bed an' I've a pain in my tummy.'

Miriam felt like bursting into tears. Why do you keep picking on me? she asked the Almighty, viciously, as she got out of bed for the second time that night. Ben snored serenely in the darkness. Miriam was almost overwhelmed by an urge to thump him. She was as entitled to a night's sleep as he was. They were *his* children as well as hers. She restrained her violent impulse and went over to her eldest daughter. The smell of vomit assailed her nostrils.

'It's all right, pet,' she soothed. It wasn't Connie's fault, there was no point in taking it out on her. 'Come on down to the sitting-room and I'll give you a little wash in Rebecca's bath in front of the fire, and I'll put clean pyjamas on you.'

'In Webecca's bath?' Connie immediately cheered up. Getting washed in the small bath Miriam had for the baby was worth going blah for. The small bath was much more exotic and exciting than the cold white enamel one in the bathroom.

Miriam removed Connie's soiled pyjamas and wrapped her in a blanket. 'Stay in front of the fire until I get hot water for the bath,' she instructed. Connie shivered. Her eyes were bright and watery, her forehead was hot to the touch. If she wasn't better in the morning, Miriam would call Doctor Elliot, she decided.

She nearly got lockjaw, yawning, as she stood in the kitchen waiting for the kettle to boil. She filled the bath with lukewarm water from the tap, added the kettle of water and carried it into the sitting-room. The weight of it made her back ache. Connie perked up when she saw the bath. She really did look wishy-washy, Miriam thought, feeling a twing of guilt for her bad humour.

By the time she'd washed Connie, changed the bed, put her and Rebecca's sheets and clothes to steep, Miriam had developed a thumping headache. She took two Anadin and lay down beside her daughter who was feeling sick again. Eventually they both dozed off. Miriam woke to hear Connie retching over herself, instead of into the potty beside the bed, placed there for such a purpose.

As she went through the whole ritual of washing and changing once more, Miriam felt utterly pissed off. She was dead tired. She had a headache and a backache, in a few hours time she was going to have to get up and face the day ahead. It was now lashing rain, she'd never get her clothes dry. Emma wanted her to look after Julie Ann for the morning because she was going to a coffee morning in Ballsbridge. Mrs Munroe wanted her to bake a batch of scones for a sale of work in the guild and Ben needed his good suit pressed because some big noise from head office was visiting his department.

The cock on Boyle's farm crowed loudly in the distance. It was still pitch-dark and his timing was completely off.

'Shut up, you stupid bird,' Miriam gritted as she got into bed beside her comatose husband and resentfully tweaked the bedclothes over her, not caring whether she woke him up or not. If Connie got sick once more, *he* could take care of her. It seemed as though she'd only just got to sleep when Rebecca's cries, shrill and insistent, woke her.

'Ben,' she dug her husband in the ribs, 'go and see to the baby, I've been up all night.'

'But it's quarter past seven – time for her feed – and I can't breastfeed her,' Ben said indignantly, as he rubbed his side. 'And there's no need to be so vicious.'

'She's going on the bottle next week, I've had enough of this lark,' Miriam grumbled as she got out of bed and lifted Rebecca out of her cot.

'You're in a very bad humour.' Ben yawned.

'So would you be if you'd been up all night with Rebecca and Connie.'

'What's wrong with Connie?'

'I don't know. She was sick twice, all over herself and the bed, and she's feverish. If she's no better I'll get Doctor Elliot for her today.'

'You should have called me,' Ben said as he let Rebecca grip his finger with her little hands.

'Huh,' Miriam snorted derisively. 'I did call you, for all the notice you took. You just turned over and snored. I'm going to bed the minute you come home tonight and you can look after them all. I'll express some milk for Rebecca and you can try her on the bottle,' Miriam declared.

'Well I can't come home early tonight, remember. I've got a union meet—'

'That's just typical,' Miriam snapped. 'I'm fed up to the back teeth having to do everything myself. Your mother wants me to make scones. I've to look after Julie Ann for the morning, on top of having to take care of a baby and a sick child. It's too much.'

'For crying out loud, Miriam, why don't you just say no to Emma and Mam. I'm fed up listening to you moaning about them. Then, when they ask you to do something, you agree immediately. If you say no they won't keep asking you,' Ben said crossly.

'That's easy for you to say,' Miriam muttered. 'Your mother would go into a huff if I said no.'

'Well let her go into a huff,' Benn said irritably as he got out of bed. They'd had this conversation a thousand times, and still Miriam wouldn't put her foot down with his mother and Emma.

'Mammy, I'm starving for my flonflakes.' Daniel appeared at the bedroom door. 'An' Connie's getting sick all over the bed, an' there's a smell off it.'

'I'll go.' Ben shuffled into his trousers and hurried out of the bedroom with Daniel trailing in his wake.

Miriam sat against the pillows, feeding Rebecca. She could hear the rain lashing against the window pane. Her bath was full of clothes steeping, she'd have to get them washed today, but Lord knows when she'd get them dry. At the rate Connie was being sick she'd have no bedclothes left, not to mention pyjamas.

She was sorely tempted to phone Emma and tell her that she couldn't look after Julie Ann today. Her hands were full with her own lot and Julie Ann was a handful at the best of times. She would phone her, she decided. As soon as she'd fed Rebecca.

* * *

'Put the little pink dress and the white cardigan on her, Vincent, and the white socks with the pink bows,' Emma instructed as she lay back against the pillows sipping the tea and eating the croissants Vincent had brought her earlier.

She marvelled as she watched her husband's gentle patience with Julie Ann. The baby was almost impossible to dress with all her squirming and wriggling. Emma found it a dreadfully tiresome chore but Vincent had a real knack for it. It helped of course that he was absolutely besotted by his daughter. Emma would have been quite jealous had she not been so relieved to have her husband do most of the babyminding. He always fed her when he was there. He dressed her and bathed her and changed her nappy before he went to work. And then when he came home in the evening he fed her and changed her and put her to bed. If

226

she cried at night, it was Vincent who tended to her. It suited Emma. Even though it meant that she didn't have one hundred per cent of his attention any more. A mother she was not cut out to be. She'd admitted that to herself from the start.

She'd been petrified out of her wits for the first few weeks that Julie Ann was home. If she gagged on her bottle or went scarlet in the face howling with colic, Emma burst into tears. She'd lived in fear of anything happening while she was on her own with her in the house. It had been a nightmare. Although she was a bit more confident now, Emma did not relish the role of motherhood. Making bottles and changing dirty nappies were not her forte. She liked it when Julie Ann was dressed prettily and looked adorable and everyone oohed and aahed over her. But unfortunately babies dribbled and puked and did other unmentionable things and the pristine state rarely lasted long.

It was all so repetitive, so *boring*. So time-consuming. Everything had to be planned around Julie Ann. Freedom was something she wouldn't have for years and years to come.

Julie Ann upchucked her breakfast all over her good pink dress.

'Oh for God's sake, Vincent, look what she's done now. And it's all over the quilt as well!'

'Calm down, I'll wipe it off.' Vincent loped into the bathroom and got a damp cloth.

'I wanted her to wear that pink dress today,' Emma said petulantly.

'I'll put the lemon one on her.' Vincent tickled his daughter under her chin and she gave a dainty little chuckle.

'Well make sure to change her socks and put the white ones with the lemon bows on,' Emma said crossly as she marched into the bathroom. No child of hers was going out in public with clashing socks. Colour co-ordination was everything.

It was with immense relief that she stood at the front door and watched Vincent drive off to Miriam's with Julie Ann tucked snugly in her wicker basket, accompanied by three made-up Cow & Gate bottles, two nappies, three bibs, a sponge, Savlon and talc and a plethora of cuddly toys.

Emma had persuaded Vincent to drop Julie Ann off at Miriam's on his way to work. Vincent protested that it was too early, but Emma insisted that she wouldn't have time to do it herself as she had to be in town early. Actually, she didn't want to see Miriam.

Her sister-in-law had phoned first thing to say that she couldn't take care of Julie Ann because Connie was sick and she was getting the doctor for her.

Fortunately, Emma had answered the phone. Vincent was in the shower. Vincent would have immediately assured Miriam not to worry, they'd make other arrangements, and Emma would have had to either bring the baby with her, or cancel her morning out altogether.

Emma had put on her most woebegone voice and said that the coffee morning she'd planned to go to was incidental. She really needed to have Julie Ann minded because she had to go and see her doctor as her anaemia seemed to have come back again. This was a bit of a fib. Her blood count, while still not perfect, was much higher than when she'd given birth. Miriam, who sounded quite frazzled, sympathized and said if that was the case she'd manage somehow.

'I'll get Vincent to drop her over, but don't say anything to him about me going to the doctor. I don't want to worry him, he's so good to me,' Emma murmured down the line, one ear cocked to make sure the shower was still on.

'Oh I won't. I hope you'll be OK. I feel desperate myself. I've just got the curse as well as everything else. The things us women have to put up with.'

'I know.' Emma sighed. She felt a little guilty, but hell, she needed a break too. Miriam was a born mother. She was used to looking after children. One more wouldn't make much difference. And it would only be for a couple of hours. Emma would look after her lot some day and give Miriam a morning off. Just then Julie Ann let out a howl giving Emma the perfect excuse to end the conversation. Which was just as well as Emma could hear that Vincent had turned off the shower.

'I better go,' she said hastily. 'Talk to you later.'

It had been a close shave. If Vincent had answered the phone there was no way she'd have been able to loll in the bath as she intended to now before dressing and putting on the glam.

She certainly couldn't have deposited Julie Ann at Miriam's looking a million dollars with all her make-up on when she was supposed to be suffering from anaemia.

Emma brushed aside her niggles of guilt. She *deserved* a morning to herself. She'd had an extremely stressful few months. Toxaemia, a premature birth, where she'd nearly *died*. All the traipsing in and out of the hospital for two months while Julie Ann was in the incubator had been horrific. Vincent had promised her he'd get a nanny, but unforunately the property market was having one of its periodic slumps and business wasn't great. He couldn't afford it right now and Emma couldn't possibly whinge about it, because Vincent was truly a husband in a million. Deep down, she knew she was an extremely lucky girl.

There was no way her friends' husbands would muck in and do all the chores Vincent did, uncomplainingly. Larry Kelly and Declan Mitchell were as lazy as sin. Declan wouldn't even put the loo seat down after him, he was so lazy, according to Lorna, his wife. It drove her nuts. Neither would he put his dirty clothes in the linen basket. And as for helping around the house ... He wouldn't know one end of a sweeping brush from the other, Lorna'd scoffed one evening after a few glasses of wine had loosened her tongue and she'd given vent to resentful feelings. They'd only been married six months and all was not a bed of roses.

Emma was secretly horrified to hear Lorna criticize her

husband to the rest of them. She'd never say a bad word about Vincent to any of her friends. You had to be loyal to your husband in public, it reflected badly on you if you weren't. Obviously Lorna didn't care enough about Declan to make the effort. Emma always spoke in glowing terms about Vincent. She was the envy of the set and that pleased her. But the nice thing was that she didn't have to tell fibs or exaggerate. Vincent *was* very good to her, she reflected as she stepped into the bath.

It was a treat to lie back in a bubble bath and not have to worry about the baby. Emma smoothed the frothy bubbles over her arms and shoulders and felt light-hearted and free. Just like when she was first married. She'd lost a few pounds through strict dieting. That pleased her enormously. The pill was terrible for putting weight on you, she thought regretfully as she ran her palm lightly over her almost flat stomach. She'd gone to London for a long weekend just before Julie Ann came home from hospital. It had been wonderful to go out on the town with her sister and, while she was there, she'd gone to a family planning clinic and got a six-month supply of the pill. This time, she was taking it religiously every night as instructed. She was never ever going to get caught again. It was much easier to get the pill in London, and a perfect excuse for a weekend away.

Vincent didn't mind her going. And he was very glad when, several weeks later, Emma decided she was safe at last and ravished him seductively one Friday night, ending several frustrating months of unwilling celibacy.

Emma felt rather horny as she remembered that night of passion. Tonight, they'd have another one, she decided happily as she lathered Avon scented soap all over her.

Two hours later, wrapped snugly in her fox fur jacket, she crossed Dawson Street and headed towards Grafton Street. She'd parked the car in Duke Street and planned a little spree in Brown Thomas before meeting the girls in the Shelbourne for coffee.

She had a delightful time testing various perfumes and

face creams before she splurged on a new Max Factor foundation that gave her skin a very smooth, sophisticated glow. A quick browse through the fashions enticed her to buy a gorgeous check mini with a wide buckled belt which would be sensational with the black figure-hugging ribbed polo that she'd bought in the January sales. Vincent loved her in minis, although Mrs Munroe frowned when Emma wore them and told her that she'd get cold in her kidneys. Emma knew her mother-in-law thought her skirts were indecent and that she was flaunting herself, but she didn't give a hoot. Vincent loved them. God had given her a great pair of legs to show off and if Ma Munroe didn't like it, she could lump it.

Emma didn't know that the women of the guild had christened her 'Mrs Mini', and that the sight of her waltzing along Main Street with her skirts 'up to her buttocks', as Bonnie Daly inelegantly put it, scandalized the older women so much that there was actually a suggestion that the parish priest should have a word in Vincent's ear about his wife's inappropriate apparel.

'Look what I treated myself to,' Emma said gaily to Gillian and Lorna as she held out the new purchase for their admiration.

'It's fab,' Gillian enthused.

'I wish I had the legs to wear it,' Lorna said enviously. Her legs were of the tree-trunk variety.

They spent a couple of glorious hours indulging in the most rewarding gossip, drinking rich dark coffee and eating little scones smothered in great dollops of jam and cream. Diets were forgotten by one and all. Emma didn't want the morning to end. She was having fun. When the girls reluctantly made a move to go, Emma decided on the spur of the moment to call and visit her mother. She knew she should go home and collect Julie Ann from Miriam's but the thought of spending yet another dreary afternoon at home depressed her utterly. It was starting to rain again as she hurried past the Mansion House and she just made it to the car before the heavens opened.

There was no way she was going to drive to Glenree in that downpour. A quick trip to Foxrock was much more inviting.

'Where's Julie Ann?' Pamela asked disappointedly.

'I didn't bring her this morning. Miriam's taking care of her,' Emma said irritably, miffed by her mother's obvious disappointment.

'I hope you're not taking advantage of that girl. You left Julie Ann with her last week as well,' Pamela scolded.

'Miriam doesn't mind. Besides she's company for Rebecca.' Emma scowled. Pamela had a knack of making her feel like a neglectful mother. She was beginning to regret her impulse to call and visit.

'How's Sheila?' Pamela inquired as she put the kettle on to boil.

'Oh up to her eyes as usual,' Emma said offhandedly as she flicked through a copy of *Vogue*. 'Interfering like mad, telling Ellen how to take care of Stephanie, according to Miriam.'

'Who's Stephanie?'

Emma's hand shot involuntarily to her mouth. She and Vincent had never told Pamela about Ellen's pregnancy.

'Who's Stephanie?' Pamela repeated, surprised by Emma's reaction.

'Er . . . no-one, really.'

'Emma . . . Who?' Pamela was not to be fobbed off.

'Ellen got pregnant and had a baby at Christmas,' Emma muttered. She was raging with herself. Now she was going to have to endure an interrogation that would leave the Spanish Inquisition in the junior league.

'Why didn't you tell me before now?' Pamela was stunned.

'It's none of my business.' Emma tried to sound indifferent.

'Don't talk nonsense, Emma.' Pamela was unimpressed. 'Why didn't she marry the father?'

'He wouldn't marry her.' Emma wished with all her

232

might that her mother would change the topic. 'Will Dad be home for lunch?'

'Not today. Now why wouldn't this chap marry Ellen? The poor unfortunate girl. She must be in a terrible state.'

'I don't have much to do with her. I don't know.' And I don't care, she would have liked to add. Damn Ellen and her stupidity.

'That's terrible,' Pamela tutted as she made coffee. 'Poor Sheila must be devastated. I thought she was in very bad form when we had them over at Christmas. The poor woman never said a word about it. I suppose she's mortified.'

'Hmm,' Emma agreed.

'Was Ellen going with this chap for long?'

'I don't know.' Emma was evasive. Pamela was surprised at her daughter's reticence. It wasn't like her at all. Usually Emma would be full of the gory details. It wasn't that she was protecting her sister-in-law. Emma couldn't stand Ellen. Pamela knew that for a fact.

'Wait a minute. I vaguely remember you telling me that Ellen went out with Chris after your wedding.' Pamela stared at Emma.

Emma flushed and looked away.

'Is Chris the father, Emma?' Pamela was horrified.

There was no point in denying it, Emma knew. Pamela would get to the bottom of the matter one way or the other.

'Is he?'

'Yeah.'

'The pup!' Pamela exclaimed. Disgusted. 'He's just got engaged to Suzy. They're getting married in June. Does Ellen know this? Does Suzy know about this child? Is he taking his responsibilities to the child seriously?' The questions came quick and fast.

Emma's heart sank even further. You'd think it was all *her* fault the way her mother was going on. She didn't know whether Suzy knew about Ellen or Stephanie. She had a feeling that she didn't. But it was none of her business and she certainly wasn't going to interfere.

'You must know something, Emma.'

'Mum, Chris is a big boy now. He doesn't tell me the intimate details of his relationships. I didn't know about him and Ellen for ages. And I haven't a clue as to whether he's told Suzy or not. That's their business, not mine.'

'Wait until I see him, I'll have a few words to say to him I can tell you. How embarrassing that a member of our family should be the cause of such a scandal. I'll have to ring Sheila and apologize.'

'For God's sake, Mum!' Emma exclaimed in dismay. 'Just say nothing and keep out of it. It's nothing to do with you.'

'Indeed it has,' Pamela retorted. 'Chris is our relation and he's left that girl in the lurch. He didn't even have the decency to marry her. Sheila and Mick are *entitled* to an apology.' Pamela was furious that Chris had put her in such an awkward position. 'You should have told me about this long before now. I'm very annoyed, Emma. Very annoyed indeed.'

Not half as annoyed as Vincent's going to be when he finds out I've let the cat out of the bag. Emma frowned as she sipped her coffee. Hail, rain or snow she should have gone straight home to Glenree instead of coming to Foxrock and opening her big mouth.

* * *

'It's life and there's nothing you can do about it. One has to keep going. But thank you for ringing, Pamela. Give my regards to the judge,' Sheila said crisply. Although outwardly composed, she was absolutely mortified. To have Pamela Connolly ring her up and commiserate about Ellen's pregnancy was a heart-scalding embarrassment that she would never forget. Pamela, to give her her due, had been very nice. Not a bit patronizing. Sheila got the impression that the other woman was as embarrassed as she was. And Pamela was certainly furious with Chris Wallace. She'd been scathing about his lack of responsibility.

'Not perfect husband material at all,' she clipped in her posh south Dublin accent. 'That girl he's engaged to needs her head examined.'

It's Ellen he should have married, Sheila wanted to retort, but she restrained herself. It wasn't Pamela's fault, even if Chris Wallace was related to her. It was a shock to hear that he'd just got engaged to be married. Secretly Sheila had always hoped that he'd reconsider and marry Ellen. She'd give her right arm to see her daughter respectably married. It was a relief when the conversation was over. She put the receiver back on its cradle and stood for a moment trying to regain her composure. Earlier she'd heard Ellen laughing and playing with Stephanie. Now there was silence, the baby must have gone to sleep.

How could Ellen laugh? Sheila wondered crossly as all the feelings of anger and resentment resurfaced. Stephanie was a little dote, she couldn't deny it. And she was the apple of her grandfather's eye. But what sort of life was she going to have? She'd be asked about her father in years to come. What sort of answer would Ellen have? It would have been better if Ellen had put a ring on her finger and moved to Dublin where no-one knew her. She could have pretended that she was a widow. She might have had some chance of meeting another man. Some chance of getting married. In Glenree, she had nothing, just a reputation that was in tatters. Tears stung Sheila's eyes. Angrily she brushed them away. She'd shed enough tears over her wayward daughter. She'd shed no more.

*   *   *

'You're so pretty, my precious,' Ellen cooed proudly at her baby daughter who was lying on the bed, stark naked, waiting for a clean nappy. The bedroom was snug and cosy. A crackling fire flamed in the grate, protecting them

235

from the cold biting winter wind that whistled down the chimney. The rain hurled itself against the window and Ellen was glad to be at home in the peace and quiet of her bedroom, away from the prying eyes and the pointing fingers.

They spent a lot of time together in the bedroom. Ellen looked around at the room that had been hers since childhood. A comfortable old armchair decorated in faded chintz sat beside the fire. It was a lovely chair, perfect for curling up in to have a snooze or a read. Now it was an ideal place to feed Stephanie. A mahogany double-doored wardrobe stood along the wall between the fire and the doorway. It was as old as the hills and had the battle scars to prove it. Ellen thought longingly of Emma's modern fitted wardrobes.

The big brass bedstead gleamed in the firelight. It had been her grandmother's. A huge colourful patchwork quilt covered the bed and Ellen had added a couple of cushions in squares of dusky pink and eggshell blue for effect. They picked up the faded dusky pink of the walls, and the pale blue of the curtains.

Stephanie's crib stood beside the bed. Mick had made a marvellous job of it, Ellen thought gratefully as she fastened the safety pins on her daughter's nappy and pulled on the plastic pants. A sash window gave views of the garden and the valley beyond. In the distance Ellen could see the lights in Miriam's bungalow. Vincent and Emma's house was in darkness. The lights of Glenree pierced the gloom of a wet afternoon as the rain dripped steadily down. Ellen often sat for hours in the window seat immersed in the view.

Stephanie yawned and scrunched up her eyes. Ellen leaned down and kissed her on the tip of her little turned-up nose. She had the cutest nose and the bluest eyes. She didn't look a bit like Chris . . . yet . . . Well around the eyes, perhaps, Ellen conceded.

She sighed deeply as she slid the little vest down over Stephanie's dark downy head. Maybe if Chris saw his daughter he might have a change of heart. For the last few days she'd thought of nothing else except bringing Stephanie to Chris. She was such an irresistible baby, how could he possibly turn his back on her? Maybe if the weather improved tomorrow, she'd go into Dublin to his new office. Miriam had found out from Emma where it was. At least he wouldn't be having a dinner party there, Ellen thought bitterly, remembering the night she'd gone to his house.

She'd hoped that once she'd had the baby the loneliness would ease but, if anything, it was worse. She so badly wanted to share the joy of Stephanie with Chris. And her baby was a joy to her. A great joy and blessing and Chris was missing all of it.

Dusk had fallen as she finished dressing the baby in her nightclothes. The darkened room was lit only by the light from the flickering flames. Stephanie was almost asleep. She always slept after her feed. Ellen was reluctant to switch on a lamp. She sat for a while with her baby in her arms, enjoying the peace and solitude. This room was her sanctuary. Her place to hide from the world. She didn't want to leave it.

The phone rang downstairs. Ellen could hear the murmur of her mother's voice. She supposed she should go down and offer to get the tea. She placed Stephanie gently in her crib and covered her up warmly. She heard Sheila hang up. The conversation hadn't been a long one, who-ever it was.

Reluctantly, she slipped out of her room and closed the door quietly. The lamp was on in the hall, lighting her way down the stairs. Sheila was standing by the phone looking flushed and agitated.

'What's wrong?' Ellen asked in concern.

Sheila glared at her. 'That was Pamela Connolly, she'd heard about you having a baby.'

'Oh,' Ellen murmured.

'Oh, indeed,' Sheila snapped. 'At least Pamela had the manners to apologize for the behaviour of that . . . that . . .

rake. You can forget about him, my girl, if you've been cherishing any secret notions that he might change his mind and marry you. Because he won't! He's just got engaged to that other floozy he was carrying on with.' Sheila was deeply angry. She swept past Ellen into the kitchen and slammed the door behind her.

Ellen stood in the hall shocked to her core. Deep down she'd always hoped and believed that Chris would have a change of heart and marry her. It had been the dream that kept her going. Even after every setback. Now she had no hope. He was getting married. Slowly she turned and walked back upstairs. She wanted to scream and cry and curse his name to the four winds. This was the deepest hurt of all. She could hardly breathe because of it. She slipped into the room, lay down on the bed and buried her face in a cushion. Hot wet tears coursed down her cheeks, as she muffled her sobs in the cushion. What in the name of God was she going to do? She'd have to think of something. She couldn't stay in Glenree with Sheila. The tension was unbearable. She'd have to get a job and try and make some sort of a life for herself. Stephanie slept soundly in her cot, blissfully unaware of her mother's anguish, while Ellen cried as though her heart would break.

* * *

Ellen looked wretched, Miriam thought as her sister-in-law let herself in through the back door. Miriam was sitting by the fire, exhausted. All the children were in bed. She'd tidied up the house and she was seriously considering going to bed herself, even though it was only half past seven. Ben was at his union meeting.

She was still feeling mad with Emma. She hadn't arrived home until four-thirty that afternoon to collect Julie Ann, who had screeched for the entire duration of her stay.

That was it, Miriam promised herself. No more childminding. She had enough of her own.

'Would you like a cup of tea?' she asked Ellen, hoping

238

the other girl would refuse. She was too tired to get up and put on the kettle.

'Yes please, Miriam.' Ellen sank into a chair and began to cry.

'What's wrong? Is Stephanie OK?' Miriam asked in concern.

'Stephanie's fine.' Ellen gulped. 'It's Chris. He's getting married and I don't know what to do. I always hoped we'd get back together. I really love him, Miriam. I know you think I'm nuts but I just can't help it. I don't want to love him. I don't want to be thinking of him. How do I get him out of my head?' She rubbed her knuckles into her eyes and sobbed like a child.

Miriam pitied her from the bottom of her heart. She couldn't understand how Ellen could possibly love Chris after the way he'd behaved towards her. But no matter how much she pointed out his flaws, Ellen never listened. She just made excuses for him and kept on loving him.

'I'll have to get a job. I'll have to make some sort of a life for Stephanie. I can't just stay up in my bedroom for ever.' Ellen raised red-rimmed eyes to Miriam.

'I know it's a huge favour to ask, Miriam. But I can't ask Mam. I don't want to ask her. I was wondering if I asked Dad for my old job back for the time being, would you look after Stephanie until I get something sorted?'

Miriam's heart sank. She longed to refuse. She couldn't face looking after another baby as well as Rebecca and her two toddlers. She could barely look after them as it was. But how could she say no to the shattered woman in front of her? How could she possibly turn her back on Ellen?

'Of course I will,' she heard herself say, as Ellen sobbed in her arms.

She'd manage somehow. She was the one person Ellen depended on and Miriam wasn't going to let her down.

Chapter Thirteen

'I still can't believe it.' Suzy removed the tissue paper from her veil and gazed at it with pleasure. It was her wedding day and she was deliriously happy.

'Believe it!' Alexandra grinned. 'I told you if you listened to me you'd get the ring on your finger.'

'You're the best friend a girl could have.' Suzy flung her arms around Alexandra and hugged her tightly. 'Now we have to find someone for you.'

'I'm not that pushed to be honest.' Alexandra returned the hug. 'Come on, time's running out. We better get dressed if you want to be there on the dot. We don't want Chris getting cold feet at the last minute.'

'I'm not going to be a second late. I think brides who are twenty minutes late and more are really pushing their luck . . .'

Alexandra gave a non-committal 'um' and busied herself laying out make-up on the dressing-table. It was obvious that Suzy, even at this late stage, was still unsure of Chris's commitment. Alexandra knew she was petrified he would stand her up at the altar. Not a great start to marriage, she thought wryly. Maybe once they were married he'd change and settle down. But did a leopard change his spots? That was the million-dollar question. Still Suzy was mad about him. Chris was what she wanted and Chris was what she was getting.

Half an hour later she stood back and admired her handiwork. Suzy was a vision in her exquisite raw silk white sheath. Baby's breath entwined in her blonde hair which shone beneath her fine white veil. Alexandra adjusted the little Juliet cap on Suzy's head and pronounced herself satisfied.

'Let's go, kid! This is it. Time to face the world.'

Suzy's hand shook as she took the bouquet of orchids from the dressing-table. She was desperately nervous. This was supposed to be the happiest day of her life but she was in flitters.

In the last few weeks, Chris had gone all moody and quiet, and found fault with everything she did. She'd been afraid to ask him what was the matter in case he'd say he didn't want to go through with the wedding. She was so unnerved. What would she do if he didn't turn up at the church? She wouldn't put it past him. That was how confident she was about her husband-to-be. Deep down Suzy acknowledged that she'd always be worried about Chris's commitment to her. It was something she tried not to think about and it was something she was going to have to cope with as best she could. Maybe it was *she* who should consider not turning up. But that was unthinkable. She adored Chris. She wanted to be with him for ever.

It's only pre-wedding nerves, Suzy told herself fiercely. Stop it now. Of all the women he'd dated, she was the one he'd asked to be his wife. *That* had to mean something. Of course he loved her. She was just being silly. Besides he'd have to turn up. This was the society wedding of the year. The reception was being held in the Gresham Hotel. Two hundred guests had been invited. The crème de la crème of Dublin's high society. Some of Chris's clients and their wives were on the guest list. He couldn't stand her up in front of them.

She took a deep breath, smiled at Alexandra, her greatest ally, and opened her bedroom door. Her mother burst into tears when she saw her and it was only with great difficulty that Suzy managed not to do the same herself.

*　　*　　*

Chris surreptitiously loosened the knot on his tie. It was a hot day and a stream of sunlight shone through the ornate stained-glass window of the church, bathing him in unwelcome light. He'd a fierce hangover after a night out with his friends.

He found it hard to believe that he was actually sitting in church waiting to get married. It was a terrifying thought. Did all bridegrooms go through this or was it just him? What was so wonderful about marriage anyway? He'd been perfectly happy the way they were. Of course it was his own fault proposing out of the blue at Christmas just because he felt under pressure over Ellen and the baby. He'd panicked and made a bad decision and now six months later it was too late to get out of it. He couldn't let Suzy down. It was bad enough to have ruined one woman's life.

Oh hell! Don't think of Ellen today of all days. Don't start feeling guilty now for heaven's sake, he thought miserably. But guilty he did feel. Usually he pushed such feelings to the deepest recesses of his mind. He didn't like admitting to himself that he had treated Ellen like dirt. He'd abused her love and broken her trust. He wasn't proud of that. Women! They were the devil's invention.

Chris wished he was a million miles away. He didn't want to get married. He didn't think marriage was a very realistic institution. Was it fair to expect a couple to stay together for possibly forty or more years? It was very unreasonable. Sure, Suzy was a great girl and they were good together but it made him feel claustrophobic to think of all those years ahead. What was he letting himself in for? A ripple of excitement spread through the assembled guests as the wedding march boomed from the vast organ at the back of the church. Chris swallowed hard. His heartbeat raced. His palms were sweaty. This was it. He stood up slowly and turned to greet his bride.

*   *   *

Glenree was *en fête*. It was a balmy Saturday afternoon. The annual sale of work was being held on the large circular green opposite the primary school. Bunting fluttered from the shops, some of which, Mick's butcher's shop included, had been given a fresh coat of paint in honour of the occasion. The new young manager of the Glenree Arms had risen to the occasion and brought tables and chairs from the bar out to the pavement. Several jaunty sun umbrellas shaded the thirsty customers who sat sipping beer as they surveyed the proceedings. It was all very Continental and added greatly to the air of fun and frolics.

Stalls edged the perimeter of the green. Book stalls, cake stalls, clothes stalls, bric-à-brac stalls, home-grown fruit, veg, jam and chutney stalls. There were crowds around all of them. A huge white marquee stood in the centre of the green and a steady stream of people entered its cool portals in search of refreshments and a respite from the hustle and bustle. Emma sat in the white shaded coolness sipping coffee. She was bored out of her mind. Resentment surged through her. She should have been at Chris and Suzy's wedding instead of stuck here in the back of beyond with a crowd of clodhoppers who were wetting themselves with excitement because of a silly old sale of work. Julie Ann whimpered in her pram and Emma's heart sank. 'Don't wake up please,' she muttered crossly. Julie Ann was teething and was as cranky as could be. It was very wearing, especially when she started howling and couldn't be pacified. Emma never knew what to do with her. If she started howling now, she could forget her coffee. She rocked the pram gently and felt most relieved when Julie Ann fell back asleep.

It was mean . . . very *mean* of Vincent to refuse to go to her cousin's wedding because of Ellen. That was all water under the bridge now. Why should Ellen's stupidity be the cause of Emma missing the wedding of the season and a great day out as well? Everybody was going to that wedding. Everybody except her, she thought sourly.

She'd argued for days when the invitation arrived, but to no avail. Vincent could not be prevailed upon to change his mind. She kept at him until one evening he'd turned on her in fury, his eyes like two chips of ice. 'I'm not going to that bastard's wedding to watch him enjoy himself without a care in the world, while my sister is here, devastated, her life ruined, her reputation in tatters, with a child to bring up because of him. No way, Emma!' He was emphatic. 'I'm surprised you'd even consider going.'

'Ah, Vincent. He's my cousin. And it takes two to tango. It's not *all* his fault you know,' she flared back.

'I know that, Emma. That's not the point. He behaved like a shit. You might think he's charming and funny and great company, but your cousin is a selfish, devious, amoral, lying cheat. He was seeing that girl when he was carrying on with my sister. Does *she* know he slept with Ellen and got her pregnant? Was he sleeping with the two of them in turn? Was he telling her he loved her, when he was saying the same thing to Ellen? What sort of a man does that? Does Suzy Kenny know any of this and, if she does, how in the name of God can she marry him? How can she trust him? How can she respect him?' Vincent's rage was palpable.

'These things happen in life, and Ellen knew what she was getting into. We warned her, Vincent. She brought it all on herself.'

'Maybe she did bring it on herself. That doesn't justify Chris's behaviour. Ellen fell in love with him and he encouraged her. He didn't give a fig for her. He just used her. And then he dumped her when she needed him most. And does he give her one thought?' He glared at her. 'I can tell you, Emma, he does not. He probably doesn't even remember her name.' Vincent's tone was bitter.

After that, Emma knew there was no point in bringing the matter up again. She hadn't realized, until his outburst, how strongly he still felt over the whole affair. He was right about Chris. Her cousin was a womanizer, always had been and probably always would be, but he was great fun and it would have been a brilliant wedding, she thought regretfully. She supposed she could have put her foot down and gone on her own but Vincent would have viewed that as a gross act of disloyalty. He was her husband and she loved him so the fleeting thought was regretfully dismissed.

Emma sighed as she bit into a limp ham sandwich. Suzy's dress would no doubt be out of this world. She had a great sense of style. Emma would love to have seen her swanning up the aisle in all her glory. Vincent's words came to mind. How could she trust Chris? How could she respect him? How could she marry him? Chris was too selfish to commit to anyone. Actually Emma felt he was incapable of loving anyone except himself. Love is blind they said and it must be, because knowing Chris and his track record, Suzy was a brave woman to take him on.

*   *   *

'Ellen, would you go over to Emily Doyle's stall and get me some of her home-made chutney? Your father loves it for some reason I can't fathom. It's no different to mine.' Sheila took some coins from her purse and handed them to her. 'Leave Stephanie here and I'll keep an eye on her.'

'Right,' Ellen said heavily.

'What's the matter with you? You're in very bad form.' Sheila frowned as she arranged a plate of scones between a tea brack and a jam sponge.

'Nothing. I think I've a bit of a cold coming on,' Ellen replied hastily. 'I'll go and get the chutney before it's all sold out.'

Sheila watched her daughter cross over to Emily's stall at the other end of the green. She sighed. Ellen was very down these past few days. She was like a cat on a griddle. Well whatever was wrong with her, she'd better get over it. She had responsibilities now. Stephanie needed a mother, not a moping weeping willow.

It was hard, Sheila conceded. Having a baby was

difficult to cope with at the best of times. Having a baby out of wedlock was a terrible trial for a girl. If only she hadn't been so foolish. It was a heart-scald, that's what it was.

'Would you like me to relieve you, Sheila?' Her musings were interrupted by an unwelcome syrupy voice. Bonnie stood smiling ever so sweetly at her.

'My stint isn't over for another three quarters of an hour, Bonnie,' Sheila responded coldly. Bonnie Daly could go and take a running jump. She's been trying to edge her way back into Sheila's good books ever since the episode at the guild meeting, but Sheila was having none of it. Bonnie was supposed to have been a friend. Loyalty was the very least you expected from your friends. Bonnie's behaviour had been anything but loyal.

'I thought you might be tired. It's a very warm day.' Bonnie's smile remained fixed, her eyes little beads of insincerity.

'I'm fine, thank you.' Sheila was not impressed by Judas Daly.

'Isn't the little one a dote?' Bonnie leaned into the pram and gooed at Stephanie. Stephanie started to screech, much to Sheila's satisfaction.

'She doesn't like strangers.' Sheila's tone was acerbic as she came out from behind the stall and lifted Stephanie out of the pram.

'Shussh, there, there, alanna. Did you get a fright? Did the lady give you a fright? Never mind, pet, Nannie's here,' she crooned. Stephanie quietened almost immediately. Sheila flashed her arch-enemy a trimphant look. 'Excuse me, I'll put her back in her pram. Come back at four, you can relieve me then.' She paused and said coolly, 'Your jam sponge hasn't gone yet. Mine and Mona's went in the first five minutes. I've put yours out at the very front where people can see it.'

Bonnie's thin lips tightened. 'I'll be back at four.' This time the tone was not so syrupy, and her eyes were bright with suppressed anger. She marched off and Sheila gave a

246

dry chuckle as she laid her granddaughter back into the pram.

'Your grandmother sorted her out, didn't she, pet?' Stephanie gurgled at her, her big blue eyes huge in her little face. Sheila gazed at the baby with her mop of silky black hair, her little button nose and her rosebud mouth. She was adorable. If only Ellen had married the father and they were a proper family. But then, she thought, remembering her last encounter with Chris, he wasn't a man at all, to have said the things he'd said about Ellen. God had strange ways of working. Maybe Ellen had had a lucky escape. Maybe if she'd married him she would have had a life of misery. Sheila didn't know. All she could do was to put her daughter and granddaughter in the hands of the Almighty.

*   *   *

Ellen pushed Stephanie's pram along the winding tree-lined road past Blackbird's Field. It was aptly named, she thought as she paused to listen to the thrilling symphony of birdsong that sweetened the air. It really was the most glorious day. The sun was warm on her face, a balmy breeze lifted tendrils of hair from her forehead. The air was fresh and clean and scented with lilacs. It was nice to be on her own for a while. Especially today of all days. A lump came to her throat.

'Oh you're pathetic,' she muttered as tears stung her eyes. But she had a reason to cry today. She knew, via Miriam, that Chris was marrying his blonde bombshell. Emma had told Miriam all about the row with Vincent and how she wasn't going to the wedding. Vincent's brotherly solidarity had touched Ellen. Actually, he'd been kinder and more approachable since she'd had Stephanie and he'd suggested they let bygones be bygones. Emma remained quite frosty though. But that didn't particularly bother Ellen.

Miriam had told Ellen about the wedding so that she could forget about getting back with him once and for all.

Would she ever forget him? Was that possible? Would time heal? She fervently hoped so. The heartache was a nightmare. Sometimes she actually felt she was in a nightmare and that she would wake up and it would all be over.

She glanced at her watch. It was almost four-thirty. He'd be well married now, she thought with a desperate sadness that seemed to seep into every bone of her body. She felt such regret for what could have been. But he'd used her and lied to her. He wasn't a decent person. He was weak and selfish. This was the last time she'd grieve for him, she promised herself. Chris was her past now. She had to get on with her life and look to the future. There was an old saying, *No man is your enemy, no man is your friend, every man is your teacher*. She'd learned a hard lesson at his hands but at least she could look herself in the eye and know that she'd given true love and she'd never lied to him. He hadn't valued her, or her love, but it didn't make her any the less of a person. She would hold her head up and so would Stephanie. Ellen could live with herself, but could Chris ever truly face himself? Ellen doubted it. Chris had a great knack of burying his head in the sand.

Stephanie waved a tiny hand in the air. Ellen wiped away her tears and lifted her daughter out of the pram. 'There's my darling,' she murmured, nuzzling her soft neck. She loved the sweet talced baby smell, and the soft downy feel of her baby's skin against hers. What a fool Chris was to have disowned his daughter. He was missing so much. It was worth all the pain and heartache she'd endured to be greeted by a huge smile and have Stephanie raise her arms up to her every morning when she went to pick her up out of her cot. Chris would never know such joy with her. And it would be his great loss.

'Come on, let's go home,' Ellen declared. Enough was enough. She'd wasted too much of her life on a man who wasn't worth it. It was time to move on.

PART TWO

PART TWO

Chapter Fourteen

1968

'Suzy! Suzy! Did you iron a clean shirt for me?' Chris leaned over the banisters and yelled downstairs at his wife. She was feeding their two-year-old twins and there was such a racket going on she couldn't hear him. Chris felt so irritated he thought he was going to burst. Was it too much to ask for a goddamn clean shirt every morning? What did Suzy *do* all day, for crying out loud?

He raced downstairs and almost broke his neck over a centipede on wheels – one of the twins' toys. 'Christ Almighty! Would you get those things off the stairs!' he glowered at Suzy.

'Why don't *you* tidy them up?' Suzy flared.

'Where's my shirt?'

'I haven't got it ironed yet.'

'For God's sake, Suzy. I've a very important meeting this morning. I can't be late.'

'Well iron it yourself then.' Suzy spooned mashed Liga into Adam and then, while he was busy swallowing it, she fed Christina hers.

'I'll do that! You iron my shirt.' Chris took the bowl of Liga from her.

Suzy went out to the utility room with bad grace. Chris scowled after her. You'd think he'd asked her to walk barefoot across the Sahara. It wouldn't take five minutes to iron a shirt. He didn't know what the big fuss was about.

'Me some,' Adam demanded, as he pulled his father's

nose. Chris laughed. His son was a character. He had a strong personality, even at two years of age. Christina was more placid.

It had been a huge shock when Suzy discovered she was expecting twins. It had taken a bit of getting used to. Until her pregnancy they'd both been able to come and go as they liked. Take off for weekends at the drop of a hat. Stay out late and party whenever they wanted. That had all changed. Now, with two toddlers, they were very tied. Although he loved them, the restrictions they imposed on his life made him feel smothered. Suzy was often short-tempered and ratty and the house looked as if a bomb had hit it with all the toys that were strewn around.

It irritated Chris. He liked things to be neat and tidy. Housekeeping was not his wife's forte, he thought crossly as he eyed last night's supper dishes, still unwashed in the sink. It hadn't been too bad when there had just been the two of them. But with two demanding children, who seemed to need a lot of feeding and clothes changes, the house never looked right any more. Suzy was always nagging him to get someone in to clean even once a week.

'If Emma and Vincent can have someone in every day, surely we could have someone in once a week. We're not paupers,' she argued.

It was all very well for Emma and Vincent. They were loaded. They hadn't had to pay a penny for the magnificent site their house was on. And Vincent, with all his contacts in the building trade, had been able to build his mansion for next to nothing. Chris had had to take out a massive mortgage for the new house Suzy had demanded once the children had been born.

Certainly they'd needed a bigger house. But detached houses in Sandymount were expensive and she'd insisted on a detached house. Semi-d's did not quite suit their image. He had to agree there. After all a prestigious address did impress. And impressing potential clients was vitally important. Nevertheless he was financially stretched with his business overheads and big mortgage. A cleaning lady was not high on his list of priorities. Not when Suzy should be able to do it if she put her mind to it. The trouble was Suzy hated being tied to the house. She wanted to be gadding off into town. Alexandra was always phoning to invite her to gallery openings and book launches organized by the PR firm she worked for. Before the children were born Suzy had been able to go to them. But that had all changed. She was a mother now, a housewife. That was what she'd wanted when she'd walked up that aisle. He hadn't *forced* her to get married. He resented her nagging and bad humours.

'Here's your shirt,' Suzy snapped. 'What time will you be home for dinner tonight? Don't forget, I promised Alexandra I'd go to a make-up party she's giving.'

'But I won't be home. I told you I was bringing Des Reid and some business associates out to dinner.'

'You *never* told me that. Otherwise I would have organized a babysitter. I'll probably never get one now. It's not fair, Chris.' She was furious.

'Suzy, I did tell you. I distinctly remember saying it last week. You just don't listen.'

'Alexandra will be mad if I don't go.'

'Fuck Alexandra,' Chris snapped. 'She's always the same. It's all right for her. She can come and go as she chooses. But she can't keep expecting you to drop everything now that you've got children.'

'She's going through a bad patch. Will left her for someone else. I have to give her support. She's my best friend.' Suzy grabbed the dish of Liga from him.

'Will left her because she was mucking him around. He asked her to marry him but she couldn't make up her mind. She kept him dangling for months. And I'll tell you one thing, he had a lucky escape because she's a ball-breaker, I'd pity the man who ends up with her. The only person Alexandra gives a hoot about is herself.'

'That's a horrible thing to say, Chris Wallace!'

'Yeah, well it's the truth.' Chris pulled on his shirt and fastened the buttons.

'She's had a very hard time,' Suzy retorted.

'Well what do you want me to do about it? Burst into tears and wear a black tie? I'll see you tonight.'

Chris strode out of the kitchen and raced upstairs to finish dressing. He couldn't care less about Alexandra and her hard times. He was having a hard enough time himself as it was. He slammed the front door when he was leaving, just so Suzy would be in no doubt as to his feelings. He hadn't even had breakfast. Des Reid's wife got up and cooked him a fry every morning. And they had four children. It was a pity Suzy wouldn't take a leaf out of her book, Chris thought petulantly as he flung his briefcase into the front seat of the car and set off for work.

*   *   *

Suzy heard the front door bang. 'Goodbye and good riddance,' she muttered as she lifted the twins out of their high chairs and watched them toddle out to the hall to play. Chris could be so unreasonable, dancing around like Hysterical Hilda because his shirt wasn't ironed. Couldn't he see she was up to her eyes?

Now she was going to have to try and get a babysitter at short notice because of Des Reid and his cohorts. Suzy didn't like Lecher Reid with his leering smile and roving hands. She sighed as she ran hot water into the sink and started to wash the dishes. Life was a drag at the moment, she thought despondently. Chris was busy at work and he wasn't mucking in much with the children. They really kept her going. Nothing had prepared her for how hard it was going to be looking after two babies. At the beginning Chris had been good at helping out. But gradually, Suzy found that she was left more on her own with them. Chris spent a lot of time wining and dining clients. Or so he told her. Was he being unfaithful? Before the twins were born she'd been pretty certain he hadn't strayed. She'd made sure to socialize with him as much as possible. He'd seemed quite contented with his lot. And she'd been

254

happy. Getting pregnant had been a calculated risk. But she couldn't keep putting it off. She was in her mid-thirties. Time was running out. She wanted a child. It would bind them closer together, she'd thought.

Now she had two children and it was pushing them apart. Chris felt trapped. She couldn't give him the attention she'd given him before. She shouldn't have blown her top earlier. He hated being nagged. If she didn't watch it, he *would* end up in the arms of another woman. That was a thought that filled her with dread.

'No more nagging from now on.' She smiled down at her daughter who had trotted in to show off her dolly. Suzy loved her children. The strength of that love had surprised her at first. She'd never thought of herself as particularly maternal. But once she'd held them in her arms for the first time, she knew there was nothing she wouldn't do for them. She loved being with the twins but she hated housework with a vengeance. Washing, ironing, cooking, cleaning. It was the pits. Years of repetitious drudgery stretched ahead of her. Could some women possibly enjoy all that? Suzy often wondered.

*   *   *

'You're not coming to *my* birthday party, Julie Ann Munroe. And I'm telling my mammy what you said.' Stephanie was red-faced with frustration and temper.

'Who cares? Your scabby old birthday party's not for ages yet. Rebecca's is first,' Julie Ann retorted snootily and then, with the cruelty that only a five-year-old possesses, she repeated her taunting jibe. 'You *don't* have a daddy like me an' Rebecca an' my mummy says your mummy's a tramp.'

Stephanie didn't know exactly what a tramp was, but she knew from her cousin's disdainful tone and the way she wrinkled her nose up in distaste that it was something not very nice at all. It was all too much for Stephanie. With a shriek of anger she lashed out and landed a punch on Julie Ann's smug little face.

Her cousin howled with shock and pain as blood started gushing from her nose.

'Good enough for you,' Stephanie yelled back. 'You leave my mammy alone.'

'Auntie Miriam, Auntie Miriam, I'm bleeding,' Julie Ann screamed hysterically.

'Jesus, Mary and Joseph!' Miriam swore from the kitchen sink as she peered out the kitchen window to see what all the commotion was about.

Rebecca galloped in through the back door, breathless.

'Quick, Mammy! Stephanie an' Julie Ann are having a terrible fight. Stephanie punched Julie Ann in the snot 'cos she said Stephanie's got no daddy an' Auntie Ellen's a . . . a something! An' Stephanie said Julie Ann wasn't coming to her birthday party an' now they're fightin'.'

'I'm sick of the lot of you,' Miriam fumed. 'You can't play for ten minutes without arguing like tinkers. There'll be no birthday parties at all for anyone if you don't stop it.'

'But Mammy, I wasn't fighting,' Rebecca wailed. 'It's not fair.' She'd been looking forward to *her* birthday party for months.

Miriam flung off her rubber gloves and marched out the back door.

'Auntie Miriam, I'm bleeding,' Julie Ann screeched as blood dripped onto her white T-shirt, making a dramatic stain.

'She said things about my mammy. An' she said I had no daddy an' I do don't I, Auntie Miriam? He just lives somewhere else.' Stephanie was trembling with fury and indignation.

Miriam felt like giving Julie Ann another wallop. The little madam! Goading Stephanie like that. She was her mother's daughter for sure, with her sharp tongue. Her heart went out to her niece. Stephanie knew that she was different. She didn't have a home with a mother and father like her cousins, she lived with her gran and grandad and her mother in the farmhouse and she was looked after by Miriam until Ellen came home from work.

Miriam had a huge soft spot for her little niece and there were times when Julie Ann and her little digs made her palm itch to box her ears.

'Stop that bawling, Julie Ann,' Miriam said crossly, as she wiped her nose.

'She hit me.' Julie Ann wept.

'Why did you hit your cousin? I'm surprised at you, Stephanie,' Miriam rebuked. She had to be seen to be fair.

'She said things an' she's a liar. An' my mammy says she's a little greedy-guts 'cos Auntie Emma doesn't half feed her an' she's always stuffin' herself in Gran's pantry.' Stephanie glared at her cousin, wanting to hurt her the way she'd been hurt.

Julie Ann stopped in mid-howl. 'I'm *not* a greedy-guts, Stephanie Munroe. I'm straight telling my mummy what you said.'

'You can't. She's not here. She's on holidays!' Stephanie retorted triumphantly.

'Would the pair of you stop it this minute!' Miriam commanded. 'Stephanie, apologize to your cousin.'

'No,' Stephanie said defiantly.

'This minute.'

'No, it's not fair, Auntie Miriam. She started it.'

'Stephanie, you punched Julie Ann in the nose and made it bleed and you called her a greedy-guts, now say sorry.' Miriam was firm.

Stephanie dug her hands in her shorts pockets and shook her head. Her little face was red with emotion and her lower lip quivered.

'If you don't apologize, I'll have to send you to Rebecca's bedroom and you can't come out to play for the rest of the afternoon.'

Stephanie looked at her aunt, her big blue eyes two pools of hurt indignation and determination. Silently she shook her head.

'Go to Rebecca's room,' Miriam said quietly, feeling like a heel.

Stephanie gave her a look of deep reproach, but said

nothing. Her lip quivered even more but she wouldn't give Julie Ann the satisfaction of seeing her in tears. Stoically, she lifted her chin, cast a look of immense scorn at Julie Ann, and marched off towards the house.

'You started it, Julie Ann, and I mightn't let you come to *my* party either,' Rebecca burst out before loyally following her cousin into exile.

Julie Ann gazed at her cousins' retreating backs in consternation. She wanted to go to Rebecca's party next week. And she didn't want to be left in the garden on her own. Now she had no one to play with. Suddenly, going to the bedroom seemed a most attractive punishment.

'I think I'll go in too,' she decided.

'No, you can stay outside,' Miriam said calmly.

'But I've no one to play with.'

'Play with Daniel.'

'He's a *boy*!' Julie Ann said in disgust. 'I want to play with girls.'

'Well you've no one to play with now, because you started a fight. And I've told you before, Julie Ann, don't be making remarks about people.'

'Well Mummy said Auntie Ellen is a tramp,' Julie Ann said sulkily. 'I heard her saying it to Daddy.'

'Julie Ann!' Miriam exclaimed furiously. 'You shouldn't be listening to grown-ups talking. And you shouldn't talk about things you know nothing about.'

'I know what a tramp is! That man who comes and knocks on the door looking for jam jars and a cup of tea is a tramp,' Julie Ann retorted indignantly.

'Does Auntie Ellen go knocking on doors looking for jam jars and tea?'

'No.' Julie Ann pouted.

'Well then, that's enough of that nonsense and you can apologize to Stephanie too.'

'She didn't say sorry to me.'

'Oh for heaven's sake. I've had enough of the pair of you. Go and tidy up those toys for me and I'll go in and get the tea.' Miriam was at the end of her tether. Emma and

Vincent were due back at the weekend after two weeks abroad in the south of France and it couldn't come quickly enough.

Julie Ann was precocious and utterly spoilt. She always wanted to be the centre of attention. Miriam knew it wasn't the child's fault. Emma gave her everything she wanted in an effort to keep her distracted and out of her hair. Since she was a baby, Julie Ann had been looked after by whomever Emma employed from the town to take care of the house. Since she was born, there'd been five different housekeepers. Julie Ann took not the slightest notice of any of them and would throw ferocious tantrums if she didn't get her own way. The only people she knew would take no nonsense from her were her gran and Miriam.

Miriam sighed. Vincent and Emma were fools. Couldn't they see that the child *longed* for a bit of discipline and the security of a routine?

Julie Ann had been in bed at eight every night since she'd come to stay with Miriam two weeks ago. The first night, Julie Ann had calmly announced that she never went to bed before ten and she was allowed to watch TV.

'Goodnight, Rebecca,' she said smugly, assuming that she was going to be allowed to stay up.

Rebecca was horrified. Even Connie wasn't allowed to stay up that late. 'I want to stay up too.' She eyeballed Miriam, testing her. If Miriam allowed Julie Ann to stay up and didn't allow her own daughter to, that was disloyalty of the highest order.

'Julie Ann, when you are in this house, you obey the rules. Eight o'clock is bedtime for you and Rebecca. Now scat.'

Julie Ann's face darkened. 'Mummy said I could go to bed when I liked,' she challenged.

'Your mummy asked me to mind you for two weeks, and I hope you'll have fun with us, but it's time for bed now, lovie. So not another word. Off you pop. Rebecca, show Julie Ann where to put her toothbrush and tooth-paste and her facecloth and towel,' Miriam said cheerfully,

259

pretending not to notice her niece's outraged expression. For a moment Julie Ann looked as though she was going to argue but she decided against it and turned a sweet smile on her aunt.

'May I have a glass of orange juice, please,' she asked politely. 'My dad always gives me one.'

'I'm afraid I just have milk,' Miriam said firmly.

'I don't like milk.'

'Water then.'

Julie Ann wrinkled her pert little button nose, threw her eyes up to heaven, and said with resignation, 'It will have to do.' Her tone implied that her relations' standard of living left a lot to be desired. Miriam hadn't known whether to be angry or amused.

It was a long two weeks. Thank God it was almost over, Miriam reflected, as she watched Julie Ann swinging by herself on the old battered swing. A swing totally different from the state-of-the-art red and blue double one she had in her own back garden.

Julie Ann knew more than was good for her and was allowed to listen to adults' conversation at will, Miriam thought crossly as she whacked a fly away from her nose. Rebecca and Stephanie were much more childish in their ways than their sophisticated cousin. Yet, after a week in their company, Julie Ann played hopscotch and rounders and *O'Grady Says* . . . with gusto, forgetting her airs and graces and behaving much more like a child her age should. No doubt, as soon as Emma was home, she'd be back to her old precocious self again.

Emma was dreadfully irresponsible, to call Ellen a tramp in front of Julie Ann. Miriam scowled as she picked up crayons and colouring books that had been strewn on the lawn. There were times, though, that Ellen asked for it. Miriam sighed as she thought of her sister-in-law. In the last couple of years, Ellen had started drinking a lot more than she used to. She dated different men. Deserved or not, she was getting a name. People talked about her.

'For heaven's sake am I supposed to sit in purdah for the

rest of my life just because I made one mistake?' Ellen snapped when Miriam delicately broached the subject. 'It's all right for you. You've got a husband and a future. I've got nothing except living with a mother who hates me and a child I can't give all the things she deserves to have. I go out on Friday night. I try to forget the life that stretches out before me. If some man comes along and chats me up and I fancy him, don't expect me to turn down the chance of a kiss and a cuddle. I can pretend that someone wants me because I'm a sexy, desirable, interesting woman and not a flabby, boring, broke unmarried mother. Don't worry. I don't sleep with them. I learned my lesson with Chris.'

You wouldn't be so flabby if you stopped drinking pints of beer, Miriam was tempted to say, but she didn't. She understood Ellen's frustration and despair. But it annoyed her that Ellen was doing nothing to change her life. When her sister-in-law had asked her to mind Stephanie all those years ago, Miriam had assumed it would be a temporary measure, until Ellen left Glenree and got herself fixed up with a job and a place in Dublin. Little did she think that almost six years later, she'd still be minding Stephanie after school. And Ellen would still be working in her father's shop and living at home.

A fine one I am to talk about doing something positive, she thought dryly. Here she was, heading for forty, well thirty-seven, she amended hastily, and she still couldn't say no to people. When Emma had started dropping broad hints about how wonderful it would be to go on holidays to her friend's villa in the south of France, but that she didn't want Julie Ann to miss school, Miriam knew what was coming.

I'm saying no! she kept telling herself. I do *not* want to mind Julie Ann for two weeks. She kept repeating this to herself like a mantra. Yet, when Emma had come straight out and asked her, she'd cravenly said yes. Much to Ben's annoyance.

Miriam glanced in the direction of the bungalow. It

needed a good lick of paint. She wanted it painted before Rebecca's birthday party next week. It looked shabby and unkept compared to Emma and Vincent's mansion. The house was getting on her nerves and it was long overdue some decoration.

Earlier this summer, Emma had decorators in to paper and paint their entire house to give it a new look. Miriam wanted a whole new look too, she thought crankily. But she had a snowball's chance in hell of getting it.

'Is tea ready yet? I'm starving.' Daniel swerved down the slope of the lawn on his scooter. It seemed to Miriam that she'd only just washed up after the lunch.

'No it's not ready,' she snapped. 'And did you tidy your football gear out of the hall?'

'I'm going to do it now,' Daniel said nonchalantly. He was just like his father for putting things off, Miriam thought. Sometimes she felt Ellen was mad to want to tie herself to a man for the rest of her life. She had it good in some ways. Sheila cooked for her. Mick provided for her. Stephanie was a good child. At least Ellen didn't have three of them constantly demanding food and attention.

She looked at Daniel, scooting back up the hill, and her irritation faded. At least they weren't faddy eaters, she thought wryly. She'd make egg and onion sandwiches and suggest a picnic out on the lawn. That would go down a treat with the kids, they loved eating outside.

The late afternoon sun shone through a heat haze. They were having an Indian summer. The sound of a tractor droned in the distance as it harvested corn. The smell of freshly cut hay and grass mingled with the scents of roses and stock. The birds filled the air with their song. Bees droned lazily by, replete with nectar. An afternoon for lazing. Maybe she'd bring out her rug and lie in the sun for a while after she'd made the tea. She had a million and one things to do. Cover new school-books in crisp brown paper, darn socks, iron shirts, bake bread, make a tart for Sheila's Bring and Buy Sale. Miriam thought enviously of Emma, enjoying a holiday in the South of

France. What she wouldn't give to change places with her.

* * *

Emma wiped the perspiration from her forehead with her wristband and prepared to serve for what she hoped would be the final game, in a strenuous tennis match. She and Vincent were playing a game of mixed doubles with Gillian and Frank. Emma was bent on beating them. It was a closely fought match. Each side determined to win. Honour was at stake. The rivalry which had always underlain their friendship bubbled close to the surface. Emma positioned herself behind the baseline, bounced the ball twice, and threw it in the air. She walloped it viciously towards Gillian. She was a better player than Gillian, Emma thought with satisfaction as her friend tried to return the shot and landed it into the net.

'Shit,' Gillian growned.

'Fifteen love,' called Lorna Mitchell who was acting as umpire.

'That language wouldn't be allowed in Wimbledon,' sniggered Declan, her husband, who was sprawled on the sidelines lowering Pimm's with gusto.

Emma flashed a looked of triumph at Vincent and he grinned back at her. 'Good shot,' he murmured. Emma positioned herself to serve again. Frank was a tougher opponent than Gillian and a fast and furious volley ensued. This time it was Emma who lost the point, hitting the ball long.

'Fifteen all,' drawled Lorna who didn't care who won. Gillian and Emma had both got up her nose with their fierce competitiveness as they pranced and preened in their whites. Every time they played a game of tennis they each appeared on court in a different outfit. Lorna'd only bought the one white skirt and top and she was feeling somewhat inadequate. Today Emma was wearing a white tennis skirt with delicate scalloped pink edging, that matched the pink fringing the cuffs and neckline of her white shirt. It was, Lorna noted with envy, a Lacoste.

Emma was furious with herself. The first serve she'd played to Gillian had bounced off the top of the net. She aced her second serve right down the line. Gillian hardly saw it coming.

'Thirty fifteen.' Lorna wished they'd hurry up and get it over with.

'*Concentrate*, Gillian,' Frank gritted.

Gillian glared at him. 'Shut up,' she muttered, furious. It was bad enough losing without him showing her up.

'Keep your eye on the ball,' Frank hissed.

'Frank, piss off!' Gillian had had enough.

Emma noted her opponents' altercation with satisfaction. Nothing like getting the opposition rattled. Vincent would never put Emma under pressure when they played tennis. Frank was an asshole, Emma thought scornfully. Gillian had lost her concentration completely. Emma played her famous double-handed backhand to Gillian and almost felt sorry for the other girl as she returned the shot high over their heads and it landed a good two feet out.

'Forty fifteen,' Lorna said crisply.

Frank glared at his wife.

Vincent smiled at his.

Declan drained the last of the Pimm's and went off to replenish the jug, and have a shot of whiskey at the same time. Pimm's was all very well for cooling one down, but it didn't have the kick of a good slug of whiskey.

Lorna watched him go from her elevated position in the umpire's chair and bit her lip. Declan was well smashed, as he had been every day of their holidays. It was only half five, they were going out to dinner later and there'd be a lot more drinking before the evening was out. She felt like crying. Trust him to make a show of her. Vincent and Frank never let Emma and Gillian down the way Declan let her down.

Emma served again and watched as Gillian shot a weak

return to Vincent who aimed it skilfully along the tram-lines. Frank played a superb backhand and made the point.

'Forty thirty,' Lorna called glumly.

Emma stood poised and in control as she prepared to serve to Frank. She wanted to win this point against her friend's husband, so that he couldn't say she'd played all her shots to the weaker partner.

She took a deep breath, stared at Frank who crouched like a great hulking bear. She threw the ball high, watched it like a hawk and then, with all her might, hit it as hard and as accurately as she could. Long years of practice and skill paid off. If there was one thing she was good at, it was tennis, Emma reflected with colossal satisfaction as she watched her ace, as neat and sharp as any Billie Jean King ever served.

'Game, set and match.' Lorna's relief was palpable as she vacated the chair and none too politely grabbed the full jug of Pimm's from Declan who was weaving his way back to the group.

'Drink, Emma, Gillian?'

'Love one,' declared Emma, flinging herself onto a lounger. It had been a tough match but she could relax in the knowledge that their honour was secure. She sipped the ice-cold drink gratefully. The heat of the sun had died away and a sea breeze lifted damp strands of hair from her forehead. Emma lay back against the cushions and felt herself relax. Between the luscious bougainvillaea, mimosa and jacaranda shrubs, heavy with scarlet, purple and yellow blossoms, she admired the brilliant sapphire of the Mediterranean. In the hills below, nestled between pine and cypress trees, she could see the orange-tiled roofs of whitewashed villas. The winding road curved like a sleek ribbon down towards Cannes. The air was heavy with the scent of flowers, and the rhythmic click, click of the sprinklers which kept the lawns verdant lulled her to drowsiness. Emma wished this holiday could go on for ever.

When Lorna and Declan had told her and Vincent that a

travel agent friend of theirs was offering them a villa in the south of France, off season, at a very good rate – were they interested in sharing? Emma jumped at the idea.

'Just one proviso,' Lorna said firmly. 'No kids.'

'Perfect,' Emma agreed happily.

'I don't know,' Vincent demurred. 'Two weeks is a long time to ask anyone to look after Julie Ann.'

'Miriam will do it, she won't mind. Come on, Vincent, it'll be like a second honeymoon,' she'd wheedled.

It had taken a lot of wheedling to get him to agree. They had, after all, been to Switzerland *en famille* for three weeks. It wasn't as if they hadn't had a foreign holiday. She'd had to really rub it in about how Julie Ann loved being with her cousins and about how good the company was for her. Reluctantly, he'd agreed. Vincent didn't like taking advantage of Miriam. And he knew Emma was inclined to take her sister-in-law's good nature for granted. In the end, he'd been persuaded and, once he'd actually got to the villa, he'd relaxed and forgotten all about home. They'd enjoyed themselves immensely.

Emma sighed as the breeze rippled along her arms and legs. A delicious lethargy enveloped her as the gentle rays of the late evening sun tanned her golden. Her colour had come up a treat. Honey gold. Gillian, who had red hair and freckles and only succeeded in turning lobster, was pea-green with envy.

Emma opened one eye and saw Vincent and Frank chatting by the pool. Declan was snoring loudly on the grass. Lorna, looking unhappy, was varnishing her nails. Gillian had gone to change for a swim. Emma yawned and closed her eye again. This was her favourite time of the day. The time for recharging her batteries before the excesses of the night.

The two weeks had sped by in the blink of an eye, she mused regretfully. It was depressing even to think about it. She was looking forward to seeing Julie Ann, of course, but, if she was offered another two weeks in this paradise, she'd have no hesitation in accepting. It was complete and utter bliss. Lorna had been right to insist on not bringing the children. Having a child dragging out of you all day was so *exhausting*. Gillian had phoned home, sometimes twice a day, to check on her two. Emma thought she was mad. She had great faith in Miriam and knew Julie Ann was in safe hands. It was Rebecca's birthday next week, she'd buy her niece something nice in Monaco to show her appreciation. Miriam wouldn't thank her if she phoned home every day. Emma had only phoned twice. What was the point in going on holiday if you spent most of it phoning home? Moments later, Emma was snoring softly, deliciously worn out after her Herculean efforts on the tennis court.

*   *   *

Julie Ann felt very lonely as she sat by herself swinging on Rebecca's bockety old swing. Her two cousins weren't speaking to her and were playing in Rebecca's bedroom. Auntie Miriam was cross with her. She wished she was at home in her own house with her mummy and daddy. She missed them enormously. It was always the same. They went away and left her at Auntie Miriam's while they had fun without her.

A tear trickled down Julie Ann's cheek. Her mummy and daddy were always telling her she was the best, the prettiest, the cleverest girl in the whole wide world. If that was so, why couldn't she go on holiday with them? She'd really really wanted to go. She would have missed school. She'd have been able to show off in front of the whole class when she came home. Julie Ann loved showing off. She loved when the other girls in her class admired her. She had more friends in the whole school than anyone else. Everyone wanted to come to her birthday party. She always had a clown and a magician at her party. And loads of food. Not like Stephanie's silly old party. All you got there was banana sandwiches and jelly and ice cream and some toffee sweets. She didn't even want to go to Stephanie Munroe's stupid little party. So there!

267

She glowered in the direction of the bungalow. She could hear giggles coming from the bedroom. Stephanie's mummy had no money and *her* mummy and daddy were very rich. Auntie Ellen couldn't afford to buy brilliant birthday presents like the ones she got. This year she was getting a Sindy doll *and* a pair of roller skates for her birthday. Stephanie would probably only get a boring old teaset.

Julie Ann pushed herself forwards on the swing. It always made her feel much better to think of how rich she was. She was the richest girl in the school. She stuck her tongue out as far as it could go as she caught sight of Rebecca and Stephanie looking out of the window at her. See if she cared about them. Her mummy was the best mummy in the world. Not like strict old Auntie Miriam, and cross old Auntie Ellen, who had no house of her own and was very poor.

*   *   *

Ellen was gasping for a cigarette, but the shop was busy and she was behind with her accounts. She'd had to help out at the counter because Eamonn, the assistant, had gone home sick and her father had gone to the cattle market to sell some of his prize heifers.

She chewed the top of her pen, trying to remember whether Mrs Fleming had bought five shillings' worth of meat or seven shillings' worth. The thought of re-counting the cash to make sure gave her a headache.

The sun shone in on top of her making her feel hot and bothered. She wanted to lay her head on her arms and snooze. It didn't help that she had the remnants of a fierce hangover.

Ellen felt a surge of irritation as another customer arrived and handed her a ten-shilling note. Coming up to the weekend was always busy, but today seemed exceptionally so. She handed the woman back her change and knocked a pile of coins onto the floor. 'God Almighty!' she muttered in annoyance as she bent down to retrieve them. A sharp pain darted through her head. 'Oooh,' she groaned. 'Never again!' She was going on the dry. She was never drinking again.

What on earth had possessed her to go into Dublin on a pub crawl with Carol Allen? Because you're a fool, she thought in self-disgust. Carol Allen was an old school friend who'd married and gone to England with her husband, several years ago. She'd come home alone, to visit her elderly mother. When she'd suggested going for a drink, Ellen immediately agreed.

They could have gone to the Glenree Arms, or even Kirwan's pub, but Ellen casually suggested that they go into Dublin. Carol had no objections. All she wanted was a chat and a night out. She didn't mind where.

Ellen had taken great care with her appearance that night. She'd got her hair done at her lunch break, she wore a gold cheesecloth top with a fringed black Indian skirt and she'd spent ages applying kohl pencil around her eyes. She'd dusted Dusky Sienna rouge over her tanned cheekbones and tried out her new Tangerine Tease lipstick.

'You're dolled up to the nines.' Sheila sniffed. 'I hope you won't be in too late in case Stephanie is looking for you.'

Ellen bit back her irritation. Her mother always had to make a comment. Sheila was an expert at making Ellen feel under a compliment.

'We're just going to the pictures,' Ellen fibbed. Going to the pictures sounded much more innocuous than going for a drink. 'Carol hasn't been in Dublin for years.' It was crazy being made to feel like a fifteen-year-old when she was practically *middle-aged*. Sometimes Ellen felt like screaming her head off with rage and frustration.

'Huh.' Sheila gave one of her unimpressed snorts. 'She came to visit her mother. You'd think she'd spend a bit of time with her instead of gadding about.' *With you* was left unsaid, but the implication was unmistakable. There were times when Ellen hated her mother and this was one of them. She knew, if she let fly, Sheila would launch into a tirade about being left to look after Stephanie, and say that Ellen was a neglectful mother, that she and Mick weren't a babysitting service. Ellen struggled to keep her temper under control. It wasn't worth losing it because, in the end, she was always the loser. She was an unmarried mother, dependent on her parents for a roof over her head and a steady job. She often longed to tell Sheila to stuff it. But she had Stephanie to think of and that would always keep her Sheila's hostage.

'I won't be too late,' she said tightly and went upstairs to kiss Stephanie goodnight. Her daughter was sitting in bed, her long dark hair framing her face like a silky curtain as she bent her head over her colouring book in intense concentration.

'Look Mammy!' She proudly held up the book to show the picture of Cinderella. 'See, I didn't go outside the lines once.'

'You're brilliant,' Ellen encouraged, smiling down into the innocent, trusting bright blue eyes raised to hers. A pain like a needle in her heart, sharp, intense, unexpected, made Ellen catch her breath. Stephanie's eyes were so like Chris's. Even after all these years, she could still picture them so vividly.

She could go for months and never think about him, and then he would come into her mind, or she'd hear some snippet of news about him from Miriam that Emma had let drop, and she'd be as bad as ever, thinking about him, longing for him, wanting to know everything about him.

She hadn't heard from him in all those years, although she was sure that Pamela must have told him that he was the father of a little girl. He had two children of his own now. Did he ever even think about the child he'd abandoned? Ellen wondered bitterly. She kissed Stephanie and hugged her tightly.

'You look nice, Mammy,' Stephanie declared. Ellen caught sight of herself in the mirror. Her make-up was fine, if a bit overdone around the eyes, but there was no disguising her thick waist in spite of the loose cheesecloth top she wore. It was utterly depressing. What was the point in dressing up like the Queen of Sheba when she felt like an elephant? Suddenly, going to Dublin with Carol didn't seem such a great idea. Because, deep down, Ellen knew that the only reason she'd suggested going to Dublin was so that she could visit all Chris's old haunts in the hope of seeing him.

When she'd made the suggestion, she'd been in one of her Chris madnesses, as she called those little episodes when she started thinking about him. They happened now and again in spite of her best intentions. Then all her fantasies revolved around him seeing her looking glamorous and gorgeous. He'd fall head over heels in love with her again, leave Suzy and he, Ellen and Stephanie would live happily ever after.

This fantasy never changed. Sometimes, the place of their heart-stopping encounter differed. The outfit she wore at their reunion, the silky sexy nightdress and negligee she wore for their first night of passion after so long, changed according to her mood or the current fashion but the essence of the dream never varied or wavered.

She saw other men, men who sometimes thought they were on to a good thing because she was unmarried and had a past, and was, in their view, desperate for a man. None of them had ever made her feel the way Chris had. and in a way she hadn't wanted any of them to. It would have diminished the great love affair of her life, she thought, a little dramatically.

Ellen looked at her sideways reflection in the chipped and stained wardrobe mirror. She was wearing espadrilles; maybe if she wore her tart's trotters she'd look taller and give the impression of being slimmer than she was. Regretfully, she eased her feet out of her espadrilles. They were like gloves, they were so comfortable. She rooted in the bottom of the wardrobe under a miscellany of shoes, sandals, bags and bric-à-brac. She was definitely going to clean out her wardrobe, she promised herself as she found one patent high-heeled sandal but couldn't find the other. Eventually, hot, dishevelled and steaming with impatience, she found the other shoe hidden under an old bag beneath the bed. She repaired the damage to her hair and make-up, kissed Stephanie once more, and warned her to be good for Sheila.

Going to visit Chris's haunts was extremely stressful. Every time the door of the lounge opened, Ellen tensed as hope and anticipation turned to disappointment and despair. It was hard to concentrate on Carol rabbiting on about things which Ellen hadn't the slightest bit of interest in, when every fibre of her being willed Chris Wallace to walk through the door.

By the time they got to the Intercontinental and she'd quickly scanned the bar and seen that he wasn't there, Ellen had had enough. She proceeded to get thoroughly drunk. Throwing caution to the winds, she agreed to Carol's suggestion to go night-clubbing in Leeson Street. After consuming several bottles of plonk, provided by a ruddy-faced businessman, who perspired profusely as he bopped with enthusiasm, if not grace, around the postage-stamp dance floor, Ellen ended up in the loo, puking miserably.

Carol, wild as ever, husband and three children in England forgotten, got off with a travelling salesman and went to spend the night in his hotel. She'd always been a good-time girl. She'd slept with *loads* of men, but she'd never got caught, Ellen thought jealously as she watched her friend weave her way across the dance floor with the tall skinny man in the ill-fitting suit. It was typical of Carol to do the hot potato act. She'd always been like that, only Ellen had forgotten.

Her feet, in the black patent sandals, were absolutely killing her as she made her way to the taxi rank. Please let there be one there, and no queue, she prayed as she clattered along. If she made it home without puking all over the back seat, she'd be lucky, she thought queasily.

Ellen was raging that she'd to pay for the taxi home, by herself, with money that she could ill afford. To add insult to injury, she woke Stephanie as she got into the big double bed beside her.

'You don't smell very nice, Mammy,' Stephanie said in her usual frank way as Ellen went to put her arms around her. 'You have that funny smell out of your mouth.' Ellen knew she reeked of alcohol. She felt a wave of nausea and self-disgust.

'Go to sleep, Stephanie,' she slurred and passed out.

Getting up for work and getting Stephanie ready for school the following morning was a nightmare, especially as Sheila nagged incessantly about the hour of the night Ellen had got in at. It was a relief to get to work. But they were short-staffed and she was snowed under with work. Now she was flinging money right, left and centre, she thought, disgruntled as more coins cascaded to the floor.

Slowly, painfully, Ellen stood up and put the fallen coins back on her cash desk. The phone rang, jarring every nerve end. 'Oh, piss off,' she muttered as she snatched up the receiver. 'Hello, Munroes.'

'Is your father back yet?' Sheila's frosty tones sliced down the line.

'No.' Ellen was equally curt.

'Have you any idea what time he's going to be back?'

'I'd say he's probably gone for a few jars. It *is* market day.'

'There's a pair of you in it, can't do anything without alcohol inside you,' Sheila said sarcastically.

'Oh for God's sake, Ma, don't be ridiculous!' Ellen exploded. 'The way you talk you'd think Da was a hardened alcoholic. You know very well he always has a drink on market day.'

'I beg your pardon, Miss. The cheek of you. I'll tell you one thing though. *You'd* want to watch yourself and the way you're drinking. Don't think I don't know that you come into this house maggoty drunk after your nights out. You should be ashamed of yourself. You're a disgrace, making a show of me and your father, not to talk about Stephanie. I pity that poor child from the bottom of my heart. A fine example you're setting her,' Sheila ripped.

'You mind your own bloody business, Ma. I'm sick, sick, sick of you interfering in my life. I'm thirty-five for Christ's sake. Would you leave me alone? And don't you dare talk to me about Stephanie. She's getting a hell of a lot more love and affection from me than I ever got from you, so shag off.' Incandescent with rage, Ellen slammed down the phone.

Was it ever going to end? Was she to be trapped in this living hell for the rest of her life? It was a nightmare living at home, constantly having to bite her tongue. She hated having to curb Stephanie's childish exuberance. She was always on edge in case Stephanie would break one of Sheila's ornaments that cluttered up every nook and cranny in the house. Sheila was very strict with her granddaughter and it grated on Ellen's nerves to listen to her mother chastising her daughter.

It couldn't go on. She was desperate. If she had to stay at home for much longer, she'd crack up and go mad. Ellen sank her head in her hands. She wanted to bawl her eyes out. There was only one thing she could do. It was something she'd been thinking about for ages. She'd saved as much as she could over the years. She had a few thousand put by. She was going to ask her parents to give her a site so she could build a small house on it. After all, she reasoned, they'd given Vincent and Ben sites, surely she was entitled to one as well.

How wonderful it would be to have a little house of her own, where she'd be her own boss. She'd be able to have friends stay over. She might even get into a proper relationship with someone and be able to conduct it in peace and privacy away from her mother's prying judgemental eyes. If she didn't do something about her situation now, she'd never do it. She owed it to Stephanie.

Ellen rooted in her bag for her cigarettes and lit up. There was no-one in the shop, she might as well make the most of it. Although her father would blow a gasket if he knew she smoked in the shop. Hygiene was of the utmost importance. Well she wasn't at the meat counter, she comforted herself. She was in her little cubby-hole. She pulled the smoke deep into her lungs. Bliss. What was it about cigarettes that was so comforting? Ellen puffed away, and felt herself relax a little. She wouldn't broach the subject of the site tonight. No doubt her mother would tell Mick how disrespectful Ellen had been to her on the phone. If there was one thing Mick hated it was rows.

She'd lie low and wait until this contretemps had blown over, then she'd speak to her father about the site. Maybe after Rebecca's party next week. Mick and Sheila would be in good humour. They always were after family get-togethers. Ellen would be as nice as pie to everyone. She'd even suffer Vincent and Emma and her snooty ways and try and refrain from making any sarcastic comments.

Please, please, please let them agree, Ellen beseeched the Almighty as she stubbed out her cigarette just as Agnes Whelan, the parish priest's housekeeper, arrived to buy her Sunday roast. She gave the elderly woman a particularly choice centre cut. Maybe Agnes would include her in her prayers. She was going to need all the prayers she could get between now and Rebecca's party. Ellen toyed with the idea of phoning her mother back to apologize. Sheila might very well hang up on her and where would that leave her? No, it was too late for apologies now. Ellen would just have to ride out the row, she decided, and hope that her mother would be as anxious to see the back of her as Ellen was anxious to go.

*   *   *

Sheila scrubbed her baking trays with angry vigour. 'Shag off,' Ellen had said to her before slamming down the phone. '*Shag off!*' Imagine saying such a thing to your mother! Sheila shook her head in disbelief. After all she'd

275

done for her. Had Ellen ever shown one ounce of gratitude for what she and Mick had done for her and Stephanie? She had not, Sheila thought indignantly. All she did was cause worry and strife in the family.

She'd had exactly the same upbringing as her two brothers and they had turned out to be fine upstanding adults. How dare Ellen say she had never received love and affection. She and Mick had been more supportive than a lot of parents when she'd announced, quite shamelessly, that she was pregnant. They could have turned her out of the house and let her fend for herself. It was most vexing. She and Mick should be enjoying life, having reared their children to the best of their abilities, without having to put up with Ellen and her shenanigans. And it was hard having a lively young child around the house. Sheila just didn't have the *energy* any more.

It was difficult, too, not to interfere in her granddaughter's rearing. Ellen was so lax with Stephanie. A child needed guidance and discipline. Not that she was that bold, Sheila thought fondly. She was a good-natured little girl, the apple of Mick's eye. He was besotted with her. Although time and love for her granddaughter had eased the shame she felt over Ellen's disgrace, Sheila still felt the stigma Stephanie's birth had cast upon the family, especially when she was in Bonnie Daly's company.

Bonnie had tried to be friends many times. But Sheila treated her with brisk disdain. Almost as though she didn't exist. This really got to Bonnie, much to Sheila's satisfaction. She was always coolly polite when she discussed guild business with Bonnie, but there was no intimacy like the old days. Although Bonnie tried her best to ingratiate her way back into Sheila's good books and to resurrect the old closeness, it was to no avail. Sheila would never forgive or forget.

She sighed as she scrubbed a particularly stubborn stain. The jam had run out of her jam tarts and made a right treacly mess. Bonnie always made better jam tarts than she did, Sheila conceded. She had a lighter touch with the sponge cakes though. Bonnie had always admired her sponges. Deep down, she missed their friendship. She and Bonnie had had a lot in common. They'd confided in each other and helped each other out in times of need. Because of Ellen, that comfort was lost to her. God had obviously decided that Sheila should have some burdens to carry. Ellen was going to be a worry for the rest of Sheila's life. It looked as though she was never going to find a good man and settle down. Ellen was her burden and with the grace of God she'd bear it, she thought stoically as she dried her hands and took out her sewing basket to begin tacking the dress she was making for Rebecca's birthday present.

Chapter Fifteen

Miriam smiled as she watched Ben chase Daniel across the lawn. Her son squealed with delight as his father threw an armful of newly mown grass over him. Ben had just finished cutting the grass in preparation for Rebecca's birthday party later in the afternoon. He'd whitewashed the house and painted the window sills, fascia board and doors in Alpine blue. It looked very pretty, almost Grecian.

Miriam was delighted with it. She'd been so pleased, she'd painted the trellises and the big tubs that held masses of geraniums, petunias, busy lizzies and scented stock, the same blue. Now that the place looked presentable, she was quite looking forward to Rebecca's party.

Because the day was so fine she was going to have a buffet outdoors. They'd been blessed with the weather. The intense heat of summer was gone but it was still warm. A gentle breeze rippled through the sweet pea that tumbled down from the freshly painted trellises. Across the fields she could see neat bales of yellow hay. Down by the river a crop of late potatoes waited to be harvested, their white flowering heads like buds of cotton wool atop green velvet. Miriam loved harvest time. She enjoyed making her jams and chutneys, drying out her onions and boiling her beetroot. It gave her tremendous satisfaction to fill her pantry with the fruits of her labour.

'Hi.' Ellen popped her head around the kitchen door, much to Miriam's surprise. She wasn't expecting her sister-in-law so early.

'I brought the cake. Stephanie and I are just on our way

home from town.' Ellen produced a white box tied with green ribbon. 'I got it in the Kylemore.'

'Ah, Ellen. You shouldn't have gone to all that trouble. A cake from Kelly's would have done fine.' Miriam wiped her hands in her apron and untied the ribbon.

'A godmother has to do her duty.' Ellen grinned.

'It's lovely!' Miriam exclaimed as she surveyed the gooey creation with *Happy Birthday Rebecca* iced in large pink letters on a bed of white icing decorated with pink rosebuds. 'She'll be mad about that. But honestly, there was no need.'

'I wanted to get her something special. And anyway I wanted to buy Stephanie a new dress for the party. You know the way little girls are about dressing up.'

'Hmm. Emma told me she'd bought Julie Ann a French costume for the party.'

Ellen threw her eyes up to heaven. 'She would. She couldn't even let Rebecca have her hour of glory without letting Julie Ann take centre stage.'

'That's Emma for you,' Miriam said dryly. The years had not lessened the antagonism between her two sisters-in-law but she always tried to stay out of it. 'She looks a million dollars after the holiday.'

'Why wouldn't she, with not a care in the world?'

'Just do me a favour and try and be nice for the afternoon. She'll be here around three.'

'Is she coming on her broomstick?' Ellen couldn't help herself.

'*Ellen!*' Miriam giggled.

'Sorry. I'm off. I'll come over a bit early to give you a hand.'

'Thanks. I'm setting up the table outside. It would be a shame to be stuck indoors on such a lovely day.'

'Good thinking. See you later.' Ellen picked up her shopping, called to Stephanie who was playing on the swing with Rebecca and Connie, and headed towards home. Miriam watched her through the window. Ellen seemed to be in very good form today. It was nice to see the old bubbly sparkle. She had a lot to put up with living under Sheila's roof.

*　　*　　*

Ellen strode jauntily past Blackbird's Field with Stephanie skipping along beside her.

'Mammy, can we pick blackberries?' Stephanie stopped beside a branch laden with fat, luscious, juicy berries.

'We haven't time, pet. We've to go home and get changed and have a bite to eat. And I promised Auntie Miriam I'd help her get the party ready. Maybe on the way home.'

'OK,' Stephanie said cheerfully.

Ellen smiled as she watched her daughter hop and skip along ahead of her, her black pigtails swinging. Stephanie was bursting with energy, she couldn't stay still for a minute. She was such a good little girl too, Ellen thought tenderly. Stephanie was very affectionate and good-natured. Often she'd hug Ellen for no reason, as if she understood that there was a sadness in her life that other mothers didn't have. If it hadn't been for Stephanie, Ellen didn't know what would have become of her. She might have gone off the rails altogether.

Today for some reason she felt very optimistic. She was certain Sheila and Mick would give her a site. She'd been planning her new bungalow. Not a big one. A two-bedroom dormer type. Ellen loved dormer bungalows with their cute little bedroom windows. She'd seen beautiful wallpaper in Dublin. A pink stripe edged with blue that would look absolutely gorgeous in her bedroom. She'd have dusky pink curtains with blue tie-backs and a pelmet.

Maybe by this time next year she'd be in her own house. And Stephanie would have a home of her own. Excitement bubbled. She'd have a house-warming party. And because she was feeling magnanimous, she might even invite Emma. She smiled as she turned into the gateway of the farmhouse.

*   *   *

Emma sat on the edge of the bed. She felt most peculiar. Her head felt light. Gingerly she lay back against the pillows. The room spun. What the hell was wrong with her? She hadn't been feeling great since she'd come back from the south of France. She hoped she hadn't picked up a bug.

'Mummy, is it time to go to the party yet?' Julie Ann raced into the bedroom and repeated the question she'd asked a thousand times already.

'Julie Ann, will you calm down! I've told you I'll tell you when it's time to go,' Emma snapped. 'Go and play in your room until I call you, please.'

'But I want to go to the party.' Julie Ann pouted. 'It's not fair. I don't want to play in my room. I want to go and play with Rebecca and Stephanie.'

'If I have to speak to you again you won't go to the party,' Emma gritted. Julie Ann had got very bold. She'd really been misbehaving since they'd come back from holidays. And she was so clingy. How Emma wished Vincent was at home to handle things. But he'd gone in to work, even though it was a Saturday. He'd a lot to catch up on.

'I hate you,' Julie Ann screamed. 'You're a mean mummy.'

'And you're a very bold girl. Wait until I tell Daddy when he gets home.'

'Don't care.' Julie Ann stuck out her tongue and marched from the bedroom.

'Oh Lord.' Emma sighed. She wasn't able for her daughter's tantrums. And the thought of going to a party full of yelling kids made her heart sink. She was sorely tempted to phone Miriam and tell her she was sick. She wouldn't be telling fibs either, she thought disconsolately. She felt grotty. Perhaps she could bring Julie Ann over to the party, stay for ten minutes or so, plead a migraine and go home to bed in peace and quiet. Julie Ann would be out of her hair and she could snooze until Vincent came home. He could go and collect her from Miriam's.

Emma closed her eyes and took some deep breaths. It helped a little.

*　　*　　*

'If I were you I'd put napkins down the front of all their clothes or they'll be ruined,' Sheila declared as she cut the top off the buns she'd brought to Miriam's and piped them with cream before adding the halved tops, shaped like butterfly wings.

'Ah they'll be fine,' Ellen declared as she spooned red and green jelly into little dishes.

'I wasn't speaking to you. I was speaking to Miriam,' Sheila retorted coldly.

Ellen sighed. Sheila had been very cool since Ellen had told her to shag off. It was most frustrating. She needed her mother to be in a good humour when she asked about the site. But all her overtures had been ignored.

Miriam kept her head bent as she tucked the candles into candleholders and stuck them in the icing. She wasn't getting involved in an argument with that pair. It was very annoying though. Why couldn't they go and argue at home? They'd better not ruin Rebecca's birthday party.

'Your fairy cakes look lovely,' she said placatingly, hoping to diffuse the situation.

'Thank you, dear.' Sheila smiled. She was always susceptible to flattery.

'I think we're nearly ready. I won't bring the food out until nearer teatime. If Julie Ann was here we could start the musical chairs,' Miriam mused.

'It's after three. Do you want me to phone and see what's delaying them?' Sheila asked. Typical of Emma. Sheila always liked getting one up on her daughter-in-law. She might be a judge's daughter, but her manners left a lot to be desired. Her family might have money but they had no class. Just look at that Wallace person. Sheila's nostrils flared with distaste at the thought of *him*.

Miriam knew exactly what was in Sheila's mind. She'd seen her trying to deflate Emma often enough. But it never worked because Emma never realized her mother-in-law was trying to score imaginary points. Emma just blanked Sheila out. Something Miriam found impossible to do.

She heard the sound of a car engine. 'Here they are,' she said with false gaiety. She should have known better. She should have just had a family party for Rebecca. There'd be a row before the evening was over. She knew it. But it was impossible to have a family party. Emma and Vincent always threw lavish parties for Julie Ann who, needless to say, boasted about them incessantly. Although she and Ellen knew they couldn't compete, they felt obliged to hold parties of their own so that the children wouldn't feel deprived.

Miriam wasn't competitive by nature but she knew Connie, Daniel and Rebecca wanted to be able to invite Julie Ann to *their* parties so that she could see the fuss that was made of *them*. It was a problem that was getting worse as the children got older. She was dreading Julie Ann's Holy Communion. Emma would go all out to impress.

'Sorry I'm late. I wasn't feeling very well.' Emma breezed in through the back door. She was feeling slightly better. The dizziness had passed and she was actually feeling a little peckish because she hadn't bothered to eat anything at home. She was looking forward to a nice cup of coffee and whatever Miriam had for tea.

'We thought something might have happened. We were a bit worried. It's gone three,' Sheila said sweetly but pointedly.

'Oh hello, Mrs Munroe.' Emma ignored her remarks and peered out through the window.

'My God! How many kids are out there?' The cacophony of yells and screeches was almost deafening as

283

they played *Blind Man's Buff* with Mick and Ben. Maybe she wouldn't stay for tea after all, Emma decided hastily.

'Where's Julie Ann?' Miriam asked.

'Oh she didn't have time to come in and say hello. She's gone straight around the back to play. She's had me pestered all day to come.' Emma perched on a stool and crossed one slim tanned leg over the other. She was wearing white shorts and a black halter-neck top. Her dark hair was tied up in a ponytail making her look like an eighteen-year-old and not a woman in her late twenties. She looked stunning.

Ellen studied her with deep envy. She'd give *anything* to look like Emma. She looked ultra-classy. As if she'd stepped out of a glossy magazine. Her clothes shrieked money. The simple gold chain around her neck, and the gold bangle on her wrist, so elegantly understated, emphasized the golden even tan from her recent holiday. She hadn't an ounce of flab. Ellen felt depressed. She was wearing a denim skirt that she was bet into and a loose pink cotton top. She was definitely starting a diet, she swore. She was going to have a new figure to go with her new house. The thought cheered her up slightly as she surreptitiously put the fairy cake she'd been about to scoff back on the plate.

'What was wrong with you anyway?' Sheila asked peevishly.

'I felt very dizzy and peculiar.' Emma lit a cigarette and inhaled deeply. Miriam wished she wouldn't smoke in the kitchen but didn't like to say so.

'You wouldn't be . . . you know . . . in the family way?' Sheila suggested delicately.

'God, no! I'd hang myself.' Emma was horrified.

Sheila pursed her lips. That was no way to be talking. If you were married a child was a gift from God. The least Emma could do was give poor Vincent a son. She had life far too easy, Sheila thought, but of course she'd never say so to Vincent or he'd bite the nose off her. He was very protective of his wife.

'Maybe it's just a bug or something,' Ellen remarked.

'Probably,' Emma agreed. She eyed her sister-in-law up and down. That denim skirt Ellen was wearing did nothing for her. It was far too tight. You'd think she'd make a bit of an effort so that she could go and get a man to marry her. For Stephanie's sake if not for her own. Stephanie was a lovely little child, she had to admit. Ellen was doing a good job bringing her up. She glanced out through the window and saw Julie Ann twirling around in her full frilly skirt in front of an admiring audience. Emma had warned her not to throw a trantrum but Julie Ann could be so naughty sometimes. It was mortifying in company.

'Let's go out and get the party under way,' Miriam suggested. She led the way out into the back garden.

'Mammy, Mammy, look what Julie Ann gave me for my birthday.' Rebecca came racing over waving a Marie Antoinette doll complete with lacy fan.

'It's beautiful. Say thank you to Auntie Emma.'

'Thank you, Auntie Emma.' Rebecca beamed. 'Mammy, can we play musical chairs?'

'Yes, go and get the others to help bring out the kitchen chairs and bring out the three pouffes from the sitting-room.'

Cheers greeted this and there was a wild gallop from the assembled children, all eager to get the games under way.

'Right, Ben. Get your guitar.' Miriam grinned.

'I'll play the music but you can referee any arguments. I'm not getting involved,' Ben said firmly. 'Pa, I'm going to pour you a nice cool beer. I think you deserve it. You go and sit in the shade for a while and watch the shenanigans. I'm telling you World War Two will have nothing on this by the time it's over.'

'Stop that, Ben.' Miriam laughed.

'You know what kids' parties are like. Don't expect civilized behaviour from this gang.'

By the time the chairs were arranged in a circle the children were as highly strung as racehorses under starter's orders.

'Now listen, everyone,' Miriam warned. 'If you're out, you're out and there's to be no nonsense and no whinge-ing. OK?'

'OK,' they chorused.

'Ready?' Ben held up his plectrum.

Ellen had to laugh at the intense expressions on the faces of the children. Stephanie was flushed with excitement. She loved being with her cousins.

Ben began to play and they ran around the chairs yelling with excitement. Ben stopped. There was a mad scramble for seats. Julie Ann gave Harriet Andrews a shove that sent her sprawling and bagged the last vacant seat. Harriet opened her mouth to start bawling.

'Oh dear,' murmured Emma. 'Be gentle, darling,' she admonished her daughter. Julie Ann sat smugly on her seat.

'I think we'll have that round again,' Miriam said hastily as Ellen picked Harriet up and brushed her down.

'That's not fair,' Daniel objected.

'Be quiet, Daniel.' Miriam glowered at her son. Perhaps musical chairs wasn't such a good idea!

Ben began to play again. This time Daniel missed a seat. 'That's all her fault.' He scowled at Harriet. 'Just because she's a cry-baby. I had my seat the last time.'

Harriet promptly burst into tears.

'Excuse me, I must go to the loo.' Emma discreetly retired from the fray.

'Did you hear her? "*Be gentle, darling*." I'd give Julie Ann a good smack on the arse if she was mine. Be gentle, darling, my foot!' Ellen hissed. 'And did you ever see anything like the get-up of her in that frilly skirt? She's a right little consequence.'

'Please, Ellen, just say nothing.' Miriam was fraught.

'I won't. I won't.'

Julie Ann won the musical chairs.

'Daddy will be very pleased,' Emma approved. She'd reappeared for the grand finale.

'Let's play *O'Grady Says* . . .' Ellen suggested helpfully. This was greeted with approval.

'*O'Grady Says* stand on one leg.' Ellen stood on one leg and they all did likewise. Stephanie lost her balance and put her other foot down to help her regain it.

'You're out. You're out,' Julie Ann yelled triumphantly. Ellen felt like thumping her.

Stephanie looked at her mother. Ellen was in a terrible dilemma. She didn't want to be seen to be siding with Julie Ann, she couldn't be accused of favouritism, but she didn't want Stephanie to feel she'd let her down.

Ellen eyeballed Julie Ann. 'Stephanie knows she's out. She's not a cheater like some people. Isn't that right, Stephanie?'

Stephanie sighed and walked to the side of the group.

'Good girl, Stephanie. Cheaters never prosper.' She smiled at her daughter and winked.

'I hope that doesn't refer to my daughter,' Emma flared hotly. Ellen was so tempted to say 'If the cap fits,' but Miriam was looking at her beseechingly and Sheila was agitated. The last thing Ellen wanted to do was cause a scene, not when she had such a favour to ask of her parents.

'I think it will be time for tea soon, so we'll just do a few more O'Grady's,' she said calmly, ignoring the remark.

'Perhaps you'd help me bring out the food?' Miriam suggested to Emma. Emma glared at Ellen. The cheek of her to imply that Julie Ann was a cheat. She had no business looking down her nose at *anyone*.

Miriam could feel the beginning of a tension headache. This was definitely the last party. From now on it was immediate family only.

The children descended on the food with a savagery that would have put Genghis Khan and his followers to shame.

Julie Ann, who loved her grub, devoured as many ham sandwiches as she could and put some in the pocket of her new skirt to eat later on. Rebecca was outraged.

'Mammy, Julie Ann's after taking all the ham sandwiches. She's put a load in her pocket an' she's after taking *three* Trigger bars, an' it's my party an' I don't think that's fair.'

'She's a greedy-guts,' Stephanie chipped in. Memories of her cousin's cheating still rankled.

'Here, here, you have a packet of Perri crisps.' Miriam tried to pacify Rebecca. Honestly Julie Ann was a little glutton. She always stuffed herself when she was visiting because she was only fed packet and tinned food at home. Emma couldn't cook for nuts.

Sheila saw her chance. If Emma wouldn't chastise her daughter then Sheila certainly would. Julie Ann had to learn manners.

'Julie Ann, it's not nice to be greedy. Little girls should have good manners. Take those sandwiches out of your pocket and put back two of those Trigger bars, like a good child.'

'Mummy, can't I keep them?' Julie Ann turned to Emma.

Oh crikey! Emma thought privately, I'll kill her when I get home.

She knew she was stuck. Julie Ann was in the wrong and she couldn't be seen to condone it. Damn Sheila and her bloody interference. This whole family were a right royal pain. It was a pity Vincent wasn't an orphan with no siblings! Emma thought viciously.

'Julie Ann,' she snapped, 'do what Nannie tells you.'

Julie Ann was horrified at her mother's betrayal.

'No.' She pouted.

Please don't let her make a show of me. Emma could feel perspiration on her upper lip.

'Julie Ann, be a good girl for Mummy.'

'Leave me alone. I'm hungry. We didn't have any lunch 'cos you were in bed.'

Emma was mortified. She grabbed Julie Ann by the wrist and removed the sandwiches from her pocket. Julie Ann started to kick and screech, watched in silent fascination by the rest of the young guests who were enjoying the spectacle hugely. It was rare for Julie Ann to get her come-uppance.

'I hate you, Mummy. You're mean, mean, MEAN!'

'Give me those bars, you naughty girl.'

'No.' Julie Ann held onto her Trigger bars for dear life. Emma had had enough. She couldn't cope. She didn't want to stay a minute longer at this party playing ridiculous games and watching Julie Ann make a show of her. You couldn't bring her anywhere. If only Vincent were here. He'd handle this. She was beginning to feel dizzy again.

'Right!' she said grimly. 'We're going home immediately. You're not going to ruin your cousin's party.' Julie Ann howled with anger.

'Let her have the bars,' Miriam said sympathetically. She felt sorry for Emma. She just couldn't control Julie Ann who was a real handful at times.

'Absolutely not, Miriam. I'm sorry about this. Julie Anne is going home to bed.' Emma was scarlet with embarrassment. How could Julie Ann do this to her in front of Sheila and Ellen? She didn't mind Miriam so much. Miriam understood. But Ellen was standing with a smug look on her face that infuriated Emma.

She had to get out of here or she was going to burst into tears.

She grabbed her struggling daughter and dragged her along behind her. Julie Ann screeched her head off and, when they got to the side of the house, out of view of their enthralled audience, Emma gave Julie Ann a sharp slap on the legs. She had never slapped her before but today she was livid.

Julie Ann screamed even louder.

'You wait until I tell your daddy. How dare you make a show of me. How *dare* you! You bold, bold girl.' Emma was nearly sobbing with frustration. She shoved Julie Ann into the back of the car and got in herself. Boarding school. Definitely. That was where madam was going. She'd learn

289

manners there, Emma fumed as she drove home in utter disgust.

* * *

'Poor old Emma, she hasn't a clue.' Ben chuckled as he finished off a half-eaten slice of birthday cake.

'Your mother shouldn't have interfered.' Miriam was still annoyed.

'You know Ma, that was too good an opportunity to miss,' Ben said wryly.

'Well she helped to ruin Rebecca's party.' Miriam dried the last dish. 'And it's the last time I'm having a party for anyone except us.'

'Fine,' Ben said mildly. 'Whatever you want.'

'I mean it,' Miriam said firmly.

'Right.' Ben knew very well it would be the whole palaver over again when it was Connie's birthday.

'And I'm not minding Julie Ann any more either. She's as bold as brass. That pair let her away with far too much.'

'I feel sorry for the child.' Ben lit his pipe and put his arm around Miriam. 'Let's sit outside for a while. It's a lovely night.' They strolled arm in arm out to the back. The stars twinkled in an ebony sky. A crescent moon peeped through the branches of the whispering pines along the river bank. The fragrance of night-scented stock wafted along on the evening breeze. It was peaceful.

'Why do you feel sorry for Julie Ann?' Miriam was intrigued. She nestled close to Ben on the patio step.

'She's lost. She's no-one to play with at home. Emma's off gadding about. Vincent is too busy at work. She's looked after by a succession of babysitters and dailies. Her tantrums are a way of getting attention. When she's here with you there's never any of that nonsense. She plays away contentedly, she knows you won't put up with her impudence and that's why she never tries it on with you. You're a great mother, Miriam.'

Miriam felt a glow of happiness. Ben always made her

feel good about herself. It was thanks to him she had any self-confidence at all. She took his pipe and put it down beside him.

'I love you,' she whispered, turning to kiss him.

'I love you too,' Ben murmured against her lips as his arms tightened around her. 'I love you very much.'

* * *

'She has no control over the young one. It's a disgrace to let her carry on like that. I'm going to speak to Vincent about it,' Sheila grumbled as her knitting needles flashed in and out with great speed.

'Stay out of it,' Mick advised.

'But it's not fair on the child. She can't be allowed to grow up like that. My goodness you wouldn't see Stephanie carrying on the way she does.'

'I know that. But Julie Ann is a different kettle of fish. And if you go interfering you could cause a row. You know how touchy Emma is.'

'It's a disgrace all the same,' Sheila said crossly.

'Here's your supper, Ma.' Ellen handed her a cup of tea and placed a plate of cream crackers and cheese on the little coffee table.

'Dad, here's your cocoa.' She handed her father his big blue mug steaming with aromatic cocoa and smiled at him. Mick smiled back. No one made his cocoa like Ellen did.

'We were just saying how good Stephanie is compared to Julie Ann,' Sheila remarked.

Ellen's heart lifted. Thank God her mother was talking to her again.

'Stephanie's a good little girl. But then she's lucky that she has you and Dad to influence her.' Ellen knew she was laying it on thick but she needed all the goodwill she could get and if a bit of flattery helped, she'd flatter. Sheila nodded smugly.

'True,' she admitted with no hint of modesty.

'Mind you I know Stephanie has her moments and as she

291

gets older she'll be more lively and boisterous.' Ellen's heart raced. It was now or never. 'I've been thinking . . . Umm . . . well I've saved a few thousand pounds over the years and I was just wondering if you and Dad would give me a site so I could build a small bungalow for the two of us. It would give you a bit of peace and it would mean Stephanie could bring her friends home when she was older. And I wouldn't have to be worrying about them making too much noise or breaking ornaments or anything.' Her mouth was dry.

Sheila stared at her. 'You want a site?'

'It would be good to be a little more independent.'

'I think you've a point there, Ellen,' Mick said quietly. 'It would be good for Stephanie to have a home of her own and for you too.'

'She has a perfectly good home here, and so have you, Miss. We didn't throw you out in your hour of need. I'm not going to have the neighbours saying we're throwing you out now.'

'They wouldn't say that, Mam,' Ellen said desperately as she saw her precious chance of a new life slipping away.

'Wouldn't they indeed? I wouldn't put anything past Slyboots Daly.'

'You gave Vincent and Ben sites,' Ellen pleaded.

'Vincent and Ben didn't make a disgrace of the family. They got married. When you've got a ring on your finger, you'll get a site too.'

'Stop that, Sheila,' Mick said sharply.

'It's my land. I brought it into the family when I married. I have some say, Mick.'

'Sometimes you say too much.' Mick got out of his chair and stomped up to bed in disgust.

'Now do you see what you've done! Why aren't you ever satisfied?' Sheila demanded. 'You should be thankful we've stuck by you and given you and Stephanie a decent home. But no, you have to go and cause trouble between your father and myself. You're a trial to me, Ellen Munroe.'

'Not half as much a trial as you are to me,' Ellen said bitterly.

Sheila watched her leave the room and felt like slapping her. She'd never had a minute's peace with her only daughter. Why couldn't she be content with her lot? What did she expect? To be *rewarded* for fornicating? The cheek of her asking for a site. Sheila knew her remarks about owning the land had hurt Mick. She'd never ever said anything like that before in all the years of their marriage. But it had just slipped out. Sheila was so annoyed her needles slipped and a whole row of stitches began to unravel.

* * *

That was it. She'd blown it, Ellen thought heavily. She should have known better than to expect any help from Sheila. If only the land had been Mick's. He'd been sympathetic to her idea. All her hope and anticipation evaporated and depression left her feeling almost smothered. She stood beside her bedroom window looking out over the lights of Glenree and felt like throwing herself out the window. Was she trapped to live this life of stifling monotony for the rest of her existence?

Chapter Sixteen

'Aachoooo.' Emma gave an almighty sneeze. Pain shot through her head and her face. She felt so ill she wanted to die. It was the Monday after the party and she'd been feeling dreadful the whole weekend.

'I've phoned for the doctor, love. He'll be here after surgery.' Vincent handed his wife a tissue.

'I don't really know him,' Emma moaned.

'He's a good doctor. We can't expect your old lad to come trotting over from Foxrock.' Vincent patted the bedclothes around her. 'And Miriam will be here with you.'

'It's so annoying that Mrs Byrne has gone to have her veins done. Just when I really need her.' Mrs Byrne was Emma's daily. She also occasionally took care of Julie Ann if Emma was stuck . . . which was quite often . . . Emma had no sympathy for Mrs Byrne and her damn veins.

Just as well she had Miriam to fall back on. She'd been a bit worried that Miriam would be cool with her after Julie Ann's tantrum at the party, but Vincent said she was fine.

Emma broke out in a sweat when she thought of that dreadful afternoon. Julie Ann had made a holy show of her and she had bawled and screeched for a solid hour after they got home until Vincent had arrived back and pacified her. If this was what she was like at almost six years of age, heaven only knew what she was going to be like when she was a rebellious teenager. Emma's heart sank at the thought.

The doorbell chimed. 'That'll be Miriam.' Vincent

leaned over and kissed her on the forehead. 'I'll get home early from work.'

'Don't catch my germs,' she sniffled.

'You can give me your germs any time.' Vincent caressed her flushed cheek.

Emma managed a weak smile. 'Vincent, you're as mad as a hatter.'

'Naw. I'm just mad about you. I'm sorry I can't stay, pet. There's an auction I have to be at. I'll phone as soon as I can.'

Emma squeezed has hand. 'See you later,' she croaked.

The doorbell rang again and Vincent hurried downstairs to answer it.

* * *

Miriam stood at her in-laws' front door and felt hugely irritated. When Vincent had phoned to ask her if she'd come over and be with Emma when Doctor Elliot arrived her heart sank to her boots. She had a pile of washing to do. The house needed a good hoover after the party. Sheila had asked her to make a batch of scones for the cake sale in aid of the new Credit Union Building Fund, and the last place she wanted to be was twiddling her thumbs for the morning in Emma's spick-and-span mansion.

'I'd stay at home myself only that there's an auction. I have to bid for a client,' Vincent explained. 'I'll have dropped Julie Ann to school. Although I was wondering if she could go to you afterwards and I'll pick her up. I'll leave work as early as I can.' Why couldn't he ask Sheila? Miriam wondered crossly. Why was it always *her*? Did everyone in the Munroe family think she had absolutely nothing to do except run around after them? As well as having three children of her own to look after, she took care of Stephanie after school, until Ellen came home from work. Emma regularly asked her to mind Julie Ann for an hour or two, which invariably turned into three- or four-hour stints. Miriam could count on her fingers the number of times Emma had minded her kids.

Then ... to add insult to injury ... no sooner had Vincent hung up than the phone rang again. It was Della who announced that she was coming to Dublin on the noon train. She wanted to stay the night. That meant that Miriam was going to have to put fresh sheets on Daniel's bed. It made Miriam's blood boil to think of how her sister-in-law had practically evicted her from the family home and yet she had no qualms about phoning Miriam *expecting* to be put up for the night. Some people were as cool as cucumbers. She jabbed her finger on the doorbell again. Vincent opened the door moments later.

'Miriam, thanks a million for coming,' he said warmly. 'I hope we're not putting you out.'

'Not at all,' she fibbed politely. 'How's poor Emma?'

'In bits, the poor dote.' Vincent grabbed his car keys from the hall table. 'I have to run. If the doctor gives her a prescription would you get it in the chemist's?'

'Sure.' Miriam nodded. There was her morning gone. By the time the doctor came and she went into Glenree for the prescription it would be nearly lunchtime. *Poor dote* my foot, she thought irritably as she closed the door behind Vincent. Everyone else had to manage when they got sick. But when Emma got a cold they all had to drop everything and rush to her side. It was a wonder Vincent hadn't called an ambulance, Miriam thought with uncharacteristic nastiness as she walked silently up the deep-pile carpeted stairs to give succour to the invalid.

'Hello, Miriam. Thanks for coming over,' Emma mewed pathetically from the huge four-poster bed that dominated the bedroom.

'Not at all. Can I get you anything? A cup of tea or a hot drink?' Her good nature reasserted itself when she saw her swollen-eyed, red-nosed, puffy-faced sister-in-law cocooned in a mountain of white fluffy pillows.

'Could I have a glass of orange juice? And would you get me a fresh nightie?' Emma sneezed lustily.

'Of course. Would you like me to straighten up the bed before the doctor comes?'

'That would be nice, thanks a million, Miriam. You're very kind.' Emma's tone was heartfelt and Miriam, big-hearted as ever despite her previous bad humour, told her briskly not to talk nonsense.

While Emma was washing and changing in her ensuite bathroom, Miriam made up the bed. It was a beautiful bedroom, she reflected as she plumped up the broderie anglaise pillows. Emma had such style. She'd had the room redone in shades of lemon and pale blue. Pristine white doors, ceiling, skirting boards and dado rails complemented the snowy whiteness of the broderie anglaise bedlinen. A luxurious carpet in shades of lemon and blue stretched from wall to wall. The immense floor-to-ceiling window allowed the light to wash every corner of the room. The vista was spectacular.

Emma and Vincent's house was built on an incline and they had a view down the valley into Glenree and beyond. The trees, which were just beginning to turn gold, spread out beneath them in an immense patchwork of greens, burnished golds, russets and bronze. Miriam could see the chimney-tops of Mick and Sheila's farm and the jaunty red gable of their big red barn amidst dappled foliage. She could also catch a glimpse of her own white and blue bungalow.

The spire of St Joseph's pierced the blue sky and the tiled, slated and thatched rooftops of Main Street glinted in the early morning sun. Miriam had seen the view once after a heavy fall of snow and it looked like a scene on a Christmas card. Emma's garden was immaculate. There was order and symmetry to the plants and shrubs. A gardener tended to it once a week. Personally Miriam preferred the riotous glory of her own unruly garden. Still, Emma and Vincent's enormous garden was a showpiece and the envy of many of their friends who only had postage-stamp-sized gardens in the city.

'Miriam, I feel very shivery, could you get me a hot-water bottle?' Emma emerged from the bathroom in a frilly pink shortie nightdress. No wonder she was shivery. She'd be too in a flimsy creation like that, Miriam thought as she went downstairs and filled the kettle.

It was another hour before Doctor Elliot arrived. Miriam showed him in to Emma's bedroom, relieved that once she got the prescription she could be off home to start her housework.

'Hello, Mrs Munroe,' Doctor Elliot said kindly as he took out his stethoscope.

'Hello, Doctor Elliot. I feel really desperate,' Emma groaned.

'Well let's see what we can do for you. Take a deep breath and hold it for me,' he said briskly. He gave Emma a thorough examination and Miriam noticed him frowning as he took her blood pressure.

'You've a bad dose of flu, my dear, and your blood pressure is high. Have you had blood pressure trouble before?'

'I had toxaemia when I had Julie Ann,' Emma said weakly.

'And since?'

'It goes up and down.'

'Hmm.' Doctor Elliot took a syringe out of his bag and a small phial.

'Not an injection.' Emma cringed.

'You won't feel a thing,' Doctor Elliot assured her as he filled the syringe from the phial and aimed the needle like a dart.

'Turn over for me like a good girl,' he instructed.

'Ouch,' Emma muttered indignantly as he injected her in the buttock.

He laid the used syringe on the bedside locker and noticed a packet beside the little marble alarm clock that Emma used.

'What's this?' he queried sternly.

Emma looked at it, heavy-eyed. 'It's my contraceptive pill.'

'Good Lord, woman! What doctor prescribed that for you?'

'I get it in London,' Emma said defensively. It was none of Doctor Elliot's business whether she was on the pill or not. *He* hadn't nearly died in childbirth. If he had religious scruples, he could bloody well keep them to himself.

'If you have problems with your blood pressure this is the *last* thing you should be on. Mrs Munroe, your blood pressure is very high. I'm going to call again tomorrow to check it. You are coming off this *immediately*. Do you want to have a thrombosis?'

'But I don't want any more children,' she wailed.

'There are other ways, less injurious to your health. We'll talk about them tomorrow. Now, I'll write a prescription for you. Take the tablets three times a day after food and I'll see you tomorrow.' The doctor packed his bag, wrote his prescription and took his leave of Emma.

Once he'd left the room, escorted by Miriam, she burst into tears. It was bad enough feeling like death but to have to come off the pill and to have to start worrying about ovulation and safe times and all that kind of stuff was just unbearable. Emma cried her eyes out and not even Miriam's kind reassuring words when she came back upstairs could comfort her.

*   *   *

Ellen sat in her little cubicle trying to add up a column of figures. Usually it was no problem to her but today she just couldn't concentrate. She was too depressed. The spark of hope that had kept her going was quenched. She felt lethargic and despondent. It had been one last chance to change her life and take back some control. It had failed. She had two options. She could stay at home and be under Sheila's thumb or she could leave Glenree and get a job and rent a flat in Dublin.

If she was on her own that was precisely what she would do. But she had Stephanie to consider. It wouldn't be fair to take her daughter away from her secure and stable life and bring her to Dublin where a stranger would have to take care of her while Ellen was working. It looked as though she was well and truly trapped.

'Ellen . . . Ellen,' her father interrupted her reverie. He had closed up for the day and there was just the two of them in the shop.

'Yes, Dad,' she said heavily.

Mick cleared his throat. 'Look, Ellen, I'm sorry about the site. I'm sure you had your heart set on it. And, if you like, when your mother has cooled down, I'll talk to her about it.'

'Ah forget it, Dad. It's not worth the hassle. And besides, even if she did agree, I'd never hear the end of it. Mam's never going to forgive me for getting pregnant. God might but she won't. That's something I have to live with.'

'That's just the way she is, pet. Your mother's a good woman, she worries about you and Stephanie.'

'Oh Dad, I just find it so hard. I made a mistake, do I have to pay for it for the rest of my life?' Two big tears rolled down Ellen's cheeks.

'Ssshh, alanna, don't upset yourself.' Mick patted her shoulder awkwardly. 'We'll work something out. Leave those figures and go over and collect Stephanie from Miriam's and after tea how about if I start giving you a few driving lessons?'

Ellen wiped her eyes. 'I'd love that. I'd give anything to be able to drive.'

'Haven't you been pestering me for long enough?' Mick chuckled. 'We'll bring Stephanie for a spin to the back of the airport, she'll enjoy watching the planes. So off with you now. I'll finish up here.'

Ellen leaned across and planted a kiss on her father's ruddy weather-beaten cheek. 'I'd be lost without you,' she said a little shyly. She didn't often have personal conversations like this with her father.

'Go on with you, I'll see you at home shortly and don't worry. We'll come up with something,' Mick said gruffly.

But Ellen knew he was pleased. He was her rock, she reflected as she closed the door behind her and stepped out onto Main Street. He was quiet and stalwart. You'd never know he was there until you were facing a crisis and then, in his own quiet way, he'd take charge. It was a great comfort and she only hoped he knew how much she appreciated him. They were a good team in the shop too, Ellen smiled. He depended on her a lot so in her own way she could repay his kindness.

She couldn't believe he was going to teach her to drive. Mick was of the old school. He felt uneasy with women behind the wheel of a car. The way Emma scorched around in her Mini horrified him. He'd resisted Ellen's pleas to be taught how to drive for years.

He must be feeling really sorry for her to offer to teach her, she thought wryly as she crossed the green which was covered in a fine layer of fallen leaves that whispered along on the breeze. Denise McMahon, an old school pal, was mowing her lawn. She called out a cheery greeting as Ellen walked past.

'How's it going, Ellen?'

'Hi, Denise,' Ellen responded with false gaiety.

'On your way home from work?'

'Yeah.'

'I didn't realize it was that late. I though I'd get the garden done. There's rain forecast. I better get my skates on and get in and get Jimmy's dinner. I always like to have his dinner ready for him when he gets home.' Denise wiped her perspiring brow and grinned at Ellen. Her two little girls played hopscotch on the path. They were pretty, like their mother.

' "Feed a man properly and he won't stray," as Sister Patrick used to say,' Denise joked.

'I wonder how she knew that?' Ellen grinned. 'See ya, Denise.'

'See ya, Ellen. Come in and have a cup of coffee some day and bring Stephanie over to play with the girls.'

'I will. Thanks,' Ellen replied warmly. She and Denise

had been close enough once. They'd had great fun growing up. They'd drifted, the way friends often did, when Denise had married Jimmy MacMahon, a quiet, reserved accountant who never had two words to put together. He was a dry old stick. They really were chalk and cheese, Ellen mused. Denise was so vivacious and he was so dull. She could have had the pick of the county. Men had swarmed around her like bees around honey. Whatever magic spell boring Jimmy McMahon weaved had worked, because Denise had waltzed radiantly down the aisle six months after their first date. Maybe he was great in bed! Ellen found it hard to think of Jimmy McMahon in the throes of wild passion murmuring sweet nothings in Denise's ear. The thought made her giggle.

She seemed happy enough, Ellen thought a little enviously. How nice it would be to have Stephanie playing in her own garden and a husband coming home to his dinner every night. Denise's contented domesticity contrasted starkly with her own restless existence.

Ellen had given up the idea of ever getting married. Who'd want her now? The wrong side of thirty with a young daughter. A spinster of the parish of Glenree.

'Oh give over,' she muttered. At least she'd known the heights of passion and she'd loved deeply and whole-heartedly. No-one could take that away from her. It wasn't her fault that she'd fallen in love with a complete and utter shit. She wasn't the first to have had her trust broken by Chris. He'd left a trail of destruction in his charming wake, but she had Stephanie. The joy of her life. And for Stephanie's sake she'd get on with things as best she could.

* * *

Mick dried the gleaming silver blade of his carving knife and hung it up beside the rest of his implements. He sluiced out the sink thoroughly and wiped the blue and white tiles surrounding it. His shop was spotlessly clean. As was his freezer room and the back room he was in now.

He frowned as he polished the taps. He was very troubled about Ellen. He could understand her desire for independence and he agreed with it, even though he'd miss Stephanie very much if they left. Stephanie was the apple of his eye. He adored her. But Sheila was not an easy woman to live with and if anything ever happened to him it was going to be extremely difficult for Ellen to live under the same roof as her mother without him to act as a buffer. A site was out of the question now. Even if Sheila changed her mind – and Mick knew he could change it for her – Ellen would feel under a compliment and Sheila would hold it over her for the rest of her life. That defeated the whole purpose. Ellen needed to be free from her mother. It was a sad thing to have to admit, but it was the truth. Mick sighed deeply, his brow furrowed, as he polished his gleaming taps with vigour.

Something had to be done about it. And it was up to him to do it.

Ten minutes later he locked the door behind him. He saw Bonnie Daly and Mona Cullen coming out of the coffee shop. They'd been in selling tickets for a parish raffle. The coffee shop could do with a lick of paint, he noted. He owned the building but it was leased to the two Boyle sisters and they were getting a bit beyond it. They were in their mid-sixties. He'd organize Willie O'Donnell to come and paint it next week. It paid to keep buildings in good repair.

The butcher's shop and the coffee shop were his, he thought crossly. He was annoyed with Sheila for making the remark about the land. Marriage was all about sharing. She'd get a fine jolt if he informed her that the shops were his and nothing to do with her. He'd bought his butcher's business with his own money.

Now he was being as bad as his wife, he decided as he got into his car. That Alpine blue that Ben had used on his house was a nice colour. Maybe he'd paint the coffee shop blue and white. His eyes strayed upwards to the first floor, the windows were peeling faded green paint. A nice fresh

303

lick of paint would give the place a facelift. His eyes widened as he thought of something. It was so bloomin' obvious it had been staring him in the face. Mick grinned a huge melon-slice grin. Sheila might like to think that she was the boss but in the end, when Mick put his foot down, she knew he meant business and this time his foot was going to be put down very, very firmly.

He started the ignition and paused to bless himself as the Angelus bell rang out over Glenree.

'*The Angel of the Lord declared unto Mary . . .*' he prayed. He'd be declaring unto Sheila in a very short space of time. And if she didn't like it that was her tough luck. He finished the Angelus and braced himself for the ordeal ahead.

*   *   *

'I'm really sorry, Vincent. I just can't believe that I've to come off the pill,' Emma sobbed. 'Maybe he's made a mistake.'

'You're coming off it and you're staying off it. We'll manage fine.' Vincent gathered her up in his arms and held her tightly. 'I'll use condoms.'

'But you hate them,' Emma wept.

'Don't worry about that. We'll work it out. The most important thing is your health, pet,' Vincent assured her.

'I'm terrified I'll get pregnant.'

'You won't. I promise.'

'But I like making love whenever we like. I like seducing you unexpectedly.' Emma raised teary eyes to her husband.

'I like it too.' Vincent smiled. 'We'll just have to have more seductions the times we're allowed. We'll be panting for each other after a few days abstinence. We'll be like the way we were on our honeymoon.'

Emma's eyes brightened. 'I never thought of that.'

'Anyway there's lots of other things we can do.' He leaned down and whispered in her ear.

Emma giggled. 'I love you, you pervert.'

'I love you too, you pervertess. So stop worrying your head over silly things. I better go and collect Julie Ann. I'm very late.'

'Ah Miriam won't mind, she's the best in the world.' Emma felt very cherished as she lay in the circle of her husband's arms.

*   *   *

'Girls, have you finished your homework?' Miriam stuck her head around the dining-room door where Connie, Rebecca, Stephanie and Julie Ann were giggling and skitting.

'Yesssss,' came the chorus.

'Right, Stephanie, your mam will be here soon, tidy up your books. You too, Julie Ann. Connie and Rebecca, go and set the table for the tea.'

'Aw Mam,' Connie objected. 'We're having fun.'

'Connie, your Auntie Della is coming this evening and I want the tea over early. Do it now." Miriam was in no mood to be trifled with. She hadn't got home from Emma's until nearly two. And she'd been going like the hammers of hell ever since. But at least the washing and hoovering were done. All she had to do was change Daniel's bed.

She was walking down the hall with an armful of clean bedlinen when Sheila marched through the open front door.

'Hello, dear. I've come to collect the scones.'

Miriam's jaw dropped. She'd completely forgotten about her mother-in-law's cake sale.

'Don't say you haven't done them yet. Tsk. I've wasted my journey and I haven't got Mick's tea ready.' Sheila made no effort to hide her irritation. 'I'll collect them first thing in the morning.'

Something inside Miriam snapped. 'Mrs Munroe, I'm up to my eyes. I spent all morning over at Emma's. Della's coming to stay overnight. I haven't stopped all day and I didn't get a chance to do any baking.' She was so angry her voice trembled.

'Well that's all right, dear. They'll do tomorrow.' Sheila was taken aback.

'No!'

'I beg your pardon?'

'I'm sorry, Mrs Munroe, I won't have time to bake. You'll just have to do without my scones this time,' Miriam declared.

'Oh well if that's the way it is. I won't take up any more of your valuable time,' Sheila retorted huffily. She turned on her heel and marched out the door.

Miriam stared after her. It was the first time that she'd ever stood up to Sheila. Her palms were sweaty. Her heart was racing. She felt sick, but she was damned if she was going to bake scones after the day she'd had.

* * *

Sheila was extremely put out as she cycled home . . . sconeless . . . Miriam had been downright *rude*. She might have had a tiring day, certainly, but there was no excuse for bad manners. She'd promised Monica Anderson a batch of scones as well as the dozen fairy cakes and the two apple tarts that she'd baked. She'd just have to go home and bake the scones herself after tea. It was very vexing though. Sheila glowered as she freewheeled down Red Barn's Hill. By the time she got home she was in a thoroughly bad humour. She'd got a puncture at Daly's stables and had had to push the bike the last half-mile home.

She'd only just set the table when Mick arrived.

'I'm late with the tea. I went over to Miriam's to collect a batch of scones for the cake sale and she hadn't baked them. Nor is she going to do them for me. I feel very let down,' she grumbled as she whipped eggs for a mushroom omelette.

'That's not like Miriam. Maybe she hadn't got time.'

306

Mick sat in the armchair by the range and took out his pipe. He was dismayed to find Sheila in a bad humour.

'Hadn't got time, indeed. How did I manage with no washing-machine or hoover when I was married first? I had to scrub and hand-wash and you didn't hear me moaning about not having time. And I had three children to rear and a farm to look after. Women today just don't know what hard work is.'

'Well you should be taking things easy, Sheila. You have your children reared. We have Eoin to work the farm. It's time you slowed down a bit,' Mick said soothingly.

'How can I take things easy? Cooking and cleaning for the four of us. I'm not a lady of leisure like Bonnie Daly. She doesn't have a daughter and grandchild expecting their meals on the table.' Sheila was in martyr mode and not to be pacified.

'Well that's why Ellen wanted to get a place of her own,' Mick pointed out delicately. 'She doesn't want to be putting you out.'

Sheila, realizing that she'd walked herself into it, backtracked furiously.

'Oh they're not that much bother. And I won't have people saying we put them out on the street. I'm not agreeing to give Ellen a site if that's what you're on about.' She was raging with herself.

'If you don't want her to have the site there's nothing I can do about it.' Mick stood up. 'But I've been thinking what's best for all of us and I've decided, if Ellen would like it, that I'm going to do up the rooms over the shop and let her live there.'

'What!' Sheila's jaw dropped. 'You can't do that. What will people say?'

'People can say what they like,' Mick retorted. 'I want Ellen to have a roof over her head and a bit of independence. I don't want Stephanie to have to put up with you and her mother arguing the toss. It's not fair on the child. It's a good solution, and if Ellen agrees, that's the way it's going to be.'

'You always were too soft with her. What are the boys going to say? They're as entitled to their share in that shop as she is.' Sheila was furious. She'd been well and truly outmanoeuvred.

'The boys will be well looked after, Sheila. You know that. All our children will be treated the same. You wouldn't agree to give Ellen a site. So I'm giving her the top of the shop.'

'Oh do what you like.' Sheila was so mad she wanted to pour the bowl of whipped egg over Mick. Instead she sliced the mushrooms viciously and glared at her husband who had retreated behind the protection of his evening paper.

*　　*　　*

There's been a row, Ellen thought with a sinking heart as she and Stephanie walked in through the back door. Miriam hadn't been in good form either, so Ellen hadn't lingered.

'Hi, Grandad. Hi, Nannie.' Stephanie bounced over to Mick and planted a big kiss on his cheek.

'Hello, love.' Mick beamed and returned his granddaughter's embrace.

Stephanie skipped over to her grandmother. 'Can I help?'

'No, dear. Tea's nearly ready. Go and wash your hands and sit down.'

'Can I do anything?' Ellen asked.

'I have it all done,' Sheila replied frostily.

Suit yourself, Ellen was tempted to retort but she kept quiet.

Stephanie chattered away through the meal, but Ellen said nothing. Sheila sat rigid and ignored her husband and daughter. 'Can I go and play on the swing?' Stephanie asked when Sheila started to clear away the dishes.

'Just for a while. And come in when I call you.' Ellen smiled at her.

'Thanks, Mammy. You're the best mammy in the universe,' Stephanie declared and gave Ellen a hug that nearly strangled her. Ellen laughed. 'Go on and no arguing when it's time for bed.'

The three adults watched the little girl race out the door. Mick felt sad. He'd miss Stephanie around the house. She was a happy little soul. But childhood didn't last for ever and, as she grew older, life with Sheila and Ellen would get much more difficult.

'Ellen, sit down for a minute. I want to talk to you,' he said evenly.

Sheila clattered the cutlery in the sink.

Ellen looked at her father, wondering what was coming.

'I know you want a place of your own. And I can understand why. Your mother has her reasons for not wanting to give you a site and I have to respect her wishes. But I'd like you to have a place of your own. So, if you'd like, I'd be willing to do up the top floor over the shop for yourself and Stephanie. There's a good plot at the back you could turn into a garden.'

Ellen sat, stunned. Mick looked at her, his ruddy face anxious as he waited for her reaction. Maybe she would think he wanted to get rid of her, he thought, suddenly uncertain that he'd made the right suggestion.

'Oh, Dad . . .' Ellen murmured. Her face lit up and she jumped up and put her arms around him.

'Oh, Dad, that would be brilliant. Thanks very much. I can't believe it.'

'Well believe it,' he said, hugging her tightly.

Sheila, back ramrod-straight at the sink, watched Stephanie playing on the swing and felt strangely bereft.

Chapter Seventeen

'We could put two bedrooms and a small bathroom in a converted attic. There's plenty of room up there. And we could partition off the big room here on the first floor and turn it into a kitchen-cum-dining-room. Or you could have the kitchen separate. Whatever you like, Ellen. And that would leave this room as your sitting-room. You just tell me what you want and I'll have an architect draw up the plans.' Doug Roche hooked his thumbs into the belt of his jeans and smiled at Ellen.

Doug was the builder Mick had asked to renovate the first floor. Ellen had known him for years. They'd gone to school together as children, and hung around as teenagers. Doug had started working with his father after school and, when his father died, he'd carried on in the building trade. He was highly regarded. When Doug Roche did a job, he did it properly. He'd built Ben and Miriam's house as well as many other houses in Glenree. He was reliable and that was enough for Ellen.

'That sounds great to me, Doug. Could I have an archway from the kitchen to the dining area? I'd keep the fireplace, it would be nice and cosy.'

'Sure. That would be fine. It would work very well. I'll get a few different ideas on paper and show them to you. There's only one problem, I'm afraid, I won't be able to start work until after Christmas. I've a house to finish and a few other jobs. So you might want to get someone else.'

Ellen was disappointed. Now that this great opportunity had landed in her lap, she was anxious to get going.

She couldn't wait to move into her new home. For a moment she was tempted to tell Doug she'd look for someone else. But she knew he was good. And he'd been exceedingly helpful and patient with her queries. Doug was nice. He treated her the same as he always had since they were teenagers. He was courteous and respectful. She didn't want anyone else. She liked him.

'I'd like you to do it, Doug,' Ellen said firmly.

'Right, I'll organize the architect and get you a quote. You can start looking at curtains and paper and the like. But seeing as I won't be starting until after Christmas, maybe you should wait until the sales before you buy anything. It might save you a few bob.'

'Yeah, I'll do that.' Ellen smiled at him. He smiled back. He'd nice hazel eyes. She'd never really noticed them before. He was attractive in his own way. He was tall, with a lean muscular build. He had lovely silky chestnut hair and a neatly trimmed beard and moustache. He wasn't married. Ellen remembered vaguely that he'd been engaged to a girl and she'd dumped him a few months before they were due to be married. She didn't know if he was dating anyone now.

'See ya then.'

'See you, Doug.' Ellen watched him lope down the stairs and was glad she'd decided to wait until he was ready.

After he'd gone, she wandered through the rooms. Mick used them for storage and there were shabby pieces of furniture, rolls of lino, trunks, old newspapers and a jumble of bric-à-brac that needed sorting. She could have lived here years ago if only she or Mick had thought of it. It was dingy, dark and neglected now but, once all the stuff was cleared out of it and the papering and painting was done, it would look really nice. For the first time in a long long time, Ellen felt a little flicker of happiness.

She walked into the back room, lowered the window and leaned out to survey what would soon be her back garden.

It was a wilderness. Although Mick kept the grass cut,

blackberry bushes and brambles encroached on three sides. The garden backed onto a meadow where cattle grazed peacefully. It was a picturesque view and Ellen looked forward to clearing the hedges and brambles and planting masses of wild roses, her favourite flower. It could be really nice, she thought happily. She'd put a swing in it for Stephanie and get a little patio laid for herself and have tubs of flowers like Miriam and Ben had in theirs.

She did a little twirl. The peace here was soothing. No tension, no stress. It was going to be a real haven. All she had to do was get through the next few months, and then her life was going to change completely. She couldn't wait.

The weeks that followed were busy ones for Ellen. She was learning to drive. Mick showed remarkable forbearance and, once she mastered the gears and gained some confidence, she began to enjoy it. As soon as she had put Stephanie to bed each evening, she would go over to the shop and work upstairs for a couple of hours. Mick and Ben had cleared all the junk out of the rooms and Ellen scraped the wallpaper off the walls and prepared the doors and skirting boards for painting. It was hard work but she enjoyed herself immensely. She listened happily to Radio Caroline as she scraped and scrubbed her new abode.

Sometimes Miriam came over to help out. She was thrilled for Ellen and they'd spent a couple of delightful Saturday mornings looking at curtain materials and wallpapers in Dublin. They treated themselves to lunch and promised each other that it was something they would do on a more regular basis.

Because she was in a much more positive frame of mind and had so much to occupy her, Ellen found that she could keep to her diet more successfully than ever before. The hard physical work she was doing was also helping. By the week before Christmas, she had lost almost a stone and she was determined to keep it off. Her face had lost its bloated look, her stomach was much flatter and she had shoulders again. It was great to fit back into a size fourteen. She treated herself to some new clothes and a good winter coat in a lovely shade of royal blue. It was very smart. One day, on the spur of the moment while she was in the city, she walked into a hairdressing salon and got her hair cut in a shorter layered look that was rather sophisticated for her.

At first when she saw her reflection in the mirror she was shocked. She'd always worn her chestnut hair just below her shoulders and, because it had a natural curl, it could look a bit wild. Now it was chopped to her nape and feathery fronds framed her forehead and cheeks.

It took getting used to but it was very groomed and elegant. She liked it. It changed her appearance quite dramatically. Miriam thought it was stunning and even Emma grudgingly said that it was nice.

She had a new image for her new life. She was never going to let herself get into a rut again, Ellen vowed.

*   *   *

Sheila handed Stephanie the big baking bowl and watched as her granddaughter, who had been waiting patiently, licked the remains of the sweet fruit cake mixture. Sheila had most of her Christmas baking done but she'd promised to do a cake for the Christmas raffle in the school fair and she'd left it until the last minute. The fair was tomorrow, four days before Christmas.

She watched Stephanie up to her ears in the creamy remains, and smiled. Vincent, Ben and Ellen had done exactly the same when they were children. She was going to miss Stephanie. She was great company. She loved hearing tales of Sheila's own childhood and Sheila liked talking about the past. Life had been much less complicated then. Maybe she was looking back with rose-tinted glasses, but this new modern world got her down sometimes.

In her day, if a girl got into trouble, she'd hardly dare show her face to the world again. And here was Ellen, as brazen as you like, going to live on Main Street. God knows what she'd get up to when she was on her own.

Bonnie and the rest of the gossips would have a field day. And the worst of it was, Mick was aiding and abetting her all the way. Sheila felt tears prick her eyes. Mick was very very annoyed with her about the site. Her behaviour had been a blow to his pride. She should never have said that it was her land. That had cut him to the quick. If she hadn't been so smart, Ellen would have been living in a house just down the road, out of harm's way. Stephanie would have been able to visit every day. Sheila knew that Ellen wouldn't be too eager to come home once she had her own place. The farm was too far from Glenree for a child to walk. She'd rightly shot herself in the foot.

'Nannie, are you sad?' Stephanie stood beside her, her big blue eyes wide with worry.

'Just a little bit, dear.' Sheila wiped her eyes and hunkered down beside her granddaughter. Stephanie put her arms around her neck and Sheila took great comfort from the loving embrace. Stephanie, God bless her trusting little heart, loved her wholeheartedly. It was a very precious love, untroubled by the tensions and strife that beset her relationship with Ellen.

'I'll miss you when you move. Wouldn't you prefer to stay here with Nannie?' She knew that was a low shot but she couldn't help herself.

'But Nannie, Mammy said I could have teddy bear curtains in my bedroom, an' I'm going to have another bed for when Rebecca or Julie Ann wants to stay. But you can come and stay too,' she added kindly. 'We could have a midnight feast.'

Sheila had to laugh at the idea. 'We'll see, love.' She could imagine Ellen's face if she announced she was coming to stay for a midnight feast. She'd be lucky to get invited to see the place at all. Sheila stood up and turned on the taps to fill the sink for the washing-up. This should have been a happy time in her life. Her children were reared. Her job was done, she should be sitting back enjoying the fruits of her labour. She should be enjoying her grandchildren. Instead she was deeply troubled by

Ellen's behaviour. Mick was cool to her. Miriam wasn't as obliging as she once was. Julie Ann was as bold as brass and Vincent and Emma were letting her away with murder. And Bonnie Daly had sold more tickets than she had for the Christmas raffle and had made sure to rub her nose in it, too.

Where had she gone wrong? She'd tried her best. She'd tried to be as good a wife and mother as she possibly could. And yet God was punishing her. Now the only real joy left in her life was being taken from her. Stephanie would grow up all too soon. And without her restraining influence. Although Sheila had to admit Ellen was quite strict with her. Much more so than Vincent and Emma were with Julie Ann. Nevertheless, Stephanie was being taken from her. Ellen was positively glowing at the thought of being on her own. Sheila had never felt so downhearted in her life.

*   *   *

Doug Roche stepped out of the shower, wrapped a towel around his waist and walked into his bedroom. His muscles ached. He'd put in a punishing day but at least the bungalow he was building was near completion and then he could re-roof McNally's extension and get that out of the way before starting work on Ellen Munroe's place.

He'd seen the lights on over the butcher's shop and seen her through the upstairs window scraping the wallpaper. It had been nice to see how excited she'd been when he'd suggested the new layout. He was looking forward to getting the project under way. He could turn the upstairs flat into a very inviting home for her and her little girl. Ellen hadn't had an easy life, but he admired her spirit and the way she held her head high. And she wasn't a bullshitter. One thing about Ellen Munroe, she was dead straight and always had been.

Doug sighed as he towelled his hair dry and put on a clean shirt. He couldn't imagine Ellen doing the dirty on a man the way Geena had on him. He'd been crazy about Geena Kingston. A pert vivacious brunette with huge blue eyes, a snub nose and a pair of rosebud lips that were made for kissing. He'd fallen head over heels in love with her. Geena had danced rings around him. He'd driven her here, there, everywhere. He'd spent a fortune on her and never begrudged a penny of it. When she'd accepted his proposal, he'd been as happy as could be. Even though she'd put off setting a date for their wedding, saying there was no rush, he'd bought a site and they'd drawn up plans for a house. He was going to build it in his spare time. In the meantime, once they were married, they were going to live in his old family home until he had the house built.

Geena had seemed happy enough. But one day a mate of his, Pete, had bought him a drink in Mulligan's of Poolbeg Street, and then he'd told him that he had something to say to him. Doug listened in shock as Pete told him that he'd seen Geena in another man's company on several occasions and he'd seen them kissing. He'd seen them as recently as the previous night.

Doug felt sick. Geena had phoned him to cancel their date. She'd said that she had a migraine and that she was going to have an early night. He'd been very sympathetic and wanted to call to see her but she'd said no. It was just one of her migraines and she'd see him the next day.

When he'd confronted her with it, she'd looked him straight in the eye and said yes, she was seeing someone else. Now that Doug knew, there was no point in denying it. He'd been gutted. He'd wanted to die. He had really loved her and she'd walked all over him and treated him like dirt. Used him, and then discarded him just like that. No wonder she hadn't been anxious to set a date for the wedding. Why had she bothered going out with him, let alone got engaged to him, he'd asked himself over and over again. He was a soft touch, that was why. Geena walked out and he'd never heard from her again. She'd amputated him from her life with a callousness that he found hard to believe. He often wondered if he'd loved a split personality.

He'd heard that she'd married her lover but that she'd left him too and taken up with a married man who left his wife and three children for her. That man was a fool, Doug reflected. Geena would never commit to anyone. She was thoroughly selfish.

Doug had never trusted a woman since. He'd dated them. Taken what they had to offer, but he'd never let his barriers down again. Nor would he, he thought grimly as he finished dressing. What had brought back those sad old memories that he'd buried away? Looking back was a waste of time. What a fool he was to be grieving over that cold bitch when she was enjoying life with never one thought for him. To hurt someone deliberately the way she had hurt him was the worst thing one human being could do to another. He would make damn sure that no-one ever did it to him again. Doug brushed his hair, smoothed down his beard and put Ellen Munroe's architectural plans in his jacket pocket. If she was there he'd pop in and go over them with her. If not, he'd go for his usual Friday night pint in the Glenree Arms.

*   *   *

Ellen sat on a milk crate and waited for the kettle to boil. She was gasping for a cup of tea. It was just gone nine-thirty and she'd been working solidly since eight. She was very pleased though. Every room was ready for Doug to start work on. All the walls had been cleared of wallpaper. All the doors, skirting boards, window sills and window frames had been sanded, ready for painting. The old carpets had been lifted and the place was spotless.

All that was left to be done was the stairs and landing and she was halfway through that. The doorbell rang. She raced downstairs, thinking that it was Miriam.

Doug stood at the door, the collar of his leather jacket pulled up against the sleety rain.

'How's it going? I have the plans if you'd like to have a look at them.' His breath froze on the cold night air.

'Come in. That's great,' Ellen said enthusiastically. 'I've the place all cleared and the paper off the walls, except for the stairs and landing.' She led him upstairs and opened the door into what would be the sitting-room.

'You've done a great job, Ellen.' Doug stared around approvingly. 'I should be able to start the second week of January. If that's OK?'

'As soon as you can is fine with me.' Ellen flicked a strip of faded green wallpaper off the front of the old shirt she was wearing to protect her clothes. 'Excuse the state of me. I'm a shambles.'

'You should see me when I come in from work in the evening. It goes with the territory.' Doug picked a lump of plaster out of her hair. The kettle whistled.

'I was just making myself a cup of tea. Would you like one?'

'Why not?' Doug agreed. 'We can study the plans and see what you think while we're drinking it. Are you happy with the quote?'

'It's very fair,' she said gratefully. She had insisted on paying half of the price although Mick had argued that it wasn't necessary. Ellen wanted to use the money she'd saved. It made the place more of her own somehow.

She made the tea, put the milk and sugar on a tray and carried it over to the milk crate. Doug was in the other room measuring and marking.

'Tea's made,' she called.

'You know that's a very long landing and it's a lot of wasted space. I could make the sitting-room L-shaped and bring the door up as far as here.' He pointed to midway along the landing.

'Could you?'

'It wouldn't be a problem and it would give you an interestingly shaped room. You could put a nice fitted unit there. A friend of mine is a carpenter. He does lovely work and he doesn't cost the earth.' Doug took the mug of tea she proffered and eyed her quizzically.

'Sounds good to me.' Ellen felt bubbles of excitement.

She was *dying* to see the flat when he was finished with it.

'Let me show you three sets of plans I got the architect to draw up for you.' He knelt down and spread the plans down on the wooden floorboards. His hair glinted burnished copper under the light and Ellen found herself thinking how silky it was. Doug had always been well groomed, she thought approvingly as she knelt beside him. He explained the technical details to her. Patiently answering her questions. Between them, they decided on the best plan and she was sorry when he stood up to go.

'Why don't you call it a night?' he suggested, noting her stifled yawn as he handed her back the mug.

'Maybe I will. It's really busy at work these days with everyone buying their turkeys and hams. Thank God, Christmas only comes once a year.'

'I suppose your little girl is all excited?'

'Don't talk.' Ellen grinned. 'She's put ten letters up the chimney, just in case, and she's convinced she saw Santa's fairies flying out of Daly's chimney one evening we were walking home. It was a huge shower of sparks but she's certain sure they were fairies.'

'It's a great time for kids. I'm not mad about Christmas and I hate New Year.'

'Me too,' Ellen agreed fervently. 'This year's not so bad though. I've got my new flat to look forward to so that will keep me going.'

'Well that's something.' He smiled down at her.

'It's the first time I'll have ever lived in a place of my own. Imagine still living at home at my age.' Ellen made a wry face.

'I'm still living in my family home. When I was engaged a couple of years ago we had plans to build a house of our own but it all fell through so I didn't bother to leave.' Doug's eyes grew momentarily sad. The woman who'd let him go was a fool, Ellen reflected. There was something very manly about Doug. Not in a macho sense. But there was a strength about him. He reminded her, in ways, of Mick.

'Would you fancy going for a drink in the Arms?' Doug asked out of the blue.

'I look a bit of a sight. I'm not exactly dressed up,' Ellen murmured.

'You look fine. Just give your hair a brush, there's a few bits of plaster in it still. I might re-plaster that landing wall, it's not the best.' Doug walked out on the landing and studied the offending wall. He seemed to assume she'd go for a drink with him. Well why not, she decided suddenly. It was Friday night. She'd worked hard for weeks. She deserved a drink. And Doug was nice. It didn't matter that she was wearing just cords and a black polo. It wasn't as if it was a date or anything.

She brushed her hair, applied some lipstick and sprayed some *Apple Blossom* on her wrists and neck.

'Do I look OK now?' she asked as Doug strolled back into the room.

'I don't think they'll throw you out,' he teased. 'Do you remember the time a gang of us went over to Sweeny's pub in Fordstown, in Brendan Fahy's father's tractor and trailer, and we were thrown out. And Denise phoned up and said there was a bomb under Mr Sweeny's toupee?'

Ellen giggled at the memory as Doug led the way down the stairs.

'Denise was as mad as a hatter. Do you remember the time she told Bonnie Daly she thought she'd seen a vision on the gable wall of the church and Bonnie nearly wet herself with excitement? Denise told her to be at the church at midnight and she was hiding in the bushes with a Chinese lantern making shapes in the dark.'

Doug guffawed. 'Yeah I remember that. Then Denise told her she thought she had a vocation and Bonnie had all the women in the guild doing novenas that Denise would become a nun. She was a nutcase. She just lives across the road, doesn't she?'

'Yeah, she married Jimmy McMahon.'

'She might have been better off becoming a nun,' Doug commented drolly. Ellen burst out laughing again. They were still laughing an hour and a half later after shared reminiscences of their youth. Doug offered to take her home when she said she didn't want to stay out too late, but Ellen had Mick's car so she was OK.

It was a most pleasant evening. One of the nicest she'd had in a long time, she reflected as she undressed and got into bed. She'd forgotten what a wicked sense of humour Doug had beneath that reserved facade. She felt very comfortable with him. It was funny how she'd known him for years and never really taken any notice of him. He had beautiful eyes, she thought drowsily as she fell asleep.

*　　*　　*

Doug walked home through the dark winding lanes of Glenree. It was a bitterly cold night but the sky had cleared and the stars twinkled brightly. His breath was a frosty filigree on the night air but his leather jacket kept him warm as he strode along.

It had been a very enjoyable evening. He certainly hadn't been expecting to have such a laugh. He'd presumed it would just be a run-of-the-mill Friday night. He'd surprised himself by asking Ellen out for a drink. He'd known her for years, of course, but it had never dawned on him before to ask her out. It wasn't a big deal or anything, though he'd enjoyed her company. He'd forgotten what a dry sense of humour she had. She was easy to talk to as well. And she wasn't a bit mean. She'd wanted to buy him a drink after he'd bought the first round. Not that he'd let her. But Geena had never, in all their time together, once suggested paying for a drink. She was as tight as they come. He'd liked Ellen for offering. Beneath the tough veneer Doug suspected she was quite soft.

He was going to do a really good job on the flat. And he'd work morning, noon and night to get it finished so that Ellen could move in soon. From the little things she had let slip, living with Mrs Munroe was not a bed of roses.

Maybe Ellen might like to come for a drink with him

over the Christmas. She didn't seem to have a boyfriend as such. Doug knew that some of the blokes he drank with thought she was easy. He hadn't got that impression. He sensed she was someone who'd been very hurt. He could certainly identify with that, he thought wryly as he walked up his garden path. That was one thing they certainly had in common. It had been nice to laugh the way they'd laughed tonight. He was quite looking forward to renovating the flat for her, he decided as he let himself into his cold dark house.

Chapter Eighteen

It was bitterly cold. A biting wind stung Emma's cheeks. She inhaled the sharp piercing air and felt invigorated. It was a beautiful day. Naked trees stood silhouetted against the deep sapphire sky. The ground crunched frostily under Cleo's hooves as she cantered across the fields that ran parallel to the river. It was a perfect way to start the New Year.

She'd thought about not going for a ride this morning. It had been two a.m. before she and Vincent had got home from Gillian and Frank's New Year's Eve party. It hadn't been a great party. Declan Mitchell had got absolutely smashed as usual and puked all over Gillian's white leather sofa. It was *disgusting* and it put a real dampener on the evening. People started to drift off as early as twelve-thirty. She and Vincent had left around quarter to one and driven to Killiney Bay for a kiss and a cuddle. Emma grinned at the memory. Vincent was a great husband. He was very good to her, very protective of her. Completely different to that swine, Declan. Poor Lorna had been so upset she'd called a taxi and left. Emma pitied Lorna Mitchell. How awful it must be to know that people dreaded having your husband as a guest.

He'd better not puke in my house today, she thought grimly. But then he wouldn't have been drinking all day. She was having a luncheon party. It was a very clever move on her part, Emma thought smugly. Very sophisticated, very *in*. Luncheon parties were far less trouble than a full-scale evening do. And the joy of it was, she'd booked caterers to take care of it, so she had nothing to do. Hence her morning gallop. She was really glad she'd gone riding. Her head was clear and free from the lingering effects of last night's champagne. She'd drunk a lot of champagne. She loved bubbly. So had Suzy. She'd been fairly tipsy. Imagine having to face two little toddlers first thing this morning. Emma shuddered at the thought. Chris hadn't been in great form. He'd been arguing with Alexandra Johnston and it had turned quite nasty. A thought struck her.

'Oh my God,' she muttered. 'Did I? Oh hell!'

Emma reined Cleo in and sat deep in thought. She had. Definitely. It had popped out. Her tongue loosened no doubt by several flutes of champers. Emma gave a deep sigh and turned Cleo in the direction of home. She'd better go and get it over with and face the music. Vincent would freak . . . for sure.

*　　*　　*

'You did *what*? I don't believe it.' Vincent stared down at his wife.

'I'm sorry, Vincent. I was tiddly. It just . . . just slipped out,' Emma said penitently.

'You asked Chris Wallace and his wife to our lunch party?' Vincent shook his head in disbelief.

'Oh for God's sake, Vincent! Chris isn't a pariah. It all happened so long ago. Ellen's got over him. We keep meeting him. It's ridiculous at this stage. He's my cousin and I'm very fond of him.'

'He's also Stephanie's father. And he's never even seen his daughter,' Vincent snapped. He didn't want that bastard Wallace in his house.

'Look, Vincent. I'm sorry. I didn't do it on purpose. Maybe they won't come.' Emma looked at him, her beautiful brown eyes mirroring her distress.

He softened. 'Maybe they won't,' he agreed. 'Just don't expect me to fall all over them if they do. It's just as well Ellen is having lunch at Denise McMahon's. It would have

324

been extremely awkward if she'd been here. I'm sure she'd have felt very betrayed.'

Stuff her, Emma thought crossly. She was *delighted* Ellen couldn't make it to her party. If it was left to her, she wouldn't have invited her at all! She refrained from commenting.

'We won't say anything to Ellen about Chris being here. OK?' Vincent said sternly.

'OK,' Emma agreed, breathing a mental sigh of relief. He hadn't taken it too badly. Much better than she'd expected actually. 'I'd better go and get dressed,' she decided.

Vincent watched her walk out of the sitting-room. It was hard to stay mad with Emma for long. But he hated the idea of Chris Wallace coming into his house. Whenever they met at parties or at Emma's family gatherings, Vincent always studiously ignored him. What he really wanted to do was take him into a dark alley and thump the daylights out of him.

He and Ellen didn't always get on, but blood was thicker than water and Chris had made Ellen suffer. Vincent knew he had no real understanding of the pain his sister had experienced. He had, thankfully, never been hurt in love, but if it was anything like what he'd endured when he'd thought Emma was going to die when Julie Ann was born, it was pretty dreadful. Although Ellen exasperated him and infuriated him sometimes, and he didn't approve of what she'd done, she was still his sister and his loyalty was to her. And if Chris Wallace said one word out of place, he'd be out the door on his ear, no matter what Emma had to say about it.

*　　*　　*

'Do you want to go or don't you?' Suzy, bleary-eyed and hungover, turned over on her side and stared at her husband. Chris buried his head under the pillow and grunted.

'Answer me, will you?'

'Do *you* want to go?' Chris muttered.

'Well we haven't been invited to their house since that night you dumped me for Vincent's tarty sister. And that was years ago.' Suzy sniffed.

'Cut it out,' Chris growled. 'Who's going to mind the kids?'

'I'll ask Vivienne to. She's getting their breakfast. She'll be delighted with the extra money. You know students.'

'We've to go to Des Reid's party tonight.' Chris sat up, reached out and shook a cigarette out of the packet. He lit up and inhaled deeply.

'I wish you wouldn't smoke in the bedroom, Chris,' Suzy snapped.

'Ah give over. Is Alexandra going to this lunch?'

'I don't think so. She's not really a friend of theirs. She just knows Gillian and Frank. Why?'

'Because if she was going I wouldn't be. Smart-assed bitch!'

'Well you started it,' Suzy defended her friend loyally. 'You shouldn't have said that about her hair.'

'I only asked her was it deliberate or had her hairdresser a grudge against her,' Chris said sulkily. 'Every time I see her, her hair is a different colour.'

'Yeah, well she gave you your answer.' Suzy giggled remembering how Alexandra had swiftly riposted, 'At least I'll still have hair when you've gone bald.' Chris was extremely sensitive about his receding hairline.

'She's a big mouth and always was.' Chris scowled.

'Well are we going or not?'

'You're mad keen to go, aren't you?'

'It's up to you.'

'All right then.' Chris swung out of bed and walked into the ensuite, leaving Suzy staring after him.

Maybe she was wrong to push him, she thought. Something had happened between Vincent and Chris. She'd never asked about it, knowing that it was a subject that was taboo. It was something to do with the sister. A fleeting memory came to her. An image of a pale-faced girl standing between an older man and woman. It had been a long time ago and she'd never asked Chris about the trio who had knocked on his front door that Monday morning years ago. Instinctively, Suzy knew whatever had happened was something that could damage her relationship with her husband. It was something she didn't want to explore further. Suddenly she didn't want to go to lunch at the Munroes.

She got out of bed and walked into the bathroom. Chris was standing in the shower soaping himself.

'Maybe we'll stay at home,' she suggested.

'I'm up now, we're going. Let's see what the rich relations have done with the mansion since we were there last.' Chris grinned. He reached out his arm and pulled her in beside him.

'Chris!' She squealed as the water drenched her and made her nightie cling to her damp body.

'It turns me on,' Chris said huskily. 'Come on, baby, feel what it does to me.' He pressed himself close against her and kissed her hotly. 'Do you want me? Tell me you want me? Tell me what you want me to do to you?' he murmured against her parted lips.

'I want you,' Suzy whispered as he caressed her nipples with his thumbs. 'I want you to—'

'Mummy. Muuummyyy . . . Adam pulled my hair. Where are you?'

'Shit!' groaned Chris.

'For God's sake!' Suzy stepped out of the shower, closed the glass door and grabbed a towel as Christina barged in.

'Mummy, your nightdress is all wet!' Christina looked at her mother in amazement.

'Why aren't you down having your breakfast?'

Christina's lower lip wobbled. Her mother was cross with her. She'd been expecting sympathy. 'Adam pulled my hair!' She began to howl.

'Oh Lord,' Suzy groaned. Her daughter's high-pitched crying was giving her a headache.

'Stop crying. Stop crying,' she urged hastily. 'I'll deal with Master Adam.'

'Will you give him a slap?' Christina sniffled.

'Just go down and tell him he's in trouble when I've had my shower.' Mollified at the prospect of her twin's impending punishment, Christina raced out of the room to let him know retribution was at hand.

Suzy dropped her towel, and pulled her soaking night-dress over her head. She opened the door and stepped into the steaming cubicle. Chris wrapped his arms around her, but her desire had gone. She let him make love to her, half-expecting a return visit from Christina. Chris didn't notice her preoccupation, but then, he didn't take as much trouble to satisfy her as he had when they'd first become lovers, Suzy thought resentfully as he groaned with pleasure and climaxed.

Two hours later they drove through Drumcondra, heading for Glenree. Both were silent. Lost in their own thoughts. Suzy was sorry she'd brought up the subject of going to the Munroes. What if Vincent's sister was there? Maybe that was why Chris was suddenly eager to go. He'd had a fling with her once. Maybe he'd want to rekindle old passions. He was getting bored with her. Suzy sensed it in their lovemaking and it scared her. She didn't want to lose Chris to another woman.

Idiot! She cursed herself silently. Why couldn't you have left it alone? As the miles sped past, her stomach tensed up in knots and her head throbbed. It was her own fault, she thought savagely. This was something she'd brought on herself.

Chris tapped his fingers against the wheel. What the hell was he doing, going to Glenree? What kind of fucking asshole was he? He knew that Vincent would have his guts for garters if he could and that Emma had only issued the invitation because she was pissed.

What would he do if Ellen was at this party? What would he say to her? Maybe his daughter would be at it.

His six-year-old daughter whose birthday was St Stephen's day. He'd buried thoughts of them so deep. He'd cut them out of his life and pretended it was all a nightmare that had never happened. Ellen and Stephanie Munroe didn't exist as far as he was concerned. They hadn't existed for six long years. Until now.

He'd love to see Ellen again. The thought had consumed him since Emma had invited them to lunch. When he'd pulled Suzy into the shower that morning it wasn't her he'd been fantasizing about, it was Ellen. The thought of making love to her again excited him. Ellen had been the best lover he'd ever had. With her, there'd been no barriers. She had reached his mind, body and soul. She knew him for what he was. And she accepted him, faults and all. She had offered him unconditional love and he'd walked away from it. Walking away from Ellen had been the biggest mistake of his life.

She hadn't married. Emma would have told him if she had. He wondered did she ever think about him. Chris felt exhilarated, as if he were standing on the edge of a precipice. Maybe she'd be there. Mabye there'd still be a spark between them.

He pressed his foot on the accelerator. For the first time in months, Chris felt alive.

*　　*　　*

Ellen put the key into what would soon be her own front door and felt a little thrill of satisfaction. What a wonderful way to start the New Year. She felt optimistic. Stephanie raced up the stairs ahead of her. Ellen had been concerned about how her daughter would feel about leaving the farm; after all, it was the only home she had ever known. But Stephanie was as excited about the move as Ellen was. The idea of having her own bedroom was thrilling for her especially when she knew there was going to be a second bed for when her cousins wanted to stay over. She had often stayed with Rebecca, and very occasionally with Julie Ann, now she was going to be able to invite *them* to stay with *her*.

'I can't wait to have my bedroom in the roof.' She grinned a toothy grin. She'd lost one of her front teeth and she looked so appealing Ellen wanted to smother her with hugs.

'I can't wait for mine either.' Ellen beamed.

'Tell me again. What room is this going to be?' Stephanie danced into the bare front room.

'This is going to be our sitting-room. And this room in here . . .' Ellen led the way into the back room, 'is going to be our kitchen and dining-room.'

'Are we going to have a pantry like Nannie?'

'No, we're going to have a fridge like Auntie Miriam.'

'Are we going to have a toast maker like Julie Ann?'

'Yeah, why not? We'll buy ourselves a toaster,' Ellen declared. She was dying to have her own china and pots and pans. She'd had a most enjoyable time in the last few weeks, buying bits and pieces for her kitchen.

'Julie Ann said Auntie Emma said she wouldn't like to live over a shop.'

'Well *we're* looking forward to living over a shop, aren't we? That's all that matters. Isn't it?' Ellen smiled down into her daughter's trusting blue eyes. Emma was such a patronizing bitch and she said far too much in front of Julie Ann. Just because she'd walked into an easy set-up. Vincent slaved for her. She never had to worry about anything. All she had to do each day was to get up and enjoy herself. If she was in Ellen's situation, she'd be damn glad to live in a flat over a shop, Ellen thought furiously. Why couldn't she keep her smart comments to herself? And Julie Ann was a little brat, rubbing Stephanie's nose in it. She was always at it.

Forget it, she told herself. Don't let it spoil your day. She was looking forward to having lunch with Denise. It was an unexpected invitation. She'd gone down to the Glenree Arms with Ben and Miriam for a drink the day after St

Stephen's day. Doug had been there and he'd joined them. Then Denise and Jimmy McMahon had arrived and they'd all started talking about the old days. They'd had a great laugh. Even dour old Jimmy had had a chuckle.

'We really should do this more often,' Denise had said animatedly as she and Ellen powdered their noses in the ladies. 'I haven't had as much fun in ages. We used to have fun, didn't we, Ellen?' she added wistfully.

Ellen looked at her. Denise wasn't really happy. She could sense it. There was a strain between her and Jimmy. He kept putting her down really rudely as if he was trying to punish her for something. Doug had made some remark about the rugby season starting soon and how Mattie O'Donoghue, his neighbour's son, was likely to be selected for the reserves.

'Is he good at scoring goals?' Denise had asked politely. Sport was not really her forte, although Jimmy was a sports fanatic and always had his head buried in the sports results or the radio tuned to some match or other.

'You don't score goals in rugby. They're called tries,' Doug explained in amusement.

'Don't mind her, she's as thick as two short planks,' Jimmy grunted. Denise hadn't said anything. But Ellen was disgusted. Imagine putting your wife down in company. It definitely hadn't been said as a joke. Jimmy's eyes were full of resentment as he glowered at Denise. To think she could have had anyone and she'd ended up with him.

Ellen watched her apply some lipstick. Denise was very attractive. She was petite but very shapely and her dark brown hair had burnished glints of copper that shone under the bright hotel lights. Her green eyes sparkled with fun, but it seemed to Ellen that Denise no longer realized how attractive she was or what good company she was.

'I saw your sister-in-law the other day. She had a gorgeous sheepskin jacket. She looked like a model,' Denise remarked as she sprayed *Blue Grass* on her wrists.

'I've heard rumours she's having a lunch party on New Year's Day. Miriam and Ben have been invited. I'm trying to avoid her. I know Vincent will make her ask me out of duty and I just don't want to go. Ma and Da got out of it by offering to mind Miriam's kids,' Ellen said glumly.

'That's a bit awkward, all right.' Denise brushed her hair until it fell in a gleaming curtain around her shoulders. Her eyes lit up. 'I've an idea. Why don't I invite you and Stephanie and Doug to lunch? We've had great fun tonight. And I think you and Doug like each other.' Mischief glinted in her green eyes. In some ways she hadn't changed a bit, Ellen thought in amusement.

'You can stop matchmaking right now,' she said firmly. 'Doug's nice and I know he's going to do a good job for me. But that's as far as it goes.'

'Come to lunch all the same. I'd really like it if you would. We aren't going anywhere and the girls would love Stephanie to come and play. It's going to be great that we're only going to be living across the street from each other,' Denise pleaded.

'Are you sure? Won't Jimmy mind?'

'Him, he's on another planet these days. I never get two words out of him. All he does is give out when he's at home. He works too hard, Ellen. He's always stuck in the office. It would be good for him. Please. Please, please, please.'

It was hard to resist Denise when she put her mind to something and anyway Ellen would much prefer to have lunch with her than with Emma and her stuck-up friends.

'OK,' she agreed.

'Right,' Denise said firmly. 'Let's work on Doug.'

'What are you doing on New Year's Day?' she twinkled, sitting down beside him and slipping her hand in through his arm.

'What are you up to?' Doug eyed her suspiciously.

'What are you doing on New Year's Day?'

'I don't know yet. My sister wants me to go to her. I treat it like any other day.'

'I've just invited Ellen to lunch so that she won't have to go to Emma's. Will you come too?' Denise gazed at him in wide-eyed innocence. Doug glanced at Ellen. Inexplicably she blushed.

'Why not?' he said lightly.

'All sorted then.' Denise winked at Ellen. 'Doug, you can explain the finer points of rugby to me seeing as I'm so woefully ignorant.'

'Denise, I remember going to a soccer match with you once when the Glenree Rangers were playing and you were following the game so brilliantly you cheered when they scored an own goal. I wouldn't even *attempt* to explain rugby to you.' Doug snorted.

'I remember that,' Ellen guffawed. 'And do you remember the ball was out and it landed at Mary Boylan's feet and she gave it a kick and poor Gerard Redmond got it right in the goolies.'

'It gave him the thrill of his life. He probably hasn't had one since,' Denise chortled and they had all laughed.

Ellen smiled broadly thinking about that evening. It had been fun and she was looking forward to lunch. Emma was most surprised when she'd declined her invitation to 'The Luncheon'.

'Oh, I didn't know you had other plans.' She arched an eyebrow as if to say *who do you know that would want to invite you to lunch?*

'It's a long-standing invitation,' Ellen said sweetly. She wasn't going to tell Emma where she was going, even though she knew her sister-in-law was agog with curiosity.

No doubt she knew about it now, Ellen reflected as she dusted the window sill. She wouldn't be able to contain her curiosity for long. Vincent would have been dispatched up to Sheila to get the news. Or else, she'd ask Miriam out straight. Emma was as nosy as they come.

The doorbell rang and Stephanie rushed past her to get downstairs first. She was fizzling with excitement at going to lunch in Denise's. Michelle and Lisa were great fun. Julie Ann was jealous because they weren't really her friends. That gave Stephanie immense satisfaction.

333

Ellen followed at a more sedate pace. She could see Doug's broad outline through the glass panel.

'Happy New Year,' he greeted her, and handed her a beautiful scarlet poinsettia in a stylish ceramic pot.

'Oh!' Ellen was completely flustered. 'It's beautiful. Thanks, Doug.'

'It's to go on your new sitting-room window sill.' He smiled down at her and she was very touched. It was a kind gesture and typical of Doug.

As if it was the most natural thing in the world, Ellen reached out her free arm and hugged him affectionately. He hugged her back.

'Don't squash the plant,' he teased as she drew away.

'I won't. I'll just bring it upstairs. I've got a box of Milk Tray for Denise and some iced caramels for the kids.'

'Yum, iced caramels,' Doug said approvingly. 'I've some beer and wine in the car.' Ellen felt suddenly light-hearted. A feeling she hadn't had in years.

'Come on, Mammy. Come on, Doug,' Stephanie urged impatiently, anxious to get across the road to her new friends. Doug picked her up and swung her up in the air and she squealed with delight.

'Little Miss Impatience,' he scoffed and Stephanie grinned down at him with her wide gap-toothed grin and tweaked his beard. She liked Doug. He was good fun. He always explained what he was doing when she asked him and he'd promised to put a swing in the garden for her, first thing. He was nice and cuddly too, she thought as he yelled when she pulled his beard. If she was ever going to get a daddy, she'd like someone just like him.

Denise watched the trio through her front window and smiled with satisfaction. Ellen Munroe and Doug Roche were perfect for each other and she was going to do everything in her power to make sure they ended up walking up the aisle of St Joseph's.

*   *   *

Chris felt his heart pound. A strange heat enveloped him as he drove through Glenree at a snail's pace. He couldn't believe it. He'd hoped against hope that he'd see her. But he couldn't believe that she was nearly the first person he saw as he drove through the almost deserted main street.

It was Ellen. After all these years it was her. Thinner than he remembered. Her hair shorter and more groomed. Standing on Main Street embracing a man as a small girl skipped up and down impatiently. Chris twisted his neck to get another look. She and the man were smiling at each other. He felt gutted. Who was this man that made her look like that? She looked terrific. Somehow he'd never thought of her with another man. Because she'd loved him so much he'd assumed she'd never feel the same for anyone else. He'd kept her in a time warp.

He wanted to stop and get out of the car and go to her. He glanced in the rear-view mirror and saw the man swing the little girl up in the air. Jealousy, rage, pain nearly smothered him. That was *his* child. Not that stranger's. His emotions shocked him. How could he feel like this? He'd kept Ellen and the child he'd never seen out of his head for years. How could it be possible for him to feel so strongly about them still?

'Are you OK, Chris?' Suzy asked him. 'You've gone very pale.'

'It's just a touch of indigestion,' he muttered as he stepped on the accelerator and sped towards the turn-off that led to Vincent and Emma's.

The party was in full swing when they got there. Emma welcomed them at the door, took their coats and led them into the lounge. An enormous log fire blazed in the fireplace. A massive fir tree, strung with white and red lights, glittered in front of the floor-to-ceiling window. Red and white bows and shiny red and silver baubles hung from the branches. It was a masterpiece. Red candles entwined with white ribbons stood on the mantelpiece and small side tables. Boughs of red-berried holly decorated the walls. The Christmas decor was the height of elegance. Suzy had to admire Emma's style.

A maid in a black dress and white apron glided towards them bearing a tray of champagne. 'Help yourselves,' Emma urged gaily. 'You know nearly everyone here.'

Chris took a glass of champagne. He was dying to ask Emma if Ellen was coming. He'd seen Vincent's brother and his wife, although thankfully there was no sign of the parents. That could have been extremely awkward.

'I've just seen Angela Kennedy. I want to ask her if she's taking part in the mixed doubles at the club next week,' Suzy murmured. Chris was in a very odd mood. First he hadn't wanted to come. Then he had, now he looked as if he wished he were a million miles away. Was that girl here, she wondered, scanning the room, although the fact was, she couldn't remember what she looked like. Suzy'd been too pissed that night so long ago to remember much about the party. The sooner this lunch was over the better. She was too uneasy to enjoy herself.

'You're very down in the dumps,' Emma remarked as she watched Chris accept a second glass of champagne.

'I just saw Ellen,' he blurted out. 'Is she coming?'

'No she isn't. Thankfully,' Emma drawled. 'She had a prior engagement.'

'She was with some man. Who is he?'

'God knows!' Emma shrugged. 'It's hard to keep track with her.'

'Don't be a bitch, Emma,' Chris said sharply.

'Well I don't know who she's with. And what's it to you anyway? You dumped her as fast as you could when she got pregnant. What's wrong with you? Have you got a touch of the guilts after all these years?' Emma was amazed at Chris.

'I saw Stephanie,' he muttered.

'Oh!' Emma didn't know what to say. It must be a huge shock to see your own child for the first time. And to see her as a six-year-old at that.

'Ellen's doing a good job of raising her. She's a very nice child,' she said hesitantly.

336

'Do you have any photographs?'

'Ah Chris!' Emma was dismayed. 'Why don't you just leave it? Why torment yourself after all this time?'

'Please, Emma.' His tone was pleading.

'I'll root some out. There's one over on the TV unit, of the three cousins. Stephanie is in the middle.' She pointed to a corner of the elegant rosewood unit that ran the length of the far wall.

'Thanks, Emma.' Chris was sheepish.

'I shouldn't have invited you.' She looked troubled as she stared at him. This was a side to Chris she'd never seen before.

'I shouldn't have come,' he said heavily.

He made his way through the clusters of guests, some of whom called out greetings, until he was standing directly in front of the photograph. Hesitantly he picked it up. Three laughing little girls stared back at him. But Stephanie was all he had eyes for. She was his, unmistakably. And Ellen's. Dancing lively blue eyes smiled out at him. Silken black hair tied in two pigtails. A mouth made for laughing. She was so like her mother except for her eyes. They were his. He could see a resemblance to Christina too. It was uncanny.

Christina and Adam had a half-sister they knew nothing about. He wondered what Ellen had told Stephanie about him.

From the far side of the room, Suzy watched her husband study a photograph intently. He looked so sad, she thought in shock. Whoever was in that photo was the reason he was here. Angela Kennedy wittered on about the mixed doubles and about whether she'd run for secretary of the club again this year. But Suzy couldn't concentrate. She had to see what was in that photograph. And yet, as if she had a premonition, Suzy knew if she did it would rock the very foundations of her marriage.

*   *   *

337

'Ben, look! Look who Vincent and Emma invited to lunch.' Miriam was so stunned she just stood with her mouth open.

'Who?' Ben peered around the room. He was far more interested in having something to eat. He was ravenous, the smell wafting through the doors into the dining-room was making his mouth water.

'Look. It's Chris Wallace!' Miriam hissed.

'Good grief! What on earth would Vincent do that for?' Ben couldn't believe it.

'It was probably Emma. Still I think it's in very bad taste. Thank God Ellen's not here.' Miriam was furious. She stared at Chris Wallace. He was still the same good-looking charmer she remembered. A bit heavier around the waist, a little grey around the temples but still the same blue-eyed smoothie Ellen had fallen in love with.

Miriam wanted to give him a slap in the chops that would send him into the middle of next year. The *nerve* of him to turn up at Vincent's house as if nothing had happened. Not once in six long years had he contacted Ellen to see if she was all right or to ask about his child. He was breathtaking in his selfishness. How could Emma be so insensitive as to invite him? That girl had no cop-on at all, she thought in disgust.

'I don't want to stay for lunch. It's not right, Ben.' Miriam turned to her husband.

'Miriam, if we leave it's going to cause a row.'

'I'm sorry, Ben, I feel really strongly about this. Ellen's your sister and my best friend. If we stay here with that shit, it's as if we're condoning what he did to her. If Ellen ever found out he was here and that we'd mixed in his company, she'd be terribly hurt. I couldn't do that to her. I wouldn't.'

Ben stared down at his wife. She was very passive usually. But she was so angry now, she was flushed. She'd always been extremely loyal to Ellen. She'd shared every bit of her hurt and grief. She was right. They couldn't stay.

'I'll tell Vincent we're going.'

'No. I'll tell him,' Miriam said quietly. 'If he wants to fall out about it, he can fall out with me.'

She put her half-finished glass of champagne on a small coffee table and made her way over to where Vincent was standing with some friends.

'Hi, Miriam, Ben. Happy New Year,' he greeted them.

'Vincent, could we just have a word?' Miriam murmured.

'Sure. Excuse me.' Vincent nodded to his friends and took Miriam's arm.

'Nothing wrong, I hope.'

'Vincent. I don't want you to get the wrong idea or anything. But we can't stay in the same house as Chris Wallace. It's not fair to Ellen. If she ever found out he was here she'd be devastated. We're going to go.'

'It's nothing personal, Vincent. But Miriam's right. He never faced up to his responsibilities to Ellen and Stephanie and it looks as if we're condoning his behaviour. And I don't condone it one bit,' Ben said quietly.

'I don't either. I'd like to punch his pretty-boy jaw and kick his ass out of here. And maybe I will,' Vincent growled. 'I didn't ask him. I mean, do you think I would? Emma was tiddly at a party last night and she asked him. She didn't really mean to. She's sorry she did now. But I didn't think he'd have the neck to come. That man has no sense of decency or integrity.' He frowned. 'Look, it's not right that you should feel you have to leave. I'll ask him to leave. Emma shouldn't have invited him. I'll explain she was tiddly and that his presence here is an insult to Ellen.'

'No . . . no. Don't cause a row,' Miriam said hastily. 'We'll just go. You can explain to Emma afterwards.'

'But it's not right. I feel the way you do. I should have put my bloody foot down and made her phone him to cancel the invitation. It's just they were very close and she feels the past is the past.' Vincent jammed his hands in his pockets and glowered in Chris's direction. He didn't even notice. He had his back to them and was looking at something on the TV unit.

339

'Leave it,' Ben advised. 'We'll slip out. It's what we'd prefer. We'll be in touch.'

'I'm sorry, Miriam.' Vincent kissed her on the cheek.

'I hope you don't think I'm being unreasonable. I just don't want to be in the same room as him.' Miriam was distressed.

'I understand. And I'm sorry it happened.'

'See you then.' Ben patted his brother on the shoulder and then followed Miriam from the room.

'Are you sure you're not mad?' Miriam asked as they got their coats and left.

'Naw. You were right. Vincent is in a dilemma there. Emma just doesn't think sometimes. She's not deliberately bitchy. But she'd want to think things through. You just don't do things like that.'

'That set she hangs around with are so . . . I don't know . . . fast. Half of them are having affairs. And they're all trying to outdo each other. They've different values.' Miriam got into the cold car and shivered. 'Blast Chris Wallace. I was really looking forward to my lunch. One thing Emma *is* good at is having great food served up.'

'I know. I'm starving. If only we hadn't seen him until after we'd eaten. I don't think I could face cold turkey again.' Ben sighed.

'I'll tell you what. I have a couple of nice T-bone steaks. How about if I cook them with some fried onions?'

'No. It's your day off. I'll cook them. And I'll build up the fire and we'll have a nice cosy lunch together. We don't have to collect the kids for a while. Besides Ma would want to know why we were home so early and I think we should just keep this between ourselves.' Ben started the engine and turned on the heater.

'Oh definitely!' Miriam agreed. If Sheila Munroe knew Chris Wallace had been invited to Vincent and Emma's there'd be the mother and father of a row. And that was the last thing the Munroe family needed. Things were bad enough between Sheila and Mick over Ellen moving out. A row with Emma and Vincent could divide the family.

Especially if Emma got up on her high horse. If Sheila or Ellen heard about Chris, it wouldn't be from her lips, Miriam vowed as they drove along the winding road towards home.

*   *   *

'*Entre nous* of course but I think maids in black dresses and white aprons is just a bit OTT. I mean where does she think she is? Beverly Hills?' Gillian bitched to Diana Mackenzie as they sipped champagne and watched people go up to the enormous hot and cold buffet for seconds. She wouldn't go up for seconds. She wouldn't give Emma the satisfaction of knowing how much she'd enjoyed the delicious food.

'Typical Emma. She had to try and outdo everyone. Mind you it must be costing a fortune. It's the best of champagne and they're not skimping on it.' Diana, in spite of herself, was hugely impressed. This was a seriously posh party.

Gillian was totally pissed off. Emma's lunch was a huge success. It was like a wedding. No-one else had caterers and maids. No-one else was lashing out Dom P. as if money was no object. No-one else had a red and white Christmas tree with dinky little bows. Her own tree, which she'd thought was a classic, had baubles of every size, shape and colour and seemed a tinselly gaudy mess in comparison.

Even Declan Mitchell was relatively sober too, she thought resentfully. She'd never forgive him for puking all over her sofa. It was the last party of hers he was ever being invited to. Lorna could come on her own or not at all. Friendship only went so far.

'Great party isn't it?' Frank said cheerfully as he arrived back to the table with another huge helping of Boeuf Stroganoff. 'This is scrumptious.'

'Oh you're easily impressed, Frank,' Gillian derided. 'It's only beef stew with a posh name you know.'

'It's the nicest beef stew I've ever tasted then,' Frank

retorted as he tucked in with relish. The smell of it was too much for Diana.

'I think I might just try another little bit. I didn't have any breakfast,' she murmured. 'Excuse me.'

Gillian watched her go with slitted eyes. Diana Mackenzie might *think* she was sophisticated, but she was no more sophisticated than the man in the moon.

'Hi, Gillian, Frank. I haven't had a minute to talk to you. Everything OK? Are you enjoying lunch?' Emma sank down gracefully into Diana's vacant chair.

'Wonderful party, darling,' Gillian effused. 'The food is very tasty . . . for caterers.'

'Oh, these aren't just any old caterers.' Emma smiled sweetly. Gillian needn't think she was getting away with that bitchy barb. 'Vincent and I believe in paying good money to get the best. And that's what they are. It's terrific not to have to worry about food so that you can mingle with your guests. It's nice to have something different. People get tired of boring old cold meats and salads at Christmas. Don't they?' She stood up as Diana came back. 'I'm glad to see you're enjoying your meal, Diana.'

'It's really tasty, Emma. I'm heartily sick of cold turkey. This is delicious,' Diana gushed.

'Enjoy.' Emma smiled smugly at Gillian and then went to join Chris, Suzy, and the crowd at their table.

Gillian was incandescent. That bitch. How dare she make patronizing remarks about cold meats and salads. *That* was what she'd served up for supper last night. It hadn't been any old salads either. There'd been Waldorf salad, Caesar salad, salad Nicoise. The utter *cheek* of her. There were times when Emma Munroe was just too big for her boots. Why she stayed friends with her, Gillian simply did not know.

*   *   *

Lorna Mitchell pushed the food around her plate. She couldn't eat. Her stomach was tied up in knots. Her palms were sweaty. Her heart was racing. No-one knew to look at her that she was having a panic attack. She hated Christmas. She dreaded its coming. Declan had made a holy show of them last night. He was on the way to getting smashed again. She couldn't take this for much longer. She'd lived with it for nearly seven years. The drunkenness. The verbal abuse. The kids, white-faced, watching their father rant and rage.

She had thought Declan Mitchell was the nicest man in the world when she met him. He'd been charming, attentive, kind, funny, sexy. Everyone thought highly of him. You couldn't find a more decent chap. Even up to the last year or so, before his drinking had got out of control, people thought Declan was a great bloke. He was always ready to give a lift or a helping hand. He was a street angel and a house devil *par excellence*. No one would have believed the years of emotional abuse she'd suffered. She tried to tell them, sometimes, when she was desperate but no one believed her and in the end she gave up. Declan had everyone fooled. They didn't see the moods, the foul language, the tearing away of every bit of self-esteem and confidence she had. Only last week, they'd been watching *The Late Late Show* and she'd made some observation.

'What would you know about it, you stupid cow?' Declan grunted from where he lay sprawled in his armchair. 'You're only an imbecile.'

Lorna watched him, mauling Nina Monahan. Grinning down at her, teasing her, in that jokey intimate way he had. Nina was loving every minute of it. But then, she would. Nina was man-mad. Forty and manless, she was pretty desperate. Lorna watched her flirting with Declan. She was such a hypocrite! You'd think butter wouldn't melt in her mouth. Declan said something to her. She giggled and fluttered her eyelashes at him. They were having a fling, Lorna knew it.

Something snapped in her. She'd had enough. If Nina was so desparate that she'd take Declan knowing the sort he was now, she was welcome to him and his abusiveness, his moods and his selfishness. And Declan was more than welcome to her. God knows he'd bad-mouthed her often enough to get a laugh from friends. They were well suited. She didn't care any more.

She got up and went out to the hall. Declan's sheepskin coat was hanging up on the hallstand. The car keys were in his pocket. She put on her own jacket, traced some lipstick over her lips and slipped out through the front door.

Lorna stood on the step and took some deep breaths. Her heartbeat slowed down. Her head felt clearer. She was afraid but she was exhilarated. By the time Declan got home this evening, if he got home – sometimes he stayed out all night – she and the children would be gone. Her widowed father had often told her that she could come back home and live with him. At least she'd have peace of mind. She couldn't take the emotional torture for one more minute. It was so difficult pretending to other people that Declan's behaviour was acceptable when it wasn't. He was on his own now. He could start accepting responsibility for his actions without her to make excuses for him. Maybe she wasn't the perfect wife. Maybe she wasn't a *cordon bleu* cook or a great housekeeper. She had her faults, she knew that. But she'd been prepared to keep her vows and make their marriage work. He hadn't. It would suit him of course that she'd walked out first. Everyone would feel sorry for him, pity him. And Nina would be seen as his saviour for rescuing him. Sly Nina who'd pretended to be her friend.

Let them think it. They'd never know the hell Lorna had lived. But no more!

Feeling that a huge load had lifted from her shoulders, Lorna sat into the Peugeot and drove at speed towards home. Maura, the babysitter, would be surprised to see her back so soon. She'd ask her to help pack up all the children's clothes and toys. Needless to say Maura would tell the world and his mother about the split. It would be a juicy piece of gossip but Lorna didn't care any more. She might never see the set again. They were Declan's friends

344

more than they were hers. She was sick of them and their superficiality. All trying to outdo each other. All bitching about each other behind their backs. She'd been as bad herself. She didn't like the person she'd turned into. That was all going to change. Today was the beginning of a New Year and the start of her new life.

*　　*　　*

Chris and Suzy were chatting to Josie Donovan and her husband. Rather they were listening to Josie twittering on about how Beckett's work was poetry in its *absolute* form, according to Josie, who thought she was highly intellectual. Suzy thought she was an *absolute* bore. Chris's expression had taken on a glazed look. Suzy knew he was miles away. She eased away from them and walked towards the unit where the photograph Chris had been studying was. She didn't want to look at it. The thought of what was in it scared her. She wanted to go home but she knew wild horses wouldn't keep her from picking it up.

Suzy lost her nerve. Swallowing hard she walked upstairs and went into the pretty pink and grey bathroom. She splashed water on her face and patted it dry with some tissue. She knew Chris was restless and that her marriage was in danger and she didn't know how to rescue it. Why couldn't he be content with what he had? The twins. A lovely home. Her. Why wasn't she enough for him? She loved him. Why wasn't her love enough? What was he searching for? There'd always been a restlessness about Chris that she couldn't understand. He'd had a lot of girlfriends before he'd married her, he was no saint, she'd known that. But he'd married *her*. She was the one he'd wanted to share his life with and have his children. That had to mean something still. It *had* to. Whatever was in that photograph that had made him look so sad was from his past. It was a photograph of her rival. The woman who was suddenly a threat after all these years. Suzy squared her shoulders. She'd fought a hard battle to get Chris

345

Wallace to put a ring on her finger. She wasn't going to give him up that easily. No ex-girlfriend was going to get the better of her.

She marched downstairs and back into the lounge. Defiantly she picked up the gilt-framed photograph.

'Oh no!' she muttered as she stared into a pair of blue eyes that might have been Chris's. 'No! No! No!' Vincent's sister had had Chris's child. Christina and Adam had a half-sister. And Chris had kept this from her all through their marriage. Did he see them still? Was he still sleeping with that woman? Suzy didn't know what to think.

Bastard! Bastard! Bastard! she swore silently, her hands trembling as she put the photograph back in its place. Well that was it. That woman could have him. He was never getting into her bed again. She wanted to bawl her eyes out and claw her nails down his face. She wanted to hurt him the way he'd hurt her. But she had to stay composed. She couldn't disgrace herself in front of everyone. It would be the talk of every dinner party in the city if she did that.

I hate you Chris Wallace. I loathe you her mind screamed. *Why?* Would this damn party never end? She needed to be by herself. It was the worst day of her life.

*   *   *

'Vincent, it's a party not a funeral,' Emma scolded. She was annoyed with him. He was spoiling the party for her with his bad humour.

'Miriam and Ben left when they saw Chris Wallace was here,' Vincent retorted.

'What! I don't believe it. For heaven's sake what did they do that for?' Emma hadn't even noticed that her in-laws weren't around.

'They did it out of loyalty to Ellen. I should have put my foot down, Emma. I don't ever want to see him in this house again.'

'Well I think you're being unreasonable, Vincent. But I'm not going to fight with you about it now. I've a house full of guests to take care of but thanks very much for ruining *my* day,' Emma whispered furiously before marching away. She was really annoyed with Vincent. And with Miriam and Ben. It was the last time they'd be invited to *her* house. How dare they put Ellen's feelings before hers. This luncheon had been the most successful bash she'd ever thrown. Everyone was raving about it. But it meant nothing now because Vincent was annoyed with her. Emma could cheerfully have throttled Ellen Munroe.

*　　*　　*

'Did you enjoy yourself?' Doug asked Ellen as he held open the car door for her.

'I had a terrific time. Denise is great fun, isn't she?' Ellen waved at her friend who stood smiling at the front door. 'It was like old times. I'd forgotten how much fun we used to have when we were teenagers.'

'Me too. Life changes you, doesn't it?'

'Yeah. Look at Denise even. She used to be so vivacious. She was wild. Now she seems . . . I don't know . . . kind of crushed.' Ellen sighed. 'Mind, if I was married to Jimmy McMahon, I think I'd be crushed too. He's hard going.'

'They say opposites attract and you certainly couldn't get more opposite than those two,' Doug said wryly. 'Still, once he got into the swing of things it was good fun.'

'The best fun I've had in ages. And it was so unexpected.' Ellen turned to Stephanie in the back seat. 'Did you have a good time, Stephanie?'

'Yeah, Mammy. Michelle and Lisa have loads of Lego, even more than Julie Ann. We built a massive big house. It was brill.'

'Was it?' Ellen smiled at her daughter's enthusiasm.

'Mammy, when we move to our new house can Michelle and Lisa come and play with me?'

'Of course they can, pet.'

'If you like, when I'm building your new bedroom I

347

could put a play corner in your room with little presses for your toys,' Doug suggested.

'Like in *Mary Poppins*? In the nursery?' Stephanie asked, wide-eyed. The nursery in the film had fascinated her. Ellen often heard her telling her dolls they were going to the nursery.

'Sure. We'll make a nursery.' He winked at Ellen.

'Oh Mammy, I'm so excited. I wish I could be like *I Dream of Jeannie* an' blink my eyes an' wiggle my nose like she does an' we'd be in our new house.'

'It won't be long now. Doug will be starting on it soon.' Ellen found it hard to contain her own excitement. To have her independence after all these years was a dream come true.

'Are you in an awful rush home?' Doug started the engine and looked at her.

Ellen was surprised at the question. 'Not really.'

'How about if we drive into Dublin and show Stephanie the Christmas lights?'

'Please, Mammy, please can we?' Stephanie pleaded, her eyes like saucers at this unexpected treat.

'Are you sure, Doug? I thought you were going to call on your sister,' Ellen demurred.

'It's still early, another couple of hours won't make any difference. It's up to you.'

'Thanks, Doug. We'd love to,' Ellen agreed happily. It was so long since a man, apart from her father, had treated her with kindness, she'd forgotten what it felt like. She felt very comfortable with Doug. He was good company and he treated her with respect. It felt nice. This was definitely the best New Year she'd had since Chris. Maybe her luck was changing at last.

*   *   *

'Why didn't you ever tell me you'd got Vincent Munroe's sister pregnant? Was it before we were married or after?' Suzy couldn't contain her anger. They were driving back towards the city. It was almost four and the pinky purple hues of the setting sun cast a pastel tinge over the still countryside.

Christ shrugged. He'd seen Suzy study the photo. Seen her sudden pallor and knew that she knew. There was nothing he could do about it. It had been bound to come out sometime.

'Are you still seeing them? Have you been seeing them all along? Christ, Chris, just tell me the truth for once in your goddamn life.' Suzy started to cry.

'I haven't seen Ellen since before the child was born so I've never seen her at all. I didn't know what she looked like until today,' he said flatly.

'Do you support them?'

'No.'

'How do they manage?'

'I've no idea.'

'Where does she live?'

'On Main Street, I think. Her father has a butcher's shop.'

'Have you ever been in her house?'

'No. I told you I've never seen her since we split up. She lived at home when I knew her.'

'Were you having an affair with her when we were together? Were you having sex with her when you were having sex with me?'

'Ah Suzy! What the hell difference does it make now? It was a long time ago. I'd broken up with her before we got engaged,' Chris said wearily.

'It makes a hell of a damn difference, you bastard! I feel used and dirty,' Suzy raged.

'For God's sake, Suzy. You're overreacting.'

'Did she mean anything to you?'

'We were . . .' Chris searched for a word that wouldn't cause Suzy pain. 'We were . . . close.'

'Why did you come to that party today? Did you hope to see her?' Suzy tried to swallow the lump in her throat.

'I dunno.' Chris grimaced. He knew Suzy was frantic.

He felt sorry for her. She was a good wife, she tried her best. It wasn't her fault he was a mixed-up mess.

'Look, Suzy, stop crying. Emma asked me to come. I like Emma, she's a mate. I shouldn't have accepted the invitation. Vincent has no intention of burying the hatchet. So forget it. I won't be going back there. Ellen has her own life. The child doesn't know me. I turned my back on them when I found out Ellen was pregnant. I'm not proud of what I did. I can't go waltzing back into their lives. I'm sure that's the last thing Ellen would want.'

'Do you want to go back into their lives? Do you want to see her again?' Suzy demanded fiercely.

'No. Now forget it, I told you, OK?' he gritted. He'd had enough of this interrogation. 'I don't want to see her again. It was over a long time ago.' He squeezed his wife's hand.

Liar! he swore silently. More than anything else in the world, he wanted to see Ellen Munroe and his blue-eyed black-haired daughter.

Chapter Nineteen

A wave of nausea swept over Emma as she looked at the runny yellow egg yolk that Julie Ann was dipping soldiers of bread into. A cold sweat broke out on her forehead and she just made it to the loo to be ill.

When it was over, she knelt on the cold hard tiles and cried her eyes out. Vincent knelt beside her, sponging her face.

'Oh, Vincent, I'm pregnant. I know it. I'm four weeks over and now this. What am I going to do? I don't want to have a baby. I don't want another child.' Great gasping sobs shook her body.

'Maybe it's a bug. Maybe it's your system getting back to normal after being on the pill,' Vincent soothed.

'No. I know I'm pregnant. That night of the party. That's when it happened. I should have been more careful. I just got confused at my counting. I thought I was still safe.' Emma wept. Arithmetic had never been her strong point. Now she was paying the price for mixing up the dates in her cycle.

Vincent led her into the bedroom and helped her into bed. 'Just relax for a while. I'll get Julie Ann off to school.'

Emma watched him leave and then turned her head into the pillow and burst out crying again. Why was this happening to her? More than anything in the world she dreaded being pregnant and having another baby. Julie Ann was enough of a handful as it was. The thought of all those nappies and bathing and feeding and the loss of her precious freedom was more than she could bear. And the idea of being fat again filled her with disgust.

She really couldn't blame anyone except herself. After the party on New Year's Day, Vincent had been extremely cool with her. He'd hardly spoken two words to her. That was most unusual for him. They rarely rowed. They'd gone to bed not talking. In the end, she couldn't stand it any longer. She'd started to cry and he'd taken her in his arms and apologized. She'd apologized for asking Chris to the party and one thing had led to another. In the heat of passion she'd miscalculated her safe period and she'd told Vincent he didn't need a condom. Just one little mistake and her life was ruined. This was if she was going to have a life. After the frightening drama of Julie Ann's birth she had visions of herself at death's door again. It was scary. Emma sobbed uncontrollably.

* * *

'Come on, Julie Ann, hurry up with your breakfast and stop messing,' Vincent said sternly. Julie Ann pouted at his tone. In spite of himself Vincent had to smile. She was so like her mother.

'Is Mummy sick, Daddy?' She licked the egg yolk from her fingers.

'She's a bit under the weather today so I want you to wash your hands and face and get ready for school, while I put the dishes in the sink for Mrs Byrne.'

'OK. Will you buy me a Trigger bar for being a good girl?'

'Yes. Now go clean up.' Vincent watched Julie Ann leave the kitchen, her blonde pigtails swinging jauntily. How would she cope with a new baby? She'd been the centre of attention for so long it would be very hard on her having to give up centre stage to a new sister or brother.

Vincent sighed as he stacked the dishes into the sink. Maybe it was a false alarm. Although he felt that was just wishful thinking. If Emma was pregnant, they were up the creek. She couldn't cope with another child. She couldn't even manage Julie Ann. Poor Emma was like a child herself sometimes, he thought ruefully. Especially when a crisis occurred. But he didn't blame her for being upset. After what she'd been through having Julie Ann it was very worrying to think of how she'd get through another birth.

What a start to the year, he thought dispiritedly. That damn New Year's Day party had been the start of all their troubles.

Ben and Miriam had walked out. Lorna Mitchell had driven off without Declan and they'd heard later that she'd taken the children and left him. That was tough on poor old Declan, Vincent thought. True he might get pissed now and again but he was a nice chap, very obliging. Leaving him in the lurch was a mean thing to do. But then Lorna was an anxious restless woman. Maybe he was better off without her. From the gossip Vincent had heard, Nina Monahan was consoling Declan and she was supposed to be head over heels in love with him.

And it had all happened at their party, Vincent thought wryly. He'd had a bad feeling at the party, probably because of that obnoxious bastard, Wallace. It had been a dreadful way to start the New Year, nearly six weeks ago. And now this. The phone rang and he went to answer it.

It was his mother-in-law, Pamela. She was distraught. Her elderly mother, who'd been in excellent health, had suffered a fatal heart attack. She wanted Emma to collect an old aunt and bring her to the hospital to say her farewells.

Vincent's heart sank to his boots. Emma was never the best in a crisis. She was going to be no help at all now because of the way things were. He knew it was an awful thing to think, but there'd been no love lost between Emma and her grandmother – who'd felt that Emma was a spoilt baggage – so at least she wouldn't be paralysed with grief at the funeral. He'd take a few days off work because Emma wouldn't be able to handle things on her own. Heavy-hearted, he went upstairs to break the upsetting news to his wife.

'Oh Vincent, why did she have to die today of all days? I feel lousy. I don't want to have to bring Aunt Edna into St Vincent's. You know the way she whines,' Emma moaned.

'Emma! Your grandmother's dead. I'm sure she didn't want to die,' Vincent said sternly.

'Yes, well she was a crotchety old interfering busybody. She didn't think *you* were good enough for me, so don't expect me to be a hypocrite and pretend I'm sorry she's dead. Because I'm not.' Emma sulked.

'Now stop it. Your mother needs you. I'll take a couple of days off work. I'll ring Miriam and ask her will she mind Julie Ann after school so that we can do whatever your mother needs us to do. Come on, get dressed.'

'You're very good to me, Vincent.' Emma touched his face.

He leaned over the kissed her. 'We'll get through this. Don't worry.'

'I know,' she sighed. *But I hate being pregnant and I don't want this baby* were her unspoken thoughts as she held Vincent's hand tightly.

*   *   *

Would Ellen come to his grandmother's funeral, Chris wondered as he sat in his office unable too concentrate on the pile of letters awaiting his signature.

Hardly. His grandmother was nothing to Ellen. Vincent and Emma would, of course, be there. And Mr and Mrs Munroe. Possibly Miriam and Ben too in a show of sympathy for Emma. But Ellen and Emma didn't get on. No! It was wishful thinking on his part.

It was almost six weeks since he'd seen her on New Year's Day and not an hour went past when he didn't think of her. It was as if the barriers he'd erected over the past six years, when he'd resolutely put her out of his head, had come tumbling down, and now all those suppressed thoughts came pouring back in a damburst of obsession.

Had she put him out of her head? Did she ever think of him? Now his fantasies were all of her. Did she ever fantasize about him? Or were her thoughts and desires all for that tall bearded man who'd made her smile? Chris was consumed with vicious jealousy when he thought of him.

It was as if he'd lost control of his life. Why now? After all these years? Was it because the thought of living the life he'd been leading — a life that had become increasingly stale — stretched over the decades to come in a flat depressing vista that filled him with dread?

He cared for Suzy, but he didn't love her. He told her he loved her. It tripped off his tongue lightly. It always had. He'd always told the women he'd been with that he loved them. They seemed to need that affirmation of his feelings for them. Deep down Chris knew that the only woman he'd ever really bonded with and loved was Ellen. And he'd been so terrified of it, so afraid of committing himself to her, he'd run away from her. Ellen had known the real him, he could never hide his feelings from her like he could from Suzy. Suzy only knew the facade. And he was trapped with her and his children. He was almost forty, life was downhill from now on.

Chris got up and walked over to the window. It was a beautiful spring day. The vivid blue sky was softened with wisps of fluffy white clouds drifting past on the breeze. A rowan tree across the road was beginning to bud and a window box in a cafe window was bursting with yellow and purple crocuses. The sight only increased his restless panic. He felt smothered, oppressed. Even his work, which had always challenged him, was a grind.

He flicked through the pages of his leather phone pad, came to the M's and found the entry marked E. That was all he'd written in the space. Just E and two numbers. Home and the shop. He dialled her work number, his heart pounding.

'Hello, Munroes.' Her voice had that same faintly husky

timbre that he remembered. She sounded light-hearted. 'Hello?' she repeated.

Chris opened his mouth but he couldn't speak. What would he say to her? Dry-mouthed, he hung up.

'Idiot!' he cursed himself as he picked up his pen and began signing his letters.

*　　*　　*

'He's so moody, Alexandra. I know he's thinking about her. He tells me he isn't. But I don't believe him.'

Alexandra Johnston raised her eyes to heaven as she listened to Suzy whingeing on the other end of the phone. That was all she did these days, moan and whinge about Chris. She was heartily sick of it. Didn't Suzy realize how bloody lucky she was with a husband and a fine house, two adorable little kids and an affluent lifestyle? She knew she was being bitchy, but there were times when she was deeply envious of her best friend. Suzy had the looks, the personality, the style and a life that Alexandra now secretly longed for. Everything dropped into Suzy's lap, effortlessly. It always had. A bit of hardship now and again wouldn't do her a bit of harm, she thought crossly as Suzy launched into a tirade about Chris.

What did she expect for heaven's sake? Chris Wallace was a womanizer and always had been. If Suzy had thought for one minute that he was going to change his ways she was a fool! That he'd lasted this long was a miracle. It came as no surprise to Alexandra that he had a love child. Men were bastards and she'd put enough of them through her hands to speak from experience.

The last man she'd been involved with, Will Fennelly, had walked out on her because she'd told him she couldn't make up her mind between him and another lover. He'd walked instead of staying and fighting for her. He'd failed the test. She hadn't cared about the other guy. She'd just wanted Will to put his foot down with her and act like a real man. But he'd wimped out on her and now she was on her own again and she hated it. She'd had enough of being single and free. That had been fine in her twenties and she'd played around with the best of them but now, in her mid-thirties, time was no longer on her side. Having your independence was nice, and it suited her, and men admired her for it, but that fine line between being independent and being left on the shelf was edging much too close for comfort. She felt like telling Suzy to bugger off.

'Look, I have to go, Suzy,' she said impatiently. 'I'll talk to you later.' She hung up and began composing a saccharine letter to a celebrity she wanted to come to a charity fund-raising dinner she was organizing for one of the firm's clients. *She* had to work for a living. Suzy didn't.

*   *   *

Suzy put the phone down and burst into tears. Everyone was deserting her. Chris might as well be on another planet these days and Alexandra didn't want to hear her tale of woe. It was very mean of her best friend. Suzy had supported her in her trials and tribulations with men. She'd always shown her sympathy when Alexandra needed it. Especially over her recent break-up with Will. It wasn't too much to expect the same consideration from her, now that she was going through a very difficult trauma. That's what friends were for. But then Alexandra had always been selfish like that. *Her* traumas were far more important than Suzy's.

Suzy walked into the kitchen and began clearing the lunch dishes. Resentment and bitterness against Chris and Alexandra filled her and, in a moment of uncontrollable anger, she lifted a cup and fired it against the kitchen wall and watched it smash into smithereens onto the floor.

*   *   *

Sheila dialled the shop's number. She was mentally selecting and discarding outfits to be worn to the removal of Emma's grandmother's remains. Pamela and her moneyed family would no doubt be dressed to the nines. They wouldn't find Sheila Munroe lacking. Vincent had phoned earlier with news of the bereavement. He said Emma was too upset to come to the phone.

Ellen answered. 'Is Mick there?' Sheila asked.

'No, he's gone to the bank.'

'Tsk. Well tell him that Emma's grandmother died suddenly this morning. I'd say the removal service will be on tomorrow evening. And the funeral the next day. We'll have to go.'

'Oh,' Ellen said.

'I presume Ben and Miriam will want to go. Are you going to put in an appearance?' Sheila asked snootily. Ellen was so busy organizing the flat these days, she was hardly at home.

'I don't think Emma would care whether I was there or not,' Ellen said matter-of-factly.

'Well you could go for Vincent's sake. He'll need the support of his family. And I want the Connollys to see that we can be counted upon for that,' Sheila declared. 'After all the girl is your sister-in-law whether you like it or not.'

'I'll see,' Ellen said irritably. 'I'll tell Dad to give you a call when he gets back. I have to go. There's a queue.'

Sheila replaced the receiver, and then dialled the hairdresser's. She'd have to get her hair set. She wanted to look her best. Fortunately Joanne, of *Joanne's, London, Paris and Rome*, was not rushed off her feet and assured Sheila that she could fit her in if she came by in half an hour. Sheila was delighted. The set would have settled nicely by the following evening.

She went upstairs to go through her wardrobe. She had a good black suit, kept for such occasions, and a little black hat with a veil. That would do for the funeral Mass. But what to wear for the removal had yet to be decided. It was a pity her pure new Irish Wool coat was red. It was very smart. She'd got it for Christmas. But red was not at all suitable for such an occasion. She took out a navy anorak and discarded it. Not half dressy enough. A bottle-green three-quarter-length coat. she could wear her navy skirt and navy court shoes . . . Perhaps.

Trust Ellen to make a song and dance about going. Typical, she thought crossly as she rooted for the navy skirt.

Sheila thought of something. Her jaw dropped in dismay. Maybe Ellen shouldn't go. That Wallace brat would probably be there. Maybe Ellen was right to keep away. After all, the delicacy of her position had to be kept in mind. Pamela and the judge mightn't want her there.

Sheila cringed. She should have kept her mouth shut. Now she was in a right pickle. She'd been looking forward to the funeral. A morning out and a chance to show the Connollys that she was as good as they were. Now, if Ellen decided to go, it would be most embarrassing. Sheila frowned. It was very vexing to say the least. She put her clothes back in the wardrobe and walked slowly downstairs. If she suddenly turned around and said Ellen wasn't to go, Ellen would get on her high horse and there'd be a row and she'd probably go to annoy her. This matter had to be treated with subtlety. She'd ring Miriam and have a chat with her. Miriam could talk to Ellen and point out the awkwardness of the situation. Sheila sighed deeply as she dialled the number. Just when things seemed to have got on an even keel again and she and Mick were the way they used to be, *this* had to happen.

*   *   *

Miriam listened in silence as her mother-in-law explained her dilemma. Her heart sank when she heard Sheila say sweetly, 'So I was wondering, dear, if you might have a quiet word with Ellen and point out that it isn't really appropriate for her to go the funeral. We don't want any unpleasantness. And we don't want the Connollys . . . you know . . . looking at Ellen and making her feel uncomfortable. I'll leave it to you to do your best. Ellen listens to you more than she listens to me. That's why I'm asking this favour. I have to go now, dear. I need to get my hair done and they said they'd squeeze me in without an appointment. Bye, bye.'

Miriam heard the click at the other end of the phone as Sheila hung up. She replaced her own receiver resentfully. It wasn't fair of Sheila to involve her in this. It could lead to bad feeling between her and Ellen. What was she going to say to her? Miriam fretted. That Sheila didn't want her to go to the funeral because she was ashamed of her? Because no matter what her mother-in-law said, no matter how she tried to cover it up with pretended concern about how the Connollys would view Ellen's attendance at the funeral, it was shame, not concern, that motivated Sheila. Her mother-in-law would always hold Stephanie's illegitimacy against Ellen. The passing of the years wouldn't change that.

She should have just said she preferred not to get involved, Miriam thought, disgusted with herself that, once more, she'd allowed Sheila persuade her to do something she didn't want to do.

*   *   *

Ellen could hear the dull insistent thud of the hammer upstairs as Doug nailed up the plasterboard on the new dining-room partition. It was music to her ears. She was thrilled with herself. The two bedrooms and the new bathroom in the attic conversion were done and the end was in sight. Soon she'd be living in her own home. Her new bedroom was light and airy, with a skylight and a little dormer window. Doug had suggested panelling the sloping ceiling in pine and it was very warm and clean.

Stephanie's room was just like hers except, true to his word, he'd got his carpenter to build shelf units that blocked off one small corner into a play area. Stephanie was beside herself with excitement.

Ellen glanced at her watch. It was almost time for lunch. She was starving. She'd made a steak casserole for lunch, the night before, and Miss Boyle in the coffee shop next door was heating it up for her. Ellen had got into the habit of having her lunch with Doug and Harry, his partner. She usually cooked stews or casseroles or hotpots and the men tucked into her cooking with gusto. It was nice to feel she was repaying Doug in some small way. He was exceptionally kind and had worked morning, noon and night to get this far in the work.

Her father arrived a few minutes later and Ellen told him the news about Emma's grandmother.

'I suppose I'll be trussed up in my good suit for this,' he sighed. 'I wouldn't mind but St Pat's are playing Bohemians tomorrow evening and I wanted to go on to the match.' Mick was a St Pat's supporter and they were having a run of good luck, the championship was within their grasp. 'Isn't that just my luck?'

'Don't go to the removal. Just go to the funeral,' Ellen suggested.

'Do you want me to be shot? Could you imagine the face of your mother if I told her I was going to a match and she could go to Dublin on her own? Because she'll be at both services, come hell or high water. Do you think she'll have the Connollys talking about her? My plans are ruined and that's all that's to it. I better go home for my lunch and see what she has to say about it.'

'She wants me to go,' Ellen said ruefully. 'To give Vincent family support. I suppose I'd better put in an appearance or I'll be the worst in the world.'

'Well you know what your mother is like, God bless her. Appearances count for everything . . . especially where the Connollys are concerned. I'll get Stella O'Neill to put in a few hours on Wednesday evening and Thursday morning to cover for us.'

'OK.' Ellen patted her father fondly on the back and then locked the shop door and went next door to the coffee shop to get her casserole.

Doug was washing his hands when she walked into her new kitchen.

'Howya, Ellen,' he greeted her in his usual cheery manner. 'That smells good, I'm famished. Harry,' he yelled up into the attic. 'Chow time.'

Harry didn't need a second summons. He clattered down the winding wooden stairs. 'Let me at it, Ellen. This is the best job we've done in years. No one feeds us like you do.'

'Oh I'm just keeping you sweet so you'll do a good job, Harry,' Ellen joked as she began serving up.

'Yeah, well I've put on half a stone since I started eating your cooking. My wife is giving out to me because my clothes are getting too tight.' Harry tucked in with gusto.

Doug looked at Ellen and winked. 'Maybe we'd better stop feeding him, we don't want him falling through the floorboards.'

'Give over!' Harry snorted as he forked a piece of steak into his mouth. Ellen gave him another helping of casserole.

'Good girl.' He beamed. The men ate with relish and later, as they drank a cup of coffee, Harry turned to Doug. 'Did you tell Ellen the plumber's coming tomorrow evening to finish up the central heating?'

'Oh great,' Ellen exclaimed.

'I suppose you'll be here?' Doug asked. 'You can do the ceremonial switching on but bring your swimsuit just in case we have to swim out of here.'

'I wouldn't miss it.' She smiled at Doug. Behind the quiet facade he had a great sense of humour and his calm easy-going way was always reassuring, especially when the flat looked as though a bomb had hit it. A thought struck her.

'I'll be later than usual. Emma's grandmother died. I'll have to go to the removal and it's on the other side of the city.'

'We won't switch on without you', Doug assured her. 'By the way, remember I told you I'd ask my mate to keep an eye out for a car for you? Well he's got a nice little

Triumph Dolomite coming in today. I'll take you over to Swords this evening if you like to have a look at it.'

'Oh Doug!' Ellen was elated. 'What colour is it?'

Doug laughed. 'That's typical of a woman. A man would ask how old it is? What's the mileage? But a woman always asks what colour is it.'

'Well what colour is it?'

'It's a surprise. But I think you'll like it.'

'Ah Doug, please.'

He raised a finger at her, 'Now! Now! patience is a virtue.'

'Doug Roche, you're a swine.'

'Thank you. Flattery will get you nowhere.'

'Ah Doug, please tell me.'

'Nope.'

Ellen leaned over and tugged at the beard on the side of his cheek. Because it was neatly clipped it was hard to get a good grip but she gave him a wigging nevertheless.

'You can torture me all you like. I'm not telling you.' Doug laughed.

'You're so stubborn.'

'That's me. You'll have a surprise when you see it. But it's really, *really* nice . . .' he teased.

'For that you can do the washing-up.' She stood up, ready to leave.

'No problem, Harry and I are very domesticated. What time do you want to go to Swords at?'

'Would eight be OK? I'll have Stephanie in bed by then.'

'Yeah, fine.' He looked at her. 'Why not go earlier and bring her with us? It would be a great surprise for her,' he suggested.

'That's a lovely idea. She'd be chuffed.'

'Right. What time then?'

'Six?'

'See ya then.'

That evening, as she cycled over to Miriam's to collect Stephanie, she smiled thinking of Doug's thoughtfulness. He was very good with Stephanie. He had a way with kids.

363

That girlfriend of his was a complete fool to have let him go. He was dead nice and she really felt she'd found a friend. She cycled faster. She was dying to see the car. She didn't stop for her usual gossip when she got to Miriam's.

'I'm galloping.' She puffed. 'Doug's friend has a car for me to look at so Doug's bringing us to Swords to see it. I'll call in later and tell you all about it,' she informed her sister-in-law who was setting the table for tea. 'Quick, Stephanie,' she called out the back door.

'Are you going to Emma's grandmother's funeral?' Miriam asked.

'Oh probably. Look I'll talk to you later. Don't think I'm being rude but I have to fly. Doug's waiting.' Ellen ushered Stephanie out the door ahead of her. 'See you later.' She never noticed that Miriam looked troubled.

'Where are we going, Mammy?' Stephanie asked as Ellen lifted her on to the carrier.

'It's a surprise.' Ellen smiled and kissed the top of Stephanie's head. She got on the bike and pedalled furiously, eager to get back to the flat where Doug was waiting.

He'd washed and changed out of his working clothes and was all ready to go.

'Hiya Doug.' Stephanie hurled herself at him.

'Hi Steffi.' Doug pulled her pigtail affectionately.

'Where are we goin'?'

'Wait and see.'

They got into Doug's cream van. Ellen was as excited as her daughter. Ten minutes later they drew into the forecourt of Rafferty's garage on the outskirts of Swords. A gleaming smart little white car with a For Sale sign caught her eye.

'Is that it?'

'Yep.'

'Oh Doug it's *gorgeous*!' she breathed. 'I'm dying to have a look at her.'

'A look at what, Mammy?' Stephanie didn't know what all the fuss was about.

364

'See that little car over there? I might be going to buy it for us.'

'Yippee,' Stephanie hollered. A car! Now they'd be like her cousins with their cars and Julie Ann wouldn't be able to say, 'You've no car and we've got two.' Their own home and a car. It was just brill.

'Let's have a look at it,' Doug suggested.

It was in immaculate condition and, while Doug and his friend poked around under the bonnet, Ellen and Stephanie sat in it and explored the interior. Ellen tried out the gears and studied the manual that came with the car.

'Do you want to take it for a trial run?' Doug stuck his head through the open window.

'Can we?'

'Yeah, here's the keys. Let's go.' He handed her the keys and helped Stephanie into the back and got in beside Ellen. 'OK, let's hit the road.'

Ellen was nervous as she started the ignition. But her apprehension soon turned to exhilaration as she steered onto the main road and put her foot down.

'Let's go as far as the back of the airport,' Doug suggested and Ellen daringly increased her speed to thirty m.p.h.

An hour later, she'd put a deposit on her first car. It was one of the proudest moments of her life. Doug had assured her that it was mechanically sound and she was getting it at a good price. She was glad to have him to rely on because she wouldn't have known from Adam whether the car was mechanically sound or not. It looked lovely inside and out but it was reassuring to know that everything was in good condition under the bonnet.

'Thanks for everything, Doug. I really love it,' Ellen said later, when he dropped her and Stephanie home. 'Do you want to come in for a cup of tea?'

'I won't, Ellen, thanks. I've to collect some timber from a fella in Drogheda and I'll have to bring him out for a pint. I'll see you tomorrow. OK?'

'OK and thanks.'

'You're welcome.' Doug smiled and once again she was struck by his good nature. Doug had a niceness about him that was genuine.

'See you tomorrow.' She stood at the front door waving after him while Stephanie rushed in to tell her grandfather that they were going to buy a car.

Mick was delighted and was full of questions about mileage and horsepower and petrol consumption. Ellen was, thanks to Doug, able to answer knowledgeably. Her father was impressed.

Sheila was at a guild meeting. She wasn't as frosty these days but she hadn't taken any interest in the renovations of the flat and had not taken up Ellen's invitation to come and have a look. She'd probably have something to say about Ellen frittering away her savings on a car but Ellen didn't care. She'd saved hard over the year. She wasn't a spendthrift. It was the first luxury she'd had since Stephanie was born and, once they were installed in their new home, she'd start saving again.

After she'd put Stephanie to bed Ellen decided to visit Miriam. She was dying to share her good news with her.

'Dad, I'm going to pop over to Miriam's for an hour. Stephanie's asleep. She was whacked out. Is that OK?' she asked her father who was reading his paper beside the fire.

'Right, see you later,' Mick said.

Ellen went over and kissed him on the cheek. 'Thanks, Da, for everything you've done for me. I could never have managed without you.'

'You'd have done fine. But I'm glad you're going to have a place of your own. It's the best for you and Stephanie.' Mick patted her shoulder. 'Do you want the car?'

'No thanks. I'll cycle. It's good exercise.' Ellen fastened her coat and put on her gloves.

'Mind yourself on that bike, there's a very bad pothole over by Red Barn's Hill. We don't want you coming a cropper.'

'I'll be careful,' Ellen promised.

As she cycled along in the dark, with just the stars and

silver moon to light her way, Ellen was almost exuberant. This was the best year she'd had in a long time. Her life was changing completely. All the old hurt and pain and anger and resentment seemed to have faded away. Her thoughts were too full of her new home, and now her new car, to dwell in the past. The old days of depression and oppression had lifted. She was in control again and it was an immensely satisfying feeling.

'Hi, Miriam,' she greeted her sister-in-law cheerily, ten minutes later.

'Hiya, Ellen come in.' Miriam was sitting beside the kitchen fire sewing a patch on Daniel's jeans. The house was quiet, the children were in bed. Ben was working late. The lamplight and flickering flames gave a welcoming snug feeling. Ellen hung up her coat and looked forward to a chat and a cuppa.

'Wait until I tell you my news.'

'What?' Miriam grinned. Ellen was in great form. It was lovely to see her back to her old self.

'I've put a deposit on a gorgeous white Triumph Dolomite. Oh Miriam, she's a little beauty. I'm so excited.' She did a little twirl around the kitchen.

'That's *great*, Ellen. I can't keep up with all this good fortune.'

'I can't either. I can't believe all the things that are happening. Doug came with me. He said it's a good buy. Did I ever think I'd see the day when I'd have my own car and my own home?' she bubbled.

'Let's have a cup of tea. I'll put the kettle on. Throw a few logs on the fire there and we'll have a natter,' Miriam ordered.

They sat by the fire, Miriam listening as Ellen told her about the central heating and the partitioned kitchen and dining-room. And how Doug had told her that she could start decorating shortly.

'I'll help with the papering and painting. We'll have it done in no time.' Miriam topped up their mugs and offered Ellen another scone.

Ellen shook her head. 'I'm too excited to eat.'

'My God, Munroe, I've never heard *you* say anything like that before.' Miriam laughed. 'You're looking great. That weight loss really suits you and your hair is gorgeous like that.'

'I've been so busy with the flat and everything. Food just doesn't seem important any more.'

'I wish I could think like that.' Miriam sighed. 'All I do is eat.'

'When I move over to Glenree, why don't we make a date that you come over to me twice a week after tea? Walk over. I won't be able to go out as much now, because I won't have Ma and Da to babysit. It would be good exercise for you.'

'Yeah. Maybe I will,' Miriam agreed.

'No maybes about it.'

'Listen, Ellen,' Miriam said hesitantly. 'Your mother phoned me to tell me about Emma's grandmother. Umm . . . are you going to the funeral?'

Ellen raised her eyes to heaven. 'Oh she was on at me this morning, saying we had to support Vincent. You know Ma! She wants to make a good impression on the Connollys. I suppose I better go, although to be perfectly honest, as you well know, I couldn't give a hoot about Emma or her grandmother. I'll go for the sake of peace.'

'Do you think it's a good idea?' Miriam asked delicately.

'Well I can't really win, can I? If I don't go, Ma will think I'm the worst in the world and if I do go, Emma will probably think I'm a hypocrite.'

Miriam took a deep breath. She couldn't figure Ellen out. Surely it must have dawned on her that Chris would be there. 'How do you feel about seeing Chris?' she asked.

'What!' Ellen looked startled.

'Well I'm sure he'll be there. He's her grandson after all.'

Ellen was stunned. The thought hadn't even entered her head. She'd been so consumed with all that was going on these past few weeks, Chris had been the last person on her mind, she realized with a little shock. She'd often imagined seeing him at some family gathering, and had she not been so occupied with all her plans it would have been the first thing she'd thought of. Maybe she *was* over him. It was a liberating thought!

'I don't think you should bother going,' Miriam murmured.

Ellen's light-hearted exuberance faded. For years she'd waited for an opportunity like this. A chance to see Chris Wallace again. In her dreams she'd imagined him looking into her eyes after being so long apart and realizing that he really did love her. She was a fool she knew. Chris didn't give a damn about her. He'd cut her out of his life with a callous ruthlessness that had caused her immense suffering. Why would she want to revive all those hurts especially now that her life seemed to have turned around so wonderfully?

'Blast Emma and her goddamn grandmother,' she muttered. 'I don't know what to do.'

'Why go and upset yourself?' Miriam asked gently. 'Leave the past where it belongs.'

'Yeah, maybe you're right,' Ellen said flatly. 'I think I'll go home and have an early night. I'm bushed.'

'It's terrific news about the car.' Miriam tried to restore Ellen's good humour.

'I'm delighted.' Ellen smiled with false gaiety. 'I'll see you tomorrow. Thanks for supper.'

She left the warmth of Miriam's kitchen with regret. Her evening was spoilt. The past had come rushing back, swamping her *joie de vivre*. Tormenting her with conflicting emotions and desires. Should she go? Should she stay? Whatever she did, she'd regret it. If she went and saw Chris and he ignored her or was coolly polite, it would kill her. If she didn't go she'd always wonder had fate given her a chance and she'd ignored it.

Mick was in bed and Sheila wasn't home, for which Ellen was very grateful. She made herself a cup of hot chocolate and sat beside the still glowing fire. Only the steady ticking of the old carriage clock broke the silence.

The aromatic smell of recently cooked brown bread lingered. The ticking and the smell she associated with her childhood. Some things never changed. And some things did, she mused. Miriam was right. the past was the past. Let it go. She drank her hot chocolate, washed and dried her cup and slipped upstairs to bed.

Sleep eluded her. She heard her mother come in and go through the routine of closing down the house for the night. A routine that hadn't changed in more than forty years.

Ellen lay in bed and all the old bitterness sharpened its teeth on her. Chris was probably hoping that she'd stay away. It would be much easier for him if she did. He'd never had to face up to the consequences of his actions. As far as he was concerned Stephanie didn't exist.

Fuck him, she thought angrily. He'd got away too easy. Too damn easy. He always had. Well she wasn't going to hide away as if she was a pariah. She was going to go to that service tomorrow and she was going to look a million bloody dollars. And so was Stephanie. Let him see that they'd managed perfectly well without him. Let him see what a little beauty his daughter was . . . and eat his heart out for what he'd missed.

She lay in the dark imagining their reunion, imagining the stunned surprise on her ex-lover's face when she walked up to shake hands with the bereaved family, as was the custom. Let *him* feel embarrassed . . . *she* would hold her head up high.

*   *   *

Sheila was agitated. Miriam had led her to believe that Ellen wasn't coming to the removal of the remains, so why was she getting out of the car with Mick at four-thirty in the afternoon instead of coming home at six as she usually did? And why was Stephanie with her? Ellen couldn't possibly be going . . . and with Stephanie! Sheila felt a hot flush start at the base of her neck and work its way right to the top of her scalp. In the name of God what could she be thinking of?

Maybe she had come home early to take care of Stephanie because Ben and Miriam were going to the service. That was it. Of course. Sheila felt almost faint with relief. Then she noticed that Ellen had had her hair styled. She watched with dread as her daughter and granddaughter walked towards the door.

'Hurry up now, Stephanie, wash your face and hands and I've left your good pink dress on the bed. Change into it when you're ready,' she heard Ellen say as they came into the house.

Stephanie galloped upstairs. She adored outings.

'You're not bringing Stephanie to the church? She's a bit young. Why don't you stay at home and go to the funeral yourself tomorrow if you feel you need to? Actually thinking about it, there's no need for you to go at all. Emma will understand that your father has to have someone look after the business for him,' Sheila said lightly, as if she'd just thought of it.

'She's dying to go. Julie Ann's been boasting about how important she's going to be because she's to put Mass cards on the coffin. There was a row going on over in Miriam's about which of their three was going to put their Mass card on the coffin, and Stephanie is determined she's not going to be left out. So we might as well go,' Ellen declared. 'Anyway I don't want Emma saying I've snubbed her by not going. I'll just run upstairs and change.'

Sheila bit her lip. There was no answer to that. She'd been hoist by her own petard. If she turned around and said bluntly to Ellen that she didn't want her or Stephanie to go because of their situation, Ellen would explode. Mick would probably take her side. If Sheila made an issue of it there'd be another row with him and that was the last thing she wanted. The best thing to do was to say nothing and put up with it. But it was most distressing, she thought crossly as she fastened her best cameo brooch to the lapel of her coat and stood to admire her reflection in the big ornate gilt-edged mirror that hung on the wall.

* * *

Ellen slipped out of her skirt and jumper, had a quick wash and put on a straight pencil-slim skirt and a black polo jumper. It was a very slimming outfit and she was very pleased with herself. Losing that stone had made such a difference. She made up her face with extra care, outlining her eyes with a light grey kohl pencil after she'd applied her eyeshadow. She patted powder over her foundation and sucked in her cheeks to add a touch of blusher. Finally a shading of *Health Glow* lipstick and a generous spray of *Blue Grass*.

Ellen stood back to view herself critically, after all it was nearly seven years since he'd last seen her. She'd been pregnant then. Her hair worn long. She'd been pale and distressed and pleading.

No, she was not that girl today. She'd been tempered by hardship. She was much stronger than that frightened, desperate young woman. Now she was independent and in control. She was much slimmer. Still curvy, but in a more elegant way. Her hair was short and sophisticated, shiny and sleek after coming from the hairdresser's. Her hazel eyes sparkled with anticipation.

'Yes, baby. I got over you,' she muttered.

'*Liar!*' her inner voice taunted. '*Why are you dolling yourself up to the nines? Why does it matter?*'

It was pride, she told herself. Just pride. But she couldn't look herself in the eye.

'Mammy, will you do my hair, please?' Ellen was grateful for the interruption. She didn't want to be thinking dangerous, upsetting thoughts.

'You look lovely, pet,' she praised her daughter as she brushed her silky black hair and secured it high up on her head in a pony-tail. She brushed down her fringe and smiled at the solemn blue eyes staring up at her. Ellen felt a

372

huge rush of protective love for her little girl. She was so innocent and trusting. When she was younger she'd often asked about her daddy and Ellen had told her that he lived far away and that there was just Mammy to take care of her. But that Grandad, especially, and Uncle Ben and Uncle Vincent were minding her too. This had always reassured Stephanie and, so far, not having a father did not seem to be a huge problem. That would come when she was older. That and the difficult, searching questions that would have to be answered honestly.

'I love you.' She bent and kissed Stephanie and held her tightly.

'I love you too, Mammy. You look lovely. Can I have some perfume?' Stephanie flung her thin childish arms around her neck and gave Ellen her speciality bear-hug.

'Of course you can.' She sprayed a little on her wrists and Stephanie inhaled the scent with pleasure.

'*Beeauutiful*,' she murmured.

'Are you girls ready?' Mick shouted up the stairs.

'Coming.' Ellen took her good royal blue coat out of the wardrobe and put it on and buttoned it up. It fell straight and elegant from her shoulders. She wound a soft black angora scarf around the neck and stared at her reflection in the mirror. If Emma's grandmother had died six months before, she'd have looked fat and frumpy. Thank God she'd lost that weight and got her hair cut. She knew, with immense satisfaction, that she'd never looked better. It gave her the courage she needed.

*   *   *

Chris sat in the old dark ornate church that reeked of candle wax and damp and polish and watched his mother, back ramrod-straight, gazing directly ahead showing not an ounce of emotion. Typical. Katherine Wallace was as cold and unemotional as ice. Chris had never seen his mother cry. Beside her Pamela wept discreetly behind her handkerchief.

Further along the seat, Emma sat disconsolately with Vincent's arm around her. She looked wretched. Pale and red-eyed. Chris couldn't understand it. She'd never cared for their grandmother. Julie Ann was hopping up and down like a yo-yo looking for her cousins from Glenree so that she could show off. Just like her mother. Chris grinned.

He and Suzy had got a babysitter. Christina and Adam were much too young to bring to something like this. Besides they'd all be expected back at his mother's house afterwards and it would be too late for the kids to stay up. Beside him, Suzy sat aloof and unhappy. The strain between them since she'd discovered he had another child ebbed and flowed. Sometimes she was OK, other times she was cold and unloving. He wasn't helping the situation. He was moody, restless and unhappy. He wondered would Ellen show up. He was so tempted to turn around and scan the crowds but Suzy would know what was in his mind. He couldn't.

He'd seen Miriam and Ben and their children standing on the steps of the church as they awaited the arrival of the coffin but of Ellen and her parents there was no sign. He felt bitterly disappointed.

The priest began the service and everyone knelt to pray.

*   *   *

Sheila was mortified as she led the way up the side aisle of the church. Mick had got lost and they'd arrived late. The coffin was already at the foot of the altar and the priest had started. She caught sight of Ben and Miriam and slipped into the pew behind, which had some spaces. Ellen followed with Stephanie and Mick brought up the rear.

Ellen sank to her knees and blessed herself. She took a deep breath and directed her gaze to the seats at the front. Her heart skipped a beat as she saw Chris, dressed in a grey business suit, beside the ever elegant Suzy who wore a belted black coat and a fur Cossack-style hat atop her blonde bob.

Chris knelt with his head in his hands so that she couldn't see his profile. Suddenly she was sorry she'd come. Her heart was pounding, her mouth was dry and she felt light-headed. What would she say if he spoke to her? She must keep her composure. It was vital. She murmured the responses to the prayers and, although it only took twenty minutes, the service seemed to take for ever. Finally it was over and people began to form an orderly queue to go up to offer their condolences to the bereaved family. Sheila stood up. This was it, Ellen thought. Head up.

She ushered Stephanie in front of her and followed Sheila. Slowly the queue moved forward as people stopped to shake hands and murmur words of sympathy to Pamela, Katherine and their families.

Four rows to go. Chris was sitting staring straight ahead at the edge of the second row. The queue shuffled on. Someone burst into tears. Ellen's palms felt sweaty. Sheila moved slowly forward. Stephanie followed. They stopped again. Stephanie was standing directly beside her father's seat. Ellen just behind her. She was so close to him she could have reached out and touched his dark hair. That dear familiar head that had lain on her breast as she stroked his hair after their lovemaking. She saw him turn slightly. He looked at Stephanie and looked again. Shocked!

Ellen felt a surge of fierce triumph. She lifted her head and stared straight ahead but was aware with every fibre of her being that Chris had turned to look at her. She was sure he could hear the beating of her heart as she passed by him. But she didn't look. She wouldn't give him that satisfaction. Then she was past him, showing Stephanie where to put the Mass card in the basket at the foot of the coffin. Sheila was shaking Pamela's hand, murmuring something. Ellen turned and followed, acutely aware that Chris was staring as she offered her condolences. Pamela gave her a limp handshake. Ellen passed along the row, with her mother, shaking hands with the dark-garbed family.

'Thanks for coming,' Emma said politely. They didn't

kiss. Julie Ann greeted her cousin with a squeal of delight. 'Are you coming to the party after?' she asked. Stephanie looked up at Ellen.

'Do come back to Aunt Katherine's,' Emma murmured.

'It depends on Nannie and Grandad,' Ellen whispered as she prodded her daughter to follow Sheila. She kept her gaze ahead of her and followed her mother down the aisle of the church.

'I'm not going back to their house this evening. They'll have too many visitors,' Sheila declared. 'They know we came, that's all that matters.' Ellen felt an awful sense of anticlimax. Was this it? Was that all she was going to see of Chris? She hadn't even see him properly. He was still in the church and already Mick and Ben were leading the way through the throng out on the church steps to where their cars were parked.

She longed to go racing back into the church. She wanted to stand in front of him and call him all the names under the sun. The hurt that had been buried for so long was back as fresh as the day he'd given it to her. Mutely, Ellen followed her parents to the car. Tomorrow was still to come. There'd be much more of a chance to see him then. Because she wanted to see him. Badly. She wanted to look him in the eye and see if he could meet her gaze. At least he'd seen Stephanie, she thought grimly as Mick eased the car out of the church grounds, into the flow of traffic.

As they drove towards Glenree she remembered that Doug was trying out the central heating for the first time. Her heart sank. She wasn't really in the humour. All she wanted to do was to go home and wallow in old, sad memories. But she had to go. They were making a big deal of it and it would be extremely rude of her not to be there when they'd said they'd wait for her.

'Mam, I was wondering if you'd do me a favour and put Stephanie to bed for me? Doug wants me to be there when they try out the central heating so I could get Dad to drop me off before you go home. I'm sure Doug would give me a lift home,' she added.

'Certainly,' Sheila agreed in quite a pleasant tone. She was utterly relieved to be heading home, with no comments from anyone about Stephanie or Ellen.

'Thanks, Mam,' Ellen said wearily.

'Will you tell me the story of *The witch. The witch. Who lives in the woods. She's not very pretty, she's not very good*?' Stephanie asked. It was her favourite. That and *Christopher Robin*.

'I will. If you're good.' Sheila turned to smile at her granddaughter.

'Let's do *Christopher Robin* now,' Stephanie begged.

Sheila began to sing:

'*Little boy kneels at the foot of his bed,*
Droops on his little hands, little gold head.
Hush! Hush! Whisper who dares.
Christopher Robin is saying his prayers.'

As Ellen listened to Stephanie's sweet little soprano voice accompanying her mother in the old much-loved song of her own childhood, tears pricked her eyes. Sheila had sung that to her as a child. Now she was singing it to her granddaughter. At least, whatever the rift was between her and her mother, Sheila did love Stephanie very much. That was a blessing to be thankful for.

She swallowed hard and sat with her arms around her daughter as the little girl sang the whole way to Glenree.

'We'll see you later, Ellen,' Mick said when he pulled up outside the shop. Doug's cream van was there. And so was the plumber's.

'Goodnight, Stephanie, be good for Nannie. I'll be home soon.' Ellen kissed her and got out of the car. She let herself into the flat. Harry met her at the top of the stairs.

'We're all ready to go,' he informed her.

'Hi, Ellen.' Doug stuck his head around the door. He looked at her and his eyes narrowed.

'You OK?'

'I'm fine.' She pretended light-heartedness. 'Do I crack a bottle and name this ship and pray for all who sail in her?'

'Let's hope we won't be sailing anywhere,' Doug said

dryly. 'Come on. Here's your control. Just click this switch here and, if everything's all right, you'll hear a low humming. That means the boiler's ignited and the pump is going.' He pointed to the switch in the hall. 'Go on,' he urged.

She pressed the switch and a low humming broke the silence.

'We're still in one piece.' He grinned. 'Now all we can do is sit and wait for a while to make sure the water's going through the system. The kettle's boiled. Would you like a cup of tea?'

'I'd love one,' Ellen said fervently as she took off her coat.

'You look nice,' Doug remarked as he took her coat from her.

'Thanks,' she said quietly. 'Doug, would you be able to give me a lift home? I came straight from the funeral.'

'Of course,' he said. 'Just sit down there and we'll hang on for a little while to make sure this lot's all right. Here's today's paper if you want a read.'

'Thanks,' she said, grateful for his solicitude.

'If you and Harry want to head off, we'll hang on here,' she heard him say to the other two men. Ellen was relieved to hear them agree to his suggestion. She wasn't in the humour for their usual jokey teasing. She said her good-byes and sat reading the paper as Doug made the tea.

'Here you go.' He handed her a mug.

She took it from him gratefully and sipped the hot brew.

'Was it a very sad funeral?' Doug asked sympathetically, mistaking the reason for her subdued air.

She shook her head. To her horror two large tears plopped into her teacup.

'What's wrong, Ellen?' Doug was beside her in an instant. Concerned.

'Oh Doug. I saw Stephanie's father for the first time in years. He's never seen her until today. And I'm just in bits.' She burst into tears. Great heaving, gulping sobs that came from the core of her.

'Ssshh. Don't cry. It's all right,' he comforted, putting his arms around her.

'I shouldn't have gone. I thought I was over him. Will I ever get him out of my head?' she asked in desperation.

'These things scar you, Ellen. I know that. But you can't let them ruin your life,' he said quietly as his arms tightened around her and he stroked her hair as she cried like a child.

When it was over he dried her tears, very gently. 'You better go and fix your make-up before I bring you home. You don't want your parents to see you're upset.'

'You're very kind,' she gulped.

'A pal can help a pal.' He stood up. 'I'll just tidy up here while you're repairing the warpaint.'

Ellen took out her compact and stared at herself. Her mascara had run down her cheeks and her eyes were red-rimmed. She looked a disaster. She was pathetic, she thought in disgust as she redid her make-up. All her hard-won self-possession destroyed because she'd made a stupid idiotic decision to hang on to silly dreams that should have died a death years ago.

That was it now. She'd seen him, for all the good it had done her. From now on he was out of her life. She wasn't going to the funeral in the morning. She'd paid her respects to the family. Emma couldn't fault her.

'That looks better,' Doug remarked.

'I feel better,' Ellen said firmly. 'Thanks for putting up with my blubbering. I don't know what got into me.'

'Come on, I'll bring you home. You won't have time to think from now on. You can start papering. I'm finished inside. I just have to do the patio and the job is done.'

Ellen linked her arm in his. 'It's a lovely job. I'm really pleased with it.'

'You'll have your new car too.'

'I know. I'm going to put tonight out of my head and get on with it. I've a lot to look forward to.' Ellen put on her coat, tied her scarf around her neck and followed Doug downstairs. Tomorrow she was going to ask Miriam to

379

help her with the wallpapering. The sooner she moved in, the better.

Sheila was making marmalade when she got home. 'I thought you'd be later,' she remarked.

'We just had to see if the heating worked. And it's fine. Did Stephanie go to bed all right?'

'She was grand.' Sheila skimmed the top of the rich orange mixture.

'I don't think I'll go to the funeral in the morning. I'd like to be in the shop in case Doug needs to ask me anything. He's going to tile around the kitchen sink tomorrow. I paid my respects tonight. I'm sure Emma won't mind,' she said casually. She half-expected Sheila to protest but, to her surprise, her mother agreed.

'There's no need for you to go. Your father and I will be there to represent the family. Miriam can come with us if she wants to.' Sheila's tone was equally casual.

Was she imagining it or was there a note of relief in her mother's voice? Whether there was nor not, she wasn't going to the funeral. Tonight had been trauma enough.

'I think I'll have an early night. Thanks for taking care of Stephanie for me.' Ellen yawned.

'She's no bother.'

'I'll bring her to visit and she can stay over sometimes if you'd like,' Ellen said awkwardly.

'She'll probably forget all about me. She'll have her swanky new bedroom and the like.' Sheila gave one of her sniffs.

'Ma, she won't. You're her nannie and she loves you,' Ellen said firmly, determined not to rise to the bait. She didn't want a row, neither did she want to pander to Sheila's martyrdom. 'Goodnight, Ma,' she said quietly and walked from the room.

She felt weary as she undressed and slipped between the sheets. It had been a long draining day. She'd gone from the heights of exhilaration to the depths of depression. Ellen lay in bed thinking of what had happened. The old unhappiness lay heavy on her heart. Seeing Chris had brought back all the pain and hurt. It was her own stupid fault for indulging herself. She could lie in bed and wallow in misery or she could finally put the past behind her.

She thought of him, suave and sexy in his business suit. She thought of the shocked expression on his face when he saw Stephanie. She thought of his shiny hair and how she'd been tempted to run her fingers through it, she'd been so close to him.

'Stop!' she muttered, clenching her hands as little quivers of want and need tormented her. She could hardly remember the last time they'd made love, it was so long ago. Tonight she wanted Chris, badly.

With fierce determination, Ellen changed the scenario. Slowly, in her mind's eye, room by room, she decorated every inch of her new home. She was halfway through her third colour change in the bathroom when she fell asleep.

*   *   *

Doug sat at his desk studying plans for a house he was going to build as soon as he'd finished doing Ellen's place. He found it hard to concentrate. Poor Ellen, she'd been very upset. It must have been tough to see the father of her child after all those years. He'd no doubt she'd been deeply in love with him. And it seemed as though she still was.

Doug chewed the top of his pen. He understood her feelings but she was wasting her life loving someone who'd obviously done the dirty on her. He'd been there. He knew what it was like. But he'd made himself get over Geena Kingston. And he was over her, he thought, a little surprised. Whoever was with her now was welcome to her. She was utterly shallow and loved only herself.

The man Ellen loved, didn't love her. If he had, he'd have stuck by her. He'd missed out on a hell of a lot. Ellen was a lovely woman.

Over the past couple of months as he'd got to know her better, Doug had grown to like Ellen a lot. She'd a droll sense of humour that appealed to him and there was a kindness beneath that sometimes tough facade that was endearing. He *liked* Ellen. She was a very good mother. Stephanie was a great little kid. That man had lost out never knowing what a little gem his daughter was.

Doug had felt very close to Ellen when he'd comforted her. It was nice. He'd felt needed. He hadn't felt needed for a long time. He was going to keep in touch with Ellen after he'd finished working for her. They were friends. She'd become very dear to him.

*   *   *

Chris lay in bed listening to Suzy's deep heavy breathing as she lay asleep beside him. He envied her deeply. He was whacked. All he wanted to do was sleep, but sleep would not comfort him. His mind raced. Twice this year so far, he'd seen Ellen and his daughter. And he couldn't get them out of his head.

He couldn't get over how well Ellen looked. She'd changed. She was still beautiful in the way he remembered her, but her face was thinner, more defined, and her hair suited her in the shorter sophisticated style. That royal blue coat really complemented her dark colouring. The voluptuous girlish Ellen that he'd known had gone. But the woman she was now was far more exciting and sexy. There was an air about her. A strength about her, as she'd ushered their daughter ahead of her up the aisle. He'd watched, fascinated, drinking in every detail of Ellen as she'd turned to shake hands and offer condolences to the family. His plams were sweaty, he'd felt uncharacteristically tense. She hadn't looked in his direction once. He wasn't even sure if she'd seen him.

He'd hurried out of the church as soon as it was polite to leave, hoping against hope that she'd be outside. Desperately, he'd scrutinized the crowd looking for her, willing her to be there waiting for him. She would have known that he'd be at the removal. Surely she'd be as curious about him as he was about her. She'd been crazy about him once.

He was shocked when he realized that she was gone. She hadn't even waited for him to come out of the church. The old Ellen would have found some excuse to come and talk to him. The old Ellen would have forgiven him on the spot if he'd asked her. The old Ellen was a real softie. Had that changed, as well as her appearance? God! He hoped not. Ellen's soft-heartedness was one of the traits that had really attracted him.

He was going to make sure he spoke to her at the funeral in the morning – if she was at it. He was going to get back with Ellen. He needed her softness and understanding. He needed nights of wild passion like they used to have. He was going to resume their love affair if it was the last thing he did. She'd fallen for him once, Chris knew he could make her fall for him again.

Chapter Twenty

She hadn't come. Chris's disappointment was so strong he could almost taste it. He felt empty and depressed as he sat drinking coffee in the hotel the mourners had repaired to after the burial. He could see Mr and Mrs Munroe chatting to Pamela. Miriam was with them but Ellen obviously hadn't wanted to see him again. Chris felt angry. She'd let him down.

He saw Emma sitting forlornly by herself. Vincent was at the bar with Julie Ann, buying her a lemonade. What was wrong with Emma anyway? She wasn't her usual vivacious self.

'I'm just going over to Emma for a minute,' he said to Suzy. She hardly acknowledged him. They'd had sex early this morning when both of them were half-asleep and he'd muttered Ellen's name. Suzy had freaked. He didn't blame her. It was a stupid hurtful thing to do. He'd had Ellen on his mind and it just slipped out. That would be him in the doghouse for the foreseeable future.

He walked over to Emma and sat down in Vincent's seat.

'What's wrong with you, you're in very bad form?'

'Nothing,' she said forlornly.

'Come on, spit it out. Are you prostrate with grief because dear old granny won't be leaving you a legacy?'

Emma gave a wan smile. 'Very funny.'

'Is Vincent having an affair? Is your mother-in-law for real?'

'Stop it, Chris.' Emma giggled.

384

'That's better. Tell Chris what's the matter.' He patted her hand.

'I'm bloody pregnant,' she murmured.

Chris was dismayed. He knew Emma was dead set against having any more children. 'You poor little sod,' he said sympathetically.

'I haven't said anything to anyone. I don't want people congratulating me. You know the way I feel about kids.' Emma looked at him with an expression of utter defeat.

'I'm sorry, love. Nothing I'll say is going to make it any better.'

'At least I know you're not going to say congratulations. That helps. Don't tell anyone.' Emma squeezed his hand.

'Poor old Ems.' Chris hugged her affectionately. He and Emma understood each other.

'I saw Ellen and Stephanie last night,' he said quietly. 'I thought she might be here today.'

'She's getting some job done in the flat over the shop. She wanted to be around in case the builder needed her. So her nibs' – she nodded in Sheila's direction – 'told me. She's moving out of home.'

'Oh!' Chris murmured. 'She looks well.'

'Are you serious! That suit is out of the ark and she's going to take the eye out of someone with that feather in her hat,' Emma scoffed, thinking he was referring to Sheila who was chatting animatedly to Pamela, the feather in her hat bobbing up and down at a rate of knots as she emphasized a point.

'I meant Ellen,' Chris said offhandedly. He was dying to talk about Ellen but he was afraid to say too much in case Emma got suspicious.

'Oh her,' Emma drawled dismissively. 'I hadn't noticed.'

'When is she moving in to her new pad?'

'Fairly soon I think. Chris, Vincent's coming back and you're not exactly his favourite person. You better go.'

'Tell you what, let's have lunch some day next week. You can have a good moan,' Chris suggested.

385

'That would be lovely.' Emma brightened up.

'Right. I'll phone you and fix a time and day,' Chris said hastily, anxious to get away before Vincent arrived.

So Ellen was getting a place of her own, he mused as he threaded his way between the tables. That was interesting. He felt a little more cheerful as he sat down beside Suzy and lit a cigarette.

* * *

'Good morning, Doug,' Ellen said brightly as she let herself into the shop. She was embarrassed after her outburst the night before.

'Morning, Ellen. You OK?' Doug smiled at her.

'I'm fine.'

'Good. See you at lunchtime?'

'Yeah.' She smiled at his easygoing direct way. She felt much better this morning. She was proud of herself. She hadn't given in to weakness. Her life was her own. Chris Wallace had been banished to where he belonged . . . oblivion.

Around eleven, when she had the orders and deliveries organized, she headed off to the bank with the previous day's takings. It was a fresh spring day and she enjoyed the short stroll. She was walking back to the shop about twenty minutes later when she saw Denise walking towards her house.

'Hi,' she called.

Denise turned to face her.

'Are you all right, Denise?' Ellen was shocked by the sight of the haggard woman in front of her. Her eyes were red-rimmed and circled with dark shadows. Her face had a waxy pallor. She was smoking a cigarette and her fingers trembled.

'Denise, what's wrong with you? Are you sick? Do you need the doctor?'

Denise's face crumpled and she began to sob. Ellen could see Monica Anderson bearing down upon them so she gave Denise a hasty shove into the garden and stepped in behind her. She led the sobbing woman into the house to the kitchen and sat her down at the table.

'What's the matter, Denise? Tell me.' She took her friend's hand in her own and made her look at her.

'Oh Ellen! It's Jimmy. He's having an affair. He's been messing about all through our marriage. Jesus. I can't believe it. *Jimmy*. I thought I could really trust him. I never thought he'd look at another woman.'

'My God!' Ellen was flummoxed.

'All the time he said he was working late in the office, and I believed him, and he was off having his little flings. He's having an affair with Esther Dowling. He had a one-night stand with Cora Nolan who works in his office. And the whole time he was fucking them he was sleeping with me.'

Ellen opened her mouth but nothing came out. She couldn't believe her ears. Jimmy McMahon . . . a womanizer . . . It couldn't be true.

Jimmy McMahon sat in the front seat of the church and was first up to receive Communion every Sunday morning. Jimmy McMahon was on the church committee. Jimmy McMahon did the church collection every Sunday at eleven-thirty Mass. Ellen couldn't believe her ears. Jimmy McMahon had had not one but *two* affairs. He was nearly as bad as Chris. But Chris was a sexy hunk, for God's sake. Under no circumstances could Jimmy McMahon be described as a hunk. He had bandy spindly legs, lemonade bottle shoulders and lank brown hair. What *was* his attraction? Ellen resolved to study him closely the next time she encountered him.

'How did you find out?' she asked gently.

'Oh, the one in the office phoned me to tell me. They'd had a one-night stand and she thought they were mated for life. She'd *followed* him to Esther's place and saw them kissing. She went crazy and caused a right rumpus on the street and then she phoned me to ask did I know that my darling husband was cheating on her *and* on me. He must have known she'd do something like that because he came home pissed and told me he was having an affair with that Dowling cow.'

Esther Dowling! Ellen shook her head incredulously. She was the bank manager's secretary. She was so prim and proper, it made it all the more shocking.

'Wasn't she going to be a nun one time? She was a real goody-goody. Do you remember her at school? She wouldn't say boo to a goose. She'd blush if you looked sideways at her. She never went dancing or out to the pub when we were growing up. Sister Patrick used to say the quiet ones were the ones to watch. How right she was. How in the name of God did she and Jimmy get together?'

'They know each other from way back when we were young. He used to sit beside her counting the church collection on Monday nights. He had an affair with her when I was pregnant with Lisa. That's how long it's been going on. Three years. He was so pissed last night it all came pouring out of him. I just couldn't believe it. When I tackled him again this morning he was sober and he didn't deny any of it.' Denise broke down sobbing.

'Don't cry, Denise. They're not worth it and I'm telling you that from bitter experience.' Ellen felt a surge of hate for Jimmy and Chris and all the bastards like them.

Denise lit another cigarette as Ellen poured the tea.

'Jimmy wouldn't talk to me. He'd come home and bury his head in the paper or watch TV but he was never really a talker so I was used to that. I really believed him when he said he was working late in the office. We were still having sex. I never refused him. I'd breathe heavy and groan and moan and tell him he was wonderful just to bolster his ego and he never bothered to find out if I was satisfied. He was a selfish bastard in bed. Maybe he was saving it all for his mistresses.'

'Maybe he wasn't any good with them either,' Ellen said gently.

'Well he must be good at something. Cora is besotted

with him. If she gets her hands on Esther she'll swing for her.'

'What do they see in him?'

'Oh, the same as I did, I'm sure. Jimmy has a great *poor little me* act. He's very good at making people feel sorry for him. He probably told these bitches that I was neglecting him or not feeding him or didn't have time for him because of the children. He probably said I didn't understand him. I've never met anyone who can feel quite as sorry for himself as Jimmy can if things aren't going his way. But I never thought he had it in him to be unfaithful. I've been married to him twelve years, Ellen, and after what he told me last night all I can say is he's a stranger to me. He's such a fuckin' hypocrite. Everyone in Glenree thinks he's a pillar of the community. For all I know he's been out with prostitutes. I could have diseases I don't know about.' She buried her head in her hands and cried like a baby.

'What am I going to do, Ellen? What am I going to do? I've no job. I'm dependent on him. What am I going to tell my kids?'

'Maybe he'll end it,' Ellen said helplessly.

'I don't want him. He's the scum of the earth as far as I'm concerned.' Denise's face was contorted with anger, pain, worry.

'Denise, I'm sorry. I don't know what to say to you. All I can do is listen. And if it's any use to you, after Chris left me when I told him I was pregnant, I thought I'd die. I really wanted to end it all. But I got through it. I had to for Stephanie. You'll have to do it for your children. It's not easy. But you do get through these things, the pain does ease. I'd be a liar if I said it goes away. It doesn't. But you fill your life with other things and, though it's still there, you bury it deep and it only comes back now and again.'

'God I feel such a failure.' Denise sank her head in her hands.

'I know,' Ellen empathized. 'You say to yourself, was it me? Was I not loving enough, interesting enough, sexy enough? It does your head in and it's so unfair. Look, it's Jimmy's loss. He's a fool.'

'I did something wrong. If he wasn't happy in our marriage it was my fault somewhere along the line.'

'Stop that, Denise, right now! He wasn't happy because he was probably feeling as guilty as hell for cheating on you. Don't you dare take the blame for his shitty behaviour,' Ellen fumed. 'Look, I have to go. I'll call in after work to see how you are.'

'Thanks, Ellen. You're a pal. Don't tell anyone. Well you can tell Doug if you want to, but no-one else. I'm sure it will all come out eventually but I don't want to give the gossips a field day.'

'Don't worry,' Ellen said grimly. 'I know all about the gossips in this place. I'll never forget what I went through when I was expecting Stephanie. Don't mind them. They preach Christian charity but they certainly don't practise it. I'll see you later.'

She was still stunned as she walked across the street to the shop. Poor Denise was going through a desperate trauma. The betrayal of trust was a terrible thing to suffer. Ellen pitied her from the bottom of her heart. She knew what the grief, the fear, the pain and anger were like. But in the long run, no matter how sympathetic friends and family were, only Denise could endure it and get over it.

For the week that followed Ellen made sure to call in and see her after work every evening. Denise veered from anger to deep sadness, her moods swinging wildly.

'Why? Why did he do that to me? How could he hurt me like that? Doesn't he have any feelings for me at all?' she'd ask over and over. Ellen couldn't give her an answer. Life was full of whys and hows. Who knew that better than she did?

Jimmy was there one evening when she went in. He muttered a greeting and disappeared upstairs. She watched him lope out of the room. Sean Connery he ain't, she thought, fascinated by the fact that he had women falling at his feet. Ellen felt like thumping him. She stayed with

Denise for a little while and then went to collect Stephanie from Miriam's.

'Are we wallpapering tonight?' Miriam asked eagerly.

'If you don't mind.' Ellen grinned.

'I can't wait.'

Doug had finished the inside of the flat and it was all ready to be decorated. The hard work she'd put in, bonding walls and sanding doors and skirting boards, meant that they were ready to start papering and painting. Ellen had bought paper and paint ages ago.

It was exciting as the sheets of wallpaper went up on the wall. The sitting-room took on a whole new look. Miriam was as enthusiastic as if it were her own place and they worked together, enjoying seeing the fruit of their labours take shape. Ellen was delighted with it. It was so fresh and clean.

Over the next fortnight they worked hard. The sitting-room was yellow and cream, the dining-room pale green and white, her bedroom pink and blue and Stephanie's blue and white, just like the nursery in *Mary Poppins*.

When the papering and painting was finished, Ellen started furnishing her home. Sheila and Mick had bought her a new three-piece suite in yellow and blue chintz for the sitting-room. She tried it in different variations until she was satisfied. One armchair in front of the window, the settee against the wall opposite the fireplace and the other armchair beside the fire. Vincent and Emma had given her a new coffee table and she placed that in the centre of the room. She'd bought several lamps which she arranged in various corners. She'd bought an old bookcase which she'd stripped and varnished. That went along the wall beside the fire. Once she'd placed her books on the shelves, Ellen really began to feel at home. She'd never taken an interest in decorating before and she was thoroughly enjoying herself.

Miriam and Ben gave her money to go towards her dining-room suite and she'd bought a round pine table and six chairs to match the pine dresser she'd bought at an auction.

Stephanie was beside herself with excitement the day the truck arrived with two new divans and a double bed. The divans were arranged side by side with a small white locker in between and she hopped from one bed to another trying to decide which one she'd sleep in. Ellen and Miriam made them up and the cheery patchwork quilts that Sheila had made looked lovely and inviting. The new longed-for teddy bear curtains fluttered in the breeze of the open window. All Stephanie's toys lay neatly on the shelves Doug had built for her. She was in seventh heaven.

Sheila was very subdued on the Saturday that the final move took place. Stephanie was bursting with excitement as all her clothes were packed into Mick's car. Ellen saw the tears in her mother's eyes and found it in her heart to feel sorry for her.

'Will you come and help us settle in?' she asked hesitantly. 'I'd really like you to see the place and be the first person to have a cup of tea with us.'

Sheila went red as she tried to compose herself.

'Thank you, dear. I'll come over with your father,' she said awkwardly.

It had been years since her mother had called her dear. Ellen felt like crying herself. It was very strange to be leaving the home she'd lived in all her life. The last years had been unhappy ones but now that it was time to leave, it was a wrench.

'Come on, come on,' Mick said briskly, aware of the underlying emotions. He was trying to keep Sheila's spirits up, he knew how desperately sad she was at Stephanie's going. He was the same himself but he wouldn't let Ellen see it.

Ellen's new Triumph was packed to the gills with all her possessions and, as she sat behind the wheel and drove down the drive of the farm to start her new life, she felt a myriad of emotions. Exhilaration, sadness, relief, anticipation. She followed Mick's car, and never looked back. One chapter of her life had closed, a new one was beginning.

That night as she lay in her new double bed looking up at

the skylight through which a thousand stars twinkled, Ellen felt at peace. She loved her new bedroom with its wooden sloping ceiling and the pink striped wallpaper. The pink lamp beside her bed cast a warm glow. The pink and blue floral curtains on the dormer window were reflected in the white and gold kidney-shaped dressing-table with the three mirrors that could be angled any way. It was dainty and feminine and completely different from the battered old mahogany one with the chipped stained mirror that she'd had at home. She had a matching white wardrobe trimmed with gold and a small chest of drawers which was now filled with all her undies and jumpers. She was as pleased as Punch with her modern furniture. She'd spent most of her savings but she'd start saving from scratch again, she assured herself.

She lay contentedly, knowing that Stephanie was sound asleep in her 'nursery' in the adjoining bedroom. It had been a long exhausting day but she was too wound up to sleep. The first night in her new home was one to savour.

* * *

Sheila lay in the dark with tears streaming down her face. The day she'd been dreading for so long had finally arrived. She'd borne up well until now. She'd been most impressed with the flat. Doug Roche had done a magnificent job. She could hardly recognize it from the shambles it had once been. And Ellen had decorated it so nicely. It had surprised Sheila who had never given her daughter much credit for that kind of thing.

When she saw Stephanie's bedroom, she could understand her granddaughter's excitement and delight. It was a beautiful room with the two beds and the lovely little play corner. Doug had built in a window seat for her. Stephanie had made her sit in it to try it out. Then she'd made her lie on both beds.

'Which one would you pick, Nannie? I can't make up my mind.'

Sheila had pretended to consider and had chosen the one by the window.

'That's the one I'll sleep in. Will you sing *Christopher Robin* for me? I'm in my nursery now and I'm sure Mary Poppins sang it to Michael and Jane.'

Sheila swallowed the lump in her throat remembering the pair of trusting blue eyes raised to her own. Stephanie was so precious to her. She was her favourite grandchild, though she'd only admit that to herself. It had been strange in Ellen's flat. She was a guest. Her daughter was mistress of her own home now. They were equals in the flat. Sheila no longer had control. She felt old, and powerless and unneeded. The house seemed hollow and empty like she did. Just herself and Mick now. Once it had been full of life. Full of young people when the children were growing up. Now it was a shell. The tears came faster. Mick stirred beside her and put her arms around her.

'Stop crying, pet. It's for the best,' he murmured.

'I miss them.' Sheila wept.

'I do too,' Mick said sadly as his arms tightened around her. 'I do too.'

*   *   *

'We'll call in after Mass. I'm dying to see the place.' Emma snuggled in to Vincent. 'Miriam said it's lovely.' Her curiosity was getting the better of her.

'OK,' Vincent agreed drowsily. Emma nibbled his ear.

'Go asleep,' Vincent murmured.

Emma slid her hand along his chest, down to the hard plane of his lean flat stomach.

'Stop, you witch.' He groaned as her hand explored further.

'Make the most of this, because when I have the baby, we're never having sex again,' Emma said huskily. She wanted to forget that she was pregnant. She wanted to try and ignore the thickening of her waist and the new fullness of her breasts. Sometimes she felt she was living in a nightmare. She was filled with dread and fear. Only in Vincent's arms could she find comfort from the ordeal that her life had become.

'Kiss me, Vincent. Hold me. Tell me it's going to be all right,' she whispered against his ear.

'It's going to be all right. When you've had the baby, we'll get a nanny. Don't worry. And the gynaecologist said you were fine and he'd do a Caesarean the minute you need it.'

'I'm really scared.'

'Don't be. I'm here. I'll look after you.' Vincent held her tightly. He could feel the frantic beating of her heart through the flimsy nightie she wore. He felt utterly helpless in the face of his wife's fear. He was never allowing her to go through this again. He was going to go to England to get sterilized. Deep down though, he hoped the baby would be a boy. He'd love a son, he thought as he responded to his wife's caress and kissed her passionately.

* * *

'It's very nice, Ellen.' Emma peered around with interest. She was amazed. She'd expected, well not a hovel exactly, but certainly nothing as nice as the bright airy pretty home that she and Vincent were standing in.

'Thanks. I'm delighted with it.' Ellen beamed. Not even her snooty patronizing sister-in-law could affect her mood today, she thought happily as she served tea and biscuits to her unexpected guests. She should have known, of course, that Emma would have to come and poke around. She was as nosy as they come.

Ellen had got up early and gone to eight o'clock Mass. She was having her parents and Doug to dinner as a little thank-you gesture. It was twelve-thirty, she had the roast in the oven and the vegetables and potatoes were all ready to cook. The smell wafting from her new kitchen was mouth-watering.

She could see Emma staring at the pine table, set for five.

Ellen had gone the whole hog, she had bought a bottle of wine, and she had prawn cocktail for starters. Crisp white linen napkins arranged in a fan shape looked very pretty.

'Are you having guests?' Emma pried.

'Yes,' Ellen nodded. She didn't elaborate. She could see that Emma was consumed with curiosity. Well she could be consumed. She probably knew that Mick and Sheila were coming but the fifth setting would be a mystery to her. Madam Emma would find out sooner or later, no doubt. But Ellen wasn't going to satisfy her curiosity.

'We met your parents at Mass. They said you were having them for lunch.' Emma was not one to give up easily.

'It's the least I can do, they've been very good to me.' Ellen handed Vincent the plate of biscuits.

'We've a bit of news for you,' he said diffidently. 'We told Mam and Dad this morning at Mass. Emma's expecting a baby.'

'Oh!' Ellen was taken aback. She knew Emma didn't want more children.

'It was a bit of a shock to me too,' Emma said dryly. 'I can't say I'm too thrilled but that's the way it goes.'

'I hope everything will be all right for you.' Ellen didn't really know what to say. 'I suppose Julie Ann's thrilled.'

'Oh we haven't told her. Not for a while yet. I couldn't cope with the questions,' Emma said hastily.

'It's early days,' Vincent said. 'We'll tell her nearer the time.'

'Mummy, I want a nursery like Stephanie, and I want teddy bear curtains.' Julie Ann marched into the room.

'But darling you've a lovely bedroom at home and your curtains were very, very expensive,' Emma said weakly. Ellen bristled. How typical of Emma to rub it in about her *very* expensive curtains. And how typical of Julie Ann to covet what Stephanie had.

'But Mummy. It's not fair! I want teddy bear curtains too. And I want a winding stairs. And a room in the attic.' Julie Ann pouted. She was so like Emma, Ellen thought.

Very dainty with expressive brown eyes and a little heart-shaped face. But she was spoilt rotten.

'Don't be silly, Julie Ann,' Vincent said sternly.

'I am *not* silly.' Julie Ann glowered at her father. 'Stephanie just thinks she's great. *My* bedroom is much bigger than hers.'

'Julie Ann!' Vincent warned.

'Leave me alone,' Julie Ann said huffily and flounced out of the sitting-room.

Emma was mortified. 'It's time we were going.' She stood up.

If Stephanie ever carried on like that she'd know all about it, Ellen thought to herself. That child was let away with murder.

'It was very nice of you to call,' she said politely.

'Good luck in your new home.' Vincent kissed Ellen on the cheek.

'Thanks and thanks very much for the coffee table.' Ellen was relieved they were going. Emma always put her on edge.

'Come on, Julie Ann,' Vincent called up the stairs.

'I don't want to go home,' Julie Ann shrieked. 'Can I stay, Auntie Ellen, please?'

'Please, Mammy, can she stay?' Stephanie peered down the banisters, adding her pleas to those of her cousin.

I'll kill her, Ellen thought. What a position to be put in.

'Auntie Ellen is having visitors,' Vincent said.

'Please, Daddy.' Julie Ann turned on the waterworks.

'Please, Mammy. You said I could have Julie Ann and Rebecca to stay,' Stephanie wheedled. Ellen promised herself she was going to have a good talk with her daughter. She didn't mind having her nieces to stay, but it should be when she chose.

'Julie Ann, cut it out.' Emma scowled. Julie Ann howled louder.

'Let her stay. I can drop her home later,' Ellen offered politely.

'No, no,' Vincent protested.

'If you're sure you don't mind,' Emma said.

Typical, thought Ellen. Offload her whenever you get the chance.

'She can play with Stephanie for the afternoon.' Ellen was silently raging. Stephanie needn't think she was going to get away with manipulating her the way Julie Ann did Emma.

'Can I have dinner in your house?' Julie Ann piped up, the waterworks ceasing as if by magic.

'Yes of course.'

'Oh goody,' Julie Ann said ecstatically. 'Are we having crispy roast potatoes?'

'We are.' Ellen had to smile. Julie Ann loved her grub.

'My mummy's roast potatoes are never crispy like yours. Can I have two?' Julie Ann asked artlessly.

'Yes, go on up and play now while I get the dinner.' Ellen changed the subject when she saw Emma go a deep shade of puce.

'Are you sure about keeping her?' Vincent wasn't too happy.

'She's fine. Don't worry.'

'You're very good,' Emma said tightly.

And you're not very good at cooking roast potatoes, Ellen thought smugly. She knew she was being a bitch but she enjoyed her sister-in-law's discomfiture.

She waved them off and hastened to her kitchen to put on the veg.

*   *   *

'Did you hear that little madam? I'll have a word with her when I get her home,' Emma fumed.

'So will I,' Vincent agreed. 'Playing up like that. I'm sure Ellen has enough to do without having Julie Ann for the afternoon.'

'Oh she won't mind that,' Emma said dismissively. 'She'll be company for Stephanie. Anyway now we can go somewhere and have lunch on our own. Won't that be a treat?' She was delighted Julie Ann was off her hands for the afternoon. She could be so wearing sometimes.

'I wonder who the other guest was. Ellen didn't say.'

'Haven't a clue.' Vincent held the car door open for her.

'She's looking very well these days. Even Chris commented on it at the funeral,' Emma said without thinking.

'It's none of his bloody business what way Ellen's looking,' Vincent growled and Emma could have kicked herself. What a stupid thing to say.

'Don't go so fast, I've dreadful heartburn, and I feel dizzy,' she fibbed.

Vincent instantly slowed down. 'Sorry, love. If you don't feel like going out to lunch I'll make it,' he offered solicitously.

'Oh I think I could manage a mouthful or two somewhere. It would be nice to be on our own for a little while. Let's go to Malahide,' she suggested.

'OK,' he agreed.

Emma relaxed in the seat and let her mind drift. Was Ellen seeing someone? Was he coming to lunch to have crispy roast potatoes? That rankled. She wouldn't have cared if Julie Ann had said it in front of Miriam but in front of Ellen! It was mortifying. She'd give Julie Ann a piece of her mind when she got home, after she'd grilled her about Ellen's mysterious dinner guest.

*   *   *

Ellen lay relaxing in a scented bath that night. She was very pleased with herself. In spite of Julie Ann, the lunch had been a great success. Doug and Mick got on famously and Sheila was most gracious. She'd even complimented her on her Yorkshire pudding. Ellen knew she was being polite. Her Yorkshire pudding had drooped dismally, compared to Sheila's perfectly risen masterpieces. But, apart from that, lunch had been very tasty. Doug scoffed everything on his plate and had seconds as well.

Julie Ann had eaten every mouthful with great relish. She'd chatted away confidently to Doug who found her very amusing.

When Sheila and Mick had gone home, Ellen suggested a walk on the beach in Portmarnock. This idea had gone down a treat. They'd all piled into her new car and she'd driven to Portmarnock, only crashing her gears once.

It had been lovely to walk along the wide golden beach inhaling the salty sea air. People were walking their dogs. Couples strolled hand in hand. Children raced along exuberantly enjoying the fresh air. Stephanie and Julie Ann had studied pools of clear water looking for crabs and sea urchins. She and Doug strode along chatting companionably. Doug treated them to tea in a little beachside cafe. It had been a perfect way to end the day.

Ellen stretched out in the bath. It was a lovely bath. It was pale green to match her sink and toilet. The bathroom was warm and she had towels heating on the radiator. It was luxurious compared to what she'd been used to at home. The great white enamel bath had needed gallons of hot water to fill it up and the bathroom was always cold in the winter, despite the electric bar on the wall.

Ellen lolled, enjoying the warmth and the scented air. She cleansed her face, steamed it, moisturised it and lay back with cold tea bags on her eyes. She'd never have been tempted to linger in a bath at home. This was decadence, she thought happily.

An hour later, she sat curled up in an armchair reading the Sunday newspapers. She was tingling from head to toe. She'd smoothed body lotion all over her, her hair was freshly washed and shampooed, her eyes shining and clear after their tea bag treatment. She had her clothes and Stephanie's school uniform ready and ironed for the next morning and she was enjoying her read beside the blazing fire. Stephanie was fast asleep. She nearly was too, she yawned, reaching for her hot chocolate.

The doorbell chimed and she glanced at the clock, puzzled. It was nine-thirty. Who'd be calling at this hour?

Maybe Ben and Miriam were going for a drink in the Glenree Arms and they'd popped in to say hello. Hardly though. Miriam had said something about finishing a jumper for Ben. Saturday night was their usual night out. Denise came to mind. Maybe there'd been a row or something. She tightened her dressing-gown belt around her waist and walked downstairs. It wasn't Denise. The outline at the door was a man's.

Doug must have forgotten something, she thought although she couldn't think what. She glanced at herself in the oval mirror that hung on the hall wall. She looked fine. She didn't mind Doug seeing her in her dressing-gown. It was a nice new one that Ben and Miriam had given her for Christmas. It was candlewick, in pale lilac, and it was as warm as toast. The colour suited her.

She opened the door with a smile on her face and her heart almost stopped as she stared into a pair of unforgettable blue eyes and she heard Chris Wallace say,

'Hello, Ellen.'

Twenty-One

'Chris! *Chris!*' Ellen didn't know what to say. She couldn't believe that he was standing on her doorstep. Why? After all this time.

'Can I come in?' he asked.

She looked into his eyes, as vividly blue as she remembered, and felt her heart thud against her ribs.

'Please, Ellen?'

Ellen stepped aside and he walked past her into the hall. She closed the door behind him and turned to face him.

'What do you want?' She was dry-mouthed.

'You.' His voice was husky. His eyes darkened as he leaned down and kissed her fiercely, hungrily.

Stunned, she pushed him away. 'For God's sake, Chris!'

'I'm sorry. I've missed you so much.' Chris stared down at her.

'You've missed me!' Ellen felt an explosion of anger. 'After all this time you think you can just walk in here as if nothing had happened and kiss me. Who do you think you are, Chris Wallace? What do you think I am?' she added bitterly.

'You've every right to be angry. I know that,' he muttered. 'There's no justification for what I did. But I want you to know that letting you go was the biggest mistake I ever made. And I've regretted it ever since.'

'You're a bastard, Chris! You walked out on me. You never even got in touch to find out about the baby. And you waltz in here, almost seven years later, and start kissing me and think it's what I want. And you expect me to forgive you. Go fuck yourself.' Her eyes blazed with fury.

'I'm sorry, baby. I'm really sorry.' His arms tightened around her.

The old endearment touched something deep inside her. She started to cry.

'Why, Chris? *Why* did you do it to me? Do you have any idea how much you hurt me? Do you have any idea how much I loved you? Didn't I mean *anything* to you?'

'Yes! Yes you did.' He took her face in his hands and stared down at her. 'I never felt for any woman what I felt for you. I was scared, love. I was immature. I couldn't handle the idea of being a father. I felt trapped.' His eyes pleaded for her understanding, for her forgiveness.

'But how could you not get in touch? Didn't you care about us? Didn't you think about me at all?' The questions she'd asked herself over and over came pouring out. She needed to know the answers.

'I *did* think about you. All the time,' Chris fibbed weakly. 'I just felt you were better off without me.' He hung his head in that boyish way that always worked with women.

'Oh Chris, don't say that,' Ellen sighed, reaching up to touch his cheek. He felt a wave of relief. She wasn't going to turn him away. Ellen still loved him just as he'd known she would. Once she'd got the blast of anger and bitterness out of her system, things would be as they once were. He bent down and very gently kissed her on the mouth. This time she responded, her lips soft against his own.

She knew she was crazy, but feeling his arms around her and the firm warm pressure of his mouth on hers was a thousand times better than all the dreams and fantasies that had kept her going over the years.

Chris was back. Holding her tight. He *had* to love her. Otherwise why was he here? She knew she was a soft fool not to send him packing but this was the moment she'd dreamed of. How often did dreams come true? He'd said he missed her and thought of her. If he was happy with

Suzy, he wouldn't be standing here kissing her now. The thought made her triumphantly happy. She'd been so jealous of that blonde woman whom she didn't even know. That woman who had taken the love that was hers. Now she could reclaim it.

Their kiss deepened. She savoured the old familiar taste and scent of him. His hands moulded her to him, it was as though all the years slipped away and they had never been parted.

'I want you,' Chris murmured. 'Ellen, Ellen, it's been so long. It's driving me crazy. You're all I can think about.' He was so aroused he wanted to take her there, pressed up against the wall in the hallway.

Ellen stared into his eyes, which were glazed with desire. He was pressing against her, his hands frantically trying to undo the knot of her dressing-gown belt.

'I want you. I want you, baby.' His breathing was harsh, hot against her neck as he nuzzled into her. His hunger aroused her. She wanted to touch him, taste him. She wanted to feel him inside her. Although she'd kissed and cuddled with other men, she'd never had full sex with anyone since Chris. He was the deepest, truest love of her life. He was the only one she wanted.

The sound of a sleepy childish cough, upstairs, penetrated her sensual daze.

'Stop, Chris. Stop!' Ellen twisted away from his kiss.

'No, no. Please, Ellen. Please let me make love to you.'

'I can't. It's not right. Stephanie might hear,' Ellen whispered.

'We'll be quiet. Come on, love.' Chris sought her lips again.

'Let me go, Chris.' She turned her head away.

'Aw, Ellen.' Chris rested his head on her shoulder. They stood, holding each other. After a while he said, 'I'm sorry. That wasn't in the script.' He smiled wryly. 'You always did get to me.'

'Only when it suited you,' Ellen said sadly.

'Can't we be friends?' His tone was weary.

Ellen looked at him. He'd been vigorous, full of energy and enthusiasm and ideas when she'd known him, but the Chris she was looking at now seemed tired and spent. His boyish good looks were coarsened by age, a hint of jowls marred his once firm jawline. Incredibly, Ellen found herself feeling sorry for him.

'Let's go upstairs and have a cup of tea.' She walked ahead of him and led the way into the sitting-room.

'This is nice.' He looked around approvingly.

'Sit down, Chris. I'll make the tea.'

'I'll come out to the kitchen and talk to you while you're doing it.'

Ellen was in such a tizzy, she didn't know if she was coming or going. She was immensely conscious of Chris watching her as she filled the kettle. Her hands shook as she took down cups and saucers from the dresser.

'Why did you come?' she blurted out.

'Are you sorry I did?'

'Yes . . . No . . . I don't know.' She was utterly confused. The peace of mind she'd struggled so hard to achieve over the years had just shattered into a thousand pieces. She was back to square one.

'I wanted us to be friends. I wanted to see my daughter,' Chris said.

'How can we be just friends? There's too much between us. Look what happened in the hall,' Ellen argued.

'If you want to be more than friends, I'd be very happy.' Chris looked her straight in the eye.

'But what about your wife?' She had to ask the question.

'Look, Ellen. Suzy's a great girl. But I should never have married her. She wanted it and she pushed until she got it. I've stuck it until now but I'm miserable because I can't stop thinking about you. She shouldn't have married me. She thought she'd change me but she won't. You're the only one who understands me.'

'Oh, Chris, how typical. Everyone's to blame except

405

you. *Suzy* shouldn't have married you. You're miserable because of *me*. Grow up and take responsibility for your actions.' Ellen angrily clattered teaspoons onto saucers.

'You've changed.' Chris frowned. His eyes were bleak. The old Ellen would never have said that to him.

'Don't be ridiculous. Of course I've changed. I *had* to. I had a child to bring up. I had to put up with a mother who will never forgive me for the shame I brought on the family. I had to survive the gossip and slurs and judgement of so-called Christians here in Glenree. There were times when I wanted to kill myself. Times when I wanted to give in to myself and wallow in misery. But I couldn't allow myself the luxury of it. I had to get on with life for Stephanie's sake. I had to face my mistakes and accept them. But it made me a much stronger person. I don't expect anything from anybody. I take responsibility for myself. So yes, I've changed, Chris. I had to.'

'You must really hate me,' he said forlornly.

She looked at him. Her anger dissipated. She'd never been able to stay mad at him for long. And he *had* come to try and make up . . . even if it *was* six and a half years too late.

'I don't hate you. You know that, Chris.'

'Do you forgive me?' He cocked his head to one side the way he used to when he'd stood her up, or let her down in some way.

Ellen was silent. She knew he hadn't the slightest idea of what she'd suffered. Do you forgive me, were only words to him.

'Do you?'

'Does it really matter to you, whether I forgive you or not?'

'Yes it does, Ellen.' He was emphatic.

'I wish I could believe that,' Ellen retorted.

'Believe it, love, please.' He came and stood in front of her and put his arms around her. 'I'm desperately sorry for what I did to you. I want us to be friends. There's nothing more I can say than that. I understand if you can't forgive me.'

'I do forgive you,' Ellen murmured against his chest. She could feel the steady beat of his heart beneath his shirt.

'I want you to be part of my life again. I want to get to know Stephanie.'

'I don't know, Chris. Maybe we'd be better off leaving things as they were,' Ellen said doubtfully. She was disconcerted. She had Stephanie to think about. And Chris had a wife.

'Just let me phone you, then. To talk, the way we used to. I could never talk to anyone the way I talked to you.' He was very insistent. Ellen found it difficult to say no to him.

'I'll tell you what. I'll give you a few days to think it over. And then I'll phone you and, if you want to keep in touch, you tell me. And if you don't, I won't bother you again. How about that?'

'OK.' It would give her time to think.

'Could I have a peep in at Stephanie?'

'Oh Chris. I don't know. This is painful for me. I feel very angry and very resentful that you feel you can walk in here and just pick up where we left off as though nothing had happened,' Ellen snapped.

'I just wanted to see her once,' he said sullenly. 'She *is* my daughter after all.'

'It's a bit late for you to think of that now. Don't give me that crap,' Ellen said bitterly.

'Ah, Ellen, don't be like that.'

'I'm sorry.' It wasn't in her nature to be unforgiving. Her heart softened as she looked up at him and saw the hurt in his eyes.

'Come on.' She took him by the hand and led him out to the hallway. She walked up the winding spiral staircase to the attic. He followed quietly behind.

Stephanie was fast asleep, her dark hair spread across the pillow, her cheeks rosy in sleep. Her battered old teddy was clutched in her arms. She looked peaceful and untroubled. Ellen watched Chris looking down at her and felt a lump in her throat.

'She's beautiful,' he whispered. Ellen switched off the bedside lamp.

'Yes she is,' she said quietly.

They went back to the kitchen where their tea remained untouched. Neither of them wanted it.

'Will you give me your home number?' Chris asked.

Ellen knew it was time to make a decision. She could say no outright and never see him again or she could let him into her life once more. She knew what she should do, but it wasn't what she wanted.

She went over to the dresser and got a pen and a slip of paper and wrote down her phone number.

Chris took the number and put it in his inside pocket.

'I'll call you in a few days,' he said quietly.

'Maybe you'll change your mind.' Ellen fiddled with the cord of her dressing-gown.

'I won't.' He took her face in his hands. 'It was good to see you, Ellen.'

'It was good to see you too,' she said awkwardly.

'I'll go, then.' Chris looked at her questioningly.

'OK. I won't come down with you. Just pull the door behind you.'

Chris looked disappointed. Well what did he think? That she was going to take him by the hand and bring him into the bedroom and let him seduce her? Did he think she was that much of a pushover?

It wasn't until she heard the click of the front door as he closed it after him and she exhaled, that Ellen realized she'd been holding her breath.

She sank down into the armchair. Her heart was pounding. It was hard to take in. After all this time, Chris had turned up out of the blue. He'd told her all the things she'd wanted so badly to hear. Especially that he'd made a mistake marrying Suzy. But could she believe him? Chris was very plausible, but lies had tripped off his tongue so easily in the past.

Why had he come tonight? Obviously things weren't going too well with Suzy. Maybe he was horny and frustrated and he thought he'd have a bit of diversion with good old Ellen.

Her cheeks burned as she remembered how she'd responded to him. The arrogance of him, to walk into her home after all these years without a word, and to start kissing her the way he had. What did he think, that she was some kind of a doormat? Ellen stood up and began to tidy up. She was angry. Once again, Chris had turned her life upside down. She folded up the paper, put the fireguard in front of the fire and switched out the lights. She went downstairs and locked the front door. The mirror reflected the soft peach light and her own troubled gaze.

'Oh, Chris, Chris. What have you done to me?' she whispered. He wanted to come back into her life. And that was what she'd always wanted. Wasn't it? Why wasn't she happy?

She went to bed and lay in the dark turning over every second of their encounter in her mind as she argued fiercely with herself.

He's using you.

He really loves you, just like you knew he did.

He's a lying, cheating bastard.

He does care about you, otherwise he wouldn't have come back.

He really wanted you.

You really wanted him.

He's married.

That's her hard luck. All's fair in love and war.

If he can deceive her, he can deceive you.

But if he was happy with her, he wouldn't have been standing on your doorstep. Maybe you're getting a second chance.

What about Stephanie? What are you going to tell her if you let him back into your life? Is it fair to her?

Is it fair to her to keep her father from getting to know her? She has a right to have a relationship with her father. And he wants to get to know her.

Ellen lay tossing and turning. After all this time, she'd

lost hope that Chris would ever come back to her. And now he had. There had to be a reason. He must love her. He *did* love her. And she loved him. God knows she did. Seeing him again had unleashed all the emotions she'd buried away. Now that he was gone, she was beginning to regret letting him go. What if he didn't ring as he said he would? Was it promises promises like the old days? Ellen turned over on her side and curled up in a ball. She knew she'd be on tenterhooks until he called. Some things never changed.

*   *   *

Chris let himself quietly into the house. There were no lights on downstairs. Suzy was in bed. He walked into the lounge, switched on a lamp, poured himself a brandy and sat down in his armchair.

He couldn't believe that he'd driven over to Ellen's. She'd been on his mind constantly since he'd seen her. Suzy was like a scorpion, bitter and angry over his admittedly unforgivable faux pas, when he'd breathed Ellen's name during sex, the morning of the funeral.

The tension and rowing between them had been so bad over the weekend he'd felt like packing his bags and walking out. In an effort to pour oil over troubled waters, he'd suggested she get a babysitter so they could go out to dinner that night.

'Take your tart out to dinner, and leave me alone,' she'd snapped.

He was so angry he'd stormed out of the house and driven off in a temper. Before he knew it, he'd found himself heading in the direction of the northside. To hell with it, he'd thought. He'd had to see if Ellen would have him back.

As he sat in the lonely quiet of his home, Chris sipped his brandy and thought about his meeting with Ellen. He'd wanted her the minute he'd seen her and it gave him fierce satisfaction to know that she'd wanted him too. The passion was still there.

But she was an angry woman. And a changed woman. She was a much stronger person, he thought in grudging admiration. The old Ellen would never have blazed away at him the way she had. Several times he'd thought that she'd tell him to get out. But then there'd been times when the old, soft, loving Ellen had resurfaced and he'd hoped he was in with a chance.

Maybe he'd lost his touch, he thought with uncharacteristic uncertainty. In the old days she'd never have pushed him away from her. He'd always been able to seduce her. Maybe when he phoned her, she would tell him to get lost, when she had time to remember how badly he'd treated her.

If Ellen turned him away he'd go nuts. He needed her love and her compassion and her tenderness badly. He needed to feel cherished and comforted the way she'd always made him feel. He was going through a bad patch. Suzy didn't understand. She was too demanding. He couldn't cope with it. He needed an escape. He needed Ellen.

He'd better not put the pressure on too soon, he decided regretfully. He'd leave it until Thursday to phone. That was about as long as he'd last, he thought, pouring another measure of brandy. He wasn't at all sure what her answer would be. The new Ellen was an enigma. And a challenge. It excited him. It was a pity Suzy was in a huff, he thought crankily. He was as horny as hell and he needed sex. But he wouldn't be getting it from her. And right now he wasn't sure if he'd be getting it from Ellen either.

*　　*　　*

Suzy tensed as she heard the key in the front door. So he was home. She'd half-expected that he'd stay out all night. She wondered where he'd gone. It wasn't that late.

Had he gone to see *her*? The mother of his illegitimate child. *Bastard!* she fumed. How dare he . . . how *dare* he say that woman's name when he was making love to her?

411

She wanted to kill him with her bare hands. How could he do that to her? How could he make her feel so dirty? She'd never be able to let him make love to her again. She'd always be afraid he was thinking of that woman. Tears trickled down Suzy's cheeks. She'd always hoped she'd satisfied Chris. She'd taken pleasure in knowing she turned him on and believed it was because he fancied her and wanted her. She'd enjoyed sex with him. But not any more. By calling out Ellen's name he'd taken away her trust and her self-confidence. He'd demeaned and diminished her and for that she'd never forgive him. He could sleep in the spare room from now on. Her bedroom door was well and truly locked.

Chapter Twenty-Two

'I'll take this one, please.' Chris indicated the eighteen-carat rope chain and matching earrings to the assistant who was serving him. He watched as she placed the jewellery in black velvet boxes.

'Would you like it gift-wrapped, sir?'

'Please.'

This was costing him a small fortune. But it would pay dividends. What woman could resist expensive jewellery? He'd never known one who could.

As the assistant wrapped the jewellery, Chris browsed absent-mindedly along the display cabinets. He noticed a half-price offer on a selection of birthstone rings. They looked pretty, and more expensive than they were. Perfect! Chris thought. Now, when was her birthday? Chris cast his mind back and concentrated hard. It was around this time of the year. Soon after the first time they'd met.

'What's the birthstone for February?'

'The amethyst,' the assistant said helpfully.

'I'll have one of those birthstone rings too.'

'They're only gold-plated.'

'That's fine. Wrap them separately,' Chris said briskly as he took out his chequebook to pay.

* * *

'I'm telling you, Alexandra, he's having an affair. I bet he's going out to see that woman,' Suzy raged down the line to

413

her best friend. 'He's damn well not getting into my bed again.'

'He *will* have an affair if you keep that up, Suzy. Why on earth would he want to have an affair with some hick out in the sticks? He's told you he hasn't seen her since before the child was born. Why would he want to go and see her now all of a sudden? And do you seriously think that, even if he did go and see her, she'd want to have anything to do with him now? Chris treated her like dirt. She'd send him packing with a flea in his ear,' Alexandra scoffed.

'Well I don't know what's wrong with him then. He's as moody as hell. And he did say her name when he was making love to me.'

'Look, Suzy, maybe he's feeling neglected because of the kids. He was the centre of your universe for a long time. Start paying a bit of attention to him,' Alexandra advised.

Suzy could sense the irritation in her tone. Obviously her best friend was getting annoyed listening to whingy phone calls.

'I'll let you go,' Suzy said dolefully. 'See you.'

'See you.' Alexandra hung up immediately as if glad that the conversation was terminated.

Suzy glowered resentfully at the receiver. It galled her to think of all the hours she'd spent listening to Alexandra moaning about her troubled love life. Her friend couldn't even spare ten minutes out of her busy schedule for her.

She went out to the kitchen and made herself a cup of coffee. Was Alexandra right? Even if Chris went to see that woman, would she want anything to do with him after the way he'd treated her? Hardly, if she had any pride at all.

Maybe she *was* neglecting Chris, she reflected as she listened to the twins squabbling in the playroom. How did you balance it all? Husband, children, housework, social life. Men had it so easy.

She glanced at her watch. Four-fifteen. She supposed she should start making dinner. It was such a chore, day in, day out. Before they'd had children they used to eat out all the time. Suzy went to explore the fridge to see what culinary delights she could fling at her unappreciative husband.

She had just put the twins to bed and was straining the spaghetti when she heard Chris's key in the door.

'Hello,' he said warily when he walked into the kitchen.

'Hello,' she answered coolly. 'I'm just going to serve up dinner.'

'It smells nice.' He lifted the lid off the saucepan where the meaty bolognese bubbled, and sniffed approvingly.

Well that was something, she thought. Lately he never commented one way or another on the food she cooked for him. He placed his briefcase on the worktop and clicked it open. He drew out a long slim gift-wrapped package and a smaller square one.

'Here's a present for you. I'm sorry I upset you. And I want you to know that Ellen means nothing to me. I finished our relationship before I got engaged to you. That was a long long time ago. You're my wife, Suzy. I love you and I hate it when we row.' He handed the two packages to her.

Suzy was stunned.

'Open them,' he urged, giving her that charming boyish smile that was so hard to resist.

With trembling fingers she opened the oblong box. The sight of the exquisite gold rope chain made her gasp.

'It's beautiful, Chris.'

'It's eighteen-carat gold. I got you earrings to match,' he said proudly. 'Here, let me put it on.' He took the chain and fastened the clasp around her neck. She could feel the warmth of his breath on her neck.

'I know I've been hard to live with lately. Work's been tough. I'm sorry.' He kissed the nape of her neck.

'Is there someone else?' Suzy whispered.

'No. I swear to you, love. I haven't been seeing anyone. You're the only one I want.' He turned her to face him. 'I love you,' he said.

'Do you?' Suzy badly needed reassurance.

'Yes I do.' He kissed her. 'Let me show you.'

Suzy remembered the hurt she'd felt when he'd said that woman's name during lovemaking. She hated him for it. But she had to believe him when he told her he loved her. Otherwise she'd go crazy. It was horrible to be fighting all the time. She'd let him make amends – just this once. She needed to be hugged and cuddled, and to be told that he loved her.

'What about dinner?' she murmured.

'We can have it later.' Chris slipped his hand under her jumper and cupped her small breast.

'I want you,' he said huskily.

'I want you too.' Suzy's arms tightened around him. Sleeping alone was no fun. Did she want to be miserable for the rest of her life? He wouldn't have bought her such lovely expensive jewellery if he didn't love her. She had to keep that thought in her head. She was being paranoid and silly and she was going to stop it right this minute.

'Let's do it here, now,' Chris urged as he hurriedly undid the zip of her jeans.

It was the best sex she'd had in months.

*   *   *

Chris sat watching *The News*. He could hear Suzy humming to herself in the kitchen. She was making coffee. He smiled. That trip to the jeweller's had been a brainwave. Suzy's fears had been allayed. Things were back to normal between them. He didn't want strife. What she didn't know wouldn't hurt her.

If Ellen agreed to see him, it would be the most wonderful thing. If she didn't . . . well that was something he didn't care to think about. But, either way, at least Suzy wouldn't be giving him grief any more. The less hassle he had to cope with, the better.

*   *   *

The phone rang. Ellen's heart started to pound. Maybe it was him. What would she say? She was nervous.

416

'Hello,' she said quickly.

'Hi Ellen.' The sound of Miriam's voice made her feel ridiculously disappointed.

'I was just wondering if you could babysit for us tomorrow night. Ben won two complimentary tickets to the theatre in a competition at work. If you could, it would be great. You and Stephanie can sleep in our room. We'll sleep on the bed settee.'

'Sure, Miriam, no problem,' Ellen said brightly but her heart sank. What if Chris phoned tomorrow evening? He might think she was avoiding him. Now that she'd seen him, Ellen wanted very much to see him again. For one brief moment she was tempted to tell Miriam that he'd called. She'd been dying to tell her at teatime, when she'd driven over to collect Stephanie, but something held her tongue. Miriam would not be impressed. Ellen was afraid of what she might say. But it was difficult keeping her momentous news to herself.

They chatted for a while and all the time Ellen was conscious that Chris might be trying to get through. She knew he'd said he'd give her a few days to think about it but deep down she hoped that he'd phone sooner.

When she went to bed around eleven, she found it hard to sleep. She kept thinking about the way he'd kissed her with such passion. She knew she was weak and pathetic but it made her feel so good about herself and her love for him, to know that he'd come back to her.

By the time Thursday arrived and he hadn't phoned, she was in the depths of depression. Babysitting on Tuesday night had been a nightmare. She kept imagining that he was phoning and she wasn't at home to answer it. Even at work, every time the phone rang, she'd wondered if it was him. But each time it wasn't and she was gutted. He'd changed his mind. It hurt. Desperately.

She'd just put Stephanie to bed that evening and was washing up the tea dishes when the phone rang. She raced into the hall to answer it.

'Hello.'

'Hello, Ellen.'

Oh thank you, God. She sent up a silent prayer as she heard his deep voice at the other end.

'Can I come and see you again?'

'Yes,' she said softly as happiness and relief flooded through her.

'When?'

'When would suit you?'

'Now?'

Ellen laughed. 'Chris,' she remonstrated.

'I mean it.'

'Could you come tomorrow? I'll ask Mam if Stephanie can stay over.' There was silence at the other end of the phone.

'Does tomorrow not suit?' She couldn't keep the disappointment out of her voice.

'Tomorrow's fine. So we're going to be alone?' He sounded surprised.

'Yes.' Ellen bit her lip. She knew she should play it cool and keep him dangling but she'd never been good at playing games.

'I won't be able to keep my hands off you.'

'I don't want you to.' There! She'd said it.

'Ellen.' She knew he was smiling.

'What?'

'I'm dying to see you.'

'I'm dying to see you too.' Ellen was so happy she thought she was going to burst. A thought struck her. 'Listen, will you bring a . . . well you know. I don't want to take any risks.' She blushed.

'I'll look after it. Don't worry. I love you, Ellen.' All the hurt and unhappiness he'd caused her couldn't diminish the joy she felt at his words.

'I love you too, Chris. Will I cook dinner for you?

'That sounds good. I'll be over around seven.'

'Chris, would you park across the road? I have to be careful. I have Stephanie to think of.'

'Of course. I'll be very discreet,' he assured her. 'See you tomorrow.'

Ellen replaced the receiver and caught sight of herself in the mirror. She was glowing. Her eyes sparkled. She felt incredibly happy. Miriam would call her a fool. Sheila would go spare, if she ever found out, but Ellen didn't care. She had to live her own life. And after all the years of misery she wasn't going to pass up this chance of happiness. She and Chris were destined to be together. No matter what anyone else thought.

She lifted the receiver again and dialled her mother's number.

Sheila answered.

'Mam, Stephanie was saying she'd like to stay over with you some night. I was wondering if she could stay tomorrow night, seeing as she won't have to get up for school on Saturday morning. I'll collect her early,' she fibbed.

'That would be lovely. I've promised her we could make chocolate Rice Krispies. And was she saying herself that she wanted to stay?' Sheila sounded pleased.

'Oh she was. She misses you and Dad,' Ellen assured her mother.

'I'll look forward to that immensely,' Sheila said crisply. 'Will I keep some dinner for her? I could collect her from Miriam's.'

'If you like. If it's no trouble.'

'I'll make steak and kidney pie, it's her favourite.'

'She'll be thrilled Mam, thanks.'

'Do you want me to put your name in the pot?'

'No, I'll be grand. I'll eat with Doug at lunchtime. Thanks, Mam. See you.' Ellen hung up. She felt slightly guilty. That was low, using her mother to babysit so she could have a night of passion with the man her parents thought was the lowest of the low. She banished the thought. It was ironic, she reflected ruefully, but, since she'd left home, she was getting on much better with her mother. Sheila would probably never speak to her again, if she knew about Chris.

She ran upstairs to Stephanie's room. Her daughter was reading *Rupert Bear*.

'Guess what?' Ellen sat down beside her and gave her a cuddle.

'What?' Stephanie was immediately intrigued.

'Nannie wants you to go and stay with her tomorrow night. She's going to cook steak and kidney pie and she's going to get you to help her make chocolate Rice Krispies.'

'Yummy!' Stephanie exclaimed approvingly. 'Is it like going on my holidays?'

'It certainly is. We'll pack your case in the morning. And you can tell Nannie and Grandad I said you can stay up late.'

'Goody.' Stephanie yawned. 'Can I bring Mister MacPhearson?'

Mister MacPhearson was her teddy.

'Of course you can. Lie down now, pet. It's getting late. I'll see you in the morning.' Stephanie wrapped her arms around her neck and kissed her.

'Night, Mammy.'

'Night, love.' Ellen smiled down at her and tucked her in snugly. She wondered how Stephanie would get on with Chris. She'd have to play it by ear and see how it went. She wasn't going to let him become part of Stephanie's life until she was sure it would be good for her.

It was a pity things were so complicated, she thought sadly as she went downstairs. But that was the way it was and she couldn't do anything about it. There was no point in wishful thinking.

By the time Mick closed up shop the following evening, she was a nervous wreck. Even Doug had commented at lunchtime when he'd noticed her picking at her meal.

'You're like a cat on a hot tin roof. What's wrong with you?'

'Nothing.'

'And I'm a Dutchman.'

'Stephanie's dad got in touch with me,' she blurted out.

'Oh!' He eyed her quizzically. 'And?'

'I'm seeing him tonight.' She couldn't figure out why she'd told him that.

'Don't get hurt again,' he said quietly.

'I won't, Doug.'

'Just be careful,' was all he said. But it touched her that he was concerned for her. He was almost finished building the patio for her. She'd miss his company at lunchtimes.

She thought of Doug that evening as she prepared chicken supreme for Chris. She wondered if he thought any the less of her for seeing Chris. His good opinion mattered, she thought in surprise. She hadn't told him that Chris was married. He hadn't asked anything about him. Doug was a nice man. A decent man. A man of integrity. Unlike Chris. The thought came unbidden and she pushed it away, cross with herself for making unfavourable comparisons.

She had the dinner ready and was bathed and dressed when the ring of the doorbell made her heart somersault wildly. She took one last look in her bedroom mirror, for reassurance. Her hair was washed and shining. Her make-up was fine. Her flowing chiffon skirt and silky red blouse looked very sophisticated. She was sick with nerves as she hurried downstairs to open the door.

Chris's eyes widened with pleasure when he saw her.

'You look gorgeous,' he approved as he stepped into the hall. He put the bottle of wine he was carrying on the hall table and took her in his arms.

'Oh Ellen, I've thought of nothing else,' he murmured as he bent his head and kissed her passionately.

Ellen kissed him back hungrily. Now that he was here, her nervousness was gone. It was paradise to be back in his arms. They kissed lustfully, touching, tasting, frantic for each other. He opened her blouse and she strained against him quivering as he slipped his fingers inside her bra and caressed her.

'Oh Ellen, Ellen. You're beautiful. You're so sensual. You're a real woman,' he muttered, cupping her breasts. He'd always loved her breasts. Suzy was small and flat-chested compared to her. 'Let's go to bed?' He drew away and stared down at her, his eyes dark with passion.

'Yeah, let's,' Ellen breathed. She wanted him as much as he wanted her. They got to the top of the landing before turning to kiss again. She opened his shirt buttons and caressed his chest, bending her head to kiss his nipples. He groaned as her fingers struggled to undo his belt. When she touched him, he was so aroused he thought he was going to come.

'Ellen, Ellen,' he muttered harshly, desperate for her. He pressed himself against her as he eased her blouse off and unfastened her bra. The feel of her semi-naked body against his drove him crazy.

'I can't wait. I want you,' he groaned as he unwrapped a condom from its foil and put it on.

'Yes, yes,' Ellen whimpered as he slid his hands under her skirt and removed her panties. The feel of his hands touching her sent a frisson of need through her that was almost unbearable.

'Oh Chris, do that again,' she begged as he stroked her lightly with his thumb. He eased her down onto the floor. And then he was on top of her and inside her, and both of them were arching and thrusting wildly, moaning with passion and pleasure and relief. 'You're the best, baby. You do it to me. Aww Ellen, Ellen, Ellen,' Chris muttered frantically as he came in a long shuddering climax, as he held her tightly, his face contorted with pleasure.

Her insides quivered as she felt his heat and the ripples of her orgasm engulfed her. She cried his name aloud, her hands digging into his shoulders.

They lay on the hard floor, panting, their hearts pounding in unison.

'That was incredible, love.' He raised himself on his elbows and stared down at her a little later when his breathing had returned to normal.

Ellen smiled and touched his jaw. 'You'll never know how much I missed you. There hasn't been anyone else, since you.'

'I missed you too. I'm sorry,' he said huskily. 'I'm glad there's no-one else. I was sure you'd have someone.'

'I've dated, petted. But I've never slept with another man. I couldn't get you out of my head.'

'I couldn't get you out of mine. I called Suzy your name once when we were having sex,' he said ruefully.

'Oh!' Ellen murmured. But she couldn't help feeling pleased. It was gratifying to know she'd been part of his fantasies during lovemaking. It wasn't all one-sided after all.

They lay cradling each other, reluctant to break the intimacy. The smell of dinner wafted up the stairs. After a while Chris said, 'Whatever you're cooking smells delicious. And I'm ravenous. Should we eat and get our strength back for later?'

Ellen giggled. 'You haven't changed a bit.'

'I'm older and greyer and you made me feel like an out-of-control teenager when we made love just now. But I'm not finished with you yet, girl. After dinner, I'm going to make it up to you, for all those years we missed. Do you want me to tell you what I'm going to do to you?' His eyes glittered into hers.

'Yes,' she whispered, feeling desire flare again.

He placed his mouth against her ear and whispered into it. 'Oh Chris,' she murmured, wishing that dinner was over as he told her in intimate detail everything he was going to do to her, the next time they made love.

He devoured his dinner with relish. He'd always enjoyed her cooking. They drank the wine he'd brought, and lingered over coffee, slipping into the old familiar intimacy. He told her about work and how difficult it had been going out on his own at the beginning.

After a while he leaned across the table and kissed her. 'I have a little birthday present for you. I know it's not the exact date but it's around this time.' He took a small gift-wrapped box out of his jacket pocket and handed it to her. 'I think it will fit.'

Ellen tore open the wrapping and opened the black velvet box. 'Oh Chris, it's beautiful,' she cried in delight when she saw the ring.

'It's your birthstone.' He took it out of the box and slid it on to the third finger of her right hand.

'You remembered my birthday!' Ellen couldn't believe it.

'I knew it was around Valentine's Day. The day we met.'

She gazed down at the ring sparkling in the lamplight. It meant more to her than anything. This ring was an affirmation of his love for her. She would wear it as long as she lived.

'Let's go to bed.' Ellen reached for his hand and led him upstairs.

This time they didn't rush things and Chris proved that he'd lost none of his expertise as he satisfied every fibre of her being with his skilful lovemaking. Ellen lay in his arms, replete, wishing the night would never end.

Around eleven-thirty, he reluctantly eased himself out of her arms.

'I'd want to be going. I don't want to be too late getting home.'

'I wish you could stay the night.' Ellen sighed.

'I wish I could too, love.' Chris hated getting out of the snug bed. 'I'd better have a quick shower.'

She watched him walk naked from the room, into the bathroom. Her body felt cold, incomplete, without him lying against her. Would it always be like this? Would she ever have him to herself and not have to worry about him going home? she wondered sadly. Once it has been she who'd had to get dressed and leave, now it was he who had to do it. Would they, could they, ever be together? Or was it a dream that could never come true? It would cause a huge scandal if he left his wife for her. Would he even consider it?

Stop thinking like that, she thought angrily. *Be content for the moment.*

She lay curled up in bed and watched him dress. He was heavier than before, thicker around the waist, with the beginnings of flab on his stomach and shoulders. His skin was pasty white and she realized with a little shock that he wasn't as sexy in the flesh as he was in her dreams. He wasn't lean and fit and tanned like Doug.

Why on earth was she thinking such thoughts, she wondered irritably as she watched him knot his tie.

'When will I see you again?' How many times had she asked that question in the past?

'I'll have to wait and see how things go next week. I'll phone you.' Chris sat down on the bed and tied his shoelaces.

'Promise,' she said, suddenly unsure.

'I promise,' he said. 'Ellen, I don't want us to be parted ever again.'

'I don't either.' They kissed and then reluctantly drew apart.

'You stay in bed. I'll switch off the lights and pull the door behind me.' Chris tucked the quilt up around her. It made her feel cherished.

'I love you,' she said.

'I love you too. See you soon.' Chris grinned happily at her. Ellen grinned back. She was happier than she'd ever expected to be again.

She heard him move around downstairs and then the front door closed behind him. She stretched luxuriantly in the bed. Her body smelt of him. She loved it. She knew she should go down and wash the dinner dishes, and clip the latch on the door, but she was too relaxed and comfortable. Her body tingled, her face felt prickly from beard rash. It was so long since she'd felt like this, she wanted to savour every moment. If only she could hold on to the happiness she felt. It was such a rare and joyful feeling. She could count on the fingers of one hand the times she'd felt like this. Once or twice with Chris, and once when Stephanie was born. She switched out the light and lay in the dark, remembering every precious second, until her eyes began to droop and she could stay awake no longer.

Ellen slept like a baby.

*   *   *

Suzy glanced at the luminous dial on the alarm clock beside the bed. It was nearly half-twelve. Chris must have taken his new clients to a club on Leeson Street. Right this minute he could be dancing with some sexy siren who was single and free. She hated when Chris had to take clients to dinner. It was often the early hours when he got home and, though he swore he hated having to entertain people, and that it was work, Suzy knew he enjoyed it. Grumpily she thumped her pillow just as the beam of headlights pierced the darkness of the bedroom. She heard the sound of tyres on gravel and felt guilty for thinking mean thoughts about Chris. Here she was thinking he was dancing the night away in Leesson Street and he had just arrived home. He was probably exhausted. It had been a long week.

'Hello hon,' she whispered when he slipped quietly into the bedroom. 'Are you tired?'

'I'm whacked.' Chris yawned. 'Thank God I got away without having to go clubbing. But at least I got the account. It's an important one. It will bring other clients to us so I'll probably be wining and dining clients a lot more. I'd better join a gym or something. All this eating and drinking will give me a paunch.'

'Maybe we should join a gym,' Suzy suggested. 'It would be nice to do something together.'

'Good idea.' Chris yawned.

He didn't sound too enthusiastic, Suzy thought glumly. She'd have to think of something else he'd like. She liked the idea of joining a gym though. Maybe she would. At least he was home, where he belonged. With her. She could put her niggling suspicions to the back of her mind for another night.

*   *   *

Chris snuggled down into bed and put his arms around Suzy. He was very pleased with himself. It was a joy to be with Ellen again. He felt alive and vigorous. The sex had

426

been mind-blowing. She was so responsive. He smiled in the dark thinking of their lovemaking. It had been really nice talking afterwards. Ellen was a great listener. He'd call her soon and make a date for midweek. Now that he'd told Suzy about the new clients, he'd have an excuse for the odd extra night out. He wished he was still with Ellen. He couldn't wait to see her again.

* * *

What was Ellen Munroe doing to herself? Emma thought enviously as she watched her sister-in-law stride jauntily into Miriam's. She was glowing. She looked as fresh as a daisy. Beside her Emma felt pale and washed-out.

It was Saturday morning and she'd called into Miriam's to see if she'd mind Julie Ann while she and Vincent went into town to buy some new clothes for herself now that the ones she had were getting too tight.

Emma felt utterly depressed. She hated the fullness of her breasts and the thickening of her waist. It was so unfair. She strove hard to keep her slim figure and now she was going to look like a whale. To think that Ellen Munroe was soon going to be slimmer than she was, was the pits. She was in such bad form, she decided not to wait for the tea Miriam was making.

'I'll go, Miriam, if you don't mind. I want to get into town before the crowds,' she fibbed.

'Are you sure? The kettle's just boiled.' Miriam heated the teapot.

'No I'll go. Thanks a million for looking after Julie Ann for me.'

'That's OK.'

Was it Emma's imagination, or was Miriam not over-enthusiastic about minding Julie Ann? She saw a glance flash between her two sisters-in-law.

'I'm going, bye,' she said curtly and marched out the door. Bugger them! No doubt they'd have a good gossip about her when she was gone. Let them. What did she care, Emma thought grumpily as she got into the car and scorched off home.

* * *

'That one is something else,' Miriam said crossly as she poured the tea. 'Imagine arriving with Julie Ann unannounced, expecting me to look after her on a Saturday morning? Then she says she's having tea, and then she says she's not and she goes off in a huff. It's a bit much!'

'She's a moody wagon, she barely said hello to me. Why didn't you say no and make up some excuse?' Ellen picked a corner off Miriam's freshly baked soda scone and ate it with relish.

'It's very hard when she's standing there. I've three kids of my own, I've loads to do,' Miriam moaned. 'Where's Stephanie?'

'She stayed at Mam's for the night. I'm on my way over to collect her.'

'That's nice. I know your mother really misses her.' Miriam sat down at the kitchen table opposite Ellen. It was nice to have a few minutes peace and quiet. The children were out playing on the swings and Ben had gone over to Swords to get a new lawnmower before he went to work a late shift.

'I was going to ask you if you'd like to come out to a few garden centres in Malahide. I want to get some spring bedding, and I thought we might have a cup of coffee afterwards. I suppose we could bring the kids, now that you're stuck with Lady Jane.'

'What time were you thinking of going?'

'Maybe we should go early before the crowds,' Ellen said wickedly and Miriam laughed.

'Don't be nasty. Emma's not well. I feel sorry for her.'

'So do I. But that's not going to change the fact that she's a stuck-up spoilt little madam,' Ellen declared. She yawned and put her hand up to cover her mouth. Miriam noticed she was wearing a very pretty ring.

428

'That a lovely ring.'

Ellen's jaw dropped and, to Miriam's surprise, she blushed.

'Ooooh,' she teased. 'Did Doug give it to you?'

Ellen looked flabbergasted. 'Doug! No. Why would Doug give me a ring?'

'Well he likes you.' Miriam looked at her in surprise. If it wasn't Doug, who was it? Ellen hardly had the money to spend it on treats like that for herself.

'We're friends, Miriam, that's all,' Ellen murmured. 'It wasn't Doug, it was someone else.'

'Who?' Miriam was agog.

Ellen raised her chin and stared Miriam straight in the eye. 'It was Chris.'

Miriam couldn't believe her ears. She was stunned. '*Chris Wallace?*' she stuttered.

'Yeah, Chris.'

'Why did he give you a ring? When did you see him?' Miriam felt as if she'd been hit with a cold codfish. She listened as Ellen told her a saga that left her open-mouthed with shock, especially when she heard that he'd been to see her the previous night.

'Did you sleep with him?' she asked, horrified.

'Yes I did, Miriam. I love him.' Ellen was defensive.

'You love him!' Miriam exploded. She just couldn't figure Ellen out. 'You *love* him! Are you crazy, Ellen? After what he did to you? How can you let that . . . that *toad* back into your life? Ellen, he's a shit!'

'He loves me, Miriam. He told me he did. That's why he came back to me. He's always loved me,' Ellen explained.

Miriam looked at her in amazement. How could she be so gullible?

'How can you believe those lies? He does *not* love you. If he loved you, Ellen, come hell or high water, he'd have been there for you when you were having Stephanie. He wouldn't have run away like the gutless creep he is. Do you remember how you cried your eyes out over him? The pain, the misery, you felt. How many nights did you sit in

429

this kitchen, in bits? Where was he then? He was off having a ball, that's where he was. Where was he when Stephanie had pneumonia and you were trotting backwards and forwards to the hospital? Where was he when she cut her first tooth, walked her first step, had her first day at school? How can he have the nerve to swan back into your life after all this time when he never got in touch with you *once*? How can you have so little respect for yourself, Ellen?' Miriam was so angry her voice was shaking.

'You don't understand, Miriam,' Ellen said heatedly. 'You don't know what it's like. I love him with all my heart. I don't want to love him. I know he treated me badly. But he came back to me after all this time. That has to mean something. And maybe I'm being given a second chance. I've lived a very lonely life, Miriam. You've always had Ben. You don't know what it's like not having someone to share with. Don't judge me.'

'And what about his wife?' Miriam demanded furiously. 'While you're having a second chance, what about her and their children? What about the vows and the commitment he made to her? Were they just words? Did they mean nothing? He doesn't love you. He doesn't love *them*. There is only one person in this universe that Chris Wallace loves, and that's himself. And if you can't see that you're thick!'

'It's really none of your business, Miriam.' Ellen jumped up, enraged.

'It *is* my business. You're my friend and I had to listen to you when you were breaking your heart over that bastard. Well I won't do it again, Ellen, I'm warning you. If you want to make a mess of your life, just when everything's going right for you, go ahead and do it. But don't come moaning to me when that skunk does the dirty on you again. He's only using you. And you know it. The truth always hurts. But you're going to get it from me, whether you like it or not. And don't forget there's someone else you have to think about. What are you going to tell Stephanie? How are you going to explain Chris to her? You're not a love-struck young girl any more, Ellen.

You've got responsibilities. You're going into this with your eyes wide open. If you're stupid enough to want to get hurt again . . . fine. But I think it's really selfish of you to get involved with him again when you've got Stephanie to think about.' Miriam's voice rose an octave.

'Don't worry, Miriam. You'll be the last one I'll come running to if I have any problems. And don't worry about Stephanie. I've never let her down yet and I'm not about to now,' Ellen snapped furiously. 'And you needn't worry about minding her any more. For all I know you moan about looking after her behind my back the way you moan about Julie Ann. Well, you'll have nothing to moan about from now on. We won't burden you with our problems for another second. And all I can say is, it must be wonderful to be perfect. I hope you never make a mistake in your life. And if you do, I hope no-one ever rubs your nose in it the way you just rubbed mine in it. So butt out of my life and mind your own bloody business.' Ellen grabbed her jacket and banged the kitchen door behind her.

Miriam stood in shock staring after her. She had never felt so angry in her life. If Ellen Munroe thought she was going to take her back as a friend she had another thing coming. She had stuck by Ellen through thick and thin. No-one had been a better friend than Miriam. If Ellen thought more of Chris Wallace, let her, Miriam thought furiously as she gathered up the teacups and nearly flung them into the sink.

She'd looked after Stephanie for years. Certainly Ellen had paid her well but that wasn't the point. What thanks had she just got . . . None.

To hell with Ellen, she could find someone else to mind Stephanie because from now on, as far as Miriam was concerned, the friendship was over.

Chapter Twenty-Three

Ellen drove out of Miriam's in a temper. She felt like bursting into tears. Miriam had just spoilt all the joy and happiness she'd been feeling over her reunion with Chris. She'd made it sound sordid and dirty, as if she was having some sort of sleazy affair or something.

It was all right for Miriam to talk. She didn't understand anything. She had Ben and she loved him and he loved her. It was a steady sort of love. She'd never had the highs and lows of a passionate tumultuous love like the love between Ellen and Chris.

Ellen knew Chris was a shit. Miriam didn't have to keep rubbing it in. Chris was selfish. He only thought about himself. That was the way he was. It didn't stop Ellen from loving him. If you loved someone, you loved them faults and all. It wasn't much of a love otherwise, she thought angrily as she drove at speed along the winding road.

She pulled in by the gate at Blackbird's Field to calm herself down before she went to her mother's to collect Stephanie. She bitterly regretted calling into Miriam's. What had hurt the most was the way Miriam talked about Ellen's responsibility to Stephanie. It was almost as if she was saying that Ellen wasn't a good mother. What did she think she was going to do, make love to Chris in front of Stephanie? Her daughter was her number one priority and always had been. That wasn't going to change, it was mean of Miriam to suggest otherwise. She glanced down at her treasured ring. Should she take it off in case Sheila noticed it?

Why couldn't Chris have realized years ago that she was the woman he wanted? Then she could have worn his ring with pride. They could have married and been very happy. Now it was complicated. She had to be secretive and that was horrible.

Reluctantly she slid her ring into her pocket and started up the car. What had started out as a wonderful day had been well and truly spoilt.

*   *   *

'If I have to go in to you pair once more I'll wallop you,' Miriam shouted at Connie and Rebecca who were arguing loudly in their bedroom. It was ten p.m. and they still hadn't gone asleep. She set a place for Ben at the table. He'd be home from work soon. She'd made macaroni cheese for his supper. It was in the oven. She always cooked him a light meal when he came off late shift.

She went in to the sitting-room and tried to concentrate on *The Late Late Show* but her mind kept reliving the argument with Ellen. It was the first time they'd ever had a row. And to have it over that selfish, two-faced, womanizing rat was sickening.

'Butt out of my life,' Ellen had said. That was very hurtful, Miriam thought resentfully. If it wasn't for her, Ellen might have had to give up work. She'd been a *really* good friend to her. That was why she'd said what she said, to try and make Ellen see sense. She should have known better. Ellen was obsessed by Chris Wallace.

She heard Ben's car in the drive and went out to put the kettle on.

'Hiya, Miri.' Ben gave her a hug and a kiss when he walked into the kitchen. She clung tightly to him.

'Hey, what's wrong?' He looked at her in concern.

Miriam burst into tears. 'I had a row with Ellen.'

'Why?' Ben was mystified.

Miriam poured out the whole sorry story.

Ben looked grim. 'She's nuts. She'll never have a minute's happiness with him. He'll use her and keep her dangling. I'd like to break his neck.'

'What are you going to say to her?' Miriam wiped her eyes.

Ben was silent for a while. Then he said, 'What can I say? She's a grown woman, Miriam. She knows her own mind. She has to live her own life. If I start interfering, there'll only be a worse row. I don't want that. I don't want bad feeling between the children. You know the way these things escalate.'

'She said she's going to get someone else to mind Stephanie.'

'Who is she going to get? *Mam!*' Ben scoffed. 'She'll be back when she's cooled down. The two of you said things in the heat of the moment. Ellen needs you.'

'Well she can bloody well apologize to me,' Miriam said crossly as she began to serve up the supper.

Ben threw his eyes up to heaven. Ellen was a fool. And now she and Miriam were fighting. That was a fine thing to hear when you came home from work, tired and hungry. Women! He'd never figure them out. He was staying out of it. Let the pair of them sort it out between them.

*   *   *

It was Sunday evening, Chris hadn't phoned and Ellen was so down in the dumps she felt like crying. Hadn't Friday night meant anything to him? Surely he could have managed a quick phone call just to say hello and to let her know that he was thinking of her.

As well as despairing of Chris, she was in a right pickle about Stephanie. She was damned if she was going to go crawling back to Miriam, she thought stubbornly. She had no business talking to her like that. Ellen stared unhappily into the fire. It was raining outside and the gloomy skies darkened by dusk did nothing to lift her spirits. Stephanie was across the road playing with Denise's children. She'd

434

give her another ten minutes and then she'd go and collect her, Ellen decided.

She wondered what Chris was doing. He was probably sitting at home with his wife, reading the Sunday papers. Or maybe they were entertaining and they were preparing dinner. She felt fiercely jealous. Maybe Miriam was right. Maybe she was crazy to take him back. But he *had* come back. She had to give him a chance.

She'd just slipped into her coat when the phone rang.

'Hello, baby. How's my girl?' Chris said.

Ellen grinned from ear to ear. She was thrilled to hear his voice.

'Hi.'

'I miss you. Can I come over for an hour or two tomorrow night?'

'Oh yes. I'd love that.'

'Straight after work?'

Ellen's heart sank. 'It's a bit early. I'd prefer if Stephanie was in bed,' she murmured.

'I can't be too late coming home. I don't want Suzy to get suspicious. Anyway I'd like to get to know Stephanie.'

'Not for a while, Chris. Let's see how things go.'

'Well then I can't come tomorrow night,' Chris said huffily.

'Don't bother then!' Ellen snapped and slammed down the phone. Damn him. He hadn't changed. He was always the one to make the rules. It was what he wanted and what suited him. Well not this time.

She'd just closed the door behind her when she heard the phone ring again. She fumbled with her keys, dropped them, cursed loudly, picked them up and got the door open. She grabbed the phone.

'Hello.'

'Sorry. Are we still on for tomorrow?'

'You'll have to come when Stephanie's in bed, Chris,' Ellen said firmly.

'OK. Look, I have to go, I'm phoning from home,' Chris said hastily. 'See you tomorrow.'

Ellen hung up. She felt drained. They hadn't been together more than a week and already they were fighting. She didn't know whether she was on her head or her heels.

'Give it a chance,' she muttered. 'It *will* get better.' At least he'd phoned. He'd been thinking about her, and he wanted to see her again. Tomorrow. Let Miriam think what she liked, Chris loved her and she loved him. Ellen closed the door behind her and walked across the street towards Denise's. Stephanie loved going over to play with Lisa and Michelle. Ellen hoped that Denise didn't mind her being there. She had enough on her hands with Casanova McMahon.

'Hi, Ellen,' Denise greeted her. She looked pale and strained. Ellen felt sorry for her.

'Thanks for letting Stephanie come over to play. I'll take the girls next weekend. You might like an afternoon to yourself.'

'Stephanie's no trouble. The three of them entertain themselves. I'd a lazy afternoon sitting by the fire reading the papers.' Denise led the way into the kitchen.

'Where's Jimmy?'

'Poor little Wishy-Washy Dowling has the flu and Doctor Kildare legged it over to make her dinner. He never bloody did anything like that for me,' Denise said bitterly.

'What's going to happen between you two?'

'I want him to go. I don't want him in my life any more, but Cowardy Custard Dowling is afraid of the scandal and is worried about her precious reputation. I think she's backing out. He's like a demon when he's at home. He barks at the girls and he treats me like dirt. Everyone thinks he's Mister Nice Guy. If only they knew! If I wasn't dependent on him financially I swear, Ellen, I'd change the locks on the door and kick him out.'

'Oh!' Ellen had a brainwave. 'Would you be interested in making some extra money every week? Miriam's got a lot on her plate lately and it would be great if I could have Stephanie looked after for a couple of hours after school until I finish work. Would you be interested?

'Yeah, sure. I'd be interested.' Denise brightened up. 'Just to have some money of my own would mean a lot.'

'Could you start tomorrow?'

'Yep.' Denise grinned.

'Are you sure? I don't want to put you on the spot.'

'I'm certain.' Denise was emphatic.

'Brilliant.' Ellen beamed. *Stuff you, Miriam*, she thought triumphantly. *I don't need you.*

* * *

'That's it, Ellen. Are you happy with it?' Doug stood with his hands shoved into his jeans pockets as he watched her surveying the finished patio.

'It's lovely, Doug. I'm delighted with it. Thanks a million.' Ellen gave him a hug and he hugged her back. He was sorry to have finished her job. He'd enjoyed doing it. He really liked Ellen. He hadn't realized how much until he'd heard about this bloke who'd come back into her life. He actually felt jealous of him. It was clear Ellen was crazy about him, the lucky blighter. Doug didn't think much of him for leaving Ellen in the lurch when she was expecting Stephanie. He hoped she wouldn't be hurt again. Just his luck to fall for someone who loved someone else, he thought wryly as he followed Ellen inside for their last lunch together.

'What's your next job?' Ellen asked as she put a plate of steaming corned beef, creamed potato, cabbage and parsley sauce in front of him.

'I'm building a house on the airport road for Niall Reynolds. And you know the worst thing?'

'What?'

'He can't cook.' Doug grinned at her.

'Just because you've finished the job doesn't mean you can't have lunch with me now and again.' Ellen sat down opposite him.

'Thanks, Ellen. I'd like to keep in touch,' he said quietly.

'I hope you do, Doug. We're friends. And thanks for all

you've done for me.' She reached across the table and squeezed his hand.

Doug squeezed back. He wanted to say, I want us to be more than friends. But it would have distressed her, he could see that she was preoccupied. With thoughts of that bloke, no doubt.

Even though it was a very tasty dinner, Doug just didn't seem to have an appetite.

Afterwards, Ellen walked downstairs with him. 'Keep in touch,' she said. He hoped she meant it.

*　　*　　*

'Mammy, Stephanie went home with Lisa McMahon.' Rebecca flung her coat and bag on the rocking-chair in the kitchen. 'She said Lisa's mammy is going to mind her. Why isn't she coming to our house any more? I miss Stephanie.'

Miriam was stunned. She'd been expecting Stephanie to walk in the door with Rebecca as usual. Tears smarted her eyes. Ellen was a bitch. She'd lost no time in dropping Miriam like a hot potato and finding someone else to use.

'Go and change out of your uniform and I'll have your soup ready in a few minutes,' Miriam said flatly. She'd never had a serious row with anyone before. It was desperately upsetting. Ellen had always been her ally. They'd been friends for a long time. To think that Ellen would end their friendship because of an argument hurt desperately. Did the friendship mean nothing? Did she mean so little to Ellen? It looked like it, she thought bitterly. Well if that was what Ellen wanted, Miriam wasn't going to go running after her. She was angry. What made people think they could walk on her? Sheila, Della, Emma and now Ellen. Miriam was sick of it. They could all go and piss off. She was going to do only what she wanted to do from now on.

*　　*　　*

Ellen couldn't relax. She was petrified Stephanie would wake up and come downstairs. She never woke at night once she fell asleep but Ellen was edgy.

'Relax, baby.' Chris nuzzled her ear.

'Sorry,' she murmured.

'Come on, kiss me. Don't you want to? Don't you want me to make love to you?' Chris said huskily as he slid his hand up along her thigh. Ellen turned and kissed him passionately. She was very happy he was here. She wanted to make love, but the niggling unease was spoiling it.

'I thought about you the whole weekend,' Chris whispered, his breath warm against her ear.

'I thought about you too.' Ellen wrapped her arms around him. It was *wonderful* to have him in her life again, she thought gratefully as he unbuttoned her blouse. They made love on the settee and it was good to satisfy him the way she'd always been able to. But when it was over, she slipped on a dressing-gown and hurried upstairs to check on Stephanie. Her daughter slept soundly. Ellen closed the bedroom door with relief.

She went back to Chris and cuddled into him. 'Was it good for you?' she asked anxiously.

'It was the best.' Chris smiled at her, his eyes drowsy. 'I wish I could stay here all night.'

'I wish you could too.' Ellen ran her fingers through his silky hair and kissed him on the forehead. 'When am I going to see you again?'

'I'll phone you. Maybe Thursday. I better stay at home next Friday night. I'll try and come Thursday and then maybe I could get over for an hour or two on Sunday evening. We'll see how it goes.' Chris stroked her cheek with his finger and Ellen savoured his caress.

He didn't make it on Thursday or on the Sunday evening. The twins came down with the mumps on the Thursday morning and were very sick. Suzy was frantic and told him in no uncertain terms what he could do with the clients he'd planned to take to dinner. He was housebound, much to his disgust.

439

Over the weeks that followed, Ellen experienced the highs and lows that had always characterized her relationship with Chris. She waited for his phone calls. Made plans to be with him, often had them changed at the last minute, but was always very happy when they were together.

She hadn't seen Miriam for almost a month. One evening when she was locking the shop, Mick asked her why Miriam wasn't looking after Stephanie any more.

'She has her hands full with her own three. And Emma's always getting her to look after Julie Ann and that bugs her. So, when I moved to the flat, I decided I'd ask Denise if she'd be interested in minding her. It means that I don't have to go over to Miriam's after work to collect her, so we can have our dinner that bit earlier. It works out better.' Ellen embroidered the truth a little.

'Oh I see. She's in very bad form lately though. Sheila asked her to sell tickets for some raffle and she said she was too busy. That's not like Miriam at all,' Mick commented.

'I must give her a ring,' Ellen murmured, pretending all was well between them. To tell the truth, she really missed Miriam. She missed confiding in her. She missed their chats and gossips and moans and giggles. Miriam was more than a great friend, she was closer than a sister. This row was very painful. After the initial anger had faded Ellen wanted to make up. She didn't want to have to choose between Miriam and Chris. But that was what Miriam was forcing her to do. As long as she was seeing Chris, there would be a rift between them until Miriam was prepared to accept her relationship with Stephanie's father.

That night she dialled Miriam's number. She'd make the effort, she decided firmly. Ben answered.

'Hi, it's me, can I talk to Miriam?' she asked quietly. She'd met Ben on the street once and he'd spoken to her. But she'd felt awkward and embarrassed. No doubt Ben knew about Chris. It wasn't fair, but she almost felt like a scarlet woman.

'Hello.' Miriam sounded decidedly frosty. Ellen's heart sank.

'Hello, Miriam,' she said hesitantly. 'I was wondering how you are?'

'Fine, thank you,' Miriam said curtly.

'Miriam, please. Don't be like this. Can't we be friends?'

'What's wrong? Can't Denise McMahon mind Stephanie any more?'

Ellen was taken aback. 'Is that why you think I'm phoning?'

'I don't really know. Are you in trouble? Are you pregnant? That's the only reason you'd need me. Isn't it? Good old Miriam comes to the rescue,' Miriam said bitterly.

'Oh, Miriam! That's an *awful* thing to say.' Ellen was shocked.

'Yeah, well it's the way I feel. Goodnight, Ellen.' There was a click and Ellen heard the dial tone as Miriam hung up. She couldn't believe it. She felt sick. She burst into tears.

She told Chris what had happened the next night he called.

'Tell her to get lost.' He scowled.

'But she's my best friend. How could she say something like that?' They were lying on the rug in front of a blazing fire. The wind howled outside and rain lashed against the windows. Ellen felt cosy and happy in Chris's arms.

'She's probably jealous,' Chris teased. 'Forget about her. Do you think I should take on Arthur Grey as a junior partner?' He got back to the topic of conversation that had dominated their last two encounters. Chris was thinking of expanding and he needed her advice. Ellen sighed as she pushed her own problems to the back of her mind.

A few days later, she met Miriam face to face after Mass. Stephanie was thrilled to see her cousins. She turned to Ellen and asked, 'Can they come back to our house? Mammy, please, please, please.'

'You'd better ask Auntie Miriam,' Ellen said.

'Please, Auntie Miriam?'

Miriam looked flustered.

441

'They can stay for a while if it's all right with you,' Ellen said quietly, 'I'll drop them home.'

'I don't know, they have to have their lunch.'

'Please, Miriam, they haven't seen each other in ages. I'll bring them home in time for lunch,' Ellen pleaded. She didn't want Stephanie to be estranged from her cousins because of the row.

'All right, then, if you're sure.' Two red spots stained Miriam's cheeks.

'I am sure. What time do you want me to have them home?'

'Half one?'

'Fine. Come on, you guys, let's go home before it starts raining again.' Ellen pretended cheeriness.

The children had great fun playing in Stephanie's 'nursery' and Ellen was happy to have them there. Whatever happened between her and Miriam, she hoped Stephanie and her cousins would always be friends.

At one-thirty promptly, she drew up outside Miriam and Ben's. She opened the door for Connie, Daniel and Rebecca but she didn't go in. She knew she wouldn't be welcome.

The days lengthened as spring blossomed. Ellen's life continued to revolve around her snatched evenings with Chris. When she was with him she was happy, but her life was unsettled and she lived from one phone call to another.

One Friday near the end of April, Chris called to ask her to go to dinner with him. Suzy and the kids had gone to Wicklow to a birthday party and they were staying over. Chris had the night free. It sounded wonderful. Ellen felt light-hearted and happy. She phoned Sheila to ask if Stephanie could stay over. She told her mother that an old school friend had invited her to dinner in her house.

Sheila was delighted to have Stephanie stay and Ellen tried to banish the guilt she felt about telling her lies. She brought Stephanie over to the farm and then raced home to doll herself up. It was such a thrill to be going out to dinner

442

with Chris, knowing that he could come back to her flat and spend the night making love.

She bathed, and dressed with care. She wore a slim-fitting dusky pink fine wool dress which emphasized her curves. She looked sensuous and sexy. It was Chris's favourite dress. She was putting the finishing touches to her make-up when the phone rang. Her heart sank. Was it Chris phoning to cancel?

It was him. 'Listen, I've been delayed here. Could you drive into town to meet me? I've booked the table for eight and we won't make it on time if I have to drive out to Glenree. I'm sorry, love, it's just one of those things.'

'OK, I'll drive in.' Ellen sighed. She'd been looking forward to being chauffeured around like a lady. It wasn't quite the same having to drive into town alone and then having to drive home.

Chris had booked a table in a small restaurant off Stephen's Green. She had to circle twice before she found a parking space and she was cross as she walked towards Grafton Street where the restaurant was. He was waiting for her when she arrived and, when he took her in his arms and kissed her, her irritation melted and she gave herself up to the unexpected and rare pleasure of being out with him.

They enjoyed a delicious meal and lingered over coffee and liqueurs chatting, holding hands, enjoying each other's company.

'Let's go back to my place,' Chris murmured as he kissed the side of her neck.

'*What!*' Ellen looked at him in amazement. She'd assumed they'd be spending the night in her house.

'Let's go back to my place, now.'

'I can't go back to your house, Chris.' Ellen was dismayed and greatly offended.

'Why not?' Chris looked at her in surprise.

'*Chris!* You shouldn't even ask me. I can't go into Suzy's house and make love to you there,' she exclaimed heatedly.

'For God's sake, Ellen, don't be daft. Suzy's not there. She's not going to know.'

'That's not the point, Chris. She's your wife. You should have some respect.'

'How can you say that, Ellen? We're having an affair. What does it matter if I make love to you in Glenree or in my place? We're still committing adultery,' he said sulkily.

'I'm not going back to your house. Now or ever. And don't ask me again, Chris. I can't believe you'd even suggest it.'

'Oh for God's sake, Ellen. It's a bit late for your conscience to act up now.'

'It's nothing to do with my conscience. I'm not sleeping with you in your wife's home. That's low, Chris. I do have *some* standards. Can't you understand that? Are you just thick or totally insensitive?'

'Don't be a bitch, Ellen. It doesn't suit you. I told Suzy to ring me around half eleven. So I'll have to be there or else she's going to get suspicious. I can't come out to Glenree.'

'Fine,' Ellen said coldly. 'Thanks for dinner, I'll see you.' She stood up and walked out to the foyer. She put her coat on. Chris didn't follow.

To hell with you! she thought angrily as she stalked out. She was furious with Chris. Just what did he think she was, expecting her to sleep with him in his wife's bed? Had he no sense of decency at all? Had he no respect for Suzy even if he didn't love her? Obviously not. Had he any respect for *her*? Ellen wondered agitatedly. He'd said he loved her. Did he? If he did he wouldn't make her feel so cheap. She felt terribly insulted, hurt, and demeaned.

Ellen drove home to Glenree, deeply unhappy.

*   *   *

Chris lit another cigarette. Fuck Ellen, he wasn't going chasing after her. If she wanted to be huffy, let her. What was the big deal? Why did it mater where they slept? Suzy wouldn't know. So how could it affect her?

He couldn't go out to Glenree. He had to be home when Suzy phoned. She was beginning to get suspicious again, always questioning him about where he was and who he was with.

He'd deliberately told her to phone him at home tonight to prove that he wasn't out on the tiles. He'd told her he was going for a drink with some of the lads but that he'd be home by eleven-thirty. He knew she didn't believe him so he was all prepared to prove her wrong. And then Ellen had gone and ruined the evening. Damn her attack of scruples. He'd been eagerly anticipating a night of wild sex where they could moan and groan and let it rip without having to worry about anyone hearing. He'd been looking forward to waking up in the morning with Ellen in his arms and doing it to her when she was half-asleep. And now he was going to spend a lonely night feeling bloody frustrated. She was a damn stubborn woman now. In the old days she'd never have walked out on him.

He paid the bill and strode out into the night, feeling totally fed up.

*   *   *

He wouldn't be there, Suzy kept telling herself as the time edged slowly towards eleven-thirty. He'd only told her to phone him to shut her up. She couldn't help it. She just knew in her heart he was seeing someone. He was in great form. He'd got his vigour back. He was very relaxed and contented. Like the old Chris. And she knew it wasn't because of her.

At eleven-thirty on the dot, she lifted the receiver and dialled. It had hardly rung three times when she heard his voice on the other end of the phone. Suzy's jaw dropped.

'Hello, Suzy is that you?'

'Hi,' she said, hardly able to contain her surprise. 'I didn't think you'd be home.'

'I told you I would be,' he said irritably.

'You sound cross.'

'I'm tired. I had a long day. I'm just going to get ready for bed.'

445

'You do that,' Suzy murmured. She still couldn't believe he was at home. 'I'll see you after lunch tomorrow.'

'OK, mind yourself.'

She heard him yawn. 'Goodnight, Chris.' Suzy slowly replaced the receiver. It was good enough for her, for being suspicious, she reproved herself as she went downstairs to rejoin her friends.

At around two-thirty, Suzy called it a night. As she sat on the bed undressing, her hand hovered over the phone. What would she do if she phoned and there was no answer? She'd know for definite he was up to something then. Maybe he'd gone out after she'd phoned. She had to know.

She dialled the number. Her heart started to thump.

Please, please let him answer, she prayed. The phone was beside the bed. It shouldn't take him long.

'Hello?' His voice was groggy with sleep.

Suzy hung up. 'Thank you, God. Thank you,' she murmured. For some inexplicable reason she felt like crying.

*   *   *

He didn't phone her that weekend. Ellen veered between intense anger and profound sadness. She knew deep down that her relationship with Chris was not making her happy. She was totally unsettled and off balance. He controlled her. He made the arrangements. He broke them. She never knew from one day to the next when she'd see him. There was no emotional security. Was this the way she wanted to live her life? Were the brief moments of happiness when she was with him worth the restless unhappiness that seemed to be a constant in her life now? It was a question she was afraid to answer.

Monday . . . Tuesday . . . Wednesday there was no word from him. She was very tempted to lift the phone and ring him at work to tell him to get lost. She resisted the urge. She hadn't the courage to finish it.

446

She was pressing Stephanie's uniform late on Thursday evening when the doorbell rang. Ellen nearly jumped out of her skin. Was it him? She raced downstairs and opened the door to find Chris standing there.

'Hiya, tetchy.' He grinned his wicked boyish grin. What could she do only laugh? When Chris put his mind to it, he could charm the birds out of the trees.

'Bastard!' she said as she stepped back to let him in.

'You'd want to lighten up, baby,' he teased as he bent and kissed her.

'You'd want to cop on to yourself,' she retorted as she hugged him tightly. Now that he was here she was happy again . . . at least for the time being. He followed her upstairs and flung his briefcase onto a chair. He pulled her down on to the settee. They made love quickly, passionately. Ellen clung to him when it was over.

'Hold me, Chris,' she whispered.

'I'm holding you, love.' He looked down at her surprised by the intensity of her tone.

The doorbell shrilled.

'God! Who's that?' Ellen nearly had a heart attack. She pulled on her jeans and jumper and hurried over to the window.

'Jesus! It's my mother and Brona Dwyer. Quick, Chris, you'll have to go out the back way. Go out the side gate and into the lane.'

'For fuck sake,' Chris cursed as he threw the used condom into the fire and pulled on his clothes and shoes. He grabbed his jacket and followed Ellen down the stairs. She let him out the door that led to the back.

'I'll talk to you tomorrow,' he whispered.

'Yeah, go, Chris.' Ellen was in a panic. She closed the door and hurried along the hallway. She paused to run her fingers through her hair. She smelt of sex. 'Oh Lord,' she muttered as she straightened her jumper and zipped up her jeans. She took a deep breath and opened the door.

'Mam, Brona. Hello.' She stepped back to let them in.

'Hello, Ellen. We're just on our way home from the guild

meeting and I've got a puncture on the bike. I want to phone your father and get him to come and collect me,' Sheila explained.

'There's the phone, Mam, go ahead.' Ellen closed the door hastily. She didn't want them to see Chris crossing the street to his car.

'I'll put the kettle on for a cup of tea while you're waiting.'

'Thank you, dear.' Sheila picked up the receiver and began to dial.

'Come upstairs, Brona,' Ellen said weakly. She led the way upstairs and brought Brona into the kitchen.

'You've done a very nice job here, Ellen,' Brona approved as she had a good look around.

Ellen's hands shook as she filled the kettle.

'I'll show you around.'

'Could I use your convenience?' Brona asked delicately. She was afflicted with weak kidneys.

'Certainly. Just go up the winding stairs. It's the door at the end.' Ellen felt sick. Brona scuttled off.

Ellen went in to the sitting-room to put away the ironing board. Her heart nearly leapt out of her chest when she saw Chris's briefcase in the armchair. She kicked it behind the sofa just before Sheila marched into the room.

'Your father will be here in ten minutes. Where's Brona?'

'She's gone to the loo.' Ellen folded the ironing board. Her face was scarlet with guilt. But Sheila didn't appear to notice.

'Sit down, Mam, I'll bring you in a cup of tea.' Ellen carried the ironing board out to the kitchen and put it away. Her nerves were shattered. It had always been her greatest fear that Sheila and Mick would find out about Chris. Now that the long dark nights of winter were giving way to brighter, longer evenings, it was going to be much more difficult to conceal his visits. She lived on Main Street, people were always passing up and down. Inevitably, someone was going to see him. She'd been lucky to get away with it for so long, she thought glumly as she cut and buttered slices of Madeira cake.

Sheila and Brona chatted away and she must have made the right responses although, if anyone was to ask her what the conversation was about, she'd never have been able to tell them. It was with immense relief that she heard the doorbell ring, alerting them to Mick's arrival.

'Thanks very much for supper,' Brona said warmly.

'You're welcome.'

'Goodnight, Ellen. I've left my bike in the parish hall, I'll get Mick to collect it in the morning. We'll escort you home, Brona.' Sheila pulled on her gloves and picked up her handbag.

Ellen followed them downstairs and opened the door to her father. It had started to rain.

'Brona, I'll stick your bike in the boot and run you home,' Mick instructed.

'Not at all,' Brona protested.

Just go home, Ellen urged silently. She was petrified Chris might come back for his briefcase.

They argued the toss for five minutes and Ellen thought she was going to scream before Brona finally agreed to the lift home. Wearily Ellen closed the door and climbed the stairs. She was numb. She kicked off her shoes and sank onto the settee. That had been the most nerve-racking hour of her life.

She wondered would Chris call back. It was just gone eleven. She pulled the briefcase out from behind the setteee. It was black leather. Expensive. Classy. Her fingers hovered over the gold locks. She clicked them. They flicked open.

'Put it away,' she told herself. Rooting through some-one's briefcase was like reading someone's diary. It was an underhand thing to do. But what did he keep in it, she wondered. Curiosity consumed her. She was disgusted with herself but she couldn't help it. She opened the lid.

Chris kept a neat briefcase, she thought with approval. There were several files. A notepad with headed notepaper. A bundle of *With Compliment* slips clipped together, all in the main compartment.

A red, blue and black biro nestled in a side pocket. A box of paper clips and a nail-clipper filled another one. A folded piece of paper shoved down into a small pocket in the lid caught her eye. She took it out. It was a receipt. Handwritten. *Holden Jeweller's*. That was where Chris had bought her ring, she thought idly. It was the name on her ring box.

Ellen glanced at the receipt. She sat up straight and read it again. Her heart somersaulted. She felt sick, humiliated, hurt beyond belief.

'Oh Chris,' she murmured as tears blurred her eyes. She'd been the biggest fool in the world.

Chapter Twenty-Four

It was time to face reality and stop deluding herself. Ellen knew it as she stared down at the receipt in her hand. Whoever had written it had nice writing, she thought numbly.

Three items of jewellery. Eighteen-carat gold chain and matching earrings. And a birthstone ring. *Sale price* in brackets. The ring certainly wasn't gold, she thought when she saw the price Chris had paid for it. The chain and earrings had cost ten times as much.

Who had he bought them for? It could be anyone. Maybe he had another mistress on the side. She wouldn't put it past him. She didn't trust Chris any more. He lied so easily. Truth and honesty meant nothing to him.

Maybe he'd bought them for Suzy. It didn't matter. All Ellen was worth was a cheap ring bought in a sale. He hadn't valued her seven years ago. He certainly didn't value her now. What more proof did she need? She was good old reliable Ellen who'd never turn him away no matter how badly he treated her, as long as he needed her.

And he did need her. Ellen recognized that. There was some need she filled that had drawn him back to her, and it wasn't just sex. There was a bond between them. A deep unspoken bond that had survived their parting.

But it didn't change the way things were between them. That would never change. He would take, take, take and she would give, give, give. It was the nature of their relationship and always had been. Chris was a selfish man. She wasn't going to change that. He had to be the centre of everything. When she held him in her arms after love-making it was always his problems that they talked about. He'd ask her questions about herself now and again, but for the most part Chris was consumed by himself and what was going on in his life. If he was in the dumps, she had to coax him out of it. It didn't work the other way around. He was so busy thinking about himself, he didn't have time to think of her and that had always hurt.

When he'd come back to her, she'd fooled herself that things would be different because she so badly wanted them to be. Nothing had changed. She was living on her nerves, waiting for him to call. When he was with her she worried that Stephanie would wake up and see him there. Or that someone would see him entering or leaving her house and tell Mick or Sheila. It hadn't troubled her so much when the winter nights were dark, but the evenings were longer now, and in summer it would be bright until after ten. Glenree was a terrible place for gossip. There'd be plenty of it, if it was known she was having a male visitor once and maybe twice a week.

Ellen worried too about Stephanie. Chris kept pressing to get to know her. But so far some instinct had made Ellen resist that pressure. Probably because she'd known in her heart that the relationship wasn't a good one no matter how much she wanted it to be.

This time around had been even worse than their first affair and one of the reasons was that Ellen felt guilty about Suzy.

She sat by the dying embers of the fire, twisting his ring around her finger. She'd never acknowledged her guilt until now. Miriam's words about Chris's vows to Suzy had touched a nerve. Ellen knew that Suzy loved Chris too. He was a most lovable man. He was charming and funny and great company. When he put his mind to it and turned on the charm, there was no one quite like him. And he was a sensual, sexy, passionate lover. Sex with Chris was very, very satisfying. No doubt Suzy had fallen in love with Chris for those very qualities. Maybe she was suffering the way Denise was because her husband was cheating on her. It made Ellen feel bad to think about it.

She shouldn't be feeling bad, and guilty, and scared of her relationship with Chris being exposed. She shouldn't be living her life as if she was on the edge of a precipice. And she always would feel that way as long as she was with him, no matter how much she loved him. He couldn't commit to her because he had no right to now. He was a married man. All she'd get was second best.

She didn't want that any more. She wanted her life to be on an even keel again. Even if it meant a life without Chris.

There! She'd acknowledged the unthinkable. If she ended it this time, she'd never go back to him. And if she ended it, she wanted him out of her life for good. But could she make the break? Was she strong enough? Ellen shivered in the chilly night air. She glanced at her watch and saw with dismay that it was nearly one a.m.

She went to bed, but lay tossing and turning. It was dawn before she finally fell asleep.

She was like a wet rag at work the following day and, when she got home that evening, she sat dozing by the fire after dinner. She was glad it was Friday night. She could look forward to a lie-in on Saturday morning. She only went into work for an hour on Saturday evenings to count the day's takings and balance the books.

She was half-asleep when the phone rang.

'Hi gorgeous. I left my briefcase in your house.' Chris sounded cheery, she thought resentfully. But then why wouldn't he? He had a wife at home and an undemanding mistress on the side. What more could a man want? He was having his cake *and* eating it.

'I have it here. When are you going to collect it?'

'I'll try and get over Sunday evening. I'll tell Suzy I'm going in to work. I'll tell her the auditors are coming the next day.'

Ellen said nothing. She didn't want to be part of his lies any more. She didn't want to be the reason for them. If he could lie so easily to his wife, God knows what lies he was telling her. It made her feel horrible. It was hard to have respect for him. A relationship without trust and respect was hard to sustain, no matter how deep the love.

She thought of Doug for some reason. Doug was a *real* man. Not real in a physical sense. Real, morally and emotionally. He was dead straight. He had integrity. He didn't play games with women and mess them about. He'd never do to her what Chris was doing to her. Compared to Doug, Chris was weak and shallow. Why did she love him so much? What was it that drew her to him? Would she ever stop loving him? Or would those feelings always haunt her?

'Are you there?' Chris interrupted her musings.

'Yeah, I'm here,' she said heavily.

'Well you might talk to me seeing as I've taken the trouble to phone you.' She could hear the sulkiness in the tone. Typical of Chris. He didn't even ask her why she was in bad form.

'I'm tired, Chris. I didn't sleep very well last night.' She wanted to tell him that it was over, finished between them. But she couldn't bring herself to say the words. She couldn't take that final step.

'Was it because of your mother arriving unexpectedly?'

'Something like that.'

'Well, you go and have an early night and I'll be over on Sunday to revive you. And let's hope we don't have any unexpected visitors. Goodnight, love.'

'Goodnight, Chris.' Ellen felt very lonely. She hung up the receiver and started to cry.

The next day, a travelling circus and funfair visited Glenree and set up in a field outside town. Stephanie pestered Ellen to go and finally she gave in. She didn't like the circus. Clowns never made her laugh and she hated seeing animals caged. But she agreed to go to please her daughter. Denise said she'd bring her girls and go with them. She'd heard about a brilliant fortune-teller who travelled with the circus. *Madam Valda*'s reputation had preceded her and there were queues outside the little caravan where she read palms, the tarot and the crystal ball.

'Are you going in?' Denise asked.

'I am not,' Ellen scoffed. 'The last time I went to a fortune-teller was one summer when I was sixteen and I was nuts about Billy McDonald. And she told me that before I had feasted on my Christmas dinner he would have declared himself to me. She told me I'd be a queen among women and that we'd have two children. If I was still waiting for Billy McDonald to declare himself, I'd be waiting a long time, now wouldn't I, considering he became a priest.'

'Did she say *what* Christmas? Maybe he'll leave the priesthood for you.' Denise giggled.

'Give over. Anyway I don't believe in that sort of rubbish. You go. I'll mind the kids,' Ellen retorted. 'I'll take them in to the circus if you want to go and queue.'

'Are you sure you don't mind? I'd really like to go to her. I want to see if she'll tell me what's going to happen to me and Jimmy.'

'I don't mind. Go on,' Ellen urged. She could understand Denise's need to try and make sense of the shambles her life had become. If going to a fortune-seller helped, she might as well go to her.

Two hours later, after the circus performance, Ellen and Denise sat in the marquee drinking tea. The children were tucking into a feast of sausage and chips. A rare treat. They were chattering away, ignoring the adults.

'Well? What was she like?' Ellen asked, keeping her voice down.

'Ellen, she was *brilliant*. I'm telling you.' Denise was wide-eyed. 'How could she know about me and Jimmy? She did the cards and picked up on him immediately. She described him to me. She told me how he never looks you in the eye. And you know?' Denise looked at Ellen. 'She's right. He doesn't. She told me he was immersed in his work. She told me he was having an affair but that he wouldn't stay with her. Seemingly Wishy-Washy Dowling

455

makes him feel like a child and he finds that exciting. She showed me a card with a child on it. But he'll end it. She told me he'd come back to me, if I wanted him. But that he'd do the same thing to me again. She said he was an egotistical man with a gamey eye. He'd always have a woman but he'd never commit to one. It was incredible. She showed me another card. It had a hunched-up character looking over his shoulder going past railings, I think. She said that was him sneaking around. Can you believe it?' Denise was deeply impressed.

'Did she tell you anything good?' Ellen was intrigued in spite of herself.

'Yeah, she said I was going to go into business. And it was going to be successful. She said I'd find peace of mind in my independence.' Denise made a face. 'How am I going to go into business? I've two daughters to look after and a philandering husband? Maybe it's just a load of bull, but a lot of the things she told me were very accurate.'

I wonder what she'd say to me? Ellen found herself thinking as she sipped the hot tea and nibbled on a cream slice.

She kept thinking about the fortune-teller all that night and the following day. Stephanie had gone to a school friend's birthday party and, on impulse, she pulled on her jacket, put on some lipstick, and left the flat to walk to the circus. There were four people ahead of her outside *Madam Valda*'s caravan.

Ellen was tempted to leave, but she'd made the effort to come so she waited along with the others.

She was calling herself all kinds of a fool when it was finally time for her to enter the spotless caravan with its gay chintz curtains and furniture covers.

'Sit down, dear,' *Madam Valda* instructed. She didn't look like a fortune-teller, Ellen thought in surprise as she handed over her money. The woman seated in front of her wasn't wearing a scarf and gypsy earrings. She was middle-aged with grey hair, small and plump. She had kind eyes.

She took Ellen's palms in her own and scrutinized them intently. Ellen felt a flutter of nervousness.

'Don't be afraid, dear. Think of me as a guide. We all have our gifts and this is mine. You've had hard times, haven't you?'

Ellen nodded.

'You've a good lifeline. They'll have to poison you to get rid of you.' She smiled at Ellen. She pulled her thumbs. 'You've strong thumbs. You're tenacious. You don't give up easily. You've a compassionate nature. But you're too soft, dear. You let your heart rule your head. It should be the other way around. You love very passionately. It's all or nothing with you.' She paused and stared intently at Ellen's palms. 'A man has hurt you deeply. There's a child. A little girl. You're not married.'

Ellen nearly fainted.

Madam Valda looked at her sternly.

'That man. He is still with you?'

Ellen could only nod.

'He's not for you. Get rid of him. Shuffle the cards for me.' She handed Ellen a large pack of cards. 'Give them a good shuffle.' Ellen did as she was instructed.

'Now.' *Madam Valda* took the cards from her and spread them out. 'Pick fifteen.' Ellen did so. *Madam Valda* arranged the fifteen cards that Ellen selected in front of her.

'Ummm,' she murmured, fixing her gaze on Ellen. 'I know you'd love me to say that this man is the man for you, but my dear, he isn't. The bond between you is deep. He runs to you and he runs from you. He's a self-centred man who cares only for himself. He doesn't accept his responsibilities. He lies. He doesn't mean what he says. He drains you of your energy. As long as he is in your life, you'll be unhappy. You know that. Don't you?'

Ellen nodded again. This was uncanny. She was half-afraid of what *Madam Valda* would say next.

The fortune-teller smiled. 'There is a deeper love than what you have now, waiting for you. A man with a far stronger character is for you. He will be a great friend first.

Friendship will turn to passion but that will only happen when you let that other man go out of your life. He will block you as long as he is with you. He is far too negative. Get rid of him and open the way towards happiness.'

'When will this happen?' Ellen asked hesitantly.

'Whenever you let it.' *Madam Valda* smiled. 'And I see two little females around you. It's in your palm. You'll have two more daughters. I also see a life of hard work that will prove very satisfying. Your life is going to change completely, my dear. There is happiness there for you. But first you have to have courage, and for a while, you will suffer grief and pain. It will pass and you'll be a much stronger person. Now go and have a good life because you die at the end of it.'

Ellen left the caravan utterly astounded. Everything that woman had said to her about herself and Chris was true. It was frightening. But it was exhilarating as well. A deeper love than what she felt now. Could that be possible? Could she ever love anyone the way she'd loved Chris? Well *Madam Valda* was right about one thing, she'd never be happy as long as he was in her life. It was time to let go. And this time it would be for good.

Ellen was calm when Chris arrived that night. It was as though a burden had lifted. All she had to do was to get over the ordeal of telling him.

'Hello, light of my life.' He stood framed in the doorway smiling at her. Her resolve weakened as her heart lifted at the sight of him.

'Hi, Chris.' She stood passively in his embrace.

'What's wrong?' He looked at her in surprise. He was used to rapturous greetings.

'Chris, we have to talk.'

'Sounds ominous,' he joked as he followed her upstairs. 'What have we to talk about?' He looked suddenly worried. 'Jesus, you're not pregnant, are you?'

'No, nothing like that,' Ellen said quietly. 'Chris, I want to end it. I don't want to see you any more. I don't want to hear from you. I want to make a fresh start.'

'*What!*' He was astounded.

'It's over.'

'What the hell is wrong with you, Ellen? What do you mean it's *over*? You love me. I love you. I need you and you need me.' Chris gripped her by the arms. 'Is it because of your mother calling the other night? Love, I'll be as discreet as I can. I promise.'

'Chris, it's over,' Ellen reiterated. 'I can't live my life like this. I'm not happy. You're married to Suzy, she has a right to expect a commitment from you. You didn't love me enough to make that commitment to me.'

'I made a mistake. I told you. Suzy means nothing. It's you I want. I love you. How many times do I have to tell you?'

'Chris, you don't love me. You don't value me or the love I have for you. I don't think you're capable of loving anyone. You're too wrapped up in yourself,' Ellen said quietly.

'Is this because I wanted you to stay at my place? For Christ's sake, Ellen, grow up—'

'No, you grow up,' she flared. 'I'm sick of waiting for phone calls. I'm sick of making arrangements and having them broken. I'm sick of looking over my shoulder. I don't want my daughter to look at me with disrespect in years to come. I have her moral welfare to think about. I've been very selfish. And I don't like it. I have responsibilities to Stephanie whether I like it or not. I'm not going to run away from them, just so I can have a few snatched moments of happiness once or twice a week. There's more to life and I want it. I want peace of mind again, Chris, and I'll never have that with you.'

'But I thought you loved me.'

'I do. More than you'll ever know or understand. I love you. You'll always be in my heart, but I deserve better than you, Chris. You take my love for granted as if it was your due. Well it isn't. You don't respect me or cherish me. And I won't live my life this way any more.' She took off the ring and handed it back to him.

'Please go, Chris.'

'What the fuck has got into you, Ellen?' Chris couldn't believe his ears. 'You love me. You know you do. We're good together. We talk, we have fun. The sex with you is the best I've ever had. And the best you've ever had too.'

'I know all that,' Ellen said heatedly. 'But I want *more*. I want what you won't give me. I want emotional security. I want to be cherished and made to feel special. I want to share. You know something, Chris. We always talk about you. We never talk about me. My life is an afterthought when you're around.'

'You sound like one of those goddamn women's libbers with their psychobabble and jargon,' he snapped defensively. 'I do cherish you. I do make you feel special. If you want me to leave Suzy, I'll leave her.'

'I don't believe that.' Ellen was shocked. She never thought he'd take that step.

'Believe it,' he said fiercely. He bent his head and kissed her. It was an angry passionate kiss.

'I love you.' His eyes glittered down into hers.

For a moment she was so tempted to believe it. In his own way, maybe he did love her. She thought of the ring. The cheap token to keep her sweet. It strengthened her wavering resolve.

'I'm sorry, Chris. I'm sorry. I want you to go. I can't handle this any more. Please go now and don't contact me again.'

'Do you want me to beg? Is that it?'

'Do you think this is some kind of game I'm playing? You're so bloody arrogant, Chris. I don't want you to beg. I just want you out of my life. I want peace. Now go.'

'I'll never be out of your life. Stephanie's my daughter. I have rights.'

'You have no rights, you bastard,' Ellen raged. That was low. Typical of Chris. He could dish it out but he couldn't take it.

'She's my daughter. I'll have my say in her upbringing.'

'Your name isn't on her birth certificate. That gives you

no rights at all. So you can forget that. If Stephanie wants to have anything to do with you when she's older, that's up to her. But by God, Chris, you forfeited any rights over Stephanie the day you walked out on us before she was born. And don't you dare think I'll let you near her. It's over. Now go.'

'Why are you being such a bitch, Ellen?' He shook her.

'Chris, you're hurting me!'

'Sorry,' he muttered, easing his grip.

'Oh Chris, please go. I don't want to fight,' Ellen said wearily. 'I love you but I can't go on. I'm tired of it all.' She felt exhausted. She sat down on the sofa.

Chris looked at her, shocked as he realized that she really did mean what she said. He picked up his briefcase, put the ring in his pocket, turned on his heel and walked out.

'Oh God! Oh God!' Ellen swallowed hard. She'd done it. She'd ended it. Her heart was pounding. She was terrified. What if she'd made a mistake? She did love him. Maybe that fortune-teller was wrong. He'd said he'd leave Suzy. That had to mean he loved her.

Think of Stephanie.

Think of the ring.

Think of the night he wanted you to sleep in Suzy's.

Think of all the times you waited for him and he never showed up.

'You did the right thing,' Ellen told herself fiercely. 'You did the right thing.' But her heart was breaking.

*   *   *

She doesn't mean it. She's probably getting her period or something. That always makes her tetchy. She loves me, she's *crazy* about me, Chris kept telling himself as he drove back towards the city.

He was bewildered by her outburst. What had brought this on all of a sudden? He thought she was reasonably happy. She was always very glad to see him. Their passion

461

for each other was stronger than it had ever been. He wanted her. He wanted to be with her. Maybe saying he would leave Suzy was a bit over the top but, if saying it would calm Ellen down a bit, he could always make excuses when it came to the crunch.

She'd seemed so definite about ending it though. He *couldn't* believe that Ellen meant what she said. She couldn't be serious that he wasn't to have anything to do with Stephanie. He wanted to get to know his daughter. She was a lovely little girl. He hadn't rushed Ellen about that because he'd hoped, as time went on, Ellen would relent about letting him see her.

This was weird. Totally unexpected. He knew that he made arrangements and sometimes broke them but Ellen had to understand that he didn't do it on purpose. It was difficult having an affair when he had a wife as suspicious as Suzy was. And he'd thought she did understand . . . until tonight.

Maybe she was feeling neglected. He'd give her a few days to cool off and then he'd bring her back her ring and a bottle of champagne and some flowers. Women loved flowers. He'd bring her red roses. There was no way that Ellen wanted to finish with him, Chris told himself as he headed on to the airport road. He was the love of her life. Ellen had the softest heart of anyone he knew. It was one of the things he loved about her. She couldn't turn her back on him even if she tried. She'd proved that when she took him back. He wanted to turn the car around and go back to Glenree. He wanted to make love to Ellen and have her tell him that she loved him. They were always extra close after they'd made love.

He pulled up, tempted to do a U-turn and go back the way he'd come. He dithered, which was most unusual for him. What if he went back and she got really mad with him? She was in a funny humour.

But maybe she wanted him to come back. Maybe she regretted her outburst. He waited until there was a gap in the traffic and then he swung back the way he'd come. He was back in Glenree in ten minutes. He felt very confident as he rang the bell. Ellen loved him. This was a misunderstanding they'd soon sort out. Once he had her in his arms, they'd be fine.

*   *   *

Ellen froze when she heard the doorbell. She'd looked out the window and saw Chris's car across the street. She'd wondered if he'd come back and now, here he was. Ellen knew she was doomed if she let him in. She wouldn't be strong enough to tell him to go a second time. Because she did love him.

He rang again. She was afraid the bell would wake Stephanie. She ran downstairs. She could see his outline through the glass panel. She was really torn.

'Go away,' she whispered. He rang the bell again, this time keeping his finger on the buzzer. That was mean, she thought, suddenly angry. He'd wake Stephanie and he didn't care. His return showed that he hadn't taken anything she'd said seriously. Good old Ellen didn't mean what she said. Well she did. This time she did, she thought grimly. She opened the bell box attached to the wall in the hall and took out the batteries. The ringing ceased although she knew that Chris's finger was still on the buzzer.

After a while Chris went away. She felt like Judas.

*   *   *

He couldn't believe it. He'd seen her run downstairs through the frosted glass. He'd felt triumphant. He'd felt horny. But she hadn't answered the door. He'd rung the bell again and kept his finger on the buzzer and then there'd been silence and he'd known she'd taken the batteries out. She wasn't going to answer.

It was the worst feeling he'd ever experienced. He felt lost, cast adrift, bereft, afraid, alone . . .

The only time he'd ever felt like that was on the day of his wedding. But that had been mild compared to the way he felt now. He felt like crying. What if Ellen really *was* serious? He didn't want to think of a life that didn't include her. Ellen was the only person in the world that he felt he could tell everything to. There was total intimacy between them. He'd never had that with anyone else. Certainly not Suzy. He never talked to Suzy the way he talked to Ellen. He never shared his secret fantasies with Suzy the way he did with Ellen. Suzy was much more inhibited than Ellen was. She didn't possess the earthy carnal sensuality that he loved in Ellen. He always felt comforted when he was with Ellen. It wasn't like that with Suzy. Now that he'd experienced that again he didn't want to lose it. How could Ellen do this to him? How could she? Was this what they meant by karma? What goes around, comes around.

He'd cruelly and callously dumped Ellen once. And now she was dumping him. And the worst thing was, she wasn't being vindictive. Because Ellen wasn't like that. If she'd been vengeful and spiteful, it would have been much easier to cope with. He could have been angry. He could have let himself hate her for causing him such torment. But it wasn't like that with her at all. She really did mean it when she said she wanted peace of mind even if that meant a life without him. Chris reversed the car and turned in the direction of Dublin. He felt as if his world had just turned upside down. Sadness seeped into every bone. Had he blown it? Ellen had accused him of only loving himself and maybe she was right. But now that he was in danger of losing her, now that *she* had ended it, Chris knew he loved Ellen more deeply than anyone else in his life. He wouldn't let her go. He couldn't. He *needed* her.

It failed to cross his mind that maybe Ellen didn't need him any more.

*   *   *

Suzy was surprised when she heard Chris's key in the door. She'd phoned the office to see if he was there and when she'd got no answer she'd immediately started thinking he was off with some woman. She wasn't expecting him home for hours, and she certainly wasn't expecting him home with a face like a thundercloud.

He'd been in great form lately. And she'd made an effort to believe that everything was all right between them. But when he pulled stunts like telling her he was going to the office and then didn't answer the phone, what was she supposed to believe?

'What's wrong, you don't look very happy?'

'I hate bloody auditors,' he growled as he threw his briefcase on the sofa.

'I rang the office. You didn't answer.' Suzy knew she sounded accusing but she couldn't help it.

Chris flashed her a look of fury. 'Was that you? I was up to my eyes in figures and I was damned if I was answering that bloody phone. I had to start all over again,' he lied.

'Sorry,' Suzy said meekly, taken aback at his anger.

'What did you want anyway?'

'Alexandra phoned to know if we'd like to go to a film premiere. Some people didn't turn up and she had spare tickets.'

'Who does she think we are, rent-a-crowd? If she couldn't invite us as guests why should we go as spares when she needs to fill seats?'

'Oh for Christ's sake, Chris, don't be so nasty. The girl was being nice.'

'Huh! That'll be the day.' Chris snorted. 'I'm going to bed, I've a headache. Goodnight.' He gave her a perfunctory kiss on the cheek and stomped upstairs.

Suzy didn't know what to think. A headache . . . Chris! Maybe he *had* been working on figures in the office. Maybe she *had* disturbed him. If only she could believe it, she thought glumly as she snuggled into the big armchair and determinedly immersed herself in her latest Harold Robbins blockbuster. If she kept thinking about whether

Chris was being unfaithful to her, she'd drive herself crazy.

*   *   *

'Ellen, Ellen,' Chris breathed harshly in the dark. He willed Suzy not to come up to bed until his fantasy was over. He groaned thinking of what he would have done to Ellen and what she would have done to him.

Later, he lay thinking about the events of the evening. He still couldn't believe that Ellen had ended their affair. She'd come to her senses. This was just a lovers' tiff, he thought drowsily. No woman had ever walked out on him before. His Ellen certainly wasn't going to be the first.

Chapter Twenty-Five

Miriam walked down Main Street and felt the now familiar knot in her stomach as she neared Mick's shop. She hated passing it now. Before the row she'd always go in and say hello to Ellen and Mick. Nowadays she hurried past. She had her meat delivered in the mornings by the butcher-boy as usual so Mick didn't realize that Ellen and she were not on speaking terms.

She saw Denise McMahon going in to her house and felt a fierce stab of jealousy. Ellen's new best friend. No doubt they had loads of chats and cups of tea and long gossips. Connie had been to the circus on Saturday with the Nolans and she'd told Miriam that she'd seen Denise and Ellen and the children going in to the marquee for tea. Miriam felt like bawling her eyes out when she heard that. She felt very lonely these days. Ben kept telling her to sort it out. But she didn't have the nerve. She was afraid Ellen would rebuff her. She'd said harsh things to her. And then, when Ellen had tried to make it up, some perverse devil had got in to her. It had been pretty vicious to ask Ellen if she was pregnant. She bitterly regretted it.

She hurried past the shop with her head down, and only slowed her pace when she got to the church. Often she'd go in and say a prayer when she went past St Joseph's, but she wasn't in the humour to pray today. God was not in her good books. No one was, she thought crabbily. She was sick of Emma and her whinges. Sheila was driving her mad trying to persuade her to go to the quilting classes that were held once a week in the guild. She needed more people to keep the numbers up. Miriam didn't like sewing. She much preferred baking. When she'd said no, Sheila had gone all huffy. But it hadn't deterred her, she was still pestering Miriam to change her mind.

Miriam was heartily sick of all her in-laws, she decided as she marched past the church. Her heart flip-flopped when she saw Ellen walk out of the bank and head in her direction. Short of crossing the street, there was no way of avoiding her. Miriam's footsteps felt like lead as she came nearer to Ellen. She noticed that her sister-in-law looked wretched. Nothing like the glowing woman who had sat in her kitchen and told Miriam that Chris Wallace was back in her life.

All must not be well in Utopia. Serves her right, she thought with uncharacteristic bitchiness. Then, as Ellen came abreast of her and she saw how truly miserable she looked, her heart softened and she stopped.

'Hiya, Miriam,' Ellen said hesitantly.

'Hello, Ellen,' Miriam said awkwardly.

'Miriam. I . . . can't we be friends?' Ellen blurted out and burst into tears.

Miriam nearly died with dismay. Bonnie Daly was just a little way behind them.

'Shhh, Ellen, Bonnie Daly's coming. Come on, let's go back to your place. We don't want her sticking her nose in where it's not wanted,' she said urgently. She handed Ellen a tissue and they walked quickly, in silence, back towards Ellen's.

When they got into Ellen's hall and closed the door behind them, Ellen threw her arms around Miriam. 'Don't be mad at me, Miriam. I'm really sorry if I offended you. You're my best friend and I miss you.' She sobbed.

Miriam felt tears come into her own eyes.

'I'm sorry I said what I did. I was worried about you but I shouldn't have said what I did. I miss you too, Ellen. I miss Stephanie and so do the girls. I'm dead jealous of Denise McMahon.' They held each other tightly.

'What a pair we are,' Ellen gulped.

'I know.' Miriam sniffled. 'It's worse than being in love.'

Ellen giggled and Miriam started to laugh too. The relief of being friends again was overwhelming.

'We're never having a row like this again, Ellen. Promise.'

'I promise. It's been horrible. It's *really* good to see you, Miriam.' Ellen wiped her eyes with the back of her hand. 'Look, it's almost lunchtime. I'll just run in and tell Dad you're staying for lunch and he can lock up. You will stay, won't you?'

'I'd love to.' Miriam felt light-hearted. This was utterly unexpected. Thank God the row was over. 'I'll run up and stick the kettle on.'

'Do I look all right? Do I look as if I was crying?' Ellen peered at herself in the mirror. 'Lord! I look a sight.'

'You look wrecked. What's wrong with you?' Miriam was suddenly terrified that Ellen *was* pregnant.

'I finished it with Chris last night,' Ellen said quietly.

'Oh!' Miriam didn't know what to say.

'I'll tell you about it in a minute. I'd better go in to Dad, he'll be wondering why I didn't come back from the bank.' Ellen ran a comb through her hair, touched up her lipstick and went out to the shop.

Miriam walked slowly upstairs. She was very glad to hear that Ellen was finished with Chris but she knew her sister-in-law was suffering. It must be a dreadful thing to love someone who wasn't good for you, she thought as she filled the kettle and put it on to boil. Chris Wallace had caused Ellen such grief since he'd come in to her life. Miriam hoped he he was finally out of it for good.

Ten minutes later she sat and listened in silence as Ellen explained why she'd let Chris go. It surprised Miriam that it was Ellen who'd made the decision. She'd assumed Chris had done the dirty on her again. She pitied Ellen from the bottom of her heart. It was a tough decision to make, but Ellen had never lacked courage. Miriam looked her sister-in-law straight in the eye.

'Ellen, all I can say is, love shouldn't make you cry. And

you'll always be crying over him as long as he's part of your life. You're right to end it. I know you do love him. He doesn't deserve the love you gave him. He never did. But in the last few months, before he came back into your life, you were happier than I'd seen you in a long time. Try and get back to that. *You* made the decision to let him go this time and you did it for the right reasons. Put yourself first from now on.' Miriam squeezed her hand. 'And I'd love to take care of Stephanie again. Honestly she's no trouble. I never minded having her.'

Ellen grimaced. 'Miriam, it's a bit awkward. I'm going to tell you something in confidence. Denise needs the money. Jimmy's having an affair with Esther Dowling and Denise is trying to make some money on the side so she won't feel she's completely dependent on him.'

'Esther Dowling is having an affair with *Jimmy McMahon*. I don't believe it!' Miriam nearly got lockjaw with amazement. 'Jimmy McMahon, my God. It's incredible. He seems so . . . so dependable. He's very good to his mother. I often see him bring her coal and briquettes and he lights the fire for her every day because she lives on her own. I'm really disappointed in him. I thought he was . . . nice . . . decent. Poor Denise. She must be in bits.'

'She's in flitters, God love her. So would you mind if I left Stephanie with her for the time being?'

'Of course not,' Miriam assured her. 'Do you know, I always thought Esther Dowling was too sweet to be wholesome. I thought she was sly. She puts on this, *I'm a helpless female* act, when she's with men. It's pathetic.'

'I never really noticed.' Ellen poured another cup of tea for the two of them and handed Miriam another slice of cherry and walnut cake.

'Well I remember noticing it when she sprained her ankle after Mass one Sunday and Guard Malone gave her a lift home in the squad car. He had to practically carry her to the car. She was fluttering her eyelashes at him and simpering to beat the band.'

'That's right. I remember.' Ellen laughed. 'And Esther's

no lightweight either, she's heavier than you and me. He was mortified.'

'She haunted him for weeks after, Cecily Malone told me,' Miriam remarked dryly. 'It obviously doesn't matter to her that they're married once she sets her eye on them. And she's so holier than thou in public. What a little hypocrite. So Jimmy succumbed to her wiles. I thought he was more of a man than that.' Miriam shook her head in disgust.

'Don't let on I told you. Denise asked me not to mention it,' Ellen said.

'Of course not,' Miriam exclaimed. That was poor Denise's business and she certainly wasn't going to blab it around Glenree. The phone rang. Ellen jumped. She looked troubled.

'Do you want me to answer it?' Miriam asked, guessing that Ellen suspected that it was Chris.

Ellen nodded. 'Would you mind? If it's him, say that I'm not here,' she said flatly.

Miriam went downstairs and picked up the phone. 'Hello?'

There was silence for a moment. Then a man asked to speak to Ellen. It was Chris. Miriam recognized his smooth suave voice.

'She's not here. Sorry,' she said curtly. She didn't give him time to answer. She hung up straight away.

'Was it him?' Ellen asked anxiously.

Miriam nodded.

'He'll plague me. Chris will never accept that I finished it. He won't be able to cope with that. Chris has such a huge ego but behind it all he feels . . .' Ellen shook her head, 'I don't know . . . inadequate, inferior in some ways. He has this air of confidence, a facade of self-assurance that fools everyone. You'd be amazed at how much reassurance he needs. He worries if he's doing the right thing at work. Suzy isn't a bit interested in his job, as long as he pays the bills. I *know* him, Miriam. He's looking for something or someone. I don't think he even knows what he's looking for himself. There's a little lost boy in him that's hard to resist. I hope I *can* resist him.'

'Yeah, well you're not his mother and it's time he grew up. You're too soft and he knows it,' Miriam said dryly. *Little lost boy, my hat*, she thought privately. If he was her little lost boy, she'd give him a good kick in the arse for treating women the way he did. 'Why don't you get your phone number changed? A friend of Ben's works in the P&T, I'll get him to fix it up for you if you like.'

'Yeah, maybe I will,' Ellen said firmly. 'That's exactly what I'll do.'

* * *

Who was that on the phone? Chris wondered, disgruntled. He knew Ellen always had lunch in the flat. He'd often phoned her there at lunchtime. No-one else had ever answered the phone before. He flung his pen onto the desk. This was driving him nuts. He glanced at his watch. He was meeting a client in the Burlington for lunch, he'd better get a move on. He didn't feel like eating anything. He felt like driving over to Glenree and making Ellen quit this nonsense. It was pointless. They'd be back together sooner or later. He wanted it to be sooner.

Lunch was a drag. Charles Moran was a boring old fart, even if he did employ a large workforce and wanted to arrange a pension scheme for them. While they were waiting for their starters, an elegant woman in a smart houndstooth business suit and black polo-neck jumper led a party of four men to a table. She was supremely confident as she organized the seating and took charge of the ordering. Chris was impressed in spite of himself. Alexandra Johnston, for it was she, was certainly good at her job. He watched her in action. She ordered, chatted to her guests, called waiters over discreetly and she revelled in it.

She was a pushy broad, he thought contemptuously as he saw her taste the wine. She should have let one of her

472

male guests do that. No wonder she wasn't married. A man would be put off by her assertiveness. What she needed was a man who wouldn't take any shit from her. She was good-looking, tall, shapely. More on top than Suzy, but not as voluptuous and sexy as Ellen, he mused as Charles wittered on about index-linked pension plans and bonus schemes.

He wondered what she'd be like in bed. He'd soon have her whimpering and begging for more. The trouble with Alexandra was she'd always gone for wimps. She'd run a mile from a real man who wouldn't put up with her crap.

'What do you think?' Charles paused with a forkful of seafood cocktail suspended between mouth and plate.

'Interesting idea,' Chris spoofed. He hadn't a clue what the old bugger had been yattering on about.

Alexandra saw him looking at her. She arched a perfectly manicured eyebrow and stared back at him. Then, dismissively, she inclined her head and spoke to the man seated next to her.

Big-headed cow, Chris thought crossly. What was wrong with him? Had he lost his touch with women? Ellen had kicked him out. Alexandra was ignoring him. He caught the gaze of a blonde babe lunching with a well-known ex-rugby player whose red nose and florid face would be enough to put anyone off their *pâté de fois gras*.

Chris deliberately stared at the babe. She blushed. He winked. She giggled. He hadn't lost it, he thought glumly. It just wasn't working on Ellen.

The idea of going back to the office did not appeal to him so he indulged Charles as they drank brandy after a satisfying lunch. Only when he saw Alexandra's guests rise to make a move did he call for the bill.

She was paying by cheque at the desk, having seen her party off in taxis. Chris had to admire her poise. She certainly was an independent woman, able to hold her own in a man's world. He couldn't imagine Suzy emulating her now. Suzy had been like Alexandra once. Bright, full of confidence, living life to the full. Marriage and

473

motherhood had changed all that. Suzy was boring, now, Chris reflected. She was paranoid about him having an affair. She found it difficult to manage the kids and the house. She'd gone off the boil in bed. He didn't look forward to going home any more.

Chris caught a whiff of *Chanel No. 5* as Alexandra moved towards him. Charles had bumped into an old friend and they'd decided to stay and have another brandy. So Chris was free to go.

'The Divine Miss Johnston,' he drawled.

'The not so Divine Mr Wallace,' Alexandra retorted.

'Was your lunch successful? The men certainly seemed to enjoy it.'

'Why wouldn't they?' Alexandra eyeballed him. She had green eyes.

'Why not indeed? Being treated to lunch by a ... glamorous woman ... is something all men aspire to,' Chris said coolly.

'You always were a sarcastic bastard. What Suzy sees in you is beyond me.' Alexandra flashed him a look of disdain.

'My ... we're touchy today. I was merely paying you a compliment. Is the big romance still off? You know what's wrong with you, Alexandra ... you're deprived.' Chris cocked his head to one side and grinned at her.

'Well, from what I hear, you're not,' Alexandra riposted.

'What's that supposed to mean?'

'I hear you're having an affair.'

'You hear wrong.' Chris stared at her.

'Suzy's convinced of it.' Alexandra stared back.

'Is she now?' Chris raised an eyebrow. 'And what do you think, Miss Johnston?' he said quietly. 'Do you think I'm the type to have an affair?'

Alexandra held his gaze. 'I wouldn't doubt it for a second.'

'I see. Well maybe I will have an affair, and maybe I won't. She'll have to be pretty spectacular, this woman

474

I have an affair with. I'm hard to please.' His eyes challenged her.

'So am I, Mr Wallace. See you around.' Alexandra raised her chin and walked past him out of the restaurant.

Chris watched her leave. He'd known Alexandra for years. It was funny how he'd never noticed her in that way until today. She was intriguing, for sure. He could have her if he wanted, he thought confidently. Ellen wasn't the only woman in the world. *She's the only one who understands me.* Impatiently he brushed the thought aside. He paid his bill and went back to the office. The afternoon dragged.

Later that evening, when Suzy was putting the kids to bed, he dialled Ellen's number. It was engaged.

He tried again around ten when Suzy was getting the supper. It was still engaged. She must have left it off the hook.

'Damn you, Ellen,' he swore as he banged down the receiver. If she wasn't careful he *would* go off and have an affair with another woman. And he'd make sure she knew about it. That would hurt her and it would be good enough for her. It might bring her to her senses. She couldn't go around treating him as if he was nothing, he thought, aggrieved. She was as bad as Alexandra Johnston.

* * *

Alexandra mooched around her apartment, sipping wine and chain-smoking. She was restless and bored. Chris Wallace was right, although she wouldn't give him the satisfaction of letting him know it. She *was* feeling deprived. Since her affair with Will had ended she'd kept herself very busy and too tired to think. But there were times . . . like now . . . when she felt like sex.

She thought of her encounter with Chris. He had fabulous blue eyes, she thought grudgingly. He was a fine thing but he knew it. There'd always been an edge between them. She never let him away with anything. She'd always kept her distance with Chris for some reason. But today

475

had been different. The way he'd look at her had been a turn-on. Loath though she was to admit it, when he'd stood very close to her and stared into her eyes, she'd felt a . . . frisson. Chris knew how to use his sex appeal, she thought crossly. He was dead sexy, that was undeniable. He'd be great in bed. His type always were. She'd seen him operate over the years. Seen women fall at his feet. Well he needn't try his tricks on her. She was impervious to his charm.

But was *he* impervious to *hers*? Alexandra drew on her cigarette. He'd come on to her today. He fancied her. Wouldn't it be something to have a fling with him and then drop him. That would certainly give Mr Wallace a taste of his own medicine. Suzy was always saying he was having an affair. She was her own worst enemy. She irritated Alexandra beyond measure with her moaning and whinge-ing and negativity. She had her man. She wasn't on the shelf. She had so much and she wasn't satisfied. It was her own fault if Chris strayed, Alexandra thought un-sympathetically. Any man would, if he had to listen to that carry-on.

Maybe she would get Chris to fall for her. Life was so boring at the moment. They could have a wild passionate fling, until she found someone else. Someone eligible! Then she'd give him the boot. Suddenly life seemed much more interesting, Alexandra decided as she poured herself another glass of wine and sat down to plan how she'd seduce the great seducer.

*   *   *

Ellen lay in bed wide-eyed. Even though it was gone midnight she couldn't sleep. She was very aware that the phone was off the hook. She wondered if Chris had tried to phone her. Not knowing was tormenting her.

'Please, please God, put him out of my head,' she prayed in desperation. At least Miriam was speaking to her. That was a huge relief. She was going to think positive, she decided. Tomorrow she would go out into her back garden and start clearing it of weeds and brambles. It was a big undertaking. She was going to work on the garden until it was a showpiece. And hopefully she'd be so tired every night, she'd fall into bed exhausted. She wouldn't have the energy to think about *him*.

* * *

Chris was mad as hell at Ellen. Her phone was constantly off the hook. If she wanted to play dirty so would he. He phoned her at work three days later.

'If you won't put your phone back on the hook I'm going to call you at work every single day,' he threatened.

'All right, Chris. I'll talk to you tonight, but I think you're really mean,' Ellen murmured down the phone.

'No, *you're* the mean one,' Chris growled. 'I'll talk to you tonight.'

At least he had the house to himself, he thought with relief as he dialled her home number later that night. Suzy was at a make-up party.

'Hello.' Ellen sounded very hostile.

'Ellen, please can we forget this messing about? I want to be with you. I love you,' Chris pleaded.

'Chris, it's over. It can't go anywhere. You're married. You've children. You've got responsibilities to them and I've got responsibilities to Stephanie. I should never have let you back into my life. It was the biggest mistake I ever made.'

'Don't say that, Ellen. Doesn't it mean anything to you?' There was a long silence on the phone. Then he heard her crying.

'Why are you crying? Please don't cry.'

'I'm crying because you're asking me the questions I once asked you. It's so ironic, Chris. I never believed you loved me.'

'I do, I do,' he said urgently. 'Let me come and visit tomorrow. Let me show you how much I love you.'

477

'If you love me, Chris, you'll never get in touch with me again. I have to start afresh. I can't go on like this. Goodbye, love. Take care.' He heard the click as she hung up.

Chris was distraught. 'Don't do this to me, Ellen,' he muttered, staring at the receiver. 'Don't leave me.' He dialled the number again.

'Chris, for once in your life, think of someone else. Stop being so bloody selfish,' Ellen raged.

'I *need* you,' he said desperately. Ellen hung up.

'Fuck you, Ellen.' He slammed the receiver into its cradle. If that was the way she wanted it, that was the way she could have it. He wouldn't go crawling. There were plenty of women who'd give their eye-teeth to have an affair with him. Let there be no mistake about that.

* * *

He was a selfish bastard, Ellen thought in disgust. He was blackmailing her, emotionally. That had been a low-down rotten thing to do, phoning her at work and threatening to phone every day until she put the phone back on the hook. That was typical of Chris. To act like a child if he couldn't get his own way. She was damned if she was going to feel sorry for him any more, Ellen thought indignantly as she went back out to the garden and started pulling weeds with a vengeance.

He was the meanest, *pull*, most selfish, *pull*, most childish, *pull*, immature man she had ever encountered. The pile of weeds rose in tandem with her indignation. She thought of every negative thing she could think of about Chris. She thought of every horrible thing he'd ever done to her. The ways he had treated her like dirt. Her cheeks flamed when she remembered their first encounter at Vincent and Emma's wedding. Of how she'd sat waiting by the phone for him to call her and he hadn't. If they hadn't met at the house-warming party she might never have seen him again. It was a sorry day she did meet him, she thought furiously.

478

Her heart twisted as she remembered his reaction to her pregnancy. He'd have let her have an abortion if he'd known about it earlier. And then that dreadful day when Sheila and Mick had confronted him and he'd told them she wasn't a virgin.

'Bastard! bastard!' she muttered as she tugged at a particularly stubborn weed. All the times he'd hung up when she'd phoned him. He hadn't needed her then, had he? He only needed her when it suited him. He needed her now because she had dumped him. His pride was hurt, his ego was dented.

Maybe he did love her. He seemed very insistent that he did. His marriage to Suzy was a disaster, that was clear. But it was much, much too late for him to discover that he'd made a mistake. There was no future in their relationship. Ellen wasn't going to risk an almighty scandal by living with a married man. If she hadn't got Stephanie, she might think differently. But then, she thought as she wiped the sweat off her forehead, maybe not. Chris would never make her happy. She couldn't trust him. Trust was everything.

She worked like a Trojan in the garden, telling herself over and over that he was a shit and he wasn't good for her. She made positive plans in her head for the future. A future without him. Her arms and shoulders ached but that night when she went to bed she slept like a log.

* * *

C,
Let's have dinner . . . My place.
A

Chris stared at the handwritten note in elegant script that had arrived in the post for him that morning. The cream embossed envelope had *personal* written on it, so his secretary hadn't opened it.

Alexandra wanted to have dinner with him in her place.

479

Talk about being forward. He knew she meant a hell of a lot more than dinner. He couldn't believe that she'd made the first move. She couldn't even let him take the initiative, he thought in amusement. She was something else. It was obvious, though, that he hadn't imagined the spark that had been there in the restaurant.

He thought of Ellen. Bitterness surged through him. Let her play hard to get, he wasn't going to hang around. He lifted the phone and said to his secretary, 'Get Alexandra Johnson of Stuart and Stuart's PR for me, please.'

* * *

'I got your letter, Miss Johnston.'

'And . . . ?' purred Alexandra.

'Let's have . . . dinner. When suits you?'

'Tonight. Seven-thirty.'

'I can't tonight. Suzy's parents are coming to dinner.'

'Sorry . . . It's the only night I'm free.' Alexandra hung up. If he wanted to have an affair that badly . . . he'd be there.

She left work early and drove home to her apartment in Ballsbridge. She sliced smoked salmon and made up a salad with plenty of olives and prepared a dressing. She sliced brown bread in readiness, put everything in the fridge, set the table with her best crystal and her scented candles. Then she headed for the bathroom for a long lingering soak. She bathed and oiled her skin in scented creams and washed her hair. She'd had her legs waxed the previous week. Her skin was soft and silky. She shivered thinking of Chris making love to her. It would be a night to remember. She was going to be the best lover he ever had, she thought as she slipped into a satin dressing-gown.

He arrived at eight with champagne.

'Dinner's informal I see,' he remarked as he lightly ran his finger over the satin of her dressing-gown.

'Very,' Alexandra said huskily as she opened her gown

and let it slip from around her shoulders. 'Let's have starters . . .'

Chris's eyes widened in appreciation.

'I like informal dinners,' he murmured, bending to kiss the creamy roundness of her breast.

'So do I.' Alexandra took his hand and led him into her bedroom. They kissed. He was a good kisser, she thought with pleasure as she started to undress him. When he was naked, she brought him to the bed.

'Lie down,' she ordered. She knelt over him and took the soft satin belt from her gown. She took one of his wrists and tied it to the brass bedstead.

'What's this?' Chris looked astounded. Then she tied the other one.

'This is going to be the night of your life,' Alexandra murmured as she slid out of her gown and leaned down and gave him a long deep wet French kiss.

* * *

Suzy was furious with Chris. He'd raced in, rushed upstairs, pulled off his clothes and got into the shower. Then he'd calmly informed her that something had come up at work. The auditors had located a tax problem. He was going to have to spend the evening with his accountant sorting it out. He'd be very late, he told her. He was sorry about missing dinner with her parents. Her protests had been in vain. He was in and out in the space of forty-five minutes. There were times she could *kill* him, she raged as she stirred the hollandaise sauce that had gone lumpy on her. He was seeing someone. He was seeing that woman in Glenree. She knew it.

Her parents arrived. She made Chris's excuses and served up dinner. She was like a cat on a hot tin roof. She thought they'd never go home. They finally left around ten, perplexed by her fidgety humour. Suzy phoned her baby-sitter.

481

'I know it's short notice and it's late. Could you possibly come over for an hour? I need to do an errand.'

'Sure, no problem, Mrs Wallace,' Vivienne said cheerfully.

'You're a treasure,' Suzy said gratefully.

Twenty minutes later she was on her way to Glenree. She was going to confront that bastard in his mistress's house. Her father owned a butcher's shop, on Main Street and Ellen Munroe lived over it. Chris's new red Peugot wouldn't be hard to find parked outside.

She drove as fast as she dared, her heart thudding with anticipation as she left the lights of the suburbs and headed into the inky blackness of the country roads. By the time she got to Glenree she was almost sick with apprehension. She drove slowly down Main Street until she saw the butcher's shop. She pulled in a few doors up from it and looked around for Chris's car. It wasn't to be seen. Maybe he had it hidden down a back lane, she thought in despair as she gazed up at the lamplit windows. Suddenly her heart froze. The door beside the shop was opening. She could hear the sound of laughter. A small petite woman stepped out. Followed by Ellen Munroe. Suzy recognized her from the funeral.

'Goodnight, Denise, thanks for the help, see you tomorrow,' Suzy heard her say.

'You're welcome. See ya,' the woman called back. Ellen stepped back inside her hall and closed the door. Suzy stared at it in amazement. Chris wasn't there. She'd been so sure. But if he wasn't with Ellen where was he . . . and with whom?

*   *   *

Chris devoured the salmon and brown bread. He was famished. Alexandra was *wild*. Insatiable. He was exhausted. But it had been some night of passion. And he'd shown her a thing or two. She was very experienced. Far more so than any other lover he'd ever had. The sex was new, exciting. But he'd missed cuddling up afterwards the way he used to with Ellen. Alexandra was not the sort of woman you cuddled up to, he thought wryly as he watched her languorously sipping champagne. Still, it was good to be appreciated. He'd make the most of this little bonus until Ellen had cooled down and was ready to come running back to him.

Alexandra closed the door on her new lover and switched off the lights in the sitting-room. She was tired. Pleasantly so. It had been a deliciously satisfying evening. Chris was a very skilled lover. He hadn't disappointed her. And she certainly hadn't disappointed him, she thought smugly, remembering the expression on his face when she'd tied him up. *That* had driven him crazy. Alexandra smiled to herself. She had a few more tricks like that up her sleeve. She was looking forward to using them.

* * *

Suzy lay tense as a rattlesnake as she heard Chris come into the bedroom. It was gone three a.m. Could he have been out that late with his accountant?

He got into bed beside her.

'Did you get everything fixed up?' she asked tightly.

'Yeah, it was a long session. Go to sleep, love, I'm whacked.'

I bet you are, Suzy thought bitterly as she lay, racked by torment, as her husband fell instantly asleep beside her.

She wanted to rake her long polished nails down the side of his face until she drew blood. He *was* having an affair. She knew it. He couldn't look her in the eyes these days. Suzy bit her lip in the dark. Who the hell was the other woman? She'd get to the bottom of it. By God she would and when she did, there'd be hell to pay.

She lay unable to sleep, her thoughts racing. She'd always known this would happen. Chris was incapable of fidelity. She'd known it when she married him. It was her own fault. She'd made her bed and now she'd bloody well have to lie on it. Well he wasn't going to get away with it. If she was miserable, he was going to be twice as damn miserable if she ever found out what bitch he was having a fling with.

Chapter Twenty-Six

Emma dragged herself out of bed. It was a damp muggy day. She felt hot and bothered. It was the pits being seven months pregnant in the summer. The last few months had really dragged. The baby kicked lustily in her stomach. Her big, fat, round stomach, with the silver stretch marks. She hated it. She hated herself. She hated being pregnant.

Julie Ann raced into the bedroom, ponytail flying. 'Mummy, are we going to Nannie Pamela's soon?'

'Yes, as soon as I get dressed,' Emma said irritably. Julie Ann was on her summer holidays and she got bored very easily. Emma constantly had to think up treats for her.

She stared out the window. The clouds were thick and oppressive. It was humid. There wasn't a breeze to stir the somnolent leaves on the branches of the trees.

'Mummy, you look different. Your tummy's sticking out,' Julie Ann announced.

Oh Lord! thought Emma. They hadn't told Julie Ann about the baby. She'd made Vincent put it off but she was seven months now, maybe it was as good a time as any. Julie Ann hadn't seemed to notice Emma's weight gain. But the flimsy cotton nightdress she wore didn't hide a lot.

'Julie Ann, I've a surprise for you.' Emma sat down heavily on the bed and put her arm around her daughter. She'd grown so tall, she was getting to be a real young lady, Emma thought proudly.

'What's the surprise? Are we going to get a pony?' Julie Ann was excited. She'd been begging her parents for a pony for ages.

'No, even better,' Emma said with false gaiety. 'We're getting a new baby.'

'A new baby!' Julie Ann wasn't impressed. 'But what about my pony?'

'Wouldn't you like a new baby?' Emma asked, somewhat dismayed by her daughter's reaction.

'Babies cry all the time. A girl in my class, Katy Nolan, has a new baby and it makes such a fuss, Mummy. I think I'd prefer a pony.'

Privately, Emma was in complete agreement

'Is it in your tummy? Did Daddy put a seed in your belly button with his willy?' Julie Ann stared intently at her mother's protruding stomach.

Emma nearly passed out peacefully.

'Who told you that?' she asked weakly.

'Katy Nolan said that's how her mummy got her new baby,' Julie Ann declared nonchalantly as she redirected her gaze from her mother's tummy to admire herself in the mirror. 'Mummy, do you think I could let my fringe grow? Fringes are only for kids. I'm nearly grown up. I think it's time I started wearing lipstick too.'

'You can let your fringe grow. No lipstick.' Emma was mightily relieved that all talk of seeds and willies seemed to be forgotten. 'Go and get your new hairband while I get dressed.'

Julie Ann pirouetted to the door. 'Am I like a ballerina?'

'Yes, you are.'

'The next time Daddy is making you a baby and putting a seed in your belly button, can I watch?'

'Julie Ann, go and get your hairband.' Emma was at the end of her tether.

'But can I watch?'

'It's a thing that mummys and daddys do in private.'

'How's anyone supposed to find out about anything in this house?' Julie Ann flounced off indignantly. Excluded once again.

'I'll have to tell her the facts of life,' Emma moaned a

couple of hours later as she sat sipping coffee in her mother's.

'Stay calm and say nothing,' Pamela advised. 'Julie Ann will forget all about it.'

'I think we better get her a pony when the baby comes. It will take her mind off things. I don't want her nose to be out of joint.' Emma sighed.

'Good idea,' Pamela approved. She knew Julie Ann was in for a major upset once the new arrival put in an appearance. For seven years she'd been queen of the castle. It was hard to share your throne.

'How's everyone in Glenree?'

'Fine,' Emma said glumly. 'Mrs Munroe was elected president of the guild. You'd think she was the First Lady of America, the way she goes on. She's making Miriam's life a misery. She expects her to bake for every occasion.'

'How's Ellen and her little girl? I must say I thought she was a lovely little thing when I saw her at your grandmother's funeral,' Pamela remarked.

'Ellen's OK. She bought a new car last spring and she's moved into a flat over the shop. She'd done it up very nicely. The back garden is spectacular. She's worked on it for months. *You'd* love it. You're into herbaceous borders and that sort of thing. I just like looking at them. I wouldn't know one end of a tulip bulb from another,' Emma admitted.

Pamela chuckled. 'No, you couldn't be accused of having green fingers. I'm glad Ellen got a place of her own. I wouldn't say Sheila's the easiest to live with.'

'I think it's good for Stephanie. Julie Ann goes to stay with her sometimes. I know Ellen's not my favourite person but I suppose you have to admire her in a way. She's made a great job of raising Stephanie.'

'Chris treated Ellen and Stephanie very badly. I never felt the same about him after that episode even if he is my own nephew. I saw him having lunch with Alexandra Johnston last week.'

'Alexandra!' Emma was surprised. 'They don't get on very well.'

'They were getting on fine when I saw them,' Pamela remarked dryly.

'Hmm,' Emma murmured. She hadn't seen Chris in ages. Not since they'd had lunch after her grandmother's funeral back in February. She must phone him and arrange to meet him for lunch before she had the baby.

She was meeting the girls for lunch today. Pamela was minding Julie Ann for her. Emma was looking forward to a good gossip. She'd missed their last lunch because she'd been feeling rotten, but she hadn't felt too bad for the past week, so she arranged to meet them in the Intercontinental. She chatted with her mother for another half-hour until it was time to leave.

'Thanks for looking after Julie Ann for me.' She kissed Pamela on the cheek.

'You enjoy your lunch. Have some fun. Julie Ann and I are going to the pictures. If you're home before us, go and have a lie-down.'

'I will,' Emma said gratefully. She liked it when her mother took charge of things. She set off for lunch and arrived just as Gillian and Diana Mackenzie drove into the car park.

'You look blooming,' Gillian squealed a few minutes later.

'Don't rub it in,' Emma said dryly.

'You look very well, darling.' Diana kissed her on both cheeks. 'How have you been?' They walked into the foyer and headed for the restaurant.

'My blood pressure's up and down. They're watching me carefully. My gynie doesn't think he'll let me go full term after what happened the last time. I wish it was all over.' Emma was trying to keep her spirits up. She didn't want to go into a detailed account of how pissed off and poorly she'd been for most of her pregnancy.

'Oh darling, just think though, another little baby. Julie Ann will be thrilled,' Diana gushed.

'She will not.' Emma grinned as she recounted the morning's conversation. The girls howled with laughter.

'Can we watch the next time Vincent's making you a baby?' Gillian chortled.

'There won't be a next time. Vincent's going to London to have a vasectomy, seeing as he can't get it done here,' Emma informed them.

'You lucky thing. Frank wouldn't do that for me,' Gillian said enviously.

'Well I can't wait.' Emma nibbled on a bread roll. 'I hate counting dates and I hate condoms.'

'Don't we all, dear,' Diana drawled. Did Emma Munroe have any idea how lucky she was to have a husband like Vincent?

'Is Lorna coming or should we order?' Emma asked.

'She said she was. Money's a bit tight since she left Declan. I'd offer to pay but she's very proud. Do you know what Declan Mitchell did?' Gillian leaned over conspiratorially.

'What?' Emma and Diana echoed as one.

'He was pissed at a party in Marianne Deasy's house and he made a pass at Vicky Stone. Nina Monahan *freaked*. She called him all the names under the sun. Her language was vile. You know that high squeaky voice she has. She was screeching like a fishwife. Everyone was shocked 'cos she pretends she's such a lady. And he said, "Shut up you, ya ..." well he used the C word,' Gillian explained delicately.

'Oh my God! The C word. How disgusting!'

'Crikey!'

The girls were horrified. *That* was shocking.

'What happened?'

'Marianne asked them to leave. That Nina is crazy to stay with him. I wouldn't care if I was on the shelf until I was ninety. I wouldn't put up with Declan Mitchell and the way he drinks.' Gillian sipped a glass of mineral water.

'Sshh, here's Lorna,' Emma warned.

'Hi.' She stood up and kissed her friend. Lorna looked

amazingly well for a woman who'd walked out on her husband.

'Hiya, sorry I'm late. I'm on a late lunch and my replacement didn't arrive back on time.'

'How do you find the job?' Diana asked. She pitied Lorna from the bottom of her heart. If she had to go out to work and support two children, she'd die.

'I like it.' Lorna smiled. She was a receptionist in a small exclusive hotel.

'You look great,' Emma said warmly.

'I sleep well at night now,' Lorna said quietly. 'I don't have to worry about Declan coming home drunk. I don't have to put up with his abuse. I don't have much money. But I've enough and I've peace of mind. It means a lot.'

'It's more than Nina Monahan's got,' Diana remarked artlessly. Emma glared at her. Diana was as thick as two short planks sometimes.

'I couldn't care less about Nina Monahan or the state of her mind. She's welcome to Declan. I wouldn't take him back under any circumstances,' Lorna retorted coldly.

'Let's order,' Emma suggested tactfully.

They had just finished dessert when Emma gave a gasp. A pain like a vice grip took hold and she doubled up.

'Oohh!' she groaned.

'What's wrong?' Gillian looked petrified.

'I don't know.' Emma was frightened. Another spasm hit her.

'Ohmigod. Ohmigod she's having the baby,' Gillian shrieked hysterically.

'Be quiet, Gillian,' Lorna snapped. 'Emma, take my arm, we'll go to the ladies. Diana, ask them to phone for an ambulance.' The manager came rushing down to assist as people stared. Emma was in too much pain to be embarrassed. The manager and Lorna led her to his office and helped her onto a chair. Emma doubled over again, groaning. Lorna wiped her forehead. She was very calm. Emma clung to her like a lifeline.

490

'Will you come to the hospital with me? Please, Lorna,' she begged.

'Of course I will. I'm going to phone Vincent now so that he can meet us there.' Lorna was very reassuring. Emma could hear the wailing shriek of an ambulance siren in the distance. She started to cry.

'You'll be fine.' Lorna gripped her hand tightly.

'I nearly died giving birth to Julie Ann. Just say there's something wrong with the baby. I'm scared, Lorna.'

'Don't be. I'll stay with you. You'll be fine and so will the baby.'

The next hour was a nightmare. She was taken off in the ambulance and all she could remember was Gillian's tear-stained face as the door closed.

The journey was a blur. A sharp knife-edged pain was ripping her apart. The doctors and nurses were very kind and reassuring as she was rushed down the long corridor into the labour ward. She wasn't prepared for the sister's words five minutes later after she'd been examined.

'It won't be long now, Mrs Munroe. We're taking you to the delivery room. You're nine centimetres dilated.'

Jesus! thought Emma in shock. I'm having the baby *myself*. I'm not going to be put to sleep. She almost fainted with terror. Pain gripped her again and she couldn't think of anything except the agony of it as she was pushed down the hospital corridor. She groaned.

'Take a good deep breath and don't push until I tell you,' the sister instructed as she placed Emma's feet in the stirrups.

'I want to be knocked out,' Emma said in terror.

'We've no time for any of that. Push, now,' the sister commanded. Emma stared at her blankly. The pain swamped her. She screamed.

'Push. Harder. Harder. Good girl, the head is through.' Emma thought she was going to throw up. It sounded so gory. It felt so gory.

'Again,' the sister ordered. Emma gave a mighty push and fainted.

491

She came to, to hear the sound of a baby crying. Her baby. The baby she had just given birth to all by herself, with no anaesthetic. Emma felt inordinately surprised and proud of herself. 'Is it all right? Is it a boy or a girl?' she asked anxiously.

'It's a little boy, four pounds. You can hold him for a minute before we put him in his incubator,' the sister said kindly. Emma burst into tears as the mewling little bundle was placed in her arms. A son. A son for Vincent. He'd be thrilled. Emma knew he'd secretly hoped for a boy. And now she had given him one. She loved Vincent so much it was worth all the pain and the mess and being fat, Emma thought as she gazed in awe at her baby.

He was a dotey little fellow with a mop of black hair and she felt a strange unfamiliar feeling as if she wanted to protect him. It hadn't been like this with Julie Ann. The nurse took the baby from her and Emma was sorry to see him go.

'We're going to take you to intensive care for a little while, Mrs Munroe. Just until we get your blood pressure stabilized,' the nurse said gently.

'Nurse. Don't tell my husband when he comes. I want to tell him myself,' Emma said weakly.

'Don't worry. We won't say a word.' The nurse tucked a blanket around her as the orderlies lifted her on to the stretcher.

Emma lay in her little cubicle, exhausted but exhilarated. It was all over. She'd never have to go through it again. Vincent was getting the snip. She wouldn't have to worry about getting pregnant. And best of all, he had his son. Emma was immensely proud of herself. There'd been so much trauma when she'd had Julie Ann, she'd been terrified. This ordeal had only lasted a couple of hours. She'd had her baby and she'd have a nanny to help her when she went home. Second time around was much easier, she thought drowsily. She fought to keep her eyes open. She wanted to be awake when Vincent came.

She didn't have to wait long. He came in through the door, white-faced.

'Are you all right, pet? Lorna told me you'd been taken off by ambulance. Sorry I couldn't get here any quicker. The traffic was brutal. What did the doctors say?' He took her hand and stared down at her, his face creased with worry.

'Stop panicking.' Emma reached up to touch his cheek. 'Vincent, guess what?' Her eyes were bright in her pale face.

'What?'

'I had the baby all by herself. I gave birth the proper way. We have a little boy. Vincent you've got a son and I'm so glad 'cos I really love you.'

'Oh Emma. Emma.' Vincent's face crumpled as he leaned down and took her in his arms. She could feel the wetness of his tears as he held her close.

'I love you very much,' he whispered into her hair. 'I'm never going to put you through anything like this again.'

'It's OK, darling. You didn't put me through anything. It's over now. And when you get the snip we can make love morning, noon and night.' Emma gave a shaky grin.

'You lie down there,' Vincent said sternly, easing her back down on to the pillows, 'and stop thinking wicked thoughts.'

'I'm crazy about you.' Emma smiled up at him.

'You're just crazy, full stop. Make love morning, noon and night indeed. We're an old married couple. Once a week will be your limit,' Vincent teased.

'Spoilsport.' Emma felt very contented as she snuggled down under the blankets and fell asleep holding Vincent's hand.

*   *   *

Vincent sat watching over his wife as she slept. He'd got the fright of his life when Lorna had phoned him. All the horrible memories of Julie Ann's birth came rushing back.

He was petrified Emma would die. He wanted to die himself as he drove like a maniac to get to the hospital.

And now this. He couldn't believe it. *'Thank you, God.'* He sent up a heartfelt prayer of thanks. He sat with Emma until he was sure she was fast asleep and then he went down to the special care unit.

The first incubator on the right, the nurse told him. Vincent went over and looked down at his sleeping baby. Vincent couldn't get over his head of black hair. He stared down at him in delight.

'Hello, son,' he whispered. 'This is your daddy.' He was longing to take him up in his arms.

'Would you like to hold him for a moment?' The nurse padded silently up to him.

'Yes, very much,' Vincent said eagerly.

The nurse lifted the baby out and placed him gently in Vincent's arms.

'Now you can say a proper hello to him.'

Vincent could hardly speak, he was so moved. His son woke and gripped Vincent's finger with his tiny hand.

He thought of Julie Ann and how much smaller and frailer she'd been compared to her brother. He was dying to see what she'd make of the new baby. A daughter, a son, and Emma. He was a very lucky man, Vincent thought happily as he kissed his baby's silky black hair.

*   *   *

Julie Ann stared at the little baby in the funny-looking glass box. Everybody was very excited about him. He was her new brother. She felt extremely important. None of her cousins had a new baby brother. They kept asking her about him. Her mummy had gone to hospital in an ambulance three days ago and she'd got the baby out of her belly button. Her daddy kept telling her about the new baby. Julie Ann was a bit fed up hearing about it.

Then her daddy had said the words she'd been longing to hear.

'Because you're such a good girl, Mummy and I are getting you a pony.'

A pony and a new baby. *Everybody* in the school would want to be her friend. Stephanie would never get a pony because she was too poor. Neither would Daniel, Connie and Rebecca. Julie Ann felt extremely satisfied. She'd let them have goes on her pony, if they were good. She'd let them hold the baby too. What times she would have dispensing favours.

It gave a funny little squawk. Julie Ann gazed at her new brother.

'Isn't he gorgeous?' her daddy said proudly. Julie Ann fastened him with a piercing stare.

'Aren't I gorgeous too?' It was very important that he answered properly.

'You are the most gorgeous daughter in the world.' Vincent hugged her. Julie Ann nestled close to her daddy. She didn't really want to share him with *It*, she decided after all. She'd much prefer just to have her mummy and daddy to herself, and of course . . . her new pony.

* * *

'Andrew Munroe, I have to admit I like it. It has a certain ring to it,' Ellen rolled the name around her tongue. 'I'm glad they had a little boy.'

'So am I. Emma is as proud as Punch.' Miriam stretched out on a lounger on Ellen's patio. Ben had taken the children to the beach and she and Ellen were having a rare Saturday afternoon of peace in Ellen's garden. The sun was splitting the trees, and the drowsy hum of the bees as they buzzled in and out of the vibrant flower beds was soothing.

'It all happened very quickly.' Ellen smoothed some *Ambre Solaire* on to her golden limbs. She was very pleased with her tan.

'Thank goodness, the two of them are fine. I thought it would be as bad as when she had Julie Ann,' Miriam murmured.

'Talking of Julie Ann, have you heard about the pony?'

Miriam grimaced. 'I'm *sick* hearing about the pony.'

'Me too.' Ellen sighed. 'Poor old Stephanie is really getting her nose rubbed in it. No pony, no baby, and no daddy.'

'The little bitch,' Miriam said indignantly.

'Julie Ann doesn't understand. She's just a little consequence. An insecure little consequence. Some day I'm going to let her have it. But then, if I do, there'll be a row. You know how sensitive Emma is about criticism of her little darling?'

'Yeah, it's very awkward,' Miriam agreed. 'God knows how poor little Andrew will turn out. Let's hope he's not like his sister.'

'I'd say there'll be some mighty attention-seeking when he's brought home.' Ellen lay back and pulled down her sunglasses.

'I wish them the joy of it. I've been through it . . . twice.' Miriam yawned and in minutes was snoozing.

Ellen lay contentedly as the sun's rays filled every pore of her body with light and heat. It was utterly enjoyable to lie in the peace and splendour of her own back garden. Beds of petunias and geraniums, busy lizzies and antirrhinums, edged with purple and white stock, were a blaze of colour against the emerald lawn. Fuschia, heavy with blossoms, saponaria, fragrant honeysuckle, and climbing roses covered the end wall. They were young shrubs but they had bloomed well. Next year she'd have a riot of colour. Trellises with clematis and sweet pea and more roses lined the side walls. It was a garden of Eden now, it would be even more beautiful in the years to come, Ellen thought proudly. She'd really worked at it. It was her reward for banishing Chris to the deepest recesses of her mind.

It was ages since they'd split. After she got her phone number changed, he hadn't called her again. He hadn't even called her at work. He'd got the message. Whenever she missed him, she made herself go through her litany of negatives about him. She never thought about the good

496

times. It was too difficult. It was much easier to think of the times he'd let her down and lied to her.

She didn't hate him. She'd never hate Chris. She cared so much about him that she hadn't told Miriam about the ring, or the way he'd wanted her to sleep with him in Suzy's house. She didn't want to diminish him further in her sister-in-law's eyes. Those hurts she would keep to herself. There would never be anyone else like him for her. Her heart ached over him. Her love for him had been a precious thing but, as time passed and she stepped back and looked at it all with eyes that weren't clouded with passion and emotion, Ellen knew she had made the right choice. Slowly, her life was getting back on an even keel. That was the way she wanted it. Even if she was to be on her own for the rest of her days.

The nights were the worst. She couldn't escape her thoughts at night so she kept herself busy during the day, and then spent back-breaking hours in her garden. It was a great way of exhausting herself and she was certainly keeping her weight down.

Every cloud has a silver lining, she thought wryly, as she too fell asleep.

'Lazybones!' Ellen woke to see Denise grinning down at her.

She glanced at her watch and saw that it was nearly four. She'd slept a solid hour. Miriam stirred.

'That was lovely,' she murmured, reluctant to open her eyes.

'I rang the front doorbell and, when I didn't get an answer, I assumed you were out here. I came in the side gate and saw two sleeping beauties. It's so peaceful. Where are the kids?'

'Ben took them to the beach.'

'My sister took my two for the weekend. Jimmy's gone to Galway with the *femme fatale*. I hope they get a dose of the galloping trots,' Denise said bitterly. She'd told Miriam about Esther Dowling so she didn't mind saying that in front of her.

497

'He's a cool customer.' Ellen sat up and pushed her glasses on top of her head.

'He's a bastard! He lavishes attention on her. He never took me away for weekends, to Galway or anywhere else. And do you know what he had the nerve to ask me the other day?'

'What?' Ellen asked gently. She understood exactly what her friend was going through.

'He asked me if I'd mended the hole in his jeans.'

'By God, I'd give him his answer,' Miriam expostulated. 'And I'd tell him where to put his jeans. Let Butter-Wouldn't-Melt-In-Her-Mouth Dowling sew his jeans for him. I hope she does his washing and ironing for him too.'

'You must be joking!' Denise scoffed. 'I wish I had money of my own to be free of him.'

'Why don't you stay and have a bite to eat with us?' Ellen invited. 'Ben's taking the kids to a cafe for sausage and chips. Miriam and I were going to have chicken and mushroom *vol au vents* and salad.'

'Sounds gorgeous.' Denise brightened up. 'Have you enough?'

'I've loads. Come on, stay.'

'OK.' Denise didn't need to be asked twice. 'I've a bottle of wine over in the house. I'll get it.'

'Great stuff.' Ellen slipped into her towelling robe and went in to the kitchen to prepare the meal. Miriam followed her and started to chop the mushrooms. Denise came back with the wine and poured three glasses. The three of them sipped and gossiped and cooked companionably.

They set the table outside and carried out their food and wine and enjoyed a delightful meal. Later, Miriam went in and brought out a half-dozen home-made chocolate eclairs. 'I cooked these for Mrs Munroe's cake sale, but when I knew I was coming over to Ellen's for tea, I decided to keep them. I'll be in the bad books, for sure.'

'Oh for heaven's sake, Miriam. You're too soft. Mam takes advantage,' Ellen rebuked.

'These are scrumptious!' Denise ate one with relish. 'I wonder who's going to take over the coffee shop now that the two old dears have retired. Their chocolate eclairs were nothing like these.'

'I'll take it over and go into business,' Miriam joked.

'Yeah and Ellen could do chicken and mushroom *vol au vents*. And I could do my famous speciality, leek and potato soup.' Denise giggled. She was slightly tipsy. She'd gone down to the Glenree Arms and bought another bottle of wine before they sat down to tea.

'I'd say it would be a little goldmine, in the right hands,' Miriam said thoughtfully. 'The Boyles were too old to run it. It's a bit dilapidated. If it was spruced up it could do very well. It's your dad's building, isn't it, Ellen? Will he lease it out again as a coffee shop?'

'I don't really know,' Ellen said slowly. 'I don't know what he plans to do with it.' She turned to the girls. Her eyes were bright with excitement. 'But I know what *we* could do with it.'

'*We?*' Miriam echoed.

'We could turn it into a deli-cum-coffee shop. We could redecorate. Cook home-cooked foods. I mean look at your eclairs, Miriam. You're terrific at baking. I can't bake. But we can all cook. We could do home-made soups. Salads. Club sandwiches. Sausage rolls. *Vol au vents*. Food people eat for lunch. It wouldn't be like a restaurant. People could take food away. We could sell cakes and stuff, and make up sandwiches on the spot. The three of us could really make that place hum.

'Denise.' She gripped her friend by the arm. 'Remember the fortune-teller told you about going into business and that it would be successful? Maybe this is it!'

'Maybe you're right! Do you think your dad would be on for it?' Denise stopped giggling and sat up straight.

'Dad's great like that,' Ellen said confidently. 'I run the business side of the shop for him. He knows I'd be well capable. What do you think, Miriam? Do you want to be a businesswoman?'

499

'What about the kids?' Miriam asked.

'Oh! Hadn't thought of that.' Ellen was stumped for a second. Then she said brightly, 'They could all come here after school. We could break a door in from next door to give us easy access. We could give them their dinner when they got home from school. They could have their homework done before they go home. And if it was fine they could play out the back or on the green. I don't think it would be a problem. Lunchtime would be our busy time and they'd still be at school then. In the summer, well, Denise, if you took care of Miriam's three and mine and had a share of the takings you'd be financially independent. We could try it out anyway,' she entreated.

'Yeah, let's.' Denise was wildly enthusiastic.

'We're going to be career women,' Miriam said delightedly.

'And why not?' Ellen picked up her glass. 'No better women to do it. You'll be able to tell Jimmy to get stuffed, Denise. Miriam, you'll be able to make money out of something you're really good at, cooking and baking. *And* you'll be able to tell Ma, no more freebies. She'll have to buy your cakes from now on.'

Miriam laughed at the idea of it.

'I mean it,' Ellen said firmly.

'And what will you be able to do?' Denise grinned.

'I'll be able to buy my daughter a pony,' Ellen said quietly. 'Now wouldn't that be something?'

Miriam smiled at her and Ellen smiled back. She knew Stephanie would get her pony.

They drank more wine and spent the evening making plans until a clamour of childish voices broke the peace. Ben and the children were home.

'That's it. Peace and quiet over. I'll go home and take this lot out of your hair,' Miriam declared.

'Did you have a nice time?' Ellen asked Stephanie when everyone had left and they had the place to themselves again.

'I'd a great time, Mammy. We all went swimming and

then Uncle Ben helped us make a *huge* sandcastle with a moat. We had to bring trillions of buckets of water to fill it,' Stephanie informed her.

Ellen smiled as she looked at her daughter's eager little face with its smattering of freckles over a sunburnt nose.

'Did you have your tea out here?'

'I did, with Denise and Auntie Miriam.'

'Was it nice?'

'It was lovely.'

'I'm hungry,' Stephanie declared.

Ellen laughed. 'Didn't Uncle Ben bring you somewhere for chips?'

'That was *ages* ago.'

'How about if you go up and have your bath and get into your jammies and then the two of us will have supper on the patio?' Ellen suggested.

'Oh yes. Oh brill, Mam!' Stephanie agreed delightedly. This was certainly out of the ordinary.

'OK. I'll run your bath. Then I'll come down here and wash the dishes and you can have either scrambled eggs, cheese and tomato on toast, or sausage and beans. And of course . . . hot chocolate.'

'I think I'll have cheese and tomato on toast,' Stephanie decided.

'Right. Would you like some bubble bath?'

'Yes please.' Stephanie danced ahead of her into the house, full of excitement. It was long past her bedtime and she was having a bubble bath, *and* supper on the patio. This was too good to be true.

She sang away to herself as she undressed and Ellen enjoyed her antics. She was great company, she thought, as she poured a good dollop of bath foam into the bath.

'You know. I really *really* like living here. Do you, Mammy?' Stephanie said as she eased herself into the frothy bubbles.

'I do, love.'

'I like Nannie's house. But I like having our own house. You know Julie Ann is very jealous of my bedroom?' she said earnestly, smoothing bubbles all over her.

'Is she?' Ellen murmured, amused.

'Yes, she is.' Stephanie nodded. 'No-one else in the whole school has a bedroom in the attic that's like the nursery in *Mary Poppins*.'

'I see.'

'And we've more flowers in our garden,' Stephanie said airily as she blew some bubbles onto her palm. 'And I bet she's never had her supper outside on a patio.'

'I bet not,' Ellen agreed. 'I'll go down and start making it.'

'Loads of hot chocolate?' Stephanie entreated. She looked so adorable with suds on her nose that Ellen had to give her a kiss.

'Loads of hot chocolate,' she promised.

She felt very content as she tidied up. It had been a lovely day. Having supper with Stephanie on the patio would be the perfect way to end it.

She was so lucky to have Stephanie, she thought gratefully. She was worth all the pain and misery she'd endured during her times with Chris.

Ellen gazed out at her garden. The sun was sinking, and the light was soft. The perfume from the flowers was exquisite. It would never have worked with Chris, she admitted. She would never have had the peace of mind she had now. It had been painful ending it. But listening to Stephanie's childish singing floating downstairs, she knew she'd made the right decision. It would have only complicated things for Stephanie if they'd stayed together. Her daughter was a happy little girl. Secure, self-confident. Who knew what damage a relationship with Chris might have caused? What if Ellen had got pregnant again? That had always been a subconscious worry too. She did miss Chris, very much. But her life was on an even keel again.

It was for the best, Ellen reflected as she grated cheese and sliced tomatoes for her daughter's supper.

Chapter Twenty-Seven

'Well Dad? What do you think?'

Mick rubbed his jaw reflectively. 'I think it's a bloomin' good notion, Ellen. There's a new housing estate being built between here and Swords. And Green Vale is just down the road. I got more than fifty new customers from that estate when it opened. There's that new computer factory half a mile away. You'll get customers coming for lunch and sandwiches. And of course you'll always have the ten o'clock Mass crowd. That's what kept the Boyles going. Glenree is expanding all the time. Expansion is good for any business. And you say Miriam and Denise are all on for it?'

'Yeah.' Ellen grinned. 'Miriam's a terrific pastry cook, she might as well make some money out of it. Denise is going to look after all the kids and make home-made soups as well. Now I can't bake, my scones turn out like the Giant's Causeway. But I can cook, make sandwiches, make up salads for the salad bar. And I can do the books. I'd do the books for the shop, of course, as well. But you'd need someone new to take the orders and payments. How would you feel about that?'

'We're a good team, Ellen. I'd miss you in the shop. But if I was stuck, sure you'd only be next door.' Mick lit his pipe. 'I'd be very proud to know that my daughter was in business beside me.'

'Oh Dad. Thanks.' She flung her arms around him. Mick laughed. 'I suppose you're going to be knocking down walls and building arches and so on and so forth?'

'Oh yeah, we're going to redo it completely. I spent all last night planning it out in my head.'

'You'd better book Doug then. Let me know how much money you'll need.'

'Oh no, Dad. That wouldn't be fair. I can't come to you for money. Not after all you did for me with the house.' Ellen was adamant.

'Now stop that, Ellen,' Mick said gruffly.

'No, I'll get a loan from the bank.'

'And what would you be paying them fellows back interest for?' Mick retorted.

'No, Dad. I won't do it, otherwise.'

'Well how about if I don't charge you any rent until you're trading in profit? Have the place for a year, rent-free.'

'Ah, Dad!' Ellen was exasperated. He was far too good-natured.

'That's my last offer, otherwise I'll . . . I'll asked Bonnie Daly if she'd like to run it as a craft shop.'

'What!'

Mick grinned. 'Did I not tell you? You know the way she's great pals with the Boyles. Well, when they told her they were retiring, Bonnie seemingly had this brainwave that she and the daughter could open up a craft shop for the tourists. If we get two dozen tourists a year in these parts we're lucky.' He chuckled. 'She came in to me the other day and told me she was interested in leasing the premises.'

'The nerve of her.' Ellen was gobsmacked at Bonnie's cheek. 'What did you say to her?'

'I told her I'd other plans for it. Kept her guessing. Could you imagine your mother's face if I went home and told her that I'd leased it to Bonnie Daly? I'd be in the doghouse for the rest of my life.'

'And had you plans for it?' Ellen asked. She hadn't even considered that Mick might want to do something with the premises, she'd been too busy thinking of her grand scheme.

'I was going to keep it as a coffee shop. Get someone in to run it. But it doesn't sound half as exciting as a deli/sandwich bar. We might as well be living in New York.' Mick chortled. 'Put that in your pipe and smoke it, Bonnie!'

Ellen laughed. Her father had a wicked sense of humour. She'd always enjoyed it.

'Are you going to see Terry Carson about the loan?' Mick cocked an eye at her.

'Well he's the only bank manager I know,' Ellen said ruefully.

'See how you get on with him. But first of all, yourself and myself will sit down this evening and work out a business plan. These kind of things always impress bank managers. And you'll have all the answers for him when he asks about business turnover and the rest of it. Peter Doherty went to him for a loan the other day to buy a new tractor and the guff he had to listen to.' Mick shook his head in disgust. 'That Terry Carson thinks he's somebody.'

'Well I'll go and see him anyway,' Ellen said briskly. 'After I've talked to the girls.'

A few days later, Ellen walked in to the bank for her appointment with the bank manager. Esther Dowling smiled sweetly at her as she tapped away at her typewriter.

'Ellen, how are you? I'm afraid Mr Carson is slightly behind schedule, he's in a meeting at the moment. He'll see you as soon as he can.'

Ellen was tempted to ask her if she'd enjoyed her dirty weekend away in Galway with Jimmy McMahon. But who was she to cast the first stone, she thought wryly.

She sat for more than half an hour in that stuffy little room with the sun beaming down on her and began to feel as wilted as the fern on the coffee table beside her. Esther was a busy little bee, taking phone calls, typing letters. At one stage she brought two cups of coffee into the manager's office.

Ellen fumed silently. She'd been given an appointment

for eleven a.m. It was now almost eleven-forty. *Her* time was as precious as his, she thought resentfully.

Ten minutes later the door opened. Terry Carson shook hands with Sean Williams, the owner of the Glenree Arms. 'No problem at all, Sean. I'll have that for you tomorrow,' Terry said expansively.

'Bring Liz in for a meal at the weekend, on the house of course,' Sean invited.

'I'll do that. Take care now.' Terry's gaze swept over Ellen as Sean left the room. He glanced at his watch.

'Esther, come inside for a moment,' he ordered his secretary.

'Certainly, Mr Carson.' Esther fluttered around getting her notebook and pen.

Ten minutes later, Esther reappeared. 'Mr Carson will see you now,' she informed Ellen. Her reverent tone suggested that it was akin to being received by the Almighty. Ellen was not impressed. She was furious. She'd been waiting almost an hour. Stay calm, she told herself. After all, she had come for a loan.

'He won't keep you for long, he's taking a client to lunch,' Esther informed her tactlessly.

'I can't stay long,' Ellen said coldly. 'I've arranged to meet . . . Denise McMahon for lunch.'

Esther blushed to the roots of her mousy brown hair. Ellen ignored her as she walked into the manager's office. Good enough for the silly cow, she thought crossly.

'Sorry for the delay,' Terry Carson said offhandedly. 'Mr Williams needed to see me on an urgent matter.'

Lucky for him he could skip the queue, Ellen thought irritably. But then Sean Williams could offer free dinners, all she'd be able to offer was a club sandwich and side salads. The notion amused her and she almost smiled.

'Sit down, Miss . . . er . . .' he glanced at his diary of appointments. 'Munroe.'

'Thank you.' He knew very well who she was, Ellen thought contemptuously. He was trying to make her feel unimportant. Ellen sat down on the hard chair. The bank

manager lolled in a luxurious black leather one. Ellen
didn't like him. He was tall, bony, with a beaky nose and
greasy greying hair. He had a mean little mouth. She
noticed that he bit his nails. Not as self-confident as he
pretends to be, she observed. He had a patronizing air.
The expression in his old grey eyes was dismissive. Ellen
knew he felt she was wasting his time. She watched,
stunned, as he glanced at his watch, took it from his
wrist, and placed it face up on his desk. His rudeness
appalled her. *He* had kept her waiting almost an hour
while his bridge-playing crony had skipped in and taken
her appointment. And then he had the nerve to put his
watch on the desk as if she was some kid up in front of
the headmaster.

'Speak to me,' Terry clipped as he folded his arms across
his chest.

'Pardon!' Ellen was rattled.

'Tell me what you want the loan for,' he said in a weary
tone.

Ellen took a deep breath and launched into details of her
proposed business. She made to hand him a typed page
with details of what she hoped her business turnover
would be, but he brushed it aside.

'What collateral have you got?' he barked.

Ellen looked at him. She put her page back in her folder.
She stood up.

'You are an extremely rude man, Mr Carson. Pig-
ignorant actually. I don't have to sit here and be treated
like dirt by the likes of you. I've more respect for myself.
You can put your watch back on. I won't be needing any
more of your time. *My* time is far too precious to squander
on an ignoramus like you.' She marched out the door with
her head held high.

Esther nearly jumped ten foot when she saw her and
went scarlet again. Ellen glared at her and marched on.
They could stuff their loan, she thought grimly. She'd get
the money some other way. She wasn't that desperate.

She walked downstairs to the main part of the bank

area, scowling. She was so angry she didn't notice Doug come in through the front door.

'Ellen!' he called out as she strode past him.

'Oh . . . oh, Doug. Sorry, I didn't see you.'

'Who's been rattling your cage?' He eyed her quizzically.

'That . . . that *slug* upstairs,' Ellen fumed.

'What happened?' Doug frowned.

'It's a long story.' Ellen didn't want to recount the ins and outs of her dealings with Terry Carson in the middle of the bank with people all around them.

'Right, let's go and have a cup of coffee over beyond and you can tell me about it.' Doug took her arm and steered her out of the bank.

'Doug!' she protested, laughing.

'Well I haven't seen you in ages. We can catch up on the news.' Doug grinned.

'Actually I might be wanting you to do another job for me, if everything goes to plan.' She smiled at him. It was a treat to see Doug, he hadn't been around much. He was working all hours.

'Sounds interesting. There's one condition though,' he said seriously.

'What!' Ellen was dismayed at his tone.

'Lunch has to be included.'

'You messer.' Ellen gave him a dig in the ribs. 'I thought it was something serious.'

'Grub *is* serious,' Doug informed her as he led her into the lounge of the hotel. 'Can I buy you lunch? Or are you in a hurry?'

'I haven't been at work for most of the morning,' she said guiltily. 'Ah, why not?'

'We'll have a drink, and order. And you can tell me why you called that *nice* Mr Carson a slug.' Ellen giggled. Doug had a way of making her laugh. She'd missed that, she thought as he went over to the bar to order their drinks.

She watched him as he chatted easily to the barman. Doug had a very pleasant manner about him that was genuine. She liked the way that he'd immediately asked what was wrong with her. When he'd been doing up the flat he'd always been interested in what was going on in her life. Much more so than Chris. No doubt Chris was getting on with life. Enjoying himself. Chatting up women. She wouldn't put it past him to have a mistress. He probably never gave her a thought now, she thought ruefully. She could have had him and she'd let him go. Their parting wasn't the tragedy it had been for her years ago, she reflected. She'd moved on with her life. Now she was ready to take it a step further. She hadn't slipped into depression and misery like she had the first time he'd left her.

No you didn't, she thought a little proudly as she watched Doug carry over the drinks.

'Why is he a slug?'

Ellen laughed. 'Sit down. I'll tell you the whole story.'

'The bloody nerve of him,' Doug growled when Ellen told him how Terry Carson had removed his watch and put it on the desk in front of him. 'Just who does he think he is? I'll settle his hash for him.'

'How?' Ellen was mystified.

'Never you mind, I'll tell you when I'm good and ready. Now where are you going to get your loan? I think it's a great idea to revamp the coffee shop. The town is crying out for a place like that. Go for it, Ellen. How much do you need?'

'Oh a few thousand. I need to gut the place and start afresh. I need equipment and seating and stuff like that.'

'Hmm.' Doug sipped his beer reflectively. 'Just as well you know a terrific builder, who knows a carpenter or two. You know, Ellen, you could open out the top floor there too. You could have stairs leading up to the first floor area. We could do it in pine. It would be lovely. You could have pine tables and chairs, and dressers along the wall. The salad bar will be self-service so people can go upstairs to their tables if downstairs is crowded.'

'Yeah.' Ellen got really enthusiastic. 'And I could put flowers in vases and make it homely and pretty. We could light a fire in the winter.'

'What are you going to call it?'

'I don't know yet. Denise, Miriam and I are racking our brains out. But listen to me, I haven't got my loan yet.'

'Would Stephanie's father be able to help you out?' Doug stared her straight in the eye.

'We're not together any more. I don't expect to see him again.' Ellen stared back.

'I see.'

'It was the best thing.' Ellen took a sip of wine. She was glad Doug knew she was no longer seeing Chris.

'I've a suggestion.' Doug eyed her cautiously.

'What's that?'

'How about if I lend you the money?'

'You're not serious, Doug. I couldn't have that. Thanks very much. It's really kind of you but I couldn't have that,' she prattled.

'Calm down, will ya,' Doug laughed. 'How about if I put the money into a share account in the Credit Union in your name so that you can borrow against it. You pay the interest on the loan, and you can give me the dividends. Then, when you've paid it off, my money will be there plus interest earned. You'll have your deli and both of us will come out of it smiling. Look at it as a way of saving for me. It's no big deal, Ellen.'

'It is a big deal and you know it.' Ellen was very touched.

'I'd like to.'

'Why?' Ellen stared at him.

'Because I like you, Ellen. I admire you. And I think it's a great business opportunity for you. We all had to start off somewhere,' Doug said quietly.

'You're a nice man, Doug Roche,' Ellen said simply.

'Are you over him?'

The question hung in the air. She knew this was the moment she would let go of Chris Wallace for ever.

'I'm over him, Doug.' Ellen smiled at the tall bearded man with the lovely kind eyes sitting opposite her. She felt light-hearted.

He reached across the table and took her hand in his.

'I'm glad for you, Ellen. I really am.' Doug squeezed her hand very tightly.

'Me too,' she murmured as she squeezed his back.

'Will you take the loan?'

'Are you sure?'

'We're pals. I'm sure.'

'Will I call it *Doug's Deli*?' Ellen laughed. She suddenly felt ridiculously happy.

'You will not. You could call it *Slug Carson's* or *Ellie's Deli*,' Doug teased.

'Maybe I'll just call it *The Deli*.' Ellen smiled.

'Sounds good to me,' Doug approved as the waiter came to tell them that their lunch was ready.

*　　*　　*

Ellen was bubbling with excitement as she poured the entire story out to Denise and Miriam that evening.

'Doug is a dote,' Denise exclaimed. 'He's a real nice fella, Ellen. You grab him with both hands. I'd better go and get my pair in for bed.'

'Send Stephanie in as well, Denise. Doug's going to get an architect to draw up plans. I'll show them to you as soon as I have them,' Ellen explained.

'It's exciting, isn't it?' Denise couldn't wait to get things moving. 'See ya.'

'See you, Denise,' Ellen and Miriam chorused.

'You look really pleased with yourself,' Miriam observed.

'It's just the way things turned around. That slime-bag Carson made me so mad and then bumping into Doug and him offering me the money.'

'You *will* be paying it back,' Miriam said as she rinsed out the teacups. 'And I'll have my money.' Ben had insisted that they cash in an insurance policy so she could invest in her new venture. He was behind her all the way. He thought it was a perfect opportunity for Miriam. 'Doug's not going to lose any money,' Miriam pointed out.

'I know that. It's just that he's very kind. He needn't have got involved at all.'

'He's a very decent man and he likes you, Ellen,' Miriam said firmly. 'And I mean *really* likes you. I've seen the way he looks at you.'

'I like him. He makes me feel as if I'm special. He makes me feel I'm someone. He told me he admires me. No-one ever told me that before.'

'You *are* special. You *are* someone.'

Ellen was embarrassed. She changed the subject quickly. 'Well I'll tell you one thing, Miriam. We're going to show Terry Carson that we can make a go of this. We might even start a chain of delis,' she said defiantly. 'And not one penny of our profits is going into his bank. We'll lodge our millions in the bank in Swords.'

'Fine by me,' Miriam agreed. 'I think this is going to be a great partnership. Glenree, hold on to your hat, the Munroe women are coming to town.'

'Yee haw,' Ellen hollered as Stephanie came in the door.

'Mammy, you're mad.' She giggled.

'Ah sure as hell am, honey.' Ellen grabbed her hands and danced around the floor with her.

*   *   *

Doug stood atop the scaffolding of the house he was building and felt the heat on his bare back. It was a great day, he thought happily as he plastered the blocks.

Bumping into Ellen had been the best thing. He'd kept out of her way knowing that there was another man on the scene. He'd actually seen him going into Ellen's one night. A business-type sort of bloke, with expensive clothes and a big car. Good-looking too.

That had pissed him off. Big-time. Doug smiled ruefully. He'd been jealous. Wasn't that something? He never thought he'd fall for a woman again and he'd gone and fallen for Ellen Munroe. And today, when she'd told him she was finished with the other bloke, and she'd looked him straight in the eye, he'd felt he was in with a chance.

Now he was going to be able to spend time with her again doing up the coffee shop. He'd meant it when he'd said it was a good business venture. It was. It was well situated. Good cooking and baking would always draw customers. If anyone could make a go of it, Ellen would. She was very quick and capable. She ran her father's business for him, and in such a discreet way that Mick thought he was the one in charge. That was a nice thing. Doug liked her for it.

They'd had a lovely lunch. Well the meal itself had been mediocre – the Glenree Arms was not noted for its cuisine – but they hadn't noticed. They'd chatted non-stop for almost two hours. Ellen was great to talk to. He loved being in her company.

He'd asked her out for a drink on Friday night. Miriam would mind Stephanie.

Doug trowelled on the plaster smoothly. He'd something to tell Ellen the next time he saw her, something that would give her a laugh. He chuckled. Ellen had a wonderful sense of humour. It was one of the many things he liked about her. He felt like climbing off his scaffold and driving in to Glenree just to share the joke with her.

Chapter Twenty-Eight

'Are you sure about this idea of letting Miriam and Ellen take over the coffee shop?' Sheila asked Mick crossly. 'I'm worried that the children will be neglected.'

'They *won't* be neglected, Sheila. The girls have it all worked out between them.'

'Well I still don't know. When I asked Miriam what would Ben do for his dinner she told me he could get it in the canteen. Imagine having to eat *that* kind of food.' Sheila's nose flared at the thought of her precious son eating canteen cooking.

'Leave them be.'

'Huh,' snorted Sheila. 'She's going to be a working woman, and that Emma one wouldn't know how to work. Nannies my bonnet. God be with the days when I had three of them to rear and no such thing as a nanny.' Sheila buttered her toast and sliced it in half.

'It's the children that will suffer,' she muttered darkly. She wasn't a bit impressed with the idea of Miriam taking a full-time job. Mothers were supposed to be mothers. Husbands were the breadwinners. Ellen was different. Nothing could be done about her situation. She had to work. But Miriam didn't. Madame Miriam was being less than helpful to her in her reign as president of the guild. She wouldn't go to the quilting classes and only yesterday she'd said she couldn't bake for the guild's weekly cake sale because she was going into Dublin with Denise McMahon to look at menus in self-service restaurants. Such nonsense! Sheila needed Miriam's help. Being president was not an easy job. Bonnie Daly was just waiting for her to make a mistake. This was *not* the time for Miriam to go all modern and become a career woman. It was most inconvenient.

'And another thing.' Sheila paused before taking a bite from her toast. 'Who are you going to get to work in the shop to replace Ellen?'

Mick was sorely tempted to say 'Bonnie Daly', but he restrained himself admirably.

'I'll get someone. Don't worry. It's a good chance for Ellen, Sheila. She's a hard worker and it's a sound proposition. I wouldn't have let her get into it otherwise,' Mick said sternly. Sheila knew by the sound of his tone that it was better to say no more. This was one battle she was not going to win.

*   *   *

'Hello O Fertile One,' Chris popped his head around the door of Emma's room and waved a bottle of champagne at her.

'What are you doing here at this hour of the night? How did you get in?' Emma's eyes widened with pleasure.

He thought she was looking surprisingly well, compared to the way she'd looked when she'd had Julie Ann.

'Emma! What a daft question. That little blonde nurse couldn't wait to let me in to see you. I told her I was your brother, home from America.'

'You're incorrigible, Chris Wallace, but it's great to see you.' Emma threw her arms around her cousin.

'I wanted to visit, but I didn't want to bump into Vincent, if you know what I mean?' he said dryly.

'Hmmm.' Emma grinned. 'Have you loads of gossip for me?'

Chris flicked open his briefcase and took out two champagne flutes. 'I was a boy scout once, believe it or not. So I've come prepared.'

Emma giggled as he popped the cork and poured the champagne.

'So you've given the Stern One a son. Was there great rejoicing?'

'Yes.' Emma beamed. 'It's lovely. Vincent's really delighted. He's got a nanny all lined up for when I get home. Although I have to say they're so nice to me in here I don't want to go home. I've been here for nearly two weeks already and the time has flown. I've had loads of visitors. But none of them brought me champagne.'

'Well you're a special little sod. Now let's see what gossip I have. Did you hear that Carol Jones and Paul Walsh have split up?'

'I heard that. You'll have to do better.'

'Did you hear that – now this is complicated – Kenny McMurrough is having an affair with Dervla Lynch, even though, six months ago, Dervla had a fling with his best friend, Norris. And get this, Kenny is also, unbeknownst to Dervla, having a hot and heavy fling with Vicky Stone.'

'I don't believe it!' Emma was delightfully gobsmacked. 'Did you know that Declan made a pass at Vicky Stone, at Marianne Deasy's party? And then Nina Monahan went for him and there was a huge row.'

'I'd like to have seen that.' Chris grinned as he topped up the glasses. 'Nina Monahan in full flow is a sight not to be missed. Was that good gossip?'

'The best,' Emma said with relish. 'How's Suzy?'

Chris made a face. 'OK I suppose.'

'What's going on with you two?' Emma stared at him.

'Aah nuttin'. It's one of those things. We're not getting on great at the moment.'

'*Are* you having an affair with Alexandra Johnston?'

Chris's eyes widened. 'What makes you say that?'

'My mother saw you both at lunch . . .' Emma raised an eyebrow at him. 'I thought you didn't like Alexandra.'

'She's OK when you get to know her. It was business anyway,' Chris said off-handedly. He didn't want to talk about Alexandra. He wanted to talk about Ellen. He wanted to tell Emma everything. He wanted to ask her about Ellen.

516

'Are you having an affair? You can tell me. I won't rat,' Emma asked curiously. She wasn't deceived by his lame *business* excuse.

'It's only a fling. It's nothing serious.'

'Why? Don't you love Suzy?'

Chris sighed and got up off the bed.

'No. I shouldn't have married her. It was a mistake.'

'She loves you,' Emma said crossly.

'I like her. She's a great girl. I thought it would work but it isn't. I feel stifled, Emma. I want out.'

'You can't leave Suzy and the kids. For heaven's sake, Chris. When I think of all those women you've been around, surely you could have fallen in love with one of them and been happy. You should never have married the girl if you didn't love her. That was a cruel thing to do.'

Chris shrugged his shoulders. 'You can't make yourself love someone. She loved me. I thought that would be enough.'

'Idiot,' Emma scolded. She was troubled. 'Do you love Alexandra?'

'Nah.' He was silent for a while and then he couldn't help himself.

'Do you know who I love?' he asked fiercely, jamming his hands into his pockets.

'Who?'

'Ellen.' God, the relief of saying it.

'*Ellen Munroe!* Chris, are you crazy? But you walked out on her. You haven't seen her in years.' Emma was astounded.

'I have seen her, Emma. She took me back in February and we were together until the end of April. Then she dumped me,' Chris said unhappily.

'Ellen took you back after what you did to her?' Emma shook her head.

'Yes. She did. And she still loved me. That's what I can't understand, Emma. I know she loved me. Why couldn't she have stuck with it?'

'Don't be an idiot, Chris. Of course she couldn't have

stuck with it. She's got Stephanie to think of it. It would kill her parents if they knew she was with you. And it's different now. You're married. You've kids. Chris, I'm not surprised she couldn't cope with it. Children change everything. Ellen was nuts about you. I know that. I saw her fall to pieces when you left her. But she'll never go back to you again because of Stephanie, so forget it. You go and patch things up with Suzy because you're going to be one sad and lonely man if you don't,' Emma said firmly.

'I can't get Ellen out of my head. I haven't gone near her for ages, but I can't stand it. I want to go and see her. And I want to see Stephanie. She's my daughter.' Chris plonked down in the chair beside Emma's bed and scowled.

'Even *you* wouldn't be that selfish, Chris. You can't go and upset that child's life after all this time. She's a lovely girl. Leave her alone,' Emma warned. 'And let me tell you one thing, Chris. Ellen hasn't been pining for you in case you've been cherishing the notion that she has. I heard the other day that she and Miriam are going in to business together. They're full of plans.'

'What sort of business?' Chris was amazed.

'They're taking over the coffee shop and turning it into a deli. That doesn't sound like a woman who's fretting. *And* I've heard she's seeing someone.' Emma stared at him.

'I don't believe it! You've only saying that because you don't want me to see her. Who's she seeing?'

'His name is Doug Roche,' Emma said gently. 'Miriam told me about it. He's a builder.'

'What does he look like?' Chris had a sinking feeling in the pit of his stomach.

'He's tall, well built. He's got dark brown hair and a beard. He's a nice man. He's not married. Forget her!' Emma advised.

Chris felt sick. That was the man he'd seen in January, swinging Stephanie around. But Ellen had told him she wasn't involved with anyone. She'd told him she loved him. And Ellen never lied. Maybe they weren't involved. Maybe they were just friends. Maybe it wasn't too late. He was going to see her. No matter what Emma said, Chris had to see Ellen again. He'd left her alone, deliberately. He'd hoped she'd miss him and contact him. Obviously that strategy wasn't working. He enjoyed his relationship with Alexandra. It was sexy and exciting, but Ellen was the one he loved and he couldn't . . . wouldn't believe that she'd fall for someone else.

'Don't tell anyone what I've told you, Emma,' he said forlornly.

'I won't, Chris. But it's too late for you and Ellen. Sort yourself out and get on with things.'

'You're a real mate, Ems.' Chris leaned over and hugged his cousin. They'd always been close. And she was always straight with him.

'And you're a daft twit, Wallace.' Emma returned his hug affectionately.

'I suppose it's too late to see the son and heir?'

'Far too late,' Emma said firmly.

'You're lucky,' Chris said wistfully. 'You and Vincent are still mad about each other. It's the only thing that matters really when all's said and done.'

'Yeah,' Emma agreed. 'I'm very lucky.'

'I better go. It's late. I'll be in touch.'

'Stay away from Ellen and Stephanie.'

'Yep,' Chris fibbed. Come hell or high water he was going to see Ellen again and soon. All he needed was the chance to talk to her, to make love to her. Then they'd be fine. Ellen just needed some persuading. This separation had gone on far too long.

*　　*　　*

Emma lay back against her pillows. She was drained. She couldn't believe what Chris had just told her. He loved Ellen. It was incredible that the bond had endured all this time – and after the way he'd treated her. The chemistry must be there, like it was with her and Vincent, she thought as she snuggled under the blankets.

She could understand Ellen taking him back. When you loved someone deeply it must be hard to turn your back on them and put them out of your life. She'd never be able to put Vincent out of her life. She just couldn't. She'd never thought Chris and Ellen were right for each other but obviously she'd been wrong. If Chris had only realized it at the time, he wouldn't have ruined his, Suzy's and Ellen's life.

It must have been hard for Ellen to end it. Emma felt a sense of admiration for her sister-in-law. That must have been the most difficult decision of her life. Emma didn't know if she'd have been able to do it. Deep down, she didn't think she would have. She was lucky to be married to the most wonderful man. She'd never have a decision like that to make. Ellen had had a hard life, Emma acknowledged as she switched off the light and lay in the dark. She deserved a bit of happiness. Maybe this Doug guy was the one who would give it to her.

*   *   *

'Right, we're off. See you, Ellen. See you, Doug,' Miriam announced as Stephanie and Rebecca waited impatiently. It was Friday night. Doug was taking Ellen out for a drink and Miriam was bringing Stephanie home to her house.

She was delighted to do it. She wanted Doug and Ellen to be together. They were perfect for each other, Miriam thought as she watched Doug pushing the lawnmower up and down Ellen's back garden. She was damn sure Chris Wallace would never have dreamed of mowing Ellen's lawn.

'See you tomorrow, and thanks.' Ellen gave her a hug.

'See you, partner.' Miriam grinned as she ushered the girls ahead of her.

She was dying for the deli to open. It was like having a whole new lease of life. She and Denise had gone scouting around the city and had got some ideas for their self-service deli.

Mrs Munroe had been extremely annoyed when Miriam told her she couldn't bake for her. She hadn't *said* anything but her nostrils had flared alarmingly and her mouth had pursed into a thin line of disapproval.

Let her disapprove! Miriam wasn't going to take any notice any more. She had her own life to live. Sheila had nearly freaked when Miriam told her Ben could have his dinners in the canteen. She'd only said it to annoy her. As if Miriam would let Ben eat his dinner at work. She'd have a dinner ready for him, come what may. That was a priority.

Miriam smiled. Ben was as excited for her as she was. He was a pet. She was very lucky, she thought as she listened to the two cousins giggling in the back of the car. It was nice that Stephanie and Rebecca were as close as she and Ellen were. It was a precious friendship and now they were going into business together. Miriam couldn't wait.

* * *

Ellen and Doug sat on the patio drinking Coke. They'd finished doing the garden. The heat of the day had cooled to a balmy breeze, the sky was tinged with red-gold hues and the scent of night-scented stock perfumed the air. It was very peaceful.

'I'll go and have a shower in a minute,' Ellen said lazily.

'There's no rush. As long as we get there before last orders. That's if you want to. I'm easy.' Doug smiled across at her. 'It's nice sitting here. You've done a magnificent job of the garden, Ellen.'

'I'm very proud of it, I have to admit.' Ellen flicked a fly away from her.

'What do you think of the plans?'

'I think they're fabulous, Doug. It's going to look great when it's finished. Denise and Miriam are as excited. I can't believe it myself.'

'Believe it. And it's going to work out.'

'I hope so.'

'Guess what I did after we had lunch the other day?' Doug's eyes twinkled.

'What?'

'I went to see The Slug.'

'The slug?' Ellen was confused for a moment and then comprehension dawned. 'Oh you mean *The Slug Carson*!'

'The very same.' Doug grinned.

'Why?'

'Well, I didn't like his attitude to you, Ellen. There's no way he'd have treated a man like that if he'd made an appointment to see him.'

'You can bet your ass he wouldn't,' Ellen agreed hotly.

'Anyway,' Doug continued. 'I told him I didn't like the way he'd treated my business partner . . . a certain Miss Ellen Munroe, and then I closed my business and personal accounts with him and took my money over to the bank in Swords. He nearly had apoplexy. It was a pleasure to watch him stuttering and stammering and trying to make excuses. Your honour has been avenged, my dear.'

Ellen was speechless. Doug thought so highly of her that he'd gone and had it out with Terry Carson and closed his bank accounts. She burst into tears.

'Ellen, what's wrong? I didn't mean to make you cry. I meant to make you laugh.' Doug was horrified. He shot out of his chair and hunkered down beside her.

'I can't believe you did that for me,' Ellen whispered, trying to compose herself.

Doug put his arms around her. 'Of course I did it for you. You're very dear to me, Ellen. I wouldn't let anyone treat you like that.'

'Oh Doug.' Ellen didn't know what to say.

'Sshh. Don't be upset.' He hugged her. 'Go in and have your shower. I'll tidy up here.'

'OK.' Ellen gave him a wobbly smile.

'Go on, I'm only being nice to you so you'll cook me some of your steak and kidney puds,' Doug teased.

Ellen laughed. What else could she do?

She had showered and was drying her hair when the doorbell rang.

'Who's that? I'm not expecting anyone,' she said to Doug who was sitting on the settee binding the worn handle on Stephanie's tennis racket.

Ellen glanced out the window.

'Oh Jesus, Mary and Joseph!' She paled.

'What's wrong?' Doug was beside her instantly.

'It's Chris. That's his car across the street.' She felt sick.

'Do you want to see him?' Doug asked evenly. 'Do you want me to go and let you be alone with him?'

'No . . . No.' Ellen put a hand on his arm. 'I don't want you to go, Doug. I don't want to see him at all.' She took a deep breath and squared her shoulders. 'I'll go down and get rid of him.' The thought of confronting Chris made her heart sink like stone. Why was he making life so difficult for her? She didn't want to see him. She didn't want the old loving feelings to surface.

'Would you like me to answer the door for you? Would you like me to tell him to go?' Doug stared at her intently.

Ellen swallowed. 'I couldn't ask you to do that, Doug.' She stared into his kind hazel eyes.

'Yes you could. If you *want* to. It's up to you.' Ellen knew he was asking her to make a choice. She looked at him and knew she could depend on him for the rest of her life.

'I want you to.' She touched his cheek.

'I won't be long,' he said quietly.

She stood, frozen, as she heard him stride briskly downstairs and open the door.

*   *   *

Chris stared in horror at the tall bearded man who opened Ellen's front door. What the hell was he doing here? This wasn't in the script at all. It was supposed to be like his and Ellen's last reunion when they'd been frantic for each other.

523

'I'd like to talk to Ellen, please.' He found it hard to be civil. He wanted to grab the man by the throat and fling him out of Ellen's house.

'It's like this,' the bearded man said quietly, but there was a steeliness in his voice that chilled Chris. 'Ellen doesn't want to talk to you. So I'd advise you to do what she wants.'

'Or?' Chris bristled.

'Or you'll have me to deal with.'

Chris stared at the man and felt an impotent fury.

'I want to talk to Ellen. Tell her I'm here.'

'She knows you're here. She saw your car across the street. She asked me to tell you that she doesn't want to talk to you.' The man repeated himself slowly and deliberately.

'And who are you?' Chris snapped.

'I'm the man you'll have to worry about if you ever come near Ellen again. Goodnight,' he said pleasantly and then very firmly closed the door in Chris's face.

Chris was aghast. He couldn't take it in. Ellen was deadly serious. She wanted him out of her life for good. She had a new man. He walked over to the car in a daze. He'd lost her.

He sat in the car staring up at the flat. What was he to do? He could go to Alexandra, he supposed. *She*'d welcome him with open arms, he thought bitterly. Wasn't that ironic? Brittle, cool, sophisticated Alexandra would want him and the softest, kindest, most loving woman he'd ever known had just rejected him.

Chris switched on the ignition and drove slowly out of Glenree. Let Ellen have her bit of rough with her builder, he thought viciously. It wouldn't last, he *knew* it wouldn't. She'd come running back sooner or later. Ellen loved *him*. She always had and always would. That would *never* change. He blinked. A mist seemed to have formed in front of his eyes. He swallowed hard. There seemed to be a golf ball lodged in his throat. To think that it had come to this. Angrily he wiped the tears from his eyes. Was this

how she'd felt when he'd left her? But he'd come back to
her, Chris comforted himself. And Ellen would come back
to him.

* * *

'He's gone,' Doug said gently.
'Thanks.' Ellen looked up at him. He held out his arms
to her and she walked into his comforting embrace.
'Can I kiss you?' he asked as he caressed her cheek.
Ellen drew his head down to hers and felt the gentle
touch of his lips. She'd come home.

To be continued

FOREIGN AFFAIRS
by Patricia Scanlan

Four women, Paula, Jennifer, Brenda and Rachel. All at a crossroads in their lives. All with choices to make.

Paula: Beautiful, ambitious and successful, she works hard and plays hard. Men find her irresistible . . . except for the one man she really wants and is determined to have.

Jennifer: She's a true friend. Paula comes to her with man troubles. Rachel tells her of family woes. Brenda, her sister, is envious of her. But will Paula, Brenda and Rachel be there for Jennifer when tragedy strikes?

Brenda: In her late thirties, she longs for glamour and excitement. Tired of being a housewife stuck at home with her children, Brenda is determined to make changes in her life. And then the unthinkable happens.

Rachel: Shy and timid, she has always been dominated by her cold, intolerant father. But beneath the surface she is bubbling with suppressed rage. This is her last chance to break free, but does she have the courage to finally become her own woman?

When the four women stay in a luxurious villa on a Greek island, they soon realize that they have embarked on more than just a foreign holiday. Can their friendships be sustained? Indeed, will their lives ever be the same again?

A Bantam Paperback
0 553 40947 6

FINISHING TOUCHES
by Patricia Scanlan

Cassie, Laura and Aileen. Schoolmates, soulmates, they shared the dreams, secrets and desires of young girls, and the passions, problems and aspirations of young women coming into their own. Cassie put her life on hold to attend to her family's needs. Laura and Aileen soared in their careers. Now they were together again as Cassie dared to make her impossible dream come true.

Aileen crossed the world to be with Cassie; Laura was there by her side. David offered her love, support and passion to burn. And Cassie's spiteful sister Barbara schemed to undermine them all.

Cassie, the family caretaker, was liberated at last, ready to launch an interior design business with a disputed legacy that would bring out the worst – and the best – in her family, lovers and friends.

A Bantam Paperback
0 553 40945 X

A SELECTION OF FINE NOVELS
AVAILABLE FROM BANTAM BOOKS

50329 4	DANGER ZONES	*Sally Beauman* £5.99
40727 9	LOVERS AND LIARS	*Sally Beauman* £5.99
40803 8	SACRED AND PROFANE	*Marcelle Bernstein* £5.99
40497 0	CHANGE OF HEART	*Charlotte Bingham* £4.99
40890 9	DEBUTANTES	*Charlotte Bingham* £5.99
50500 9	GRAND AFFAIR	*Charlotte Bingham* £5.99
40496 2	NANNY	*Charlotte Bingham* £4.99
40895 X	THE NIGHTINGALE SINGS	*Charlotte Bingham* £5.99
17635 8	TO HEAR A NIGHTINGALE	*Charlotte Bingham* £5.99
40072 X	MAGGIE JORDAN	*Emma Blair* £4.99
40298 6	SCARLET RIBBONS	*Emma Blair* £4.99
40615 9	PASSIONATE TIMES	*Emma Blair* £4.99
40614 0	THE DAFFODIL SEA	*Emma Blair* £4.99
40373 7	THE SWEETEST THING	*Emma Blair* £4.99
40973 5	A CRACK IN FOREVER	*Jeannie Brewer* £5.99
40996 4	GOING HOME TO LIVERPOOL	*June Francis* £4.99
40820 8	LILY'S WAR	*June Francis* £4.99
50429 0	KITTY AND HER BOYS	*June Francis* £5.99
40818 6	A DISTANT DREAM	*Margaret Graham* £5.99
40408 3	GONE TOMORROW	*Jane Gurney* £5.99
40730 9	LOVERS	*Judith Krantz* £5.99
40731 7	SPRING COLLECTION	*Judith Krantz* £5.99
40206 4	FAST FRIENDS	*Jill Mansell* £4.99
40938 7	TWO'S COMPANY	*Jill Mansell* £5.99
40947 6	FOREIGN AFFAIRS	*Patricia Scanlan* £4.99
40945 X	FINISHING TOUCHES	*Patricia Scanlan* £5.99
40483 0	SINS OF THE MOTHER	*Arabella Seymour* £4.99